D0805995

The Political Dynamics of European Economic Integration

LEON N. LINDBERG

STANFORD UNIVERSITY PRESS

STANFORD, CALIFORNIA

LONDON: OXFORD UNIVERSITY PRESS

1963

Stanford University Press
Stanford, California
London: Oxford University Press

Library of Congress Catalog Card Number: 63-14129
Printed in the United States of America

Published with the assistance of
the Ford Foundation

THE POLITICAL DYNAMICS
OF EUROPEAN ECONOMIC INTEGRATION

To Beatrice and Andrea

PREFACE

THIS STUDY of the European Economic Community does not offer a definitive account of its activities, but is directed toward a limited number of specific concerns. These are spelled out in some detail in Chapter 1. I am interested in political integration, in the processes whereby a number of nation-states come to construct a single political community. The essence of a political community, it seems to me, is the existence of a legitimate system for the resolution of conflict, for the making of authoritative decisions for the group as a whole. Accordingly, my effort has been to illuminate the nature of the EEC as an institutional system, and to assess its impact on decision-making patterns in the "Europe of the Six." Field research in Western Europe was done between August 1959 and January 1961. Because of the nature of the analysis, and because the internal workings of the EEC cannot be profitably studied from afar, the most reliable conclusions can be drawn only for this period. Some effort has been made, however, to advance coverage beyond this point in the case of agriculture, for which decisions of crucial importance were taken in January 1962.

This, then, is primarily a study of certain selected features of the experience of the EEC in its first four years of operation. Most of the writing was completed by early 1962, and unless more recent events, or subsequent scholarly publications, substantially altered or invalidated the analysis, I have not taken them into account. In a strict sense, as with all analyses of contemporary phenomena, the study was dated the moment the ink dried. I tried, however, to ask questions and draw conclusions that would not depend upon the time context, and I hope I have succeeded. I have documented the emergence of an EEC procedural code, which seems to me to constitute the essence of political integration. General de Gaulle's actions since January 1963 constitute a violation of this code. It is much too early to tell what the effect of this will be. Among the possibilities are an interruption or slowing down of the processes of political integration, and the emergence of a new code.

The people to whom I am indebted for assistance are too many to acknowledge by name. Much of the material presented is based upon interviews: with officials of the EEC Commission, of the Council of Ministers, of the Committee of Permanent Representatives, of the European Parliament, of the Economic and Social Committee, of the European Investment Bank, of the High Authority of the European Coal and Steel Community, of the Commission of the European Atomic Energy Community, and of the Ministries of Economic Affairs, Foreign Affairs, and Agriculture of the Member States of the Communities; with representatives of interest groups and political parties at both the national and the Community level; and with scholars and other interested observers in this country and on the Continent. All entertained my most naïve questions with utmost courtesy and helpfulness, and to them I should like to express grateful appreciation. Where specific sources could be given, I have identified them in the Notes. I wish to thank Political and Economic Planning of London, Martinus Nijhoff of The Hague, and the University of Michigan Law School for permission to quote from their publications. No acknowledgment would be complete without special mention of Agence Europe of Luxembourg, a news agency specializing in the European Communities. It is an essential source of primary information for any student of these matters.

I owe a special intellectual debt to Ernst B. Haas of the University of California (Berkeley), who stimulated in me an interest in political integration and who presided over this manuscript from germination to publication. Richard Mayne of the EEC Commission went over the entire manuscript with meticulous care, saving me from many an error and inconsistency, and offering invaluable comments and suggestions. My thanks go also to the following, who read the manuscript in whole or in part, and who have helped me to minimize error and clarify and tighten the analysis: Chadwick Alger of Northwestern University, Bernard C. Cohen of the University of Wisconsin, Robert Cohen of the EEC Commission, Leon D. Epstein of the University of Wisconsin, Amitai Etzioni of Columbia University, Elmer W. Learn of the University of Minnesota (St. Paul), John H. Schaar of the University of California (Berkeley), and Walter Yondorf of M.I.T. Research. Whatever grace the writing may possess is due to the unfailing efforts of my wife, who also typed the first drafts, and Miss Pauline Wickham of Stanford University Press.

This study was made possible by research-training and thesis-completion grants from the Social Science Research Council, which enabled me to spend from August 1959 to January 1961 in Europe, and which provided time subsequently to complete work on the manuscript. The documentation and information services of the several institutions of the European Communities were helpful beyond the "line of duty" in providing me with documents, reports, and the like. The officers and staff of the

United States Mission to the European Communities shared their extensive knowledge with me, and helped to open doors. To Madeleine Ledivilec, librarian of the European Atomic Energy Community, must go very special thanks for unfailing help and invaluable friendship.

Any errors committed are, naturally, only my own. Unless otherwise noted, all translations are also my own.

LEON N. LINDBERG

Madison, Wisconsin
May 1963

CONTENTS

ABBREVIATIONS

Unless specified otherwise, organizations cited in a foreign language belong to the country in whose language the entry is given; thus the first organization listed is a French one, the second a German, and so on.

APPCA	Assemblée Permanente des Présidents des Chambres d'Agriculture
BDI	Bundesverband der Deutschen Industrie
BHE	Bund der Heimatvertriebenen und Entrechteten
BLEU	Belgium-Luxembourg Economic Union
CDU/CSU	Christlich-Demokratische Union
CFTC	Confédération Française des Travailleurs Chrétiens
CGA	Confédération Générale d'Agriculture
CGC	Confédération Générale des Cadres
CGIL	Confederazione Generale Italiana di Lavoro
CGT	Confédération Générale du Travail
CISC	Confédération Internationale des Syndicats Chrétiens
CISL	Confédération Internationale des Syndicats Libres
CISL	Confederazione Italiana di Sindicati di Lavoro
CNMCCA	Confédération Nationale de la Mutualité de la Coopération et du Crédit Agricole
CNPF	Conseil National du Patronat Français
CNV	National Confederation of Christian Workers (Netherlands)
COCCEE	Comité des Organisations Commerciales des Pays de la C.E.E.
COCOR	Co-ordinating Commission of the ECSC Council of Ministers
Confagricoltura	Confederation of Italian Agriculture
Confindustria	Confederation of Italian Industry
COPA	Comité des Organisations Professionnelles Agricoles de la C.E.E.
CSC	Confédération des Syndicats Chrétiens (Belgium)
DBV	Deutscher Bauernverband e.V.
DC	Democrazia Christiana
DGB	Deutscher Gewerkschaftsbund
DP	Deutsche Partei
ECSC	European Coal and Steel Community

EDC	European Defense Community
EEC	European Economic Community
EFTA	European Free Trade Association
EPA	European Parliamentary Assembly
ESC	Economic and Social Committee
Euratom	European Atomic Energy Community
FDP	Freie Deutsche Partei
FGTB	Fédération Générale des Travailleurs Belges (Belgium)
FIB	Fédération des Industries Belges (Belgium)
FNSEA	Fédération Nationale des Syndicats d'Exploitants Agricoles
FO	Confédération Générale du Travail—Force Ouvrière
GATT	General Agreement on Tariffs and Trade
ICCTU	International Confederation of Christian Trade Unions
ICFTU	International Confederation of Free Trade Unions
KAB	Confederation of Catholic Workers (Netherlands)
KNBTB	Dutch Catholic Farmers' and Growers' Union
KNLC	Royal Dutch Agricultural Committee
MRP	Mouvement Républicain Populaire
MSEUE	Mouvement Socialiste pour les Etats-Unis d'Europe
NCBTB	Dutch Christian Farmers' and Growers' Union
NEI	Nouvelles Equipes Internationales (league of European Christian parties)
NVV	Netherlands Socialist Trade Union Federation
OECD	Organization for Economic Cooperation and Development
OEEC	Organization for European Economic Cooperation
PCI	Partito Communista Italiano
PME	Confédération Générale des Petites et Moyennes Entreprises
PSC	Parti Social Chrétien (Belgium)
PSI	Partito Socialista Italiano
RGR	Rassemblement des Gauches Républicaines
RPF	Rassemblement du Peuple Français
SFIO	Section Française de l'Internationale Ouvrière (Socialist Party)
SPD	Sozialdemokratische Partei Deutschlands
UIL	Unione Italiana di Lavoro
UNICE	Union des Industries de la Communauté Européenne
UNR	Union pour la Nouvelle République
WEU	Western European Union

PART ONE

POLITICAL INTEGRATION AND THE TREATY OF THE EUROPEAN ECONOMIC COMMUNITY

POLITICAL INTEGRATION: DEFINITIONS
AND HYPOTHESES

THE EUROPE that gave birth to the idea of the nation-state appears to be well on the way to rejecting it in practice. The Treaty establishing the European Economic Community (EEC), signed in Rome on March 25, 1957, represents the latest in a series of steps designed to break down the bastions of European national separatism. Its six signatories, France, Germany, Italy, Belgium, the Netherlands, and Luxembourg, were already members of the European Coal and Steel Community (ECSC), whose foundation in 1952 had created a common market restricted to coal and steel. The experience with this first effort at sector integration led ultimately to the creation of the EEC as well as the European Atomic Energy Community (Euratom):[1]

It soon became evident that integration by sectors could only yield limited results. Its restricted scope, unconnected with the other parts of the economic and financial system, ruled out any large-scale activities and made it impossible to achieve an over-all equilibrium. To sweep away from Europe protectionism and economic nationalism with their resulting high production costs, high costs of living and economic stagnation, a different approach was required, a wide attack in more than one dimension as it were; it must have the depth of integration and the wide scope of a freeing of trade. This approach was provided first by the Beyen Plan and then by the Spaak Report, which marked the first step towards the Common Market.[2]

---

[1]Superscript numbers refer to the Notes at the back of the book, pp. 319–50, in which will be found all source citations, quotations from documents, and supplementary evidence.

The EEC has as its primary goal the creation of an area in which goods, people, services, and capital will be able to circulate freely. To achieve this, a customs union is created, but a customs union in which attention is devoted not only to barriers between states, but to economic, financial, and social reactions that may take place in the Member States. The main purpose is the abolition of trade barriers, tariffs, and quotas, which is to be accomplished more or less automatically during a twelve- to fifteen-year transition period, divided into three four-year stages. A series of targets is assigned to each stage, and these relate not only to progress in removal of trade barriers, but also to parallel measures of economic and social alignment. This process is to be accompanied by the establishment of a common external tariff, within which an alignment of the several economies is to go on in order to adjust differences in price and working conditions, and in productive resources. Advancement from one stage to another is dependent upon achieving these respective targets. All this is to be supervised by institutions specially set up by the Treaty.[3]

The economic and social significance of these developments is certainly far-reaching—one need only read the newspapers to confirm this. For the political scientist, too, they are of consuming interest, for here he can observe the actual processes whereby political actors move beyond the nation-state as a basic framework for action, appearing finally to realize the oft-proclaimed "fact" of the international interdependence of nations. Forces are at work in Western Europe that may alter the nature of international relations, as well as offer promise of a fuller and more prosperous life for the inhabitants of the region.

The stated goal of the EEC is the creation of a customs union and ultimately the achievement of a significant measure of economic integration. The fundamental motivation is political. It is, in the words of the Treaty, to establish "an ever closer union among the European peoples."[4] Our concern will be with the political *consequences* of economic integration. We shall try to measure the extent to which the creation of the EEC and the activities which take place in its framework give rise to the phenomenon of political integration. Whereas in terms of commercial policy the establishment of the EEC is "already the most important event of this century," its vast political significance is still only a potential.[5]

POLITICAL INTEGRATION

What, then, do we mean by political integration? Some writers define it as a *condition*, and others as a *process*. In the works of Karl W. Deutsch, integration refers to the probability that conflicts will be resolved without violence. The central concept is that of a "security-community," which is "a group of people which has become integrated": that is, they have attained "within a territory . . . a 'sense of community' and . . . institutions and practices strong enough and widespread enough to assure, for a 'long' time, dependable expectations of 'peaceful change' among its population."[6] Integration may come about through several types of security-communities, "amalgamated" or "pluralistic," implying respectively either the presence or the absence of any real central decision-making institutions or delegations of national autonomy. In either case, integration is achieved when the states concerned cease to prepare for war against each other.[7]

Similarly, North, Koch, and Zinnes list six criteria in terms of which one can consider integration: the probability of violence given a conflict situation (same as Deutsch); the frequency of conflicts between any given number of organizations in a given span of time; the number of compatible policy conditions; the degree of interdependency between n given organizations; the number and significance of interlocking communications systems or structures; and the extent to which membership overlaps.[8]

Such conceptualizations of political integration as a *condition* have been criticized on the grounds that they permit only a general discussion of the environmental factors influencing integration, and that they fail to provide us with the tools needed to make a clear distinction between the situation prior to integration and the situation prevailing during the process, thus obscuring the role of social change.[9] For these reasons, Haas insists that we should look at political integration as a *process*: "Political integration is the process whereby political actors in several distinct national settings are persuaded to shift their loyalties, expectations and political activities toward a new centre, whose institutions possess or demand jurisdiction over the pre-existing national states. The end result of a process of political integration is a new political community, superimposed over the pre-existing ones."[10]

In Haas's work, this definition is rigorously tied to an ideal-type analysis in which the institutions of the ECSC are compared to those of an ideal federal-type system. This kind of heuristic device is certainly above reproach and did in fact yield extremely valuable results. My own investigations, however, have led me to adopt a more cautious conception of political integration, one limited to the development of devices and processes for arriving at collective decisions by means other than autonomous action by national governments. It seems to me that it is logically and empirically possible that collective decision-making procedures involving a significant amount of political integration can be achieved without moving toward a "political community" as defined by Haas. In fact, use of this type of ideal, or model, analysis may well direct the researcher to a different set of questions and a different interpretation of the data collected:

European integration is developing, and may continue so for a long time, in the direction of different units. . . . We can only speculate about the outcome, but a forecast of the emergence of a pluralistic political structure, hitherto unknown, might not be wholly erroneous. Such a structure might very well permit to a great extent the participating nations to retain their identity while yet joined in the organizations that transcend nationality.[11]

For the purpose of this study, political integration will be defined as a *process*, but without reference to an end point. In specific terms, political integration is (1) the process whereby nations forgo the desire and ability to conduct foreign and key domestic policies independently of each other, seeking instead to make *joint decisions* or to *delegate* the decision-making process to new central organs;[12] and (2) the process whereby political actors in several distinct settings are persuaded to shift their expectations and political activities to a new center.*

Although this dual definition lacks the analytical clarity and precision of model analysis, it is, I believe, appropriate to the problem at hand. Not only does it provide us with a set of interrelated indicators by means of which to judge the experience of the EEC, but it specifies what I take to be the process of political integration. The first part of the definition refers to two modes of decision-making which are, in my opinion, intimately related, the existence of delegated decision-making being a basic precondition for progress in shared decision-making. The processes of *sharing* and of *delegating* decision-making are likely to affect the governmental structure in each state involved, creating new internal problems of coordination and policy direction, especially between Ministries of Foreign Affairs and such specialized ministries as Economic Affairs, Agriculture, and Labor that are accustomed to regarding their spheres as wholly or primarily of domestic concern. States with traditions of representative and parliamentary government are also faced with the problem created by the development of decision-making centers whose authority derives from an international, rather than a national, consensus.

The second part of the definition refers to the patterns of behavior shown by high policy-makers, civil servants, parliamentarians, interest-

---

* This definition is adapted from Haas, *Uniting of Europe*, p. 12. I have preferred to limit it to shifts in political expectations and activities, and to exclude shifts in values and any reference to a political Community end point, since it seems premature to undertake a study of value changes, even if an efficient way of measuring them could be devised. Changes in values can be expected to come about only *as a result of* new patterns of political expectations and activities.

group leaders, and other elites. Here our attention is directed to the perceptions and resulting behavior of the political actors in each of the states involved. The relationship between this set of indicators and those referring to governmental decision-making is very close. By the nature of the process, government policy-makers and civil servants are involved increasingly in the new system of decision-making: they attend meetings of experts, draft plans, and participate in an over-all joint decision-making pattern. Similarly, as the locus of decision-making changes, so will the tactics of groups and individuals seeking to influence the decision-making process. They may oppose the change, but once made they will have to adjust to it by changing their tactics, or their organization, or both, to accommodate to the new situation. In Haas's words: "Conceived not as a condition but as a *process,* the conceptualisation [of political integration] relies on the perception of interests . . . by the actors participating in the process. Integration takes place when these perceptions fall into a certain pattern and fails to take place when they do not." Moreover, "as the process of integration proceeds, it is assumed . . . that interests will be redefined in terms of regional rather than a purely national orientation."[13]

So much for defining the concept of political integration. The problem now is to try to spell out how it can be made to occur in actual life. Since there have been numerous efforts at transnational organization and cooperation that have not had political results of this kind, political scientists have tried to identify constant background, or environmental, factors or conditions upon which political integration is contingent. Thus Deutsch isolates the following conditions as essential or helpful for a pluralistic or amalgamated security-community: initially compatible value systems, mutually responsive elites, adequate communications channels, a commitment to a "new way of life," and the existence of a "core area."[14] Similarly, Haas calls for a pluralistic social structure, a high level of economic and industrial development, and a modicum of ideological homogeneity.[15]

But the examination of background factors or conditions does not help us account completely for the *process* of political integration, nor does it permit differentiation between the situation prior to integration and the situation prevailing during the process. Accordingly, it is necessary to try to identify some additional variable factors to specify *how* political integration occurs. On the basis of Haas's researches and my own experiences in Western Europe, I suggest that the process of political integration requires the following conditions: (1) Central institutions and central policies must develop. (2) The tasks assigned to these institutions must be important enough and specific enough to activate socioeconomic processes to which conventional international organizations have no access. (3) These tasks must be inherently expansive. (4) The Member States must continue to see their interests as consistent with the enterprise.

CENTRAL INSTITUTIONAL DEVELOPMENT

Central institutions are required in order to *represent* the common interests which have brought the Member States together, and in order to *accommodate* such conflicts of interest as will inevitably arise. In discussing the institutions of the EEC, I prefer to avoid the concept of "supra-nationality" and to focus instead on the extent to which the Community institutions are enabled to deal directly with fields of activity, rather than merely influencing the actions of individual governments in respect of these fields. There are four main aspects to be considered:

1. North, Koch, and Zinnes seek to distinguish between compromise and "true integration," both seen as ways of dealing with conflict.[16] Both depend upon *reducing the intensity* of the conflict by uncovering its sources, and by taking the demands of both sides and breaking them into their constituent parts. Each party to the conflict is forced to re-examine and re-evaluate its own desires against those of the other party and against the implications of the total situation. True integration is achieved when a solution has been found in which "both desires have found a place," in which the interests of the parties "fit into each other." I suggest that the central institutions of the EEC, by isolating issues and identifying common interests, may play a crucial role here in "precipitating unity."

2. The integrative impact of the central institutions will depend in part upon the *competencies* and *roles* assigned to them. Much, however, depends upon whether or not the institutions make full use of their competencies and upon *how they define their role*. The literature on organizational decision-making suggests some relevant questions in this context. What formal and informal decision-making and relational patterns will develop? What patterns of commitment will be enforced by organizational imperatives, by the social character of the personnel, by "institutionalization," by the social and cultural environment, and by centers of interest generated in the course of action and decision? I suggest that the early years of the existence of these institutions will be significant in determining their long-range competence, that patterns of internal differentiation and conflicting values will develop, that organizational behavior will be conditioned by the necessity of adjusting to the environment, and that co-optation will be used as a tactic to head off opposition.

3. Central institutions lacking real competency to affect policy-making directly may develop a *consensus* that will influence those national or international decision-makers who do determine policy.

4. Finally, the patterns of interaction engendered by the central institutions may affect *the over-all system* in which they operate; in other words, these institutions may have latent effects that contribute to political integration. As Alger points out, participants in the activities of central institutions may develop multiple perspectives, personal friendships, a comraderie of expertise, all of which may reflect back upon the national governments and affect future national policy-making.[17] Such latent effects, however, are significant only if the individuals concerned are influential at the national level, *and* if their activities in the central institutions involve significant policy-making.

ELITE ACTIVATION

Thanks to the efforts of the so-called "group theorists," political scientists today know that any analysis of the political process must give a central place to the phenomena of group conflict, to the beliefs, attitudes, and ideologies of groups participating in the process of policy formation. If political integration, as we have defined it, is going on, then we would expect to find a change in the behavior of the participants. Consequently we must identify the aims and motives of the relevant political groups, the conditions of their emergence, and the means by which they seek and attain access to centers of political power.

One of the main obstacles to political integration has been the fact that international organizations lack direct access to individuals and groups in the national communities involved. "Short of such access, the organization continues to be no more than a forum of intergovernmental consultation and cooperation."[18]

Actors with political power in the national community will restructure their expectations and activities only if the tasks granted to the new institutions are of immediate concern to them, and only if they involve a significant change in the conditions of the actors' environment. Several patterns of reaction may be expected:

1. Individual firms may undertake measures of self-protection or adjustment in the form of cartels to limit competition, the conclusion of agreements, and so on.

2. Groups may change their political organization and tactics in order to gain access to, and to influence, such new central decision-making centers as may be developing.

3. These activities may act back upon the central institutions and the Member States by creating situations that cannot be dealt with except by further central institutional development and new central policies. An example would be a developing need for antitrust legislation in response to an evolving network of agreements between firms in several countries.

4. Such activities may also have latent effects of the kind already described, operative under the same conditions.

INHERENTLY EXPANSIVE TASKS

Here is a problem of central importance because changes in the policy needs of the Member States create definite phases in the life of international organizations. To remedy this, the task assigned to the institutions must be inherently expansive and thus capable of overcoming what Haas calls "the built-in autonomy of functional contexts."

Lessons about integrative processes associated with one phase do not generally carry over into the next because the specific policy context . . . determines what is desired by governments and tolerated by them in terms of integrative accommodations. . . . There is no dependable, cumulative process of precedent formation leading to ever more community-oriented organizational behavior, unless the task assigned to the institutions is inherently expansive, thus capable of overcoming the built-in autonomy of functional contexts and of surviving changes in the policy aims of Member States.[19]

This is the principle involved in the concept of "spill-over." In its most general formulation, "spill-over" refers to a situation in which a given action, related to a specific goal, creates a situation in which the original goal can be assured only by taking further actions, which in turn create a further condition and a need for more action, and so forth. The concept has been used by Haas to show that integrating one sector of the economy—for example, coal and steel—will inevitably lead to the integration of other economic and political activities. We shall formulate it as follows: the initial task and grant of power to the central institutions creates a situation or series of situations that can be dealt with only by further expanding the task and the grant of power. Spill-over implies that a situation has developed in which the ability of a Member State to achieve a policy goal may depend upon the attainment by another Member State of one of its policy goals. The situation may show various features:

1. The dynamics of spill-over are dependent upon the fact that support for any given step in integration is the result of a convergence of goals and expectations. These often competing goals give rise to competing activities and demands, which may be the basis of further convergence leading to further integration.

2. Lack of agreement between governments may lead to an expanded role for the central institutions; in other words, Member States may delegate difficult problems.

3. At the level of elite groupings, demands and expectations for further actions may be expressed as a result of partial actions taken by the central institutions.

4. The activities of the central institutions and nonofficial elites may *create situations* that cannot be dealt with except by further central institutional development and new central policies.

5. Far-reaching economic integration, involving all sectors of the economy, as in the EEC, may offer great scope for spill-over *between* sectors. Conflicts over further integration in a given sector, involving disparate national interests, may be resolved by bargains between such sectors (e.g., agriculture and energy).

6. Participation in a customs union will probably elicit reactions from nonmember states, a situation which may create problems that can be resolved only by further integration or by expanding the role of the central institutions.

CONTINUITY OF NATIONAL POLICY AIMS

"Spill-over" assumes the continued commitment of the Member States to the undertaking. The Treaty of Rome was the result of a creative compromise, a convergence of national aspirations. Political and economic integration cannot be expected to succeed in the absence of a will to proceed on the part of the Member States. Granted that it would be difficult for a state to withdraw from the EEC, it must be stressed that little could be done to move beyond minimal obligations if one or several states were to maintain a determined resistance. It seems likely, however, that with the operation of the other integrative factors, the alternatives open to any Member State will gradually be limited so as to reduce dependence upon this factor. For the will to proceed need not have a positive content. Given only a general reluctance to be charged with obstruction, or to see the enterprise fail, the stimulus to action can be provided by the central institutions or by other Member States.

The way in which decisions are made, in which conflicts of interest among the Member States are resolved, will be of definitive importance for political integration, because the kind of accommodation that prevails will indicate the nature of the positive convergence of pro-integration aims, and of the extent to which the alternatives open to national decision-makers may have been limited by participation in the enterprise. In this connection we may ask the question, Under what conditions does conflict produce a stronger bond between the parties than that which existed before?[20] Moreover, as already mentioned, the mode of accommodation is directly correlated to the developmental potential of the central institutions.

Conflicts between states may be resolved on the basis of "the minimum common denominator," by "splitting the difference," or by "upgrading common interests."[21] The "minimum common denominator" type, characteristic of classical diplomatic negotiations, involves relatively equal bargainers who exchange equal concessions while never going beyond what the least cooperative among them is willing to concede. Accommodation by "splitting the difference" involves a similar exchange of concessions, but conflicts are ultimately resolved somewhere between the final bargaining positions, usually because of the mediatory role performed by a secretariat or expert study groups, or out of deference to third-party pressure such as might be institutionalized in "parliamentary diplomacy." This implies "the existence of a continuing organization with a broad frame of reference, public debate, rules of procedure governing the debate, and the statement of conclusions arrived at by some kind of majority vote."[22] Although such mediating organs may not be able to define the terms of agreement, they do participate in setting limits within which the ultimate accommodation is reached. Accommodation on the basis of "upgrading common interests," whether deliberately or inadvertently, depends on the participation of institutions or individuals with an autonomous role that permits them to participate in actually defining the terms of the agreement. It implies greater progress toward political integration, for it shows that

the parties succeeded in so redefining their conflict so as to work out a solution at a higher level, which almost invariably implies the expansion of the mandate or task of an international or national governmental agency. In terms of results, this mode of accommodation maximizes . . . the "spill-over" effect of international decisions: policies made pursuant to an initial task and grant of power can be made real only if the task itself is expanded, as reflected in the compromises among the states interested in the task.[23]

This last type comes closest to what North, Koch, and Zinnes call "true integration."

We now have a set of definitions, variable factors, indicators, and hypotheses with which to assess the extent to which the EEC is contributing to the process of political integration. We are concerned above all with determining the impact of the EEC on official and nonofficial decision-making patterns in the "Europe of the Six," and with analyzing the structure and content of such central decision-making as may develop.

In the rest of this section we shall analyze the key features of the EEC Treaty and its potential for political integration. In Part II we shall try to determine how the EEC institutional system has developed in practice. "Institutional system" is defined as that system within which a decision-making event takes place, a definition which embraces both the actors involved and the system of activities that results in decision.[24] In Part III, by analyzing several sequences of decision-making, we shall observe the system in action, and focus on the spill-over function and the accommodation of conflict. Finally, in the last chapter, we shall draw together our findings on the EEC and political integration.

$$\boxed{\text{II}}$$

THE TREATY AND ECONOMIC INTEGRATION

IN THIS SECTION we shall analyze the EEC Treaty and try to assess its potential contribution to the process of political integration.* More specifically we want to examine the extent to which it can be expected to affect decision-making patterns in the six Member States. Consequently we must determine (1) which policy areas normally subject to the autonomous determination of each state are affected, (2) the degree to which decision-making in these areas has been shared or delegated, and (3) the nature of the institutional system set up and of the decision-making within it. Thus, we are not centrally concerned with judging the potential or actual impact of the EEC as economic integration.[1] Nevertheless, a brief exposition of the Treaty of Rome in terms of its basic nature, that is, as an effort at general economic integration, is indispensable to an understanding of its potential for political integration. Only in this way can we gain perspective on the scope of the undertaking and the extent of the obligations accepted by the Treaty signatories.

The Treaty of Rome is a complex document, containing 248 Articles, 4 Annexes, 13 Protocols, and 4 Conventions. It represents an effort to create a single, unified market where formerly there were four (counting the three Benelux countries as one market). It is based on an infinitely varied and delicately balanced set of actions to be taken by several sets of actors at carefully specified intervals. Its *substantive provisions* will be examined in some detail under the following headings: the mission (Articles 1–3) and fundamental principles of the Treaty (Articles 4–8; 211–40), the unification of the market (Articles 12–84), the normalization of

* It will be referred to hereafter as the Treaty of Rome.

competition (Articles 85–122), economic development (Articles 123–30), and the association of overseas countries and territories (Articles 131–36).[2]

THE MISSION AND FUNDAMENTAL PRINCIPLES OF THE TREATY

According to the Treaty, "It shall be the aim of the Community, by establishing a Common Market and progressively approximating the economic policies of Member States, to promote throughout the Community a harmonious development of economic activities, a continuous and balanced expansion, an increased stability, an accelerated raising of the standard of living and closer relations between its Member States" (Article 2).

The Treaty envisages the following activities in order that these purposes be achieved:

(a) the elimination, as between Member States, of customs duties and of quantitative restrictions in regard to the importation and exportation of goods, as well as of all other measures with equivalent effect;

(b) the establishment of a common customs tariff and a common commercial policy towards third countries;

(c) the abolition, as between Member States, of the obstacles to the free movement of persons, services and capital;

(d) the inauguration of a common agricultural policy;

(e) the inauguration of a common transport policy;

(f) the establishment of a system ensuring that competition shall not be distorted in the Common Market;

(g) the application of procedures which shall make it possible to co-ordinate the economic policies of Member States and to remedy disequilibria in their balances of payments;

(h) the approximation of their respective municipal law to the extent necessary for the functioning of the Common Market;

(i) the creation of a European Social Fund in order to improve the possibilities of employment for workers and to contribute to the raising of their standards of living;

(j) the establishment of a European Investment Bank intended to facilitate the economic expansion of the Community through the creation of new resources; and

(k) the association of overseas countries and territories with the Community with a view to increasing trade and to pursuing jointly their effort towards economic and social development. (Article 3.)

The IRRI study defines the following as fundamental principles or characteristics of the Treaty: progressivity, prohibition on discrimination, irreversibility, openness, a geographically limited field of application, and coordination and harmonization.

1. The provisions for the *progressive creation of the Common Market*

as spelled out in Article 8 of the Treaty constitute one of its most notable features.[3] The transition period of twelve years (which may be extended to a maximum of fifteen years), with the system of targets already referred to, was established to allow for the necessary adaptations to the new state of affairs. However, although a specific timetable was established for the liberalization of goods, for other fields (such as agriculture) on the general goal of completion by the end of the transition period could be agreed upon. For transport, not even this general goal was specified.

2. Fundamental to any common market is a *prohibition on all discrimination* based on nationality. The Treaty affirms this general principle and assigns to the Community institutions the task of laying down such special rules as are necessary (Article 7).

3. The *irreversible* nature of the commitments entered into derives both from the scope and nature of the undertaking itself and from the fact that although there are numerous safeguard clauses that permit states to delay taking certain specified steps, these delay mechanisms are always temporary and the state is not the sole judge in the matter.[4]

4. The *open character* of the Community is attested to by the fact that any European state may become a member, subject to the unanimous approval of the Member States (Article 237), and that the Community can conclude association agreements with third countries, a union of states, or an international organization (Article 238).

5. The Treaty's scope of application is defined by the following factors: that the Treaty is *geographically* limited to the six signatories, their overseas territories, and Algeria; that it was concluded for an unlimited period of time (Article 240); and that it involves all sectors of the economy with the exceptions of coal and steel and atomic energy.

6. The signatory states have engaged to coordinate their economic policies to the extent necessary for the attainment of the objectives of the Treaty (Article 6).

THE UNIFICATION OF THE MARKET

The substantive material of the Treaty can be seen in terms of three economic axes: liberalization, normalization, and development. The *liberalization* of exchanges in goods and services, together with the freer circulation of persons, creates a new unified market within which competitive conditions must be *normalized*. The whole is then to be involved in a vast movement of *economic expansion and development*.

The liberalization of exchanges between the members, i.e., the unification of the market, consists of the establishment of the customs union, the special provisions for agriculture and transport, and the provisions for the free circulation of persons, services, and capital.

The Customs Union (Article 12–37)

The creation of a customs union implies the elimination of customs duties, of all charges of an equivalent effect, and of all quota measures. It supposes also the establishment of a common external tariff in relation to third countries.

The elimination of customs duties. It is forbidden to establish new duties (Article 12); those in force on January 1, 1957, were decreased by 10 per cent during the first year; thereafter each Member State is to reduce the total of the duties so as to reduce by 10 per cent its total customs receipts (based on value of imports for 1956), its being understood that the reduction for any particular product must be at least 5 per cent each time (Article 14, paragraph 3 and 4). This system permits some temporary protection of sensitive industries. The goals to be achieved are reductions for each product of 25 per cent at the end of the first period and of 50 per cent by the end of the second period (Article 14, paragraph 6).

The timing of these reductions, which also apply to duties of a fiscal nature, is spelled out in considerable detail (Article 14, paragraph 2): the first after one year, the second, third, and fourth at eighteen-month intervals thereafter, the fifth after another year, and the remaining reductions at intervals to be determined by the Community institutions. Customs duties on exportation and equivalent charges shall be abolished at the end of the first stage (Article 16). The institutions of the Community are charged with administering these provisions and with checking for noncompliance (Article 14, paragraph 6, Article 15, and Article 16, paragraph 4).

The elimination of quantitative restrictions. As of the coming into force of the Treaty, all new quantitative restrictions were prohibited (Articles 31 and 32). A timetable was established for the progressive enlargement of quotas. After one year all bilateral quotas were converted into global quotas open to all Member States, and these are to be increased by not less than 20 per cent each year as compared to the preceding year, with an increase of at least 10 per cent for any particular product (Article 33, paragraph 1). In the case of nonliberalized products or where the quota is very small, a quota equal to at least 3 per cent of the national output was established after one year, to be increased each year (Article 33, paragraph 2). Each quota shall be equal to not less than 20 per cent of the national output at the end of ten years (Article 33, paragraph 3).[5]

Export quotas shall be abolished by the end of the first stage (Article

34). Here again the tasks of administration and surveillance are performed by the institutions (Article 33, paragraph 4, 6, 7, and 8; Article 37, paragraph 6).

The establishment of a common external tariff. The adoption by the Member States of a common external tariff establishes the uniqueness of the Community and distinguishes it from a free trade area. The general rule adopted was that the common external tariff should be set at the level of the arithmetical average of the duties applied in the four customs territories involved: Benelux, Germany, France, and Italy (Article 19, paragraph 1; note exceptions in paragraph 2).

Exceptions exist for a number of products, however, and are all enumerated in a series of special lists appended to the Treaty.[6]

Member countries are required to reduce the gap between duties now in force for third countries and the common external tariff in three reductions of 30 per cent, 30 per cent, and 40 per cent, respectively, at the end of each of the three successive stages of the transition period (Article 23).

Special Provisions for Agriculture (Articles 38–47)

Although the common market extends to agriculture[7] and agricultural trade (Article 38), a whole set of special provisions supplementing or amending the general clauses had to be devised before an organized European market could be considered. This was made necessary by the probable repercussions that the abolition of protection would have on farm incomes, and by the fact that trade in agricultural products is hampered not so much by customs duties and quotas as by the innumerable restrictions that reflect varying patterns of agricultural marketing. These restrictions are accounted for by the special conditions of production (the small size of enterprises, their dependence on weather conditions, etc.).[8]

The fusion of the market in agricultural products is to take place against the background of a common agricultural policy that is to be elaborated during the transition period by the institutions of the Community (Article 43 spells out the procedures involved). The objective of this common policy is "to increase agricultural productivity," "to ensure thereby a fair standard of living for the agricultural population," "to stabilize markets," "to guarantee regular supplies and to ensure reasonable prices to consumers" (Article 39). The key to the common agricultural policy is to be a common organization of agricultural markets consisting of price controls, subsidies on production and marketing, arrangements for stockpiling and carry-forward, and a common machinery for stabilizing importation or exportation (Article 40, paragraph 3). Wide latitude is left the Community institutions in regard to such specifics as price levels and the form of market organization.[9]

The most concrete provisions deal with the protective devices to be retained, particularly with minimum price clauses, and the procedure by which these are to be eliminated,[10] and with ways of developing intra-Community trade by the conclusion of long-term contracts (Article 45). To avoid the possibility that these safeguard clauses might be used to frustrate the principle of trade liberalization in agriculture, the Community institutions are given powers of review and, most important, are charged with working out the criteria on the basis of which minimum prices are to be calculated (Article 44, paragraph 3).

Free Circulation of Persons, Services, and Capital (Articles 48–73)

In order to achieve a real unification or fusion of markets, the principle of the Common Market must be extended progressively to cover the liberalization of all factors of production, labor, services, business establishment, and capital, in addition to trade. Considerable attention is given to this necessity in the Treaty and also to protections against short-run social and monetary problems to which such liberalization might give rise. However, as was true in regard to agriculture, the upshot of these provisions is little more than a definition of ultimate goals, a list of general principles to be followed and a timetable for action. Further specification is left up to the institutions set up by the Treaty.

These general goals are defined in some detail for labor, services, and the right of establishment, but are extremely vague for capital movements. The free movement of workers is to be ensured by the end of the transition period and shall involve the abolition of any discrimination based on nationality as regards employment, remuneration, or working conditions.[11] Restrictions on the right to enter non-wage-earning occupations and to set up and manage firms and companies (Article 52), as well to receive payment for such services as insurance, banking and financial activities, distribution, and the professions, are to be progressively abolished (Article 59). As regards capital movement, the Treaty contains only one obligation: the freeing of current payments on capital movements (Article 67, paragraph 2). The ultimate goal is stated so generally as to lend itself to any number of interpretations. Restrictions are to be abolished "to the extent necessary for the proper functioning of the Common Market," exchange permits shall be granted in the "most liberal way possible" (Article 67, paragraph 1), and members "shall endeavor to avoid" the introduction of new restrictions (Article 71; note also escape clauses Article 70, paragraph 2, and Article 73).[12]

The institutions of the Community are given somewhat different roles in these several areas, but are in general empowered to "lay down the measures necessary" or to establish a "general program."[13]

Special Provisions for Transport (Articles 74–84)

Transport is an important service and as such is central to any common market. Discriminatory transport charges could easily wipe out customs duty reductions, thereby seriously distorting competition. Special provisions for transport services were necessary because of their intrinsic importance for the Common Market, because of their juridical status (since the railroads are government-owned and government-operated), and because of the thorny problem of competition between the different transport media. Thus the inclusion of transport is to be sought within the framework of a common policy, a policy, however, that is limited to the establishment of common regulations applicable to international transport and to the conditions under which nonresident carriers may be admitted to national transport services.[14] The application of the provisions is further limited by the exclusion of sea and air transport.[15]

Nevertheless, procedures are established to enable decisions to be reached in this restricted area, in harmony with the rest of the Treaty. In addition, more precise and immediate provisions are made for the elimination of forms of discrimination. All discriminatory prices and conditions of carriage that are based on country of origin or destination of products should be abolished by the end of the second stage (Article 79, paragraph 1), the Community institutions being empowered to lay down implementing rules (Article 79, paragraph 3 and 4). By the beginning of the second stage, the members are required to eliminate any subsidies or protection in prices or conditions of carriage that had been made in favor of particular firms (Article 80).[16]

THE NORMALIZATION OF COMPETITION

Competition in the Common Market can be distorted in numerous ways, as a result of which a country can be handicapped in competition with another, or consumers deprived of the beneficial effects of competition. The Treaty deals with such impediments to the normal circulation of goods by several means: by attempting to control agreements and monopolies, by controlling state aids or subsidies, and by correcting distortions that may arise from legislation or regulations imposed on industries.[17]

The provisions of the Treaty in this domain can be classified into two groups: those directed toward the actions of individuals or firms and those directed toward public (state) actions.

Rules Applicable to Firms (Article 85–91)

The following actions are deemed incompatible with the Common Market and are therefore prohibited:

Any agreement between enterprises, and decisions by associations of enterprises and any concerted practices which are likely to affect trade between the Member States and which have as their object or result the prevention, restriction or distortion of competition within the Common Market, in particular those consisting in:

(a) the direct or indirect fixing of purchase or selling prices or of any other trading conditions;

(b) the limitation or control of production, markets, technical development or investment;

(c) market-sharing or the sharing of sources of supply;

(d) the application to parties to transactions of unequal terms in respect of equivalent supplies, thereby placing them at a competitive disadvantage; or

(e) the subjecting of the conclusion of a contract to the acceptance by a party of additional supplies which, either by their nature or according to commercial usage, have no connection with the subject of such contract. (Article 85, paragraph 1.)

The prohibition does not apply when the agreement or practices in question "contribute to the improvement of the production or distribution of goods or to the promotion of technical or economic progress while reserving to users an equitable share in the profit" (Article 85, paragraph 2).[18] With respect to monopolies, the Treaty seeks to control the taking of improper advantage of a dominant position by prohibiting such practices as the imposition of inequitable prices or trading conditions, the limitation of production, and the application of unequal terms to different parties (Article 86). Here again it is left to the institutions of the Community to lay down such regulations as are necessary for the application of these general policies (Article 87).[19]

Dumping is categorically forbidden within the Common Market, and if recommendations by the Community institutions fail to stop such practices, the injured states are authorized to take whatever retaliatory steps these same institutions may determine (Article 91).

Rules Applicable to States (Articles 92–122)

Government aids that affect competition by favoring certain enterprises or products are deemed incompatible with the Common Market, whether provided directly by the state or from state resources (Article 92).[20] The Community institutions are given wide powers both in regard to such aids as already existed in the states, which they can require annulled or modified, and in regard to new aids, which must be submitted to them for approval; approval may be denied if the practices are found incompatible with the Common Market (Article 93).

Although the Treaty does not affect state autonomy in fiscal matters, it does impose certain restraints inherent in the principle of nondiscrimination. A state may not impose any internal charges or taxes designed to favor its producers, and all states are pledged to abolish any extant charges by the beginning of the second stage (Article 95).[21]

In addition to fiscal provisions, states may be required by the action of Community institutions to bring about greater uniformity in legislative and administrative provisions that have a direct bearing upon the Common Market (Article 100). Machinery is also provided for the elimination of disparities between the legislative and administrative provisions of the members, if these disparities distort the conditions of competition (Articles 101 and 102).

As part of this continuing principle of equalizing the costs and conditions of competition, the Treaty provides for the harmonization of social policy. It was thought that the costs imposed by social legislation would place unequal burdens on certain members. Consequently we find these commitments: to ensure the principle of equal pay for men and women during the first stage and to maintain this principle thereafter (Article 119); to "endeavor to maintain the existing equivalence of paid holiday schemes" (Article 120); and, by the end of the first stage, to adopt French practice concerning the basic level for overtime payment and the average overtime rates in industry.[22] The members agree on the general need to improve the living and working conditions of labor "so as to permit the equalization of such conditions in an upward direction" (Article 117), and assign to the institutions of the Community the task of promoting "close collaboration between Member States in the social field" (Article 118).

Some more general aspects of economic policy are also covered in the Treaty.

In economic as in social matters the guiding principle of the Treaty is to rely on the virtues inherent in the large market and on the wisdom of the common institutions which will supervise its application, but at the same time to establish at the outset certain compensatory mechanisms to assist that application and to guide it towards a fair sharing of opportunities between the regions. . . . The harmonization processes are intended to pave the way to a common economic policy by stimulating agreement on the most sensitive points. Other provisions in the Treaty, although they may have negative or safeguarding aspects, are intended to encourage a collective economic outlook and thus to correct the relatively automatic working of the mechanisms which create the customs union.[23]

The Treaty deals specifically with three aspects of general economic policy: economic trends, monetary policy, and commercial policy. The Member States have agreed that their policy relating to economic trends is a "matter of common interest," and that the Community institutions shall be consulted with regard to the measures to be taken (Article 103).

In respect of monetary policy, the Treaty leaves complete freedom to the Member States, each keeping its own currency and remaining responsible for maintaining its balance of payments.[24] Some coordination is essential, however, since a state's foreign trade policy is closely related to its monetary policy. Only very general commitments could be agreed upon: that "Member States shall co-ordinate their economic policies" through a "collaboration between the competent services of their administrative departments and between their central banks" (Article 105, paragraph 1); that a consultative Monetary Committee shall be established "to keep under review the monetary and financial situation of Member States" and to make reports to the Community institutions (Article 105, paragraph 2); that Member States shall undertake to authorize all "payments connected with the exchange of goods, services or capital, and also any transfers of capital and wages, to the extent that the movement of goods, services, capital and persons is freed as between Member States in application of this Treaty" (Article 106, paragraph 1); and that policy with regard to exchange rates shall be considered "a matter of common interest" (Article 107). Provisions are made for serious balance of payments difficulties whether resulting from the establishment of the Common Market or from other causes. Two remedies are foreseen: provisional adoption by the state concerned of safeguard measures (Article 109); and mutual assistance by its partners (Article 108). The only detailed role assigned to the Community institutions in the area of monetary policy, besides encouraging collaboration, is in determining the steps to be taken in case of balance of payments crises.

More effective coordination is provided in the area of commercial policy, probably by the force of circumstance, for here the progress toward a common external tariff makes collaboration indispensable. The Treaty requires that specific steps be taken during the transition period to lay the foundation of a common foreign trade policy and assigns the tasks of negotiation and decision to the Community institutions. During the transition period, "Member States shall coordinate their commercial relations with third countries" (Article 111, paragraph 1), shall seek to adjust their tariff agreements in force with third countries (Article 111, paragraph 4), shall harmonize their measures to aid exports to third countries (Article 112, paragraph 1), and shall consult with a view to concerting their action toward international organizations of an economic character (Article 116). At the end of the transitional period, uniform principles shall form the bases of the common commercial policy. This policy will cover tariff amendments, the conclusion of tariff or trade agreements, the alignment of liberalization measures, and export policy and protective commercial measures, including those for dumping and subsidies (Article 113, paragraph 1); it will be determined and directed by the institutions of the Community (Article 113, paragraph 2, and Article 116), which will also handle the approximations during the transition period (Article 111, paragraphs 1, 2, 4, and 5, and Article 112, paragraph 1), represent the Community, and conduct all relevant negotiations with third countries (Article 111, paragraph 2, and Article 113, paragraph 3).

ECONOMIC DEVELOPMENT

Having outlined the provisions of the Treaty as they relate to the liberalization of exchanges and the normalization of competition, we come now to our third economic axis, that of economic development. The Member States are pledged to "facilitate the economic expansion of the Community through the creation of new resources" and "to improve the possibilities of employment for workers and to contribute to the raising of their standard of living" (Article 3). Two tools have been created for these purposes: The European Investment Bank and the European Social Fund.[25]

The mission of the European Investment Bank is to contribute "to the balanced and smooth development of the Common Market" "by granting loans and guarantees on a non-profit-making basis," thus "facilitating the financing of" projects for aiding less developed regions, for modernizing or converting enterprises, or for creating new activities when these are of interest to several members and when they cannot be financed by means available in the Member States (Article 130). Its function is thus to bring into focus a common investment policy linked to the developing Common Market, although it is doubtful whether this can be achieved without a common economic policy.[26] The Bank has a capital of one billion dollars, subscribed as follows: 300 million each by France and Germany, 240 million by Italy, 86.5 million by Belgium, 71.5 million by Holland, and 2 million by Luxembourg.[27] It has a legal personality quite separate from that of the Community and a separate set of institutions charged with its administration.[28]

The European Social Fund, on the other hand, is administered by the institutions of the Community (Article 124. Also Articles 127 and 128). It is assigned the task of promoting employment facilities, and the geographical and occupational mobility of workers (Article 123). The Fund is authorized to cover 50 per cent of the expenses incurred by a State for the purpose of "ensuring productive re-employment of workers by means of: occupational retraining, resettlement allowances," and granting aids for workers whose employment is affected "as a result of the conversion of enterprises to other production" (Article 125, paragraph 1). The scope of the Fund is limited, and its effects are difficult to predict because it is restricted to supplementing national programs,[29] because it can contribute only to the expenses of workers already re-employed (Article 125, paragraph 2), and because the Treaty contains no provision for its financial resources.

THE ASSOCIATION OF OVERSEAS TERRITORIES

In spite of the difficult problems posed, and after arduous negotiation, it was finally decided to "bring into association with the Community the non-European territories" of certain of its members, so as to promote their economic and social development and to establish close relations between them and the Community.[30] This association is governed by several principles. The overseas territories are part of the Common Market and shall have free access to it for their products, while at the same time applying to their commercial exchanges with Member States the same rules applied in respect of the state with which they have special relations (Article 132). The overseas territories have special needs, and may levy certain customs duties on imports from the Community when this is necessary to their economic development and so long as there is no discrimination between the six partners (Article 133, paragraph 3). Member States have agreed to contribute to the investments required for the progressive development of these countries and territories by creating a Development Fund.[31]

The Convention annexed to the Treaty sets forth the steps to be taken during an initial five-year period, after which new provisions will be drawn up. Community institutions are assigned roles analogous to those exercised in the Common Market,[32] as well as the task of administering and directing the activities of the Development Fund.[33] During the five-year period, the Member States will contribute a total of $580,000,000 to the Development Fund. The Convention specifies not only the proportionate contributions but also the allocation of the funds among the territories, the French Territories receiving the lion's share.[34]

This summary of the substantive provisions of the Rome Treaty reveals the immense scope of the undertaking. The Treaty establishing the European Economic Community aims beyond the immediate goal of a customs union, envisaging in effect the eventual achievement of an economic union and the creation of "the foundations of an ever closer union among the European peoples" (Preamble to the Treaty of Rome). "The Member States are determined to secure the full advantages of a Common Market, and . . . this requires the control of such a market by means of common rules and common institutions."[35] The Six have made use of the method of international organization, and have committed themselves to specific obligations, with common institutions to supervise their execution. They have also laid down common rules and objectives and have agreed to follow common policies in such important areas as agriculture and foreign commercial relations. Certain limitations must be kept in mind, however. The field of competence of the European Economic Community is strictly limited to the economy, and even in this area there is no rigid system of commitments, the Treaty proceeding very flexibly from subject to subject. Furthermore, the common institutions have no general competence to take whatever measures are necessary to reach the assigned objectives.[36]

III

THE TREATY AND POLITICAL INTEGRATION

ONE OF THE TREATY'S unique characteristics, much discussed by commentators, is that, with the exception of specific obligations clearly spelled out in regard to the customs union provisions, it amounts to a general statement of goals with a set of institutions and a procedure for their attainment. This is in sharp contrast to the Treaty of the European Coal and Steel Community, which is a quite precise statement of *rules* and a machinery for their application, and gives the EEC institutions far wider latitude for quasi-legislative functions.[1] So we see the Treaty widely referred to as a "traité cadre" (framework treaty). It sets forth the basis of economic unification, leaving much of the content vague, but establishing an institutional system with the power to define the future order of things.[2] According to one observer, "this amounts to a real European legislative power. . . . The Community is going to lay down general measures in areas in which national legislatures have legislated or which have been at least in fact considered as pertaining normally to the legislature in most states."[3] The legislative power has two dimensions. The first concerns the ability of the institutions to deal directly with the substantive fields of activity of the Treaty and is expressed in the form of the actions they may take in order to achieve their aims; the second concerns the ability of the institutions to modify the terms of the Treaty itself.

According to the Treaty, the institutions may act in the following ways with regard to the Member States: they may issue regulations and directives, make decisions, and formulate recommendations or opinions.[4] *Regulations* have general application and are binding in every respect and directly applicable in each Member State. This is a real "European" power for the Community, which is here granted the right to legislate directly on the populations of the Member States without passing through national organs.[5] *Directives* are binding on any Member State to which they are addressed with regard to the result to be achieved, but leave to domestic agencies the determination of form and means. *Decisions* are binding in every respect for the addressee, which can be either a specific individual, in which case they have executory force,[6] or, more likely, a state, whose government is thus bound.[7] *Recommendations and opinions* have no binding force. Regulations, directives, and decisions must be supported by reasons and shall refer to proposals or opinions that derive from the Treaty (Article 190). If any state fails to respect these acts, it may be charged with violation of the Treaty (Articles 169–70). These various modes of action will be discussed more fully later. Suffice it to say now that they range from specific administrative and enforcement tasks, as in the customs union provisions, to the formulation of broad policy, as in the field of agriculture.

An unusual feature of the Treaty is the fact that it grants to its central institutions—as distinguished from the signatory states—the power to modify the terms of the Treaty itself. This is given its most general expression in the following statement: the Community institutions are authorized to "enact the appropriate provisions" when "any action by the Community appears necessary to achieve, in the functioning of the Common Market, one of the aims of the Community in cases where this Treaty has not provided for the requisite powers of action" (Article 235). There are numerous other instances of acts that constitute either *complements* to, or *modifications* of, the Treaty. We have already mentioned many of the activities left to the institutions, activities that are in effect complements to the Treaty: the establishment of uniform objective criteria for fixing minimum prices for agricultural goods and their substitution for national systems; laying down a general program for abolishing restrictions on the free movement of workers, on the freedom of establishment, and on the supply of services; deciding whether, to what extent, and by what procedures general transport provisions shall be extended to sea and air transport; determining new tasks for the European Social Fund, and so on.[8]

These complements are a vital part of the ability of the institutions to *act directly* in regard to the subject matter of the Treaty, a topic that will be discussed in detail later. The possibilities for *modification* of the Treaty are more relevant for our immediate purpose. Here we can identify at least ten cases when substantial changes in Treaty provisions may be made by the institutions themselves.[9] These include amending the entire timetable for the elimination of customs duties and quantitative restrictions; writing a new Convention concerning relations with the Overseas Countries and Territories; the power to increase the number of judges and advocates-general of the Court; the amendments concerning the scale of financial contributions to the Community; the authority to lay down provisions for the direct financing of the institutions from the proceeds of the Common External Tariff; determining provisions for direct election of the European Parliamentary Assembly by universal suffrage; determining the conditions of admission to membership of any other European state and the adjustments to the Treaty necessitated thereby; and concluding agreements with third countries, a union of states, or an international organization.

There is, naturally, a procedure for formal amendment, although, what with the broad discretionary powers granted to the institutions, one wonders if it will be much used. Proposals for Treaty revision, if approved by the institutions of the Community, shall be submitted to a conference of representatives of the governments of the Member States, the representatives determining "in common agreement the amendments to be made to this Treaty."[10] This is a traditional procedure for intergovernmental conventions or agreements and is the procedure followed for the Rome Treaty itself. It seems likely, however, that most modifications of the Rome Treaty will be accomplished without it.

THE NATURE OF THE EEC INSTITUTIONAL SYSTEM

We have so far demonstrated the existence in the Treaty of a legislative or quasi-legislative power that has been entrusted to the institutions of the EEC, not to mention their administrative and enforcement functions. The Member States have thus given up the power to act autonomously and unilaterally in a whole spectrum of specific and general cases by virtue of the authority and role granted to these institutions. We have not discussed the individual institutions up to this point because I have wanted to demonstrate that such legislative powers and abilities to deal directly with the subject matter of the Treaty as the institutions possess are granted to the Community as a whole and not to any one institution as was the case with the High Authority in the ECSC Treaty. For the purposes of the following discussion the EEC will be treated as an independent system in isolation from the two other Communities, the ECSC and Euratom, even though they share several of the same institutions.*

* Namely, the European Parliamentary Assembly and the Court of Justice (see Convention Relating to Certain Common Institutions of the European Communities). Each of the three treaties sets up a different set of relationships with different powers and different roles for the various institutions.

The EEC system consists of the following institutions:

The Assembly,* composed of delegates from the national parliaments who are appointed in accordance with the procedure laid down in each state. It consists of 142 members, 36 each from Germany, France, and Italy, 14 each from Belgium and the Netherlands, and 6 from Luxembourg.[11]

The Council of Ministers, with one representative delegated by each government (Article 146).

The Commission, consisting of nine members chosen for their general competence by the governments of the Member States acting in common agreement. The term of office is four years and can be renewed. Members of the Commission may not seek or accept instructions from any government, being charged with representing the general interest of the Community. Similarly, the Member States have engaged to respect this independence and not to seek to influence the members (Articles 157 and 158).

The Court of Justice, consisting of seven judges, who shall be chosen from among persons of indisputable independence, and who fulfill the conditions required for holding the highest judicial office or who are jurists of recognized competence. They are appointed for a term of six years by the governments acting in common agreement. A partial renewal takes place every three years, all judges being eligible for reappointment.[12]

The various Consultative Committees, chief of which is the *Economic and Social Committee,* composed of representatives of the various categories of economic and social life: producers, farmers, transport operators, workers, merchants, artisans, the liberal professions, and "the general interest." It has 101 members, 24 each from Germany, France, and Italy, 12 each from the Netherlands and Belgium, and 5 from Luxembourg, appointed for four years renewable by the Council acting unanimously (Articles 193 and 194).

How do these institutions exercise the powers conferred upon them by the Treaty? What are their roles?

Administrative and Executive Powers

The effective powers of the Community are concentrated in two institutions, the Commission, which is permanent and essentially administrative or technical, and the Council, which is nonpermanent and political. The Council is charged with ensuring the achievement of the objectives laid down in the Treaty and the coordination of the general economic policies

---

* The name of the Assembly was officially changed to the European Parliament in 1962. Since, however, most of the sources cited in this book refer to it as the European Parliamentary Assembly (or the EPA), I have preferred to use this form.

of the Member States, and is endowed with the major powers of decision (Article 145).

The Council as an organ of the Community is called upon to conform to the objectives of the Community and is thus faced with the double task of representing the interests of the different States and of assuring the satisfaction of the common interest as well. Thus its principal function is to find an equilibrium between opposed national interests and to harmonize them with the common objectives and necessities of the Treaty.[13]

The Commission is to watch over the general functioning and development of the Common Market. It is charged with *ensuring the execution* by the Member States of the Treaty and of the acts of its institutions. For this purpose it has a general power of recommendation and advice (Article 155), as well as numerous particular powers, such as the right to gather information and verify any matters in its jurisdiction (Article 213), and the right to require a Member State to defend its actions by submitting comments, should the Commission consider that the State has failed to fulfill any of its obligations (Article 169). The Commission represents the Community at the European Parliamentary Assembly, before which it is responsible (Articles 140, 143, and 144) in judicial matters (Article 211), in negotiations and relations with third countries and international organizations,[14] and in financial administration (Articles 205, 206, and 208); in addition, it has the duty of publishing a general report on the activities of the Community (Article 156). It has its own power of decision and participates in the preparation of acts of the Council and Assembly, and may also exercise such competence as the Council confers on it (Article 155).

REPRESENTATION IN EEC ORGANS

	Council votes	Commission[a]	Europ. Parlia. Assembly	Econ. & Soc. Committee	Votes Social Fund	Votes Development Fund
France	4	2	36	24	32	33
Germany	4	2	36	24	32	33
Italy	4	2	36	24	20	11
Belgium	2	1	14	12	8	11
Netherlands ...	2	1	14	12	7	11
Luxembourg ...	1	1	6	5	1	1
Total ...	17	9	142	101	100	100

a Although the members of the Commission are not regarded as national representatives, and although only the maximum number in the Commission, not the precise distribution, is fixed by the Treaty, the practice has been to allocate seats as shown in the figures.

Thus the Treaty envisages a very close cooperation between these two institutions.[15] Although the Council takes most of the final decisions, it can usually act only on a proposition of the Commission, which it cannot amend except by a unanimous vote (Article 149). This requirement of unanimity presumes in favor of the proposals of the Commission and, combined with the fact that the Council can rarely act on its own initiative, gives to the Commission a considerable influence over the deliberations and decisions of the Council. "The Commission is thus the driving force behind the actions of the Council, which filters, controls, and channels this force."[16] Another significant provision is that which permits the Commission to modify its proposals so long as they have not been finally acted upon by the Council (Article 149). This gives the Commission an arbitration function in that it can make changes in its proposals should this be necessary to avoid a deadlock in the Council. It also implies, of course, that the Council might refuse to consider a proposal of the Commission, unless the Commission agrees to amend.

We have seen that the Treaty envisages three combinations for decision-making so far as the Commission and Council are concerned: the Council can act alone, the Commission can act alone, or the Council can act on a proposition of the Commission. The voting procedures governing the exercise of decisional power vary depending upon the nature of the question and the originating institution. The Commission is a strictly collegial body, and all votes are, in principle, to be reached by a simple majority of its members (Article 163). The voting machinery for Council acts is far more complex and is one of the most original aspects of the Treaty. The governing principle is that of "weighted voting," and it is designed to conciliate juridical equality with the functional inequality of states at the international level. It seems likely that such provisions will be demanded in any international organization involving loss or sharing of sovereignty.[17] Certain acts of the Council require unanimity, although this is in general limited to the transitional period or to primarily political questions.[18] It is significant that "abstentions by members either present or represented shall not prevent the adoption of Council conclusions requiring unanimity" (Article 148, paragraph 3). Otherwise, according to the case, Council acts call for a simple majority, a qualified majority, or several special majorities.

The Treaty states that, except when otherwise provided for, the conclusions of the Council shall be reached by a *simple majority vote* (Article 148, paragraph 1). This seems a very large exception, since the Treaty states most precisely the majorities required in practically all cases. A simple majority is actually quite difficult to achieve, a majority of six being in fact a two-thirds majority. It places all members on an artificial level of equality and is actually applicable in only six cases in the Treaty, all of which deal either with internal matters or with relatively minor matters in which the smaller powers have a special interest.

The *qualified majority*, based on a system of weighted voting, governs a majority of cases under the Treaty[19] and "represents the common law of the Treaty."[20] The votes of the Member States are weighted as follows: Germany, France, and Italy have four votes each, Holland and Belgium two each, and Luxembourg one vote. The majority required is twelve votes of the seventeen. In cases in which the Council acts on a proposal of the Commission the majority may be reached by any combination of states, but in all other cases it must have the favorable vote of at least four states.[21] This is a concession to the small powers to compensate for the usual guarantee provided by the "European" Commission. This arrangement permits the three big powers to prevail if they are in agreement with each other *and* with the Commission. No single big power (in combination with Luxembourg) can block the work of the Council. Two big powers must obtain the support of Belgium and the Netherlands to get their view accepted. The aim was to favor agreement between the big three and to avoid the creation of two permanent voting blocks.[22] The liberalizing effect of a prior proposal from the Commission is a true innovation, "since it indirectly introduces a vote of the Community in the voting procedure of the Council."[23] It should be recalled further that even when the Council is acting by a qualified majority, it must reject or accept Commission proposals *in toto*, since they can be formally amended *by the Council* only by a unanimous vote.*

Special majorities, also based on weighted voting, are called for in case of the adoption of that part of the budget relating to the European Social Fund,[24] and for three votes concerning the administration of the Development Fund.[25] The weighting is based directly on the financial contributions of the Member States to the respective Funds. In either case the required majority is 67 votes out of 100, thus preventing a single big power from blocking decisions.

This institutional system is designed to enable the Member States to acquire a view of their common interest, and to urge them to take cooperative action. Most decisions are prepared by the Commission, which is required to reach and to defend an independent view from the standpoint of the Community. Its proposals are submitted to the Council, and it participates in all the discussions held in the Council. "Thus, from the start as well as during the debates in which each government defends, as

---

* The Commission *can* change its proposals, and may have to do so, in order to get Council agreement.

they should, their national interest, a voice speaks for the interests of the Community."[26] The Council, after thorough discussion, is urged to take action by the provision that most decisions can (or will ultimately) be taken by a qualified majority vote, and that most decisions must be made on Commission proposals and cannot be amended except unanimously. Thus decisions can be taken and actions carried out despite the opposition of a Member State. A decision taken by a majority engages the responsibility of all the members of the Council, and a Member State cannot "prevent application, as far as it is concerned, of decisions to which it has not agreed."[27]

Comparison of Weighted Voting and Financial Contribution

	European Social Fund		Development Fund	
	Weighting	Financial contribution	Weighting	Financial contribution
Belgium	8	8.8%	11	12.04%
Germany	32	32.0	33	34.41
France	32	32.0	33	34.41
Italy	20	20.0	11	6.88
Luxembourg ...	1	0.2	1	0.22
Netherlands ...	7	7.0	11	12.04
Total ...	100	100 %	100	100 %

source: Van Ginderachter, p. 387.

Before we can draw firm conclusions about the potential impact of these institutional provisions, we must specify which policy areas, normally subject to the autonomous determination of the individual Member States, are affected. We shall have to analyze in detail the *scope* of the powers that can be exercised under the Treaty. This has been done in Appendix A (pp. 299–312), and the complete catalogue of powers, procedures, forms of action, and voting arrangements is to be found there. A summary of quantitative characteristics is given in the table on the facing page.

We see that most important decisions, those that have an impact on the legislative and administrative autonomy of the Member States and on the nationals of the States (i.e., regulations, directives, and decisions), are made by the Council on a proposal of the Commission. Most of these can be adopted by a qualified majority of the Council, at least after the first four to eight years. Unanimity is required for actions of particular importance, especially those which constitute modifications or complements to the Treaty, and for actions primarily of a political nature. The Council has a limited range of actions that it can take without a proposal of the

DECISION-MAKING IN THE EEC TREATY

	Actions			
	Regulations	Directives	Decisions	Other
Council alone:				
Unanimity	3	—	7	21^a
Qualified majority	—	1	7	5^b
Simple majority	—	—	1	4
Special majority	—	—	2	—
Council on Commission proposal:				
Unanimity	14^c	12^e	5^g	5
Qualified majority	19^d	15^f	13^h	2
Simple majority	2	1	—	3
Special majority	—	—	2	—
Commission alone:				
Simple majority	5	5	21	10

a = of which 2 change to qualified majority. e = of which 10 change to qualified majority.
b = including 2 initially unanimity. f = including 10 initially unanimity.
c = of which 5 change to qualified majority. g = of which 1 changes to qualified majority.
d = including 5 initially unanimity. h = including 1 initially unanimity.

Commission, and most of these are matters either of internal organization (statute of personnel, budgetary questions) or of external relations (admission of new members, association of third states, relations with international organizations). The Commission has its own power of decision in such strictly technical areas as intervening to put various safeguard clauses into action, the calculation of duties and the arithmetic average for the common external tariff, and administration of the Social Fund. Thus the definition of policy for nonspecified objectives was left to the Council, whereas it belongs to the Commission in those technical areas in which the principles and the general policy have been defined in the Treaty.[28]

Far from establishing a rigid code of rights and obligations, the Member States have transferred to common institutions subject to their predominant influence powers and legal means necessary to carry out the achievement of the objectives and principles of the Community. While accomplishing their mission, the institutions, though bound by the more or less detailed provisions of the Treaties, have a large amount of freedom in selecting the common policies or determining the law of the Community.[29]

Most commentators agree that on the level of practical realities the Commission will exercise a very influential role. There is no doubt that the powers of proposition are a most important element. The Commission also has resources accruing from its permanence, and central facilities for study and research.[30]

If the Commissions advance only proposals that the Council may wish to hear, they may in their subservience to the Council forfeit their independence, betray the protection and promotion of Community interests, and become mere traditional governmental commissions. If, on the other hand, the Commissions pursue bold yet realistic policies, they may succeed in coaxing the Council along to take such and such action, particularly if they are supported by the Assembly.[31]

It is quite clear, however, that integration will not proceed against the will of the Member States, and that a great deal of negotiating will be necessary to establish a balance between conflicting forces and interests.

In relation with this fact it is often said that the negotiations initiated with the drafting of the Treaties continue. It should then be underlined that these negotiations initiated between the six Member States with the usual procedure and conditions of classical international negotiations continue in the different framework of the Community. The difference increases as a mutual adjustment of conflicting forces and of the framework of the Community is taking place.[32]

It is this framework and this difference with which we are concerned. The Council is made up of representatives of the Member States, and it is clear that the governmental representatives in Council will act on instructions from their respective governments. It would be misleading, however, to describe the Council as merely the sum of the governments of the different states and to consider it as some sort of permanent diplomatic conference.[33] It is a Community institution. This is evident from the fact that the decisions of the Council can frequently be taken against the will of one or more governments.[34] Even when Council votes require unanimity, it is an imputable act of an international organization rather than a matter of an international agreement, an agreement between six states.[35]

Interestingly enough, the Treaty itself makes a distinction between the Council acting by unanimity and an agreement between the six governments. This occurs in areas in which the States were seemingly most anxious to retain sovereignty, e.g., a decision on the location of the permanent seat of the Community institutions (Article 216), the negotiation of the duties for the goods on List G (Article 20), and multilateral and bilateral associations with third states (Article 238). Political circumstances will weigh heavily, too. The exercise of a veto power by a single state in an undertaking like the EEC will always be decided upon with an eye to the discomforts of being isolated in a "club de six."[36] It is possible that the veto will be a desirable instrument for compelling the Member States to attain consensus by negotiation, and that the complicated voting arrangements provided for will never be employed.

We have seen to this point that the Member States in signing the Treaty of Rome have agreed to lay down on certain specified matters a law of the Community, directly binding in each State and applied as national law. The basic outlines of this law are to be found in the Treaty itself (as in the rules of Competition in Articles 85 and 86), but it has to be completed, adapted, implemented, and applied to individual cases, a task that is to be performed by the institutions of the Community. "The authors of the Treaty were, however, aware that beyond this creation of a uniform Community law the economic integration of Europe postulated a harmonization of national law."[37] Recall the numerous specific Treaty provisions calling for harmonization and coordination of national legislation and administration in customs matters (Article 27), for the right of establishment (Article 54, paragraph 3, and Article 56, paragraph 2), for the free supply of services (Article 66), and in social affairs (Article 117).

The principle is stated in general terms in a special section of the Treaty entitled "The Approximation of Legislation" (Articles 100–102): "The Council, acting by means of a unanimous vote on a proposal of the Commission, shall issue directives for the approximation of such legislative and administrative provisions of the Member States as have a direct incidence on the Common Market" (Article 100). Since directives are binding only in regard to the result to be achieved, the form and means of their implementation are left to the State concerned. In fact it will be the Commission that selects the dispositions to be approximated, prepares the decisions, and acts as the motor of the harmonization activity.[38] The common rules, whether laid down by the Treaty or issued by the common institutions, can only be considered the law of the Community insofar as some procedure is organized to ensure their execution. The Member States cannot be the final judge of the observance of their obligations. Nor could the harmonization of legislation long proceed without a harmonization or unification of jurisprudence. To these ends the Treaty envisages the creation of a Court of Justice.

Judicial Control

The Court of Justice is charged with ensuring the "observance of law and justice" in the interpretation and application of the Treaty (Article 164). As such it may hear appeals against acts of the Council or the Commission, appeals against inaction of the Council or the Commission, appeals by the Commission against Member States, appeals by one Member State against another, appeals to pecuniary sanctions, and appeals concerning conflicts of jurisdiction. The Court also has certain other special competences:[39]

1. Appeals against the acts of the Council and Commission (other than

recommendations and opinions) may be brought by a Member State, the Council or the Commission, or any natural or legal person. Appeals by Member States, the Council, or the Commission may be brought on grounds of incompetence, errors of substantial form, infringement of the Treaty or of any legal provisions relating to its application, or abuse of power. Any natural or legal person may appeal against a decision addressed to him, or against a decision that is of direct and specific concern to him although addressed to another person (Article 173). If the appeal is well founded, the Court of Justice shall declare the act concerned to be null and void (Article 174).

2. Appeals against failure to act when required to by the Treaty may be brought against the Council or the Commission by a Member State, by the other institutions of the Community, or by natural or legal persons. "Such appeals shall only be admissible if the institution concerned has previously been invited to act. If at the expiry of two months after such invitation that institution has not stated its attitude, the appeal may be lodged" (Article 175).

3. Appeals may be brought by the Commission against a Member State for failure to fulfill any of its obligations under the Treaty. The Commission must first give a reasoned opinion on the matter after requiring the State to submit its comments. "If such State does not comply with the terms of such opinion within the period laid down by the Commission, the latter may refer the matter to the Court of Justice" (Article 169). If the Court finds against the Member State, "such State shall take the measures required for the implementation of the judgment of the Court" (Article 171). The Community has no means of enforcement against a Member State, but "failing to comply with a decision of the Court stating its obligations under the Treaty is highly improbable on the part of a Member State. A failure would mean that the Member State is questioning the 'affectio societas' without which the Community can not live and would therefore raise a basic political problem."[40]

4. Appeals by a Member State against another Member State may be brought on the grounds of failure to fulfill Treaty obligations. The matter must first be referred to the Commission, which must give a reasoned opinion within three months after requiring the States concerned to submit their comments in written and oral pleadings (Article 170). Thus, such a dispute may be settled by the Commission. "And if it goes to the Court, the views of the Commission speaking for the common interests of the Community will be taken into account."[41]

5. Appeals to pecuniary sanctions may be made if individuals or enterprises fail to comply with their obligations under the law of the Community. The Treaty itself does not institute penalties, but "the regulations

laid down by the Council pursuant to the provisions of this Treaty may confer on the Court of Justice full jurisdiction in respect of penalties provided for in such regulations" (Article 172). The Treaty provides a special system for enforcing pecuniary obligations, a system that also applies to the enforcement of the decisions of the Court. The Community itself has no means of enforcement, but the Treaty stipulates that forced execution shall be automatically ensured by the Member States.

The writ of execution shall be served, without other formality than the verification of the authenticity of the written act, by the domestic authority. . . . After completion of these formalities at the request of the party concerned, the latter may, in accordance with municipal law, proceed with such forced execution by applying directly to the authority which is competent. (Article 192.)

6. Appeals concerning conflicts of jurisdiction. When any question concerning the interpretation of the Treaty, the validity and interpretation of the acts of the institutions, and the interpretation of the statutes of any bodies set up by an act of the Council is raised before a court of one of the Member States, such a court, if it considers that its judgment depends on a preliminary decision, may request a ruling by the Court of Justice. Should there be no appeal under municipal law from the decisions of such a court, the matter *must* be referred to the Court of Justice (Article 177).[42]

7. Special competences. The Court may hear cases concerning fulfillment by Member States of their obligations under the Statute of the European Investment Bank, the conclusions of the Board of Governors of the Bank, or the conclusions of the Board of Directors (Article 180). It may rule in any case between the Community and its employees under the conditions laid down by the relevant statute (Article 179), and on the removal or suspension from office of members of the Commission (Articles 157 and 160).[43] The Council, the Commission, or a Member State may obtain the opinion of the Court regarding the compatibility with the Treaty of agreements between the Community and one or more States of an international organization (Article 228). The Court is "competent to make a decision pursuant to any arbitration clause contained in a contract concluded under public or private law, by or on behalf of the Community" (Article 181). Member States may also submit disputes to the Court for decision (Article 182). The Court is called upon to appoint arbitrators in several cases: passage from the first to the second stage after the sixth year if the required majority is not reached, or a minority state so requests (Article 8, paragraph 4); appeals to decisions taken at the end of the transition period to amend, abolish, or maintain the derogations accorded to Luxembourg (Article 1, paragraph 2 of Protocol Concerning the Grand Duchy of Luxembourg); and in the event of disagreement about whether

the level of the monetary reserves of the franc area may be considered satisfactory enough to call for the abolition of special aids (Protocol Relating to Certain Provisions of Concern to France, Article 1, paragraph 3).

Parliamentary Control

"The Assembly . . . shall exercise the powers of deliberation and control which are conferred upon it by this Treaty" (Article 137). The control function is based on the Assembly's right to receive and discuss in public meeting the annual general report submitted to it by the Commission (Article 143), to address oral and written questions to the Commission, which the latter is obliged to answer (Article 140), and to force the resignation of the Commission by adopting by a two-thirds majority of the votes cast a motion of censure concerning its activities (Article 144).

The practical effectiveness of these powers is subject to some question, however. Although the Assembly can try to influence Commission policy preparation through its committees, in practice it has had little success in gaining any *prior* control over the policy of the executive and the propositions being made to the Council. Furthermore, a vote of censure forcing the resignation of the entire Commission would doubtless weaken the position of that institution vis-à-vis the Council, a result not likely to be welcomed by the Assembly.[44] The control function is further attenuated by the fact that the most important decisions are taken by the Council. The Commission could easily hide behind the argument that its proposals had not been accepted by the Council. The Council is not responsible before the Assembly, does not have to respond to questions verbally or in writing, and has full latitude over the conditions under which it shall be heard by the Assembly (Article 140).[45] However, it is probable that the provisions of the Treaty that bind the Council and the Commission together in the preparation and promulgation of regulations, directives, and decisions, insofar as they reinforce the role of the Commission, will indirectly extend the control of the Assembly over the decision-making process.[46]

In addition to these powers of control, the Assembly has certain functions of consultation and deliberation. The Treaty stipulates no less than twenty-three specific cases in which the Council, after having received a proposal from the Commission, must submit it to the Assembly for its opinion. A complete listing will be found in Appendix B. The Commission defends the proposals before the Assembly, which then makes its opinion known by means of an absolute majority vote (Article 141). The Commission may then modify its original proposals so long as the Council has not acted (Article 149). Reuter suggests that this procedure might lead the Commission and the Council to get together prior to submitting projects to the Assembly, thus furthering a basic Treaty goal of encouraging continuous cooperation and consultation.[47]

The Commission is required to include in its general report to the Assembly a special chapter on the development of the social situation within the Community. "The Assembly may also 'invite' the Commission to draw up reports on special problems concerning the social situation" (Article 122). A consultation is almost always prescribed for important decisions in the social field, for amendments or complements to the Treaty, or for problems traditionally reserved for parliaments. Even though these consultations carry no obligatory weight, it would be difficult for the Council to ignore the opinion of an Assembly "composed of representatives of the peoples of the States united within the Community."[48] The Assembly thus participates in the process whereby the institutions of the Community complete, develop, and apply the general goals laid down in the Treaty of Rome.

The participation of the Assembly in the budgetary process requires some additional comment. Each EEC institution makes a provisional estimate of its expenses. The Commission then groups these estimates into an "avant-projet," which it sends with its recommendations to the Council. The Council must consult the Commission and, "where appropriate, the other institutions concerned."[49] The Council then establishes a draft budget, which is sent to the Assembly before October 31 of the year preceding that of its implementation. If, within a period of one month, the Assembly states its approval, or does not transmit an opinion to the Council, the budget is considered adopted. If the Assembly proposes amendments, these are transmitted to the Council, which discusses them with the Commission. These amendments may or may not be taken into account when the Council adopts the final budget (Article 23, paragraphs 3 and 4). The Commission is also required to submit to the Assembly the accounts of the preceding financial year in respect of the budget, together with a balance sheet showing the assets and liabilities of the Community (Article 206). The possibility envisaged in the Treaty of financing the Community from its own resources in order to give the Commission greater independence might be expected to result in a strengthened control by the Assembly.[50]

The Consultation of Interests

The Treaty also provides for the creation of several quasi-corporative consultative institutions. Most of these are highly specialized, such as the Monetary Committee, the Transport Committee, and a committee to administer the European Social Fund.

The Monetary Committee, consisting of two members from each country, was established in order to promote the coordination of monetary matters, and is directed "to keep under review the monetary and financial situation of Member States and of the Community and also the general payments system of Member States and to report regularly thereon to the Council and Commission; and to formulate opinions, at the request of the Council or of the Commission or on its own initiative" (Article 105, paragraph 2). It must be consulted on the following matters: the abolition of restrictions on capital movements (Article 69); the introduction of exchange restrictions (Article 71); the authorization to a state to take protective measures in case of disturbances of the capital market (Article 73); authorization to Member States to take protective measures when one Member State alters its exchange rate so as to distort competitive conditions (Article 107); the granting of mutual assistance to a Member State in balance of payments difficulties (Article 108); and decisions to require a Member State to amend or abolish safeguard measures taken unilaterally (Article 109).

The Transport Committee is composed of experts appointed by the Member States; these experts are attached to the Commission, which consults the Committee on transport questions whenever it deems it desirable (Article 83). *The Committee for the Social Fund* is composed of representatives of governments, trade unions, and employees associations, and is to assist the Commission in administering the European Social Fund (Article 124).

The Economic and Social Committee is the only one of these consultative bodies with anything like a broad mandate; as such, it is the only one likely to have any significant integrative role to play, although the others may well be important in their specialized areas.[51] The Committee includes representatives from all categories of economic and social life and is divided up into specialized sections for the main fields of the Treaty, specifically including an agricultural and a transport section (Article 197). The Committee must be consulted by the Council or by the Commission in specified cases, including most provisions involving the elaboration of "European legislation." The Council or Commission may ask for its opinion in other cases if they think fit. A list of cases in which the Committee's opinion must be sought will be found in Appendix A, p. 311.

The possibilities for a positive role for the ESC are somewhat limited by the absence of a right to issue an opinion on its own initiative or to adopt its own rules of procedure.[52] The Treaty does not stipulate how votes are to be taken in the ESC, an indication that voting as such was not considered important. What is important is to afford interested groups a forum in which to make their opinions known.[53]

SUMMARY AND CONCLUSIONS

Opinions vary about the potential significance of the Rome Treaty. Frank sees it as "an ingenious and imaginative document" that reflects "an intimate familiarity with postwar efforts to make progress in the reductions of trade barriers."[54] On the other hand, we have the following continental opinion:

The Treaty is interminable, complex, impossible to disentangle. . . . This is how Europe—still in the process of gestation—falls headlong into Byzantinism. . . . What is this mixed salad of eloquent declarations of principle, minute and at times ridiculously detailed regulations, platonic protestations to good intentions, technical rules of economic disarmament, pious wishes, principles and exceptions to principles, and exceptions to exceptions? There is not an article affirming a proposition that another article hidden in another corner of the Treaty would not render almost meaningless. The judges of the Court of Justice better have their spectacles handy! The text which it will be their chore to interpret is a "maquis," a labyrinth, a brain-twister, a puzzle.[55]

But for those of us who are concerned more with political and economic potentialities than with the niceties of legal draftsmanship, a fairer assessment is given by Stein:

The exceptions, the escape clauses and safeguards written into the Treaty, particularly at the insistence of the French, give an impression of undue complexity. But if one considers the novel character of the Treaty, its scope and the need to accommodate vital national interests, as well as the continental approach to constitutional documents, it would be naïve to expect a simple instrument. The Treaty extends to *all* economic activities of a complex industrial society.[56]

It remains to consider the general questions posed earlier with regard to the potentialities for political integration inherent in the EEC Treaty. Which policy areas normally subject to the autonomous determination of each State are affected? To what degree is decision-making in these areas shared or delegated? And what is the nature of the institutional system established? In order to summarize the provisions of the Treaty with regard to these questions, we shall argue that the Treaty involved the Member States in a wide range of commitments and obligations, and that these can be arranged along a rough continuum ranging from the specific to the most vague and general. Points along this continuum of commitment will be defined (1) in terms of whether the Member States have agreed to broad goals, and/or to implementing policies and/or rules for enforcement or application, and (2) in terms of the tasks assigned to EEC institutions. Thus we can identify the following four categories of commitment:

to goals, policies, and rules with the EEC institutions being granted regulatory powers; to goals and policies with the institutions being granted regulatory and rule-making powers; to goals with the institutions being given policy-making, rule-making, and regulatory powers; and to goals with minimal or no institutional involvement.

Goals, policies, and rules. The Treaty provisions establish a commitment to goals, policies, and rules with regard to the bulk of the customs union section. A timetable and a set of detailed actions are established. These actions are to be taken automatically by the Member States. The institutions of the Community are entrusted with ensuring that these obligations are met. The Commission plays an active role and exercises most of its decision-making power with regard to matters in this category.

Goals and policies. Significant areas of the Treaty involve agreement on goals and policies, but leave it to the institutions of the Community to specify the means and often the timing of application and regulation. Most actions in this category are taken by the Council on a proposal of the Commission, most often by majority voting after the first and second stage. Many of these provisions include what we have referred to as complements to the Treaty. This category covers the implementation of the provisions concerning transport, competition, the free supply of services, the free movement of workers, state aids and state trading, minimum prices for agriculture, capital transfers, etc.

Goals only. Often the Treaty states only a general goal, leaving the institutions to choose the necessary policy measures to be taken (as well as the means of application and regulation). Unanimity prevails more often here, and in some cases the Council may act alone rather than on a proposal of the Commission. Notable in this category is the common agricultural policy. It includes also the extension of provisions to sea and air transport, rewriting the Convention concerning relations with overseas territories, general harmonization, the regulation of capital movements, etc.

Goals only, no institutional provisions. Here the Member States were able to agree only on broad wishes for the future. In general no role for the Community institutions is specified. Exchange rates are to be treated as matters of "common interest," Member States shall "endeavor to cooperate," and so on. In this category are provisions on fiscal questions, monetary policy, taxation, and economic trends.

We have identified several variable factors or conditions as being of special relevance in accounting for the process of political integration. Economic integration can be expected to have political consequences if it leads to the development of central institutions and policies, if the tasks assigned to these institutions are important enough to concern major groups in the society, if these tasks are quite specific, and if the tasks are inherently expansive. If we look at the Treaty of Rome in these terms, it is clear that it has a wide potential for political integration. It provides for the setting up of a complex central decision-making machinery, which, though formally dependent upon the will of the Member States, does provide for an independent source of initiative and impulsion toward the Treaty's goals. With regard to relations between the Member States, or between the Member States and the Community, on matters within the competence of the Community there is established a juridical order that has the characteristics of an internal rather than an international system.[57] These institutions, furthermore, are granted significant power to make policy as well as to enforce the execution of specific obligations.

It is also clear that the tasks assigned to the institutions are of sufficient importance to activate groups in all sectors of the economy. This is true whether we consider the extent to which decisions are removed from the autonomous determination of states, or the subject matter areas themselves. Formally, the Treaty is a customs union. The effect of a customs union is to eliminate the possibility of a national policy of external exchanges. This is the minimum possibility. If the Member States are to observe the range of obligations stated in the Treaty, there is not an area that will not be deeply affected. One can indeed expect that the traditional distinction between foreign affairs and domestic affairs will cease to be a real guide to governmental operations, and that new problems will be created in the relations between the traditional governmental departments. Groups of all kinds can be expected to feel insecure and to orient themselves toward such new decision-making centers as develop.

We need not belabor the point that the Rome Treaty is unusually specific about the tasks assigned to the institutions of the EEC (although not equally specific in all areas). But it is certainly true that tension between the institutions and the Member States has been reduced by spelling out in some detail the nature of the common institutions and the areas of their competence.*

It also seems likely that there will be a gradual extension of the scope of central decision-making, that the tasks assigned to the EEC institutions will prove inherently expansive. The Treaty is in many ways only a partial treaty. If the Member States wish to create a real customs union, they will have to extend and specify the area of common or delegated decision-making. Problems that arise from the merging of the six economies will require action transcending the borders of any one state. The nature of the

---

* Thus the Treaty establishing the EEC has 248 articles, as well as lists, protocols, and annexes, whereas 14 articles suffice for the North Atlantic Treaty, 42 for the Statute of the Council of Europe, and 28 for the OEEC Convention. Beloff, p. 546.

Treaty as a "traité cadre" represents a realization of this fact; moreover, it carries it one step further: the institutions are given wide latitude to formulate policy with significant representation for the general interest of the Community as a whole in the Commission. These institutions can hardly avoid making centralizing policies. We have seen that in principle the States do not lose competences, and conversely that there is hardly an economic matter in which the Community does not have some competence. The institutions act to prohibit, or, more often, to complete, the actions of the States rather than substituting for them. Policy-making in the EEC may resemble a kind of intergovernmental negotiating process, but it is cast in a new framework that transforms its fundamental characteristics.

PART TWO

THE DECISION-MAKING CONTEXT:
ORGANIZATIONAL AND ROLE PHENOMENA

OFFICIAL DECISION-MAKERS

THE EEC TREATY came into effect on January 1, 1958. In this section we shall examine the Community's experience during these first years in terms of the political impact of the EEC, the extent to which governments share or delegate decision-making authority in areas of vital interest, and the effect of such development on political and socio-economic processes in the Member States. We shall not try to judge the EEC in terms of economic integration, nor can we even discuss all the activities of the Community, since these range over the entire sphere of economic policy.

By all indications the Community has been an unqualified success. In January 1962 the Council of Ministers approved the transition to the second stage of the Treaty of Rome, certifying that the objectives laid down in the Treaty for the first stage had been achieved. The Commission, viewing the results of the first stage, observed with some satisfaction:

It can now be claimed with certainty that the Common Market can no longer be called into question and that there will be no going back; it may also be affirmed that this economic unification is part of an advance towards political unification which is being pursued on parallel lines. . . .

The constitutional foundation for the Community's continuing advance has been laid, since it is only by unanimous decision of the Council on a proposal of the Commission that the two final stages of the transitional period can be prolonged.

The economic conditions are present, since Europe has experienced and is experiencing a much more vigorous upsurge than the other large economic units in the world.

The political, psychological and human prerequisites are also fulfilled, because the Member States and the Community institutions have shown their resolve to pursue without respite the goal that has been set, because the Community has the means to move ahead, and finally because it has the support of public opinion in taking this course.[1]

Certainly the figures on intra-Community trade are impressive. The increase in the volume of trade among countries within the EEC has been far greater than that with third countries. A distinct improvement in intra-Community trade in early 1959 coincided with the application of the first measures of tariff and quota disarmament,[2] and this improvement continued. The value of the goods exchanged (as percentage increase over that of the previous year) increased by 19 per cent in 1959, by 25 per cent in 1960, and by 16 per cent in 1961.[3]

According to the Commission:

It is . . . in the psychological effect of the introduction of the new Common Market that a determining factor should be sought. Faced with this new economic entity in process of establishment, producers have shown more interest in their vast European market where, sooner or later, all obstacles to trade will be removed. There is greater competition between the producers of the six countries and this has led them to refrain from restoring certain price reductions made during the period when business was slack, or to mark down their products to promote sales. More vigorous business relations have been established, more frequent contacts made by business people and their organizations, which are preparing both to face up to the requirements of this new market and to benefit by these advantages.[4]

The Commission reports that where the Treaty imposed specific obligations on the Member States, primarily in the customs union provisions, these have been observed virtually without exception. In the few cases in which a Member State has failed in one of its obligations, the Commission has been able to ensure that action was taken to put matters right.[5] Furthermore, there has been only a minimal recourse to escape clauses. Developments have been so favorable that the Member States agreed in mid-1960, and again in 1962, to speed up the timetable set down in the Treaty for the elimination of trade barriers, and it now seems likely that a customs union will become an established reality in eight years or less, rather than the twelve to fifteen years foreseen in the Treaty. This decision to "accelerate" was of prime importance for the Community, and is examined in detail in Chapter 9.

Frequently in the Treaty the institutions of the EEC are charged with specifying the means and timing according to which agreed policies are to be put into effect. Such implementing measures involved long study and the coordination of effort among the Member States. In most of these cases, however, specific proposals have now been made by the Commission to the Council, and in some cases the first regulations and directives have also been adopted, e.g., for removing restrictions on the free supply of services, on the free circulation of workers, and on capital transfers, as well as for enforcing the Treaty provisions dealing with rules of competition. The problems of eliminating internal charges equivalent to duties, state aids to exports, and state monopolies are still under study.[6]

Where the Treaty specified only general goals, leaving it to the institutions to define policies and implement rules, progress has been mixed, being limited generally to preliminary studies and to developing institutionalized methods of consultation and coordination: i.e., economic and financial policy, social policy, and energy policy. Only in agriculture has there been significant activity, and this is due largely to the fact that the Treaty lays down a specific timetable.[7] The development of a single common agricultural policy in the place of six different ones is the first really major project for the EEC, and has engaged all the institutions of the Community as well as interest groups in all the Member States. (This is discussed in detail in Chapters 11 and 12.)

Moreover, the wider impact of the EEC on economic and political relations within Europe, within the Atlantic Alliance, and throughout the world is undeniable. As the Commission observes:

The Community has from the outset been making its mark as a factor of real importance in international life. The steady progress in internal consolidation achieved during these years and confirmed by the acceleration measures decided on in May 1960, has strengthened the attraction which the Community exerts on the outside world. The current negotiations being held with certain European countries on the possibility of membership and the desire of other states to become associated with the Community are the most convincing evidence of the Community's power of attraction. Elsewhere, new approaches to the problem of readjusting the balance of world trade show that the Community has stirred the forces of progress in the free world.[8]

Major problems have been created for the Community by virtue of its impact on third countries, and these have been especially significant in terms of internal EEC institutional development. One of the most important issues, that of the free trade area and the subsequent problem of the Six and the Seven, is examined in Chapters 7 and 8.

Here we shall be concerned with the nature of the EEC institutional system as it evolved during the first years. By institutional system, I mean the whole system within which a decision-making event takes place: i.e., the actors and activities that result in decision. In this case, the system under study is that centered upon the EEC institutions, which comprise the *official* decision-makers of the system. Our analysis will perforce be selective. We have approached the data with certain limited questions in mind, and have not sought to make an exhaustive analysis of organizational and administrative developments. Our treatment will be restricted to those aspects of organizational development that we have identified as being particularly relevant for political integration. Who are the key Community decision-makers? What are the patterned relationships among the several institutions of the Community, and between these institutions and the Member States? Does the system approximate the formal outlines laid down in the Treaty, or has it evolved differently in response to organizational and environmental needs? What are the implications of such developments for the process of political integration?

We are also interested in certain organizational activities of nonofficial decision-makers. Such activities are part of the EEC decision-making system in that they are designed to *influence* the official decision-makers, or are the *result* of activities of the official agencies. Has the advent of the EEC and its institutional system been of sufficient importance to cause significant economic actors to restructure their expectations and activities? What are the implications of such changes for political integration?

THE DEVELOPING PATTERN

We have seen that the Treaty of Rome is in essence a "traité cadre," that, with the exception of the customs union provisions, it contains more or less precise statements of goals and sets up an institutional system to achieve them. Thus the powers given to the institutions, we have argued, are in reality legislative powers. In contrast to the ECSC, these powers were not invested in a "supranational" executive, but were given to the Community as a whole. Though most final decisions involving "legislation" are the responsibility of the Council of Ministers, representing the governments of the Member States, a proposal of the Commission requiring a unanimous vote for amendment is usually prerequisite to such decisions.

One of the lessons of the ECSC experience was that integration could not proceed against the will of the governments involved, as was revealed by the fact that the High Authority was not able to make use of its extensive supranational powers and came to consult with the Council far more often than was envisaged by the Treaty.[9] In the EEC Treaty a number of provisions seem to have been designed to ensure a continuous and close collaboration between the Council and the Commission, a formalization of the system of institutional balance that had been developed *de facto* in the ECSC. This continuous involvement of the governments of the Member States in every stage of Community decision-making, and therefore in the day-by-day process of integration, was considered by many observers to be one of the most important aspects of the Rome Treaty.

This judgment has now been strikingly confirmed. In fact the involvement of government representatives in the integration process has been carried to an extent that few could have foreseen. The Treaty, while encouraging a close cooperation between the Council and the Commission, at the same time established a procedure whereby proposals were developed by the Commission and adopted by the Council if they commanded sufficient support (after consultations with the European Parliamentary Assembly and the Economic and Social Committee).[10] In practice this distinction between the role of elaboration and preparation and that of final decision has become obscured by a vast congeries of permanent and *ad hoc* groups that have been created between the Commission and the Council. The Treaty states that the rules of procedure of the Council "may provide for the establishment of a committee of representatives of the Member States."[11] Accordingly, the Committee of Permanent Representatives was set up in order to prepare the work of the Council and to execute such other business as might be conferred upon it. It was also given the right to institute working groups and to charge them with special tasks of technical preparation and study.[12] The Committee of Permanent Representatives is made up of the heads (of the rank of ambassador) of the permanent delegations of each of the six Member States to the European Communities. They reside permanently in Brussels and meet at least once a week; and since the Council meets as a rule only once a month, they are the principal liaison between the Community and the Member States.

Before drawing up formal proposals, the Commission has made a practice of contacting the Permanent Representatives to obtain the views of the various governments, and it regularly meets with groups of experts drawn from the national administrations and convened by the Permanent Representatives. Only after such consultations does the Commission prepare its proposals. The completed proposals are then returned to the Permanent Representatives, whose task it is to prepare the meetings of the Council by preliminary exchanges of positions. Before discussing the proposal, the Committee of Permanent Representatives in its turn calls in groups of national experts (for these are highly technical matters), often the same experts who have already met with the Commission, but this time formally instructed by their respective governments. Several such groups may meet simultaneously to study different aspects of a given Commission proposal in order to reach such agreement as is possible at this technical level. The Commission is always represented in these sessions.[13] The results of the sessions are reported to the Permanent Representatives, who discuss any problems that remain unresolved; here again the Commission is an active participant.

These discussions are designed to achieve as much agreement as possible between the several Member States and the Commission before the Council itself treats the matter in its monthly sessions. The Commission can, and usually does, change its proposals, or it may make new ones in the course of the discussions in the Committee of Permanent Representatives. For a great many routine matters, agreement has been reached by this time (it being the purpose of the Committee of Permanent Representatives to achieve the widest possible consensus), and the Council merely approves the work. When questions arise on which agreement proves impossible at this level, the points at issue and the various alternatives offered will form the Council's agenda. Normally, by this time, agreement depends on political decisions or sacrifices, and involves a pattern of bargaining and compromise that can be conducted only at the highest level. The Commission participates in the sessions and debates of the Council as a *de facto* seventh member, and often plays a decisive role in bringing about compromise solutions.[14]

Such is the over-all pattern. The result is a tremendous proliferation of study groups and special committees, an impressive number of people involved, and a fairly substantial financial investment. The following chart gives the number of staff positions authorized for the various Community institutions in the EEC budgets for 1961 and 1962.[15]

	1961	1962
Commission	1,846	1,933
European Parliamentary Assembly	415	415
Council Secretariat	296	315
Court of Justice	87	92
Economic and Social Committee	59	64
Common services (legal, statistical, and press and information)	328	344

The budget of these institutions (in millions of dollars) for the two years is as follows:[16]

	1961	1962
Court, Council, and Parliament	3.3	3.4
Commission*	41.0	54.7
Total (millions of dollars)	44.3	58.1

The total EEC budget of some 44 million dollars in 1961 and some 58 million in 1962 is considerable for an international organization of six members. It is particularly remarkable in view of the fact that the budget does not include the funds allocated for the Euratom Commission, that only one-third of the total represents the expenses of the European Parliamentary Assembly, the Council, the Court, and the legal, statistical, and press and information services, which are common to all the Communities, and that only one-half of the expenses of the Economic and Social Committee,

---

* Of the figures given for the Commission, 20 million dollars in 1961 and 29 million in 1962 were allocated for the Social Fund.

which is common to the EEC and Euratom, is represented.[17] In 1961 the cost of the EEC was shared by the Member States as follows:[18]

Belgium	$ 3,666,606.38
Germany	13,158,021.60
France	13,158,021.60
Italy	10,751,661.60
Luxembourg	88,256.44
Netherlands	3,305,052.38

The size of the staffs and the amount of the budgets indicate the importance attributed by the Member States to participation in the EEC. Yet these figures fall far short of giving an accurate estimate either of the number of individuals involved in the EEC decision-making process or of the total costs borne by the Member States, because they do not account for the national experts who meet regularly by request of the Commission, nor for the Permanent Delegations, nor for the Committee of Permanent Representatives and the national experts it consults. The Permanent Delegations of the six Member States to the EEC have a total permanent staff in the neighborhood of 150, and since they are national missions, their expenses are included in the respective national budgets. The same is true of all the national experts, whether they are consulted as independent experts by the Commission, or as instructed delegates by the Committee of Permanent Representatives. In either case the *per diem* is paid by the government, the Commission or Council paying transportation only.

The Commission has the responsibility of representing the interests of the Community as a whole. It may not receive instructions from any government, and its staff is to be the nucleus of a European civil service. It is charged with carrying on the day-to-day activities of the Community, with ensuring that the provisions of the Treaty are observed, and with making technical proposals ranging over the entire area of economic policy. A large staff has been assembled for the performance of these tasks, approximately 50 per cent of which has been drawn from the administrative services of the Member States.[19] This figure, however, rises to 75 per cent for the major administrative posts (Category A), and if we take only the major policy-making posts (Categories A-1 and A-2), 57 of which are authorized in the 1961 budget, we find that *all* are drawn from the national administrations!* Furthermore, many of these officials (all those in Categories A and B, the latter consisting of specialized technicians) are only "on leave" from their national administrations, to which they expect to return. One may well question how such arrangements fit in with the idea of a European civil service.

---

* Actual figures for the various categories are given in note 19, p. 325.

EXPERT GROUPS CALLED BY THE COMMISSION[a]

General Directorate	No. of groups	Type of group			Estimated no. of meetings per year (1960)[b]					Est. range of participants per meeting
		Gov't officials	Nongov't officials	Mixed gov't & private	1–3	4–6	7–11	12–20	21 or more	
External Rels.	6	6	—	—	2	—	—	3	1	7–21
Econ. & Fin. Affairs	12	7	1	4	7	4	—	1	—	5–27
Internal Mkt.	8	8	—	—	3	2	1	1	1	11–60
Competition	28	28	—	—	20	7	1	—	—	12–30
Social Affairs	35	19	11	5	29	6	—	—	—	7–41
Agriculture	19	19	—	—	17	2	—	—	—	20–30
Transport	4	4	—	—	1	3	—	—	—	12–18
Overseas Devt.	5	4	—	1	4	1	—	—	—	6–20
Totals	117	95	12	10	83	25	2	5	2	

[a] These figures are based on internal documents of the Commission. Their significance is limited in that the information available for the various committees varied greatly: many committees met irregularly, and some had only temporary tasks; some General Directorates reported contacts both with nongovernmental groups and with groups made up of government experts, whereas most reported only governmental contacts; and, finally, the figures for the General Directorate in charge of Agriculture are certainly incomplete.

[b] The figures in this column serve merely as a general indication, since in some cases the data referred to the number of meetings actually held in 1960, and in others to the number scheduled per year (with reference to 1960 and often looking ahead to 1961). The groupings "1–3, 4–6, 7–11, 12–20, and 21 or more" in the subheading represent the estimated number of times per year that a group met or was scheduled to meet; e.g., of the six groups called by the General Directorate for External Relations, two met three times a year, three from 12 to 20, and one more than 21 times a year.

As already noted, besides its permanent staff there are all the independent experts, drawn from the technical departments and Ministries of the Member States, whom the Commission consults on technical matters. This has now become regular practice. Many of the consultations are bilateral, the Commissioners and high officials traveling to the various capitals for conferences. In addition, a large number of mixed working groups, composed of officials and experts drawn from the national administrations (and sometimes from nongovernmental groups and international organizations) and members of the Commission's staff, meet regularly in Brussels. Normally these officials are consulted by the Commission as technical experts and are not closely instructed. Groups may be convoked by one or by several General Directorates* and may include experts (usually Directors or Heads of Division) from one Ministry or from several Ministries. They meet from once a year to twice a month, and their membership varies from five to forty persons.

Their activities range over a vast field. Nine groups of national and Commission experts are at work on the problems raised by the removal of restrictions on the right of establishment and the free supply of services, examining and comparing national legislation and the administrative provisions that govern given spheres of activity (e.g., insurance, banking, crafts, and agriculture). Other groups deal with such problems as the tariff concessions to be made in negotiations with GATT (General Agreement on Tariffs and Trade), the unification of methods for analyzing business cycle fluctuations, the comparative budgets of the Member States, long-term economic expansion and structure, regional policy, state monopolies, ententes and restrictions on trade, dumping, the harmonization of tax systems, state aids to exports, state aids to such special sectors as cinematography and agricultural machinery, manpower, unemployment in specific areas, social security for migrant workers, harmonization of legislation, veterinary services, forests and conservation, railroad transport, transport infrastructure, inland waterways, and so on.

A partial survey made late in 1960 revealed a total of 127 such expert groups in existence. The accompanying chart summarizes their incidence and nature. On the basis of these admittedly inexact and incomplete figures (which do not include the bulk of contacts with nongovernmental organizations, nor the less formalized contacts with national administrators), one can calculate an annual average of about 430 meetings between national experts and Commission officials.† If we take an average figure of 20 non-

---

* Major administrative units of the Commission.

† The actual number is probably higher. In November 1960, 50 conference rooms in the Commission's headquarters had been reserved for meetings of outside experts. Assuming this rate were maintained for 10 or 11 months of the year, one would calculate an annual average of 500–550 meetings.

Community participants per meeting, we get a grand total of 8,600 participants per year, a substantial number even when we allow for the inevitable duplications. This gives us an idea of the extent to which the Commission consults government officials before it submits its formal proposals to the Committee of Permanent Representatives. Moreover, the Commission maintains contact with these work groups and with the separate national administrations also after it has submitted its proposals. Conferences of this type not only serve to coordinate national actions and to provide the Commission with much-needed technical information, but are a forum for hearing complaints of Member States against certain Commission activities or policies. Even in such a field as restrictive practices, in which the Commission has direct powers of intervention, the head of the General Directorate for Competition has called conferences on how to interpret Treaty provisions, and on which cases of restrictive practices to examine first.[20] Similarly, in the exercise of its supervisory powers, the Commission communicates at length with the national governments through various standing groups before concluding that Treaty violations may have occurred.[21]

We have seen that when the Commission has made its recommendations, many of the same experts are called back to Brussels by the Permanent Representatives to aid in the study of these proposals. From January 1958 until the end of September 1960, the Committee of Permanent Representatives had itself held 135 meetings, as against 36 held by the Council. In addition, during the same period, it had called approximately 884 meetings of working groups drawn from the various national administrations; these were convoked on an *ad hoc,* pragmatic basis. By late 1960 there were over 30 such groups. They were rationalized in October 1960, in collaboration with the Commission, when permanent working groups were set up, paralleling in large degree the organization of the Commission: that is, they covered general questions, finance, social policy, agriculture, economic and commercial policy, transport, and external relations and overseas territories.[22] Further, during the twelve-month period between September 30, 1959, and September 30, 1960, 447 meetings of expert groups were convened, and if we again take 20 as the average number of non-Community participants, we get an annual average of 8,940 participants, including duplications.[23] By adding this figure to the estimate of 8,600 non-Community participants convened by the Commission *before* formulating its proposals, we get an annual over-all total of 17,540. This is a rough index of the extent to which high national civil servants participate in the EEC decision-making process.

The Committee of Permanent Representatives, at the heart of this intensive collaboration between the Commission and the national governments, is placed at the convergence of a great many pressures and was overworked from the start, even with the individual staffs at its disposal and the services of the Council Secretariat (this body prepares positions and working papers, takes notes, sends letters, and so forth). More and more, therefore, as special problems are faced, the tendency has been to set up additional preparatory committees of approximately equivalent status to the Committee of Permanent Representatives and reporting directly to the Council. Among these are the following:[24]

The Special Committee for Article 111 (Comité Cent-Onze) set up under Article 111 of the Treaty to aid the Commission in preparing the GATT tariff negotiations.[25]

The Group for the Coordination of Technical Assistance to Under-developed Countries, made up of delegates from each Member State and from the Commission. The aims of this group are to exchange information on the activities of the Member States in the area of technical aid, to compare available resources, to study requests for aid, and to compare methods and techniques used, all with the idea of facilitating cooperation, studying initiatives, and promoting joint action.[26]

The Group for the Coordination of Policy on Credit Insurance, again joining officials from the Member States and the Commission. The aims in this case are to harmonize the policies of the Member States in the field of credit insurance for exports, to study the multilateral use of available credit resources, and to coordinate the positions of the Member States in international institutions.[27]

A *Special Committee* (now extinct) to assist the Commission in the negotiations concerning Greece's application to be associated with the Community.

Another *Special Committee* (also no longer in existence) to assist the Commission in the association negotiations with the Dutch Antilles.

The Special Committee on Agriculture, deriving its mandate from the decision of May 12, 1960, to accelerate the EEC timetable. This group was charged with the short-term task of working out the acceleration of the Treaty's provisions concerning agriculture, and with the long-term tasks of examining the Commission's proposals for a common agricultural policy and of preparing the long series of Council decisions that will be required over the years.

The *Special Committee for the Study of a European Economic Association* must also be included. This was set up by the Council in March 1959 to study the recommendations made by the Commission with regard to the problem of relations with the Community's OEEC partners. The Member States and the Commission were both represented on the Committee, with Commissioner Jean Rey as its chairman. The mandate of the so-called Rey Committee was extended subsequently to include the preparation of the EEC position in the newly created Organization for Economic Cooperation and Development (OECD), the special GATT conferences called by the U.S. Under-Secretary of State, C. Douglas Dillon, and the trade talks being held in the Committee of Twenty-One.[28]

Finally, the *Business Cycle Committee,* also set up by the Council (at the Commission's request and reporting officially to the Commission), is a high-level committee chaired by the German State Secretary for Economic Affairs, Alfred Müller-Armack. It is charged with exchanging information and trying to develop common rules and a code of good conduct for questions of business-cycle policy.[29]

These committees appear to represent a definite trend. The Committee of Permanent Representatives is serving more and more as a clearinghouse for an expanding coterie of specialized committees, reserving for itself only matters of general, or essentially political, importance. Each of the special committees can be expected to convoke working groups of national experts and so to contribute to the ever-expanding circle of involvement in EEC decision-making. All these committees form a permanent liaison between the Council and the Commission. The Commission is formally represented on the major ones and may even provide the chairman and/or the secretariat. The Commission's proposals form the subject matter of their discussions, which are designed to prepare the decisions of the Council by effecting a maximum preliminary reconciliation of national views.

But this pattern of central institutional growth has not been restricted to tasks specifically laid down in the Treaty of Rome. At the urging of General de Gaulle, the Foreign Ministers of the Six have met at three-month intervals since November 1959 for "political consultations" in which problems of foreign policy ranging from Berlin to the Congo have been discussed. The original French proposal envisaged the creation of a permanent political secretariat to be set up in Paris. This was vigorously opposed by many Europeans and by the governments of the Benelux countries, who saw it as a first step in the establishment of a Franco-German hegemony in the EEC, as a potential threat to the integrity of the EEC institutions, and as the final estrangement of the Community of the Six from the rest of Europe, especially the United Kingdom. No definitive agreement has yet been reached on this issue, although de Gaulle continues to press for closer political cooperation among the Six. The Bonn Declaration, signed on July 18, 1961, was typically vague and general.*

---

* Other steps have been taken to develop political cooperation and the harmonization of foreign policies by means of periodic meetings of the information officers of the six Foreign Affairs Ministries. An action program has been drawn up calling for harmonization in the field of information on major world problems, for closer col-

It affirmed that the Six were "anxious to strengthen the political, economic, social and cultural ties which exist between their peoples" and that their policy would be as follows:

1. To give shape to the will for political union already implicit in the Treaties establishing the European communities . . .

2. To hold at regular intervals meetings whose aim will be to compare their views, to concert their policies and to reach common positions in order to further the political union of Europe . . .

3. To instruct their Committee to submit to them proposals on the means which will as soon as possible enable a statutory character to be given to the union of their peoples.[30]

Meetings at the ministerial level have not been restricted to Ministers of Foreign Affairs. A regular series of meetings has taken place among the Ministers of Finance, Agriculture, Transport, and Labor. A representative of the Commission has normally been present at such meetings and has sometimes even presided. In the case of the meetings of the six Ministers of Agriculture, the original initiative was taken by Commissioner Sicco Mansholt. The meetings of the Ministers of Finance are perhaps the most institutionalized, a permanent secretariat having been set up to prepare their sessions.[31] To make clear the link to the Rome Treaty and its institutions, and no doubt to avoid controversy such as that over the "political secretariat," the Commission was asked to provide the permanent secretariat. The first meeting was held in July 1959, and the fifth in October 1960. They were convened out of common recognition that the Treaty of Rome posed problems in the area of financial policy that could be dealt with only through regularized contacts. Some of the matters discussed have been budgetary policy, fiscal policy, long-term trends in public expenditures, and the possibility of coordinating the positions of the Six in international financial organizations such as the International Monetary Fund.[32]

There has been some concern that these special meetings of Ministers might detract from the central role of the Council,[33] and attenuate the role of the Ministers of Foreign Affairs as chief policy-makers and coordinators in European integration affairs. The objections of the Belgian Foreign

---

laboration between governmental press services and those of the Community, especially in regard to the social objective of the Treaty, and for collaboration in promoting a better understanding of the Community in third countries. *Agence Europe*, August 2, 1960.

It is also interesting to note that the consular services of the Member States throughout the world have begun to make more or less coordinated reports on trade developments, these reports being regularly forwarded to the Commission as well as to the governments.

Minister, Pierre Wigny, to such special meetings seemed to be based on these grounds, although he may also have felt that technical Ministers were likely to be less "European" and therefore less cooperative in seeking compromises. Subsequently, the Council of Ministers decided to institutionalize all future ministerial meetings as sessions of the EEC Council of Ministers.

This, then, in summary, is a description of the institutional framework in which EEC policies are shaped. Clearly, the relational pattern is not that which had been foreseen in the Treaty. In practice the distinction between the Commission's responsibility of proposal and the Council's responsibility of decision has become blurred. A vast bureaucratic system is developing, involving thousands of national and Community officials in a continuous decision-making process.

On the national level officials of national administrations form the staff of the Permanent Representatives in Brussels, and national official experts are called in to work with the staffs of the "executives." These same officials advise their respective Ministers on the Councils as well as their own governments generally. The staffs of the Commission and of the other "executives" as well as the staff of the Council's Secretariat have been recruited to a large measure from national administrations. Some former Ministers have become members of one of the "executives" and former representatives in the Assembly have become Ministers or members of an "executive." This interplay of national and Community administrations, the growing expertise and the development of vested interests of Community officials will inevitably increase the influence of a compact bureaucracy.[34]

The growth of this "extra-Treaty" institutional system has given rise to criticism, both from Community circles and from outside observers.[35] It has been argued that the system is *slow, inefficient, and ponderous,* that the institutions are overstaffed and overorganized, that the innumerable expert groups and consultations lead to a fantastic duplication of effort as well as interminable delays, and that the Community is in danger of choking to death on its own procedures. The Commission has been accused of *watering down its own roles,* both as spokesman for the common interests of the entire Community and as originator of proposals to the Council, by excessive reliance on prior consultations with national experts. This weighty process of consultation further complicates its already tortuous internal working methods. Finally, the Council has been accused of *upsetting the "institutional balance"* of the Treaty by creating a Committee of Permanent Representatives and all kinds of special groups between itself and the Commission. This "shadow executive" has been seen as a potential rival to the Commission, and the extensive restudy of the Commission's proposals that it undertakes in company with national civil servants has given substance to fears that it will produce proposals counter to those of the Commission. Not only would this derogate from the major power of the Commission in relation to the Council, namely its monopoly of the right to make proposals; it would also affect the Community character of such proposals. According to Mrs. Camps, "Proposals from the Commission should be based on an objective appraisal of the requirements of the Community looked at as an entity. Proposals arrived at by a group of national representatives will tend to be a compromise of differing national views."[36]

It is this last point that has caused the greatest concern. The most consistent critic of the Permanent Representatives and its coterie of groups has been a Dutch Socialist member of the EPA, and a long-time "European," Jonkheer van der Goes van Naters. He had been critical of a similar organization in the ECSC, the Coordinating Commission of the ECSC Council of Ministers (COCOR), and looked upon the Permanent Representatives with equal suspicion. He is reported as saying, "Between the Council and the Commission a new organ not provided for as such has been interpolated, the Committee of Permanent Representatives, which is less and less a modest preparatory committee subordinate to the Council, and which becomes more and more a third executive, a Council of Ministers' Deputies."[37] He feels the functions of such a committee should be strictly limited to preparing Council meetings and to executing Council decisions; otherwise the Commission will be reduced to the level of a technical secretariat.[38]

The issue really came to the fore in the dispute over the Community's 1959 budget.[39] Unlike the ECSC, which has its own financial resources (from taxation), the EEC operates on a budget made up of contributions from the Member States. The Council retains effective control of the budget, adopting it by a qualified majority vote, although the Commission, the Assembly, and the other institutions do participate in its preparation according to a specified timetable. Under the Treaty, "Each of the institutions of the Community shall draw up provisional estimates of its expenses. The Commission shall combine these estimates in a preliminary draft budget. It shall attach its opinion which may contain divergent estimates. . . . The Council shall, whenever it intends to depart from the preliminary draft, consult the Commission and, where appropriate, the other institutions concerned."[40] Consideration of the 1959 budget, the Community's first full-scale budget,* ran far behind the timetable laid down in the Treaty, largely because the Council's estimates had not been submitted to the Commission on time. Instead of accepting the Commission's estimates,

---

* The 1958 budget estimates were submitted at the same time, but since they referred to the current year and to existing staff, they were accepted by the Council.

or consulting it about changes, the Council referred the budget to a committee of national experts, which was instructed to make recommendations
for substantial cuts. This committee subsequently invited the institutions
to submit new reduced estimates, on the basis of which it completed its
recommendations to the Council. On February 2 and 3, 1959, the Council
met and finally adopted the budget.

This procedure was vigorously attacked by the EPA, which adopted
two strongly critical reports, in December 1958 and April 1959. The discussions on the budget held between the Commission and the Council were
in closed session, and although the Commission's original estimates were
reduced, it did succeed in obtaining the rejection of many of the cuts
suggested by the experts.[41] Furthermore, the Commission was in close
touch with the discussions throughout the process, participating in the
deliberations of the Council, the Permanent Representatives, and the expert
group. It came to accept the Ministers' need for expert help far more than
did the EPA and was more circumspect in its criticism of the procedures
chosen.

The chief criticisms raised in the Assembly were leveled at the Council:
that it had failed to adhere to the timetable laid down in the Treaty; that
it had failed to act as if it were responsible to the Assembly as a competent
budgetary authority; that it would bring about a distortion of the Community's institutional balance if it delegated powers to its own subsidiary
organs; that it had failed to provide the Community's institutions with the
means to carry out their tasks; and that it had failed to provide properly
for the European Social Fund. In addition, the Member States were criticized for failing to choose a single seat for all the institutions.

The Assembly's debates reflected a general concern that the Council's
tendency to rely on the advice of its own subsidiary organs would jeopardize the Commission's right to carry out studies and make proposals. The
size of the staff being accumulated around the Permanent Representatives
and in the Council's Secretariat was also seen as a potential danger:

If decisions were to be left largely in the hands of civil servants responsible
only to the Ministers and not to the other organs of the Community, the establishment of the budget would, to that extent, be removed from the control of
the Commission and the comment of the Assembly would be less effective. That
the Assembly was so critical of the establishment of an entirely new body, not
provided for in the Treaty—the committee of experts—was due to its strong
feeling that the Council should take budgetary decisions on its own responsibility, as a community body, and should not take them on the advice of
national officials, expressing national viewpoints.[42]

The main conclusion of the parliamentarians was that such expert groups
were permissible only if their work were purely technical, and only if it

had no decisive influence in policy-making. As has been pointed out, however,

national experts (who are usually senior officials) are not going to meet, at considerable expense of both time and money, just to check figures, but are in the nature of things, inevitably going to exert considerable influence on policy-making. There is no middle path for a committee of national experts between checking the figures and advising on policy issues and no committee of senior officials will be content with the first function.[43]

The bulk of these criticisms are valid, as far as they go. The institutional system that has developed is certainly not the one outlined in the Treaty. It is not a rational or efficient system judged by any established principles of public administration. The decision-making role of the Council has obviously been diffused. National experts do indeed influence Community policy-making at all levels. But, at the same time, there is nothing to prove that the system has had negative effects for long-range political integration. Such a conclusion would be warranted only if it could be demonstrated that the role and influence of the Commission in the over-all process had been diminished, and that the common policies that emerged were normally of the "lowest-common-denominator" type, or of the "split-the-difference" variety.

A full understanding of these problems cannot be achieved until we have viewed the EEC decision-making system in action. Such analysis is reserved for Part III. However, measured by budgetary outlay and the size of the staffs of Community institutions, by the truly striking degree of involvement of government officials and experts in the preparation of Community policies, by the institutional developments centering upon the Committee of Permanent Representatives, and by the participation of the Commission at all levels of the process, the impact of the Rome Treaty on national decision-making processes seems firmly established. It remains for us to try to assess the organizational implications, manifest and latent, of these developments to see how they affected the competencies and roles of the several Community institutions. I shall suggest that the system developed in response to definite needs, that it is eminently rational from a political point of view, and that it represents a positive adjustment to the environment on the part of all the Community institutions, and particularly the Commission.

THE COMMISSION

It might well be expected that the institutional system we have been describing would bog down in interminable bureaucratic consultations. In most international organizations, negotiations involving government representatives "end in a compromise on the basis of a give and take bargain, or in a lack of compromise ensuring cooperation through inaction."[44] The authors of the Treaty sought to avoid this danger by providing that all major decisions of the Community were to be based on proposals of the Commission, which represented the interests of the Community as a whole. In other words, "The executive body is not meant to proceed to a preparatory negotiation between representatives of the Member States, as any committee of the Council could do. It is required to reach, and to state in all following discussions with the Council or the Assembly, an independent but responsible view on each matter concerned, from the standpoint of the Community."[45] But we have seen that the Commission does indeed engage in multiple preparatory sessions with representatives of the Member States, and we are entitled to ask if its role as animator or motor for the Community policy-making apparatus is not thereby compromised. Do the proposals made by the Commission after this elaborate process represent a Community position, or do they consist merely of what the governments want to hear? In short, has the Commission succeeded in playing a significant integrative role during the first years of the EEC's existence?

All formal organizations are adaptive social structures, and they are to some extent molded by forces tangential to their ordered structure and stated goals.[46] Organizations typically seek security in their social and political environment, a stability of authority and communication, a continuity of policy determination, and a homogeneity of outlook with respect to the meaning and role of the organization. Certain patterns of commitment are thus enforced by organizational and environmental needs and by centers of interest generated in the course of action. Such adaptations are essential, but they may bring about changes in the over-all competency of the organization and in the goals it seeks to implement. This is particularly true if these goals are precarious—that is, if they fail to command widespread approval, or if they run counter to influential interests. The organization has to learn how to reconcile internal aspirations with external environment, and the real work of organizational leadership lies in managing this process of dynamic adaptation. Several specific tasks are implied here: (1) the definition of the institutional mission and role—these must be specified and recast in terms of external and internal capabilities; (2) an institutional embodiment of purpose—purpose must be built into the social structure of the organization (by staffing and recruitment); and (3) a defense of institutional integrity vis-à-vis external forces—this involves the major adaptive mechanisms of ideology and co-optation.[47]

The members of the Commission have shown themselves well aware of these fundamentals of organizational dynamics. As the accompanying chart reveals, most of the members are not technicians, but have held posts at cabinet level or in policy-making levels of national administrations. Most have been active in politics and are able to command considerable influence in their respective countries.

The members of the Commission are firm advocates of a maximum economic and political integration, as well as of the principle of delegating national powers to Community institutions, in some cases maintaining close contact with national and Community-wide "pro-European" groups, chief among which is Jean Monnet's Action Committee for a United States of Europe.* Yet they were faced with certain inescapable facts that placed distinct limits upon their freedom to implement these goals. The formal decision-making powers assigned to the Commission by the Treaty were distinctly inferior to those of the High Authority. The superiority of the Council of Ministers over the Commission was clearly spelled out. The Commission's role was to be largely the technical one of supervision and preparation. Clearly, only by developing cooperative relations with the Council could anything be achieved. The nature of the Treaty as a "traité cadre," the great reliance upon the coordination and harmonization of national economic and financial policies, demonstrated that integration must proceed on the basis of an intensive cooperation between national and Community officials. This was especially true during the first years, when the Commission had to rely heavily on the national administrations while it developed its own staff.

The Commissioners obviously had to take into consideration the degree of support for integration in the several governments.[48] The Netherlands, Belgium, Luxembourg, and Italy were in favor of new, far-reaching integrative moves that involved the exercise of wide powers by Community institutions. Germany, on the other hand, had become increasingly divided over these issues. Ludwig Erhard, the Minister for Economic Affairs, had maintained his opposition both to the idea of a European regional economic union and to the creation of "dirigistic" institutions, a position that seemed to be gaining strength in Germany. Even Chancellor Adenauer's faith in "federalist" conceptions had declined after the defeat of the plan for a European Defense Community, and during the negotiation of the Rome Treaty the Germans consistently emphasized intergovernmental *cooperation and coordination.* The French Parliament had accepted the Treaty

---

* The Monnet Committee is made up of the top leaders of the major trade union federations of the Six and of the center and left-of-center political parties (Socialist, Christian-Democratic, and Liberal). Its influence on behalf of maximalist integration policies is difficult to measure, but is probably substantial, at least within certain limits. For a complete listing of the participating organizations, see Haas, *Uniting of Europe*, p. 302, n. 16.

EEC COMMISSION

(as of January 1963)[a]

Member	Nationality	Background	Political affiliation
Hallstein, Walter (President)	German	Professor, diplomat, State Secretary for Foreign Affairs (1951–57)	Christian-Democrat
Mansholt, Sicco (Vice-President)	Dutch	Agriculturist, Minister of Agriculture and Fisheries (1945–58)	Socialist
Marjolin, Robert (Vice-President)	French	Administrator, economist, Secretary-General OEEC (1948–55), assistant to Jean Monnet (1946–48)	Socialist
Caron, Giuseppe (Vice-President)	Italian	Small industrialist (chemicals), Senator (1948–58), administrator, delegate Consultative Assembly, junior minister	Christian-Democrat
Groeben, Hans von der	German	Civil servant, administrator (Ministry of Economic Affairs), COCOR, Spaak Committee	Not known
Rey, Jean	Belgian	Deputy (1939–58), Minister of Economic Affairs (1954–58), ECSC Council of Ministers (1954–56)	Liberal
Schaus, Lambert	Luxembourg	Lawyer, diplomat, Minister of Economic Affairs and Army, Permanent Representative to EEC (1958)	Christian-Democrat
Levi Sandri, Lionello	Italian	Administrator, professor, municipal counselor	Social-Democrat
Rochereau, Henri	French	Exporter, Senator (1946–59), Minister of Agriculture (1959–61)	Independent Republican

[a] Commissioners are appointed for a four-year term, which is renewable. Hallstein, Mansholt, Marjolin, von der Groeben, and Rey were all members of the original Commission (set up in January 1958). Caron, however, replaced Piero Malvestiti (Italy), who resigned in September 1959 to become President of the ECSC High Authority; Schaus replaced Michel Rasquin (Luxembourg), who died in June 1958; Levi Sandri replaced Giuseppe Petrilli (Italy), who resigned in February 1961; and Rochereau replaced Robert Lemaignen (France), who resigned in January 1962. Biographical information on the former members of the Commission is as follows: Malvestiti—professor, Deputy (1946–58), Under-Secretary in various ministries, Christian-Democrat; Lemaignen—businessman, business interest group official (CNPF), Independents; Petrilli—specialist in economics, finance, and social insurance, Christian-Democrat; and Rasquin—journalist, Minister of Economic Affairs (1951–58), member of ECSC Council of Ministers (1951–58), Socialist.

only after extensive concessions had been demanded of, and granted by, the other signatories. De Gaulle's rise to power in spring 1958 threatened to renew the whole question of France's readiness to accept even the stated obligations of the EEC treaty, not to mention its political implications. De Gaulle was not known as an advocate of national abnegation, and Michel Debré, his newly appointed Prime Minister, had long been a foe of the ECSC High Authority and of federalist ideology in general, consistently holding out for looser kinds of association. From outside the Community, too, came potential threats. The story of the EEC's relations with Great Britain and the European Free Trade Association is related later. Suffice it to note now that the posture assumed by Great Britain throughout the Rome Treaty negotiations and up to the present had constituted a threat to some of the basic goals of the "Europeans," a threat that was made even more dangerous by the conflicts it revealed among the Six. The Commission thus had to operate in such a way as to minimize internal EEC conflicts in order to maintain a strong position vis-à-vis the outside world.

With these limitations in mind, how has it defined its mission and role? The members of the Commission separately, and President Hallstein speaking for them as a group, are quite clear about their objective: namely, "the political unification of our continent."[49] The way to achieve this is to make economic integration irreversible.[50] Economic integration can only be made irreversible if the integrity of the Community as an economic union is preserved, if the provisions of the Treaty are fully implemented and if possible speeded up, if the independent role of the Commission is expanded or at least protected, and if the governments become so engaged in the undertaking that inaction or obstruction is impossible. Thus the Commission joined with the French to thwart the plan for a free trade area, which all the other Member States wanted, partly because it was seen as a threat to the identity of the Community. In the acceleration sequence, the Commission was motivated primarily by the need to get some sort of acceleration accepted quickly, even at the price of temporarily unbalancing the Treaty. In all this, however, the Commission has moved very cautiously.

With regard to its own role, the Commission has also been circumspect, adopting throughout a self-effacing attitude. The French in particular were sensitive about the early efforts of the Commission to assert its "political reality," as in the matter of the Commission's proposal to establish EEC diplomatic missions in London and Washington. This idea was vetoed by the French, and the Commission learned the need for caution. This can be seen in its public statements about the balance of power between the Council and the Commission. In an important speech before the EPA in October 1960, Hallstein reaffirmed that such notions as "supranationality" confused, rather than clarified, matters and gave rise to "theoretical controversies." He went on to say that "the big decisions of the Community . . . are the province of the Council of Ministers. . . . The Council is the principal institution, the one that constantly conciliates the interests of the Member States with the interest of the Community. It is in the Council that the common policies are elaborated and the policies of the Member States are harmonized. . . . This point is significant because in the last analysis, all policy is unity."[51] Nevertheless, Hallstein stressed that the Commission, too, had important functions to perform: as the initiating force that impels the Council to act and moves the Community forward; as the guardian of the Treaty; and as the arbitrator or conciliator between the governments.[52]

The Commission has maintained consistently that its role was not limited to technical and bureaucratic functions, but that it was also a policy-making and coordinating authority.[53] It has sought to expand its own role, but on a pragmatic basis. In the specific proposals that the Commission is called upon to make under the Treaty, it has tried to provide for a maximum role for the central institutions. For example, the Commission's proposals for implementing the Treaty provisions on competition envisaged extensive regulatory powers for the Commission. Similarly, in its agricultural proposals the Commission relies heavily on the creation of a number of European marketing boards, which would ultimately have the authority to set support prices that could be rejected or changed only by a unanimous vote of the Council.

The keystone of the Commission's tactics has been the effort to engage the governments in the process of preparation and decision. It has actively encouraged the system of consultation with government experts "for the purpose of coordinating the action of their services in the implementation of the Treaty . . . or to acquire better information on existing problems and the intentions of the authorities concerned, or . . . to *associate the administrations* of the six countries with the working out of the Commission's proposals."[54] Similarly, with regard to interest groups,

the Commission has decided to let its actions be fully known to the public, keeping in the picture the representatives of those economic and social groups concerned, consulting them, advising them, even *associating them* with the work where possible. . . . The Commission notes with pleasure the many endeavors that have already been made to arrange for the exchange of ideas among those responsible for the various fields of activity in the six countries or for a better understanding of the objectives of the Community; in the firm belief that such action will develop a sense of community, the Commission gives them its unstinted support.[55]

Thus the General Directorate for Agriculture has a special department for contacts with nongovernmental groups. It has been the policy of this department and this General Directorate to encourage the creation of regional interest groups by insisting that "common" opinions should be presented to the Commission rather than six sets of positions elaborated by six different national groups. Consultations are also organized with the Committees of the European Parliamentary Assembly and with the specialized sections of the Economic and Social Committee, as well as with pro-integration interest groups outside the Community institutions. Furthermore, the Commission is conscious of the need for good public relations, maintaining an active and efficient information program. And its good standing with the press has contributed much to the pro-integration climate so prevalent in Europe today.

This policy gains support for the Commission, avoids major conflicts, and, above all, helps to engage the national administrations and national interest groups in the Community policy-making system. As such, it represents a form of "informal co-optation," a process whereby the Commission seeks to accommodate itself to the sources of economic and political power within the Community by associating them with policy-making. The Commission bases its proposals on a judgment of what the governments are likely to accept. This has not meant in practice that the Commission proposed the minimum which was acceptable, but that its proposals were designed to accommodate enough from each national position to win support or acquiescence, albeit grudging. This is strikingly confirmed in its proposals on acceleration and in its two memoranda on a European free trade area. In both cases the Commission was given the task of developing concrete proposals on issues about which the governments had been unable to agree. In both cases the Commission's proposals pleased nobody, but were accepted ultimately because there seemed to be no alternative.

It appears that the EEC institutional system, despite its complexity, actually offers more opportunities for the Commission to take an active role than would otherwise have been the case. And, as we have seen, the Commission is an active participant at all stages of the process. According to one description, "The Commission, in spite of the unwieldiness of its administrative apparatus, shows considerable agility. Instead of restricting itself to the tasks set forth in the Treaty, it is trying to become an instrument of coordination, a catalyst, or, if you will, a conductor of an orchestra, who organizes, who animates, and who pulls conclusions from the meetings in which those responsible for economic policy in the Six countries participate."[56]

But the Commission may well have paid a heavy price for these "gains." By filtering its proposals through interminable committees and working groups, it further complicates an already inefficient administrative structure. According to the Treaty, only the Commissioners themselves are nationally apportioned.[57] However, a gentleman's agreement was reached among the signatories by which the Commission's staff would be recruited one-quarter each from France, Germany, Italy, and the Benelux countries. Furthermore, the over-all administrative structure of the Commission was also dictated by rather rigid national apportionment considerations. Nine General Directorates were set up, one for each Commissioner. Each Commissioner has major responsibility for the activities of his General Directorate, although it is formally headed by a group of three Commissioners. In January 1963 the apportionment of the General Directorates was as follows (the General Directorate for Administration is headed by four Commissioners, being made up of the President and the three Vice-Presidents):

External Relations: Jean Rey (head); Robert Marjolin; Giuseppe Caron
Economic and Financial Affairs: Robert Marjolin (head); Sicco Mansholt; Lionello Levi Sandri
Internal Market: Giuseppe Caron (head); Jean Rey; Lambert Schaus
Competition: Hans von der Groeben (head); Robert Marjolin; Jean Rey
Social Affairs: Lionello Levi Sandri (head); Sicco Mansholt; Henri Rochereau
Agriculture: Sicco Mansholt (head); Hans von der Groeben; Lambert Schaus
Transport: Lambert Schaus (head); Giuseppe Caron; Henri Rochereau
Overseas Development: Henri Rochereau (head); Hans von der Groeben; Lionello Levi Sandri
Administration: Walter Hallstein (head); Sicco Mansholt; Robert Marjolin; Giuseppe Caron

Each General Directorate subsumes an elaborate structure of Directorates and Divisions. Because of an accepted rule that a high official of a given nationality ought not to serve directly under a compatriot, the structure has become fairly rigid, with all high-level posts identified with a specific nationality. This provision, combined with the over-all apportioning, has resulted in a staff of uneven abilities. It is frequently very difficult to recruit qualified people to fit specific posts, although some flexibility has been achieved by "trading seats" (an Italian A-2 for a French A-2). Promotion within a given General Directorate is hard. Such advancement as is possible has usually been horizontal, i.e., to a higher post, but in a different General Directorate, a procedure that is not particularly popular with those who wish to continue to work in the field of their special interest or competence. The practice of staffing high posts with civil servants serving on leave from their own administrations poses further recruitment problems. As a matter of procedure, all appointments to high policy-making positions (Categories A-1, A-2, and A-3) are also cleared in advance with the governments concerned.

To date, it is difficult to demonstrate any adverse consequences, but it does seem that this kind of geographical distribution for staffing and recruitment might result merely in a multinational civil service, and that the ideal of a truly international one might suffer accordingly. One of the main tasks of organizational leadership is to recruit and staff in such a way as to build the purposes of the organization into the social structure of the organization. It is too early to know to what extent the Commission may eventually suffer in this regard. I suggest that a large and complex administrative apparatus, combined with a strict national distribution of policy-making positions, may not be particularly conducive, in the long run, to the development of real Community initiatives, and may weaken the authority of the Commission.

THE COUNCIL OF MINISTERS

The Treaty assigns to the Council the task of finding an equilibrium among opposed national interests, and of harmonizing them with the interests of the Community as a whole and with the common objectives of the Treaty. We have seen that this "harmonization" goes on at all levels of the decision-making process, and that the Council considers only those problems that have eluded solution at the level of the experts, or at the level of the Committee of Permanent Representatives or one of the Special Groups. Such problems involve matters of prime importance for one or several Member States, conflicts of interest that can be resolved only by means of concessions and bargaining at the ministerial level. How then does the Council define its own role? Does it see itself as a Community institution? Does it act as one?

The Council of Ministers meets approximately once a month in sessions that may last as long as three days.[58] The Member States have normally been represented by the Ministers of Foreign Affairs or of Economic Affairs, although attendance has often varied from hour to hour, with specialized Ministers sitting in for specific problems within their competence. The most frequent participants in Council sessions have been as follows:

Germany: Ludwig Erhard, Minister of Economic Affairs and Vice-Chancellor; Heinrich von Brentano, Minister of Foreign Affairs; Gerhard Schröder, Minister of Foreign Affairs (since November 1961) ; Alfred Müller-Armack, Secretary of State for Economic Affairs; Ludger Westrick, Secretary of

State for Economic Affairs; Albert von Scherpenberg, Secretary of State for Foreign Affairs; Werner Schwarz, Minister of Agriculture.

France: Maurice Couve de Murville, Minister of Foreign Affairs; Jean-Marcel Jeanneney, Minister of Industry; Wilfrid Baumgartner, Minister of Economic Affairs and Finance; Edgar Pisani, Minister of Agriculture; Valéry Giscard d'Estaing, Secretary of State for Economic Affairs (Minister of Economic Affairs and Finance since April 1962).

Italy: Giuseppe Pella, Minister of Foreign Affairs; Antonio Segni, Minister of Foreign Affairs (from March 1960 to May 1962); Attilio Piccioni, Minister of Foreign Affairs (since May 1962); Emilio Colombo, Minister of Industry; Mariano Rumor, Minister of Agriculture.

Belgium: Pierre Wigny, Minister of Foreign Affairs; Paul-Henri Spaak, Minister of Foreign Affairs and Vice-Premier (since April 1961); Jacques van der Scheuren, Minister of Economic Affairs; Antoine Spinoy, Minister of Economic Affairs (since April 1961); Jacques van Offelen, Minister of Foreign Trade; Charles Heger, Minister of Agriculture (since April 1961).

The Netherlands: Joseph Luns, Minister of Foreign Affairs; Jelle Zijlstra, Minister of Finance; J. W. de Pous, Minister of Economic Affairs; G. M. Marijnen, Minister of Agriculture.

Luxembourg: Eugène Schaus, Minister of Foreign Affairs and Foreign Trade; Emile Schaus, Minister of Agriculture.

Couve de Murville, Wigny,* and Luns attend all the sessions and provide a definite continuity of participation, although development of an institutional identity has been hampered by the relative infrequency of meetings and the changing participants. The proceedings and debates of the Council are secret, and except for press communiqués no public documents are published. The results of votes are never made public, on the grounds that the Council is a *collegiate body.*[59]

Members of the Council are subject to a variety of influences and are most responsive to national rather than Community-wide "publics." They reflect the views of their respective parties, cabinets, and heads of governments, and, through their ministries, special economic or political constituency groups. But as a body they are an institution of the Community, and public statements by spokesmen of the Council have generally emphasized its Communitarian character, as the following extract shows:

The Council and the Commission are called upon to cooperate in carrying out the Community's tasks. . . . We are trying . . . to develop within the Council the collaboration of all the Ministers responsible for different sectors, not only to ensure that the letter and the spirit of the Treaty be respected, but above all to reinforce the dynamism, the cohesion, and the efficacy of the institution and thus of the Community as a whole. [The Council is] a *Community institution,*

* Until April 1961, when Paul-Henri Spaak became Minister of Foreign Affairs.

which, by virtue of the very rules of the Treaty and by the spirit that animates it, tends more and more to answer to its Community function. After all, the practice of the past months leaves no doubt in this regard: the Council, by going through the positions of each of its members and by going beyond these positions, in fact becomes the crucible in which a Community will is formed.[60]

The Council has shown sensitivity to criticisms from the EPA and has gone to considerable lengths to emphasize that although the Treaty assigns different roles to the various Community institutions, they are all engaged in a common effort to build a united Europe. The Council has agreed to participate in an annual "colloquy" with the EPA and the members of the Commission (as well as the members of the Euratom Commission and the ECSC High Authority). These meetings, sometimes extending over several days, have involved a reasonably full and frank exchange of views, as well as giving the Council an opportunity to defend its actions. In the colloquy of November 1959 the following subjects were discussed: the relations between the Council and the Assembly, the coordination of the external policy of the Six countries, and relations with the associated overseas territories. In November 1960 the merging of the executives of the three communities was discussed, and also the foreign policy of the Community. The 1960 colloquy developed into a full-scale debate on the overall policy of the Member States regarding European integration and in particular regarding de Gaulle's proposals for a permanent political secretariat; each of the six Ministers spoke *on behalf of his respective government*, giving a "defense" of their European policies.

The Council has emphasized that it is not responsible to the EPA under the Treaty; on the other hand, it has expressed its awareness that, in practice, it cannot act independently of the EPA. In his address to the Assembly in November 1959, Pella remarked:

We know that it is often difficult to distinguish between that which belongs to the competence of the Commission and that which belongs to the competence of the Council. Moreover, you [members of the EPA] are led to think less in terms of institutional responsibility than in terms of Community responsibility, and this is readily understandable. Consequently, it is also natural that your deliberations should tend to be directed toward the activities of the Council.[61]

In this spirit, at its session of March 9–10, 1960, the Council agreed to consult the Assembly on important Community problems even though this was not required by the Treaty, to give supporting "reasons" when the Council did not comply with Assembly resolutions, to answer questions from the parliamentarians if they concerned matters the Council had already considered, and to present periodic oral reports on the activities of the Council. This decision was subsequently reported to the Assembly:

Thus, by our common efforts, we shall create the conditions that will enable our institutions to function with a maximum of efficacy for the great benefit of our Communities. . . . Difficulties will be overcome by the forces that you represent in your capacity as the European Parliament, united to which will be the forces that the Councils and the Commissions, in their turn, put at the service of the Communities. And these forces—acting in concert beyond the differences which now and then separate, but nevertheless stimulate, us—testify that the "Europe, organized and alive," that President Robert Schuman called into being May 9, 1950, is now on the march.[62]

With regard to the Commission, we have already seen that the Council has regularly included it in its deliberations and that on several occasions it has conferred additional tasks on the Commission. The most important of these, it will be recalled, were the tasks of preparing a Community position on the free trade area issue (with the Commission's subsequent chairmanship of the Rey Committee), of presenting specific proposals for the acceleration of the Common Market timetable, and of conducting the negotiations over Greece's application for association with the EEC.[63]

The goal of Council meetings is to achieve a maximum consensus among the Member States. Unanimity is sought, even where this is not required, but always on the basis of mutual compromise. The Member States have generally shown great sensitivity toward each other's needs, and the gathering has been described as resembling "more a large 'cercle de famille' than an ordinary diplomatic meeting."[64] The atmosphere is informal, for the Ministers know each other well by now, long, formal speeches are rare, laughter is easy, and there is a clear awareness of running a common project in which the problem is never whether agreement is possible, but rather what level of compromise should be sought. Participation has been in the spirit of joint problem-solving, instead of being limited to defending national points of view. No single Member State is habitually obstructive, and all have made significant compromises in the interests of achieving a Community solution. Basic confrontations of interest have occurred, but no firm pattern of blocs has been established, different members playing mediatory roles under different conditions. Thus Belgium and Italy mediated in the conflict of the Netherlands and Germany vs. France in the issue of the free trade area, France and Belgium mediated in the conflict of the Netherlands vs. Germany in the question of agriculture, and so on. The Commission, too, has played the part of mediator during sessions of the Council, both by offering compromise formulas and by changing its proposals.

This is not to say that agreement is always reached. Wide differences of basic interest and conception still exist among the Member States, and progress toward an economic union must necessarily be slow. In an address before the EPA, Pierre Wigny, President of the Council, underscored the difficulties that lay ahead:

These difficulties, however, do not stem, as some would have us believe, from the passiveness, the inaction, or in other words the ill-will, of the Councils or the Governments. They are no more than the outward signs of the struggle of which Paul Valéry speaks in his "Philosophie de l'esprit," the struggle "between yesterday, which is the past, and a certain tomorrow which is working within us," of which he rightly says that it has never been "going on more furiously than in our age" within all social groups.[65]

Disagreements between the Member States are normally de-emphasized, however, and divisive issues are always postponed, or returned to the Committee of Permanent Representatives for "further study."

THE COMMITTEE OF PERMANENT REPRESENTATIVES AND THE OTHER PREPARATORY COMMITTEES[66]

It was inevitable that the Council of Ministers would establish some sort of committee to prepare its decisions ahead of time. The Council meets infrequently, its composition fluctuates, and the Ministers who attend (often the Foreign Ministers or the Ministers for Economic Affairs) are already heavily burdened with their normal responsibilities. Such a committee (COCOR) had functioned successfully in the European Coal and Steel Community and was even more necessary in the EEC, given the enormously expanded scope of the undertaking. In the EEC the Member States are deeply committed to a process of establishing a Common Market, unifying their economies, and developing new modes of policy preparation and decision. Vital interests are constantly in the balance, and it is clear that the several governments intend to exercise as much control over the process as they can. It follows, therefore, that they will attempt to retain and develop their own independent sources of technical information so as to be able to confront the Commission and if necessary to offer alternative formulations.

As we have noted, the Permanent Representatives serve a dual function: as a preparatory committee of the Council, and as the formal ambassadors of the Member States of the Community. Each Permanent Delegation has a structure similar to that of an embassy or overseas mission. The delegations are permanently based in Brussels (also the headquarters of the Commission's Services, the Economic and Social Committee, the Council, and the Euratom Commission), and have an average staff of about thirty (less for the Belgians and Luxemburgers, who are already in Brussels). As diplomatic missions, they deal with problems of protocol, transmit notes and communications, and gather information. In their collective role they have become, in effect, an institution of the Community. Their membership is relatively stable,* they meet together at least once a week, and they are in constant contact with Community matters and Community personnel.† Their stated function is to prepare the meetings of the Council of Ministers, but has developed, as we have seen, to include normal liaison with the Commission at all stages, detailed examination of Commission proposals (and sometimes the formulation of alternative suggestions), and, above all, as much preliminary reconciliation of national views as possible.

Relations between the Committee of Permanent Representatives and the Commission were quite strained at the outset. In June 1958, President Hallstein observed before the EPA, in response to a query from van der Goes van Naters, that there was indeed a danger that such a committee might be given responsibilities that according to the Treaty should reside in the Council, and that it might create an administration which would seek to perform functions assigned to the Commission.[67] The Commission was reluctant at first to appear before the Committee of Permanent Representatives, maintaining that it was supposed to deal directly with the Ministers. Relations became particularly strained during the controversy over the 1959 budget, when the Commission interpreted the Committee's behavior as an effort to assume control and to derogate from the Commission's own role. The fears and suspicions of the Commission have all but disappeared as the actual role being played by the Permanent Representatives has become more clearly defined. The Commission still resists the periodic efforts of the governments (especially the French) to confer on the Committee of Permanent Representatives the right to make final decisions in place of the Council. The Commission has maintained that such responsibility, even on minor points, cannot be delegated by the Council; but it has accepted the development of a "rubber-stamp" procedure by which matters agreed upon by the Permanent Representatives

---

* Johannes Linthorst-Homan (Netherlands) and Albert Borschette (Luxembourg) have served continuously since 1958, and Joseph van der Meulen (Belgium) for almost as long; while Attilio Cattani (Italy) and Carl Ophüls (Germany) were Permanent Representatives from 1958 to 1961. As of April 1962, the Permanent Representatives were Günther Harkort (Germany), van der Meulen, Jean-Marc Boegner (France), Antonio Venturini (Italy), Borschette, and Linthorst-Homan.

† It is interesting to compare the number of meetings held by the Permanent Representatives and COCOR, respectively. Between September 30, 1959, and September 30, 1960, the Permanent Representatives held 66 meetings and called 447 expert working groups, whereas COCOR held only 14 meetings and called only 31 expert working groups. The figures reflect the fact that COCOR met only periodically, and that only the Italians maintained a permanent staff in Luxembourg.

can be approved by the Council *en bloc,* with no debate, if there are no objections. As with the "written procedure" already referred to, the Commission's assent is required.

A continuous dialogue has developed between the Commission and the Committee of Permanent Representatives. The Commission uses the Permanent Representatives as interlocutors to discover the "limits of the possible" before making formal proposals and as a clearing house for summoning national experts to Brussels. The Committee, on the other hand, frequently calls on the Commission for technical information or asks it to present "the dossier." The Commission is present at all the Committee's sessions, and the atmosphere is one of sincere effort to solve Community problems. All participants know each other well, and informality is the rule. They do not always talk on national briefs, and the common interest of all in achieving a compromise solution is generally stressed. A two-way influence has thus been instituted. The Permanent Representatives defend national points of view, but at the same time are influenced by their participation in Community affairs and often argue back to their national capitals in favor of Commission proposals, or in favor of making concessions to another Member State in order to achieve agreement. The Commission and the Permanent Representatives are linked, to this extent, by a "camaraderie de combat."[68] Such a process operates best with regard to technical matters or in areas in which the governments are willing to compromise. However, in a case like the dispute between the Netherlands and Germany over acceleration in agriculture, the matter had to be referred to the Council of Ministers, who were in a position to strike more fundamental bargains.

The Committee of Permanent Representatives acts as a real catalyst, and has developed strong European feelings (more so than the Council). It considers itself to be "the Commission's best friend." The extent to which individual Permanent Representatives are able to play a significant two-way role depends on how specific their instructions are and what facility they have to obtain their modification. This in turn depends to a great extent on the methods by which national policy on EEC questions is made and coordinated. The conditions that have caused the Permanent Representatives to become somewhat "Europeanized" may also diminish their influence in the respective national capitals.

The EEC concerns all national Ministries, both because of the scope of the commitments entered into and because matters previously subject to the autonomous determination of each government now involve joint or shared decision-making. Jurisdictional conflicts among various Ministries, and most particularly between Foreign Affairs and Economic Affairs, are endemic. Foreign Affairs has tried to retain control over European integration matters (viewed as external relations), but this inevitably derogates from the competence of Economic Affairs and the technical Ministries. These conflicts may arise for familiar reasons, such as the generalization of normal conflicts occurring between government departments with different technical goals or different constituencies; thus the Minister of Finance may oppose the Minister of Agriculture. Or they may mirror fundamentally different views on the whole issue of integration (arising again perhaps from different technical goals and constituencies), as when Chancellor Adenauer and his Foreign Minister and Finance Minister stood against Erhard, the Minister for Economic Affairs. Basically, however, it is a function of the incipient breakdown of the differentiation between foreign affairs and domestic affairs.*

There is the question of the extent to which governmental structures have been affected by the increasing involvement of the government concerned in the work of international institutions and, in particular, by the fact that the activity of these institutions now encompasses fields previously regarded as wholly or primarily of domestic concern. In other words, to what extent is the traditional distinction between foreign and domestic affairs as reflected in the existence of foreign offices and foreign services on the one hand, and domestic departments of government and home civil services on the other, any longer a real guide to the operations of government? There is the question as to the way in which governments regard service on the secretariat of such organizations by members of their own services, and the extent to which this has come to be regarded as part of the formal career of members of the relevant departments, and there is the further question as to the effect of service of this kind upon the subsequent outlook of the individuals concerned and their departments. . . . How far has this expansion of international activity created new problems in the relations between the traditional departments of individual governments and how far has satisfactory machinery for their coordination been achieved in particular instances?[69]

The signing of the Rome Treaty gave rise to major interministerial conflicts in all the Member States over the direction and coordination of policy in the new Community. One of the "prizes" in such conflicts has been control over the Permanent Delegations to the EEC—the appointment of the Permanent Representative, the lines of direction and responsibility, and so forth. In several of the countries, especially in France and the Netherlands, there was serious discussion about the creation of a special Ministry of European Affairs, but the Foreign Affairs Ministries have blocked such moves to date. In all cases, but with varying effectiveness, Foreign Affairs has retained formal control over the Permanent

---

* The growing number of meetings between the technical Ministers of the Six (Finance, Agriculture, Labor, and Transport) is partly an expression of these conflicts, as are the efforts of the Ministers of Foreign Affairs to control such meetings.

Representatives. The upper staffs of the several delegations are drawn from the various Ministries concerned, but all are missions of the Ministry of Foreign Affairs and report to that Ministry, and, with the exception of Belgium and the Netherlands, all the Permanent Representatives come from Foreign Affairs. This control and direction is most complete in the case of the Italian delegation, with *all* official communications going to Foreign Affairs and being dispatched from there to other Ministries. The formal role of the Quai d'Orsay is similar, but its function is more that of a messenger boy for most questions, as will be seen later. In the Netherlands and Germany, direct formal communications are permitted between a representative of, say, Economic Affairs and his Ministry, and in the German case the lack of coordination on European affairs that is evident in Bonn is faithfully mirrored in the direction given to the Permanent Delegation.

Each of the Member States has developed more or less institutionalized systems for coordinating the views of the several Ministries on European integration problems, but these do not function very satisfactorily because they are *ad hoc* developments and bound to be subject to alteration. Thus the machinery set up has in no way resolved the conflicts between Ministries. Except in Germany, this machinery has taken the form of a coordinating committee. The Germans, however, have no formal or regularized coordinating committee. Interested Ministers (or their deputies) meet on specific issues, as they arise, in order to instruct the Permanent Representative. When no agreement is possible, as frequently happens, the matter must be settled by the cabinet or by Adenauer himself. Basic differences on policy and ideology exist in the government, and, as a result, instructions to the Permanent Representative are closely negotiated and generally quite specific. The Permanent Representative is influential within Foreign Affairs and has appealed successfully for a change in instructions when this had been blocked by Economic Affairs.

Italy, the Netherlands, and Belgium all have some kind of interministerial coordinating committee. In Italy, this committee meets only before sessions of the Council (not before those of the Permanent Representatives). Foreign Affairs is in firm control, the government has been a consistent supporter of economic integration, and as yet there seem to have been no major interministerial conflicts to challenge this Ministry's position. The Permanent Representative has, as a rule, been very loosely instructed, and he plays a major role in the formation and coordination of policy in Rome, participating actively in sessions of the coordinating committee. His role in debates in the Committee of Permanent Representatives has been very positive and cooperative. The Italians have been among the most consistent supporters of the Commission. The

Permanent Delegation also sees its role as being that of "educating" Italian civil servants in European affairs. "We force Rome to think," one is told.

The situation in the Netherlands is quite different. A coordinating committee exists, under the direction of Foreign Affairs, but basic differences between Ministers persist (Economic Affairs is in general more "European"), and each Ministry tries to cling to its sphere of jurisdiction. The Committee for Coordination meets in The Hague before every session of the Committee of Permanent Representatives and decides on precise instructions on every point of the agenda. The Permanent Representative does not play a very significant part in the coordinating committee's discussions. No bargaining room is provided, and if an unexpected item comes up in a session of the Permanent Representatives, the Dutch Representative is unable to take any position at all. This is a general principle in the Netherlands, where Cabinet meetings often deal with minute details, and is no doubt a function of its delicately balanced political system. Nevertheless, it is at least partly responsible for the reputation for intransigence and stubbornness that the Dutch have earned in Community circles.

The problems of coordination and instruction are far less troublesome for the Belgians because the bulk of the Community's work is carried on in Brussels. The Permanent Representative depends on Foreign Affairs, and the Foreign Minister has kept full control. An Interministerial Committee for Economic Affairs (CEI) seeks to provide coordination, and the Permanent Representative plays an active role in its deliberations. He may even call it into *ad hoc* session on his own initiative, and has done so in order to obtain a modification in his instructions. The Belgian Permanent Representative, as well as the Belgian representative in Council meetings (usually Wigny), has consistently supported "European" solutions.

But none of these systems is considered satisfactory by those who participate in them. Only the French have a relatively efficient system of coordination, and this is largely because the Interministerial Coordinating Committee for Questions of European Economic Cooperation has an established status based on an agreement between all the Ministries. It has a permanent secretariat, through which pass all communications and instructions. Meetings of interested Ministries are called when it is necessary to elaborate a position. Agreement is usually reached at the level of *fonctionnaires,* but if not, the matter goes to the Ministers themselves. For the bulk of matters concerning the Rome Treaty, however, the Ministry of Financial and Economic Affairs is the most influential, and the position of Foreign Affairs is relatively weak. The reverse is true for issues that go beyond the Treaty, as in matters of external relations, acceleration, and so on. The Permanent Representative does not seem to play a major role in the coordination process.*

It is not yet clear whether (or to what extent) the other interstitial groups that have been established parallel to the Committee of Permanent Representatives will develop along similar lines. The continuous meeting together with Commission officials in the course of trying to develop common policies for the Six will surely have its effect. It should be recalled that the atmosphere of these sessions is one of problem-solving, common interests being stressed throughout, and not that of the point-by-point bargaining typical of classical intergovernmental negotiations. Nevertheless, we have seen that the part that such groups as the Committee of Permanent Representatives is able to play is largely dependent on its membership being drawn from high-level officials with access to national policy-making processes.

The Rey Committee (the Special Committee for the Study of a European Economic Association), which bears primary responsibility for preparing the Community's position on relations with third countries, was the first of these specialized committees, having been set up in March 1959. Its membership has been drawn from high levels,† and it has played an increasingly wide role in policy formation, especially in regard to relations with the European Free Trade Association (EFTA). The influence of the Commission (through the Committee's chairman, Commissioner Rey) has been striking, and is one of the more notable examples of the interpenetration of functions that characterizes the EEC.[70] The Special Committee on Agriculture began to function in the fall of 1960, and there are signs that it will play at least an equivalent role.‡ This Committee is

---

* In COCOR, the French delegate was usually the Assistant Secretary-General of the Interministerial Coordinating Committee, and thus coordination was even closer.

† The original members were as follows: Baron Snoy et d'Oppuers (Belgium), Secretary-General of the Ministry of Economic Affairs; Olivier Wormser (France), Director-General of Economic Affairs at the Ministry of Foreign Affairs; Alfred Müller-Armack (Germany), State Secretary of the Federal Ministry of Economic Affairs; Attilio Cattani (Italy), Permanent Representative to the European Communities; Albert Borschette (Luxembourg), Permanent Representative; Ernst van der Beugel (Netherlands), special adviser to the Ministry for Foreign Affairs; and, of course, Jean Rey (Belgium), of the Commission. EEC Commission, *Bulletin*, No. 2 (1959), p. 22.

‡ The national delegations are made up of high officials from the Ministries of Foreign Affairs, Agriculture, and Economic Affairs, but it is interesting to note that, with the exception of Luxembourg, the heads of delegations are all responsible to the Foreign Affairs Ministry. The French and Italian delegations are headed by the Permanent Representatives. *Agence Europe*, September 12, 1960.

at the center of the long and incredibly complex process by which the Community is developing a common agricultural policy. It is a committee of the Council, using the Council's Secretariat, and its chairmanship rotates on the same basis as that of the Council and the Committee of Permanent Representatives. There was support from four of the six governments for making Commissioner Mansholt the chairman and for allowing the Commission to provide the Secretariat of the Committee.[71] This idea was rejected, but since the Committee's task is to examine the proposals of the Commission, the latter has retained the initiative. In practice the Commission prepares the meetings, calls experts, presides over their meetings, makes reports, and even acts as an executory organ for the Committee.[72]

Perhaps the chief significance of all these committees, as of the hundreds of expert study groups drawn from the national administrations, is the expectation that, in the long run, national bureaucrats and technicians will be so involved in the decision-making process at the Community level that they will become committed to that process, that they will become "engaged." According to Haas, "The concept of 'engagement' postulates that if parties to a conference enjoy a specific and well-articulated sense of participation, if they identify themselves completely with the procedures and codes within which their decisions are made, they consider themselves completely 'engaged' by the results even if they do not fully concur in them."[73] Before long, vast numbers of national administrators will have participated in innumerable conferences and will have become well acquainted with their opposite numbers in Bonn or The Hague, with whom they have worked and perhaps "fathered" a policy decision in which they take pride.[74] It is no longer necessary for contacts between national administrators to be channeled through the Ministry of Foreign Affairs and the other appropriate Ministries: "We just pick up the phone." Such multiple contacts at all levels foster reciprocal understanding and good will, which a strict definition of roles would not do. Indeed, "one may be happy that the technicians become interested in European problems and may hope that they will help stop being citadels of protectionism and become the instruments of integration."[75]

A particularly interesting reflection of the impact of the EEC on national administrations is seen in the area of personnel policy. As the distinction between matters of external concern and matters of domestic concern has slowly eroded, changes have begun to appear in governmental concepts of service in EEC institutions. This is clearly apparent in the case of France. The French administration has accepted the notion that the EEC Treaty is no ordinary international document involving matters of concern only to a few specialists. On the contrary, the accepted principle is that all civil servants with significant responsibility must become fully competent in European affairs. This has led the French to favor a system whereby national civil servants could be "detached" for four to five years for service in the European Commission, after which they would return to Paris to important posts in the French administration. The aim of the French is that their entire administrative elite should pass through the Commission. This position has brought them into conflict both with the other Member States and with the Commission, and was largely responsible for the long delay in agreeing on an EEC personnel statute. The Commission and the "Europeans" have regarded the French attitude as a threat to their goal of building a high-quality, permanent, and independent "European" staff for the Commission. The French, on the other hand, have argued that this sort of "co-penetration" would promote, and even accelerate, the development of "Europe," which would not be achieved by the creation of competing national and international bureaucracies.

The French have undoubtedly several motives for setting forth these ideas, but it is difficult to deny their contention that French civil servants working on the Commission staff have so far been among the most valuable and enthusiastic "Europeans." Furthermore, if our analysis of the EEC system is correct, the French proposals would only formalize an already existing pattern, since many of the high officials of the Commission were working on a "detached" basis during the years the EEC was without a personnel statute (1958–62).[76] This included the bulk of the French, who were encouraged to return to Paris after several years by the provision that they would continue to advance in the national hierarchy even while working for the Commission. The other Member States did not share the French view, and provisions for "detachment" were not so favorable. In Italy they extended only to members of the Diplomatic Corps, and then, as in Belgium and Germany, there was no provision for automatic advancement in the national hierarchy. Dutch civil servants can only be detached for one year, and if they leave the service, they lose all benefits they might have accrued. The Dutch position is conditioned by the low level of salary in the Netherlands, as well as by the fact that so many top-level administrators were leaving for greener pastures in Brussels.

When the Treaty of Rome was drawn up, many people questioned the wisdom of establishing a system which, though it would probably result in shared or joint decision-making, would do so at the expense of national parliaments. The EPA has no powers of effective control, nor can it deal directly with substantive policy areas, although it may develop its ability to influence the actions of policy-making institutions. The system of bureaucratic development and interpenetration we have described reinforces these original fears. One is led to speculate, in fact, about the long-range significance that the centralization of bureaucracies has been shown to have for the development of centralized states, for example, the role of the bureaucracy in Ancient Egypt, in the France of Louis XIV, and in the unification of Germany. Under the EEC as it actually operates, members of the executive branches of government, whether acting through working groups called to advise the Commission or the Permanent Representatives, or through the Permanent Representatives or the other interstitial committees, or through the Ministers in Council, are assuming important responsibilities in many matters hitherto within the jurisdiction of the national parliaments. The individual Ministers may still be responsible before their parliaments, but parliamentary control cannot be very effective when the Minister may be outvoted in the EEC Council of Ministers.[77] We are witnessing, therefore, the development of an amorphous system of power whose ultimate form cannot be predicted.

THE EUROPEAN PARLIAMENTARY ASSEMBLY

How does the Assembly fit into this system? According to Stein,

[The Assembly] has been remarkably successful in establishing practices and procedures which ensure cooperation with the High Authority and the Common Market and Euratom Commissions, and which provide a basis for a measure of control over these executive bodies. On the whole these bodies appear to have willingly submitted to these procedures and the public record abounds with professions of their desire to cooperate with the Assembly and to encourage its growth. It would be difficult, however, to demonstrate at this juncture that the Assembly has already succeeded through these procedures in actually influencing and controlling the activities of the "executives" in a significant way. . . .

The Assembly has had a measure of success in developing techniques for bringing its views before the Councils of Ministers. However, the evidence of any real control or influence over the Ministers appears non-existent at this time.[78]

This judgment is confirmed in the general survey we have made of the Community's first years of existence and in the case studies that follow. The Assembly does not participate directly in the EEC policy-making process as we have described it. Nor have its activities contributed to the institutional developments upon which we have laid so much stress. Indeed, the Assembly has often been suspicious of, or even hostile to, these developments, warning the Commission against relying so much on the national governments and pointing out that the Commission's preliminary conferences with national experts have no legal standing.[79] Nor have the parliamentarians made any effort to coordinate the debates in Strasbourg and in the national parliaments.[80] As Haas has pointed out in reference to the EPA's precursor organization, the Common Assembly of the ECSC,

In jurisdictional and organizational terms, the outstanding parliamentary artificiality of the Assembly remains its inability to bind the parent legislatures, to administer its own composition, to control its two executives meaningfully, or to co-ordinate the debates and votes of the national parliaments. . . . In the absence of these powers the Assembly's routine work takes place in a vacuum; the national legislatures remain free to act as they did before; there is no evidence that they defer in any way to the resolutions of their delegates in Strasbourg.[81]

The Assembly's short-run significance for policy formation has been limited to providing a public forum for the debate of major Community issues, and as such it has been very useful for the Commission, and often embarrassing for the Council and the governments. As the most actively "European" of the institutions, it can generally be counted upon to support the Commission against the Council and to seek to maximize integrative policies. The Assembly has repeatedly urged the Commission to exercise its powers more vigorously, to implement a liberal interpretation of the Treaty, to deal firmly with national measures intended to circumvent Treaty provisions, to develop rapidly an "antitrust" statute, and to do more in the social field and in the coordination of economic policies.[82] This is not to say that the Assembly is *always* in agreement with the Commission upon the details of policy, nor that sharp differences do not occur within the Assembly itself. In either case, however, each of the divergent positions adopted has almost always advocated an extension of the role of the central institutions and has thus contributed to spill-over. (For details see Chapter 11).

The Commission uses the Assembly as a sounding board for all major policy statements. It actively seeks support and appears readily before its committees. Yet it does not consider itself bound by these consultations:

The Commission has kept the European Parliament fully informed of its plans and, during 1959 and the first quarter of 1960, has sought the Parliament's opinion each time that a major political problem arose, even though it was not required to do so by the Treaty. The Commission has also, on several occasions taken an active part in debates in the Parliament dealing with the Community's external relations or with agricultural policy. It recently opened the general policy debate in the Parliament with an account of the recommendations it had submitted to the Council on speedier implementation of the Treaty and has taken into account *as far as possible* the resolutions adopted by the Parliament at the conclusion of these debates.[83]

The Assembly has sought to expand its participation in the policy-making process by asking the Commission to consult it *before* making proposals to the Council. The foremost example was the common agricultural policy. The Commission acquiesced and participated in the ensuing debates, but made it quite clear that it would nevertheless "feel entirely free in making its proposals, for it knew the Assembly would not want to usurp the place of the Executive."[84] Thus the role being played by the EPA vis-à-vis the Commission is analogous to that of a pressure group. It represents *one* source of opinion and pressure among the many to which the Commission must remain sensitive.

But the Assembly has a significant long-range potential for influencing policy. It seeks constantly and aggressively to expand its role; it keeps a close watch over the activities of the Commission, the Council, and the governments, both by means of seven or eight public plenary sessions a year, which last from two days to a week, and by means of thirteen standing committees,* which meet throughout the year on an average of three to four days a month. Most of the Assembly's work is done in these committees, which study the activities of the "executives," and draft reports and resolutions to be submitted to the Assembly. In addition, they receive testimony from members and officials of the Commission, interest group representatives, and independent experts. The committees have made every effort to influence the Commission at all stages of the process of proposal preparation. The forms and procedures, if not the content, of parliamentary control have evolved, and presumably the content will eventually follow, since it appears inevitable that the Assembly will gain more power if the integration process continues. The members of the Assembly are working hard toward this end. The goal of the great majority of parliamentarians is gradually to transform the Assembly into a Federal Parliament of a unified Europe, with real legislative powers, control of the purse, and effective supervision over the executives. They have pushed for a merger of the three nongovernmental executive bodies (the EEC Commission, the High Authority, and the Euratom Commission), and have recently completed work on a convention for the election of the EPA by direct universal suffrage.[85] According to one report,

Even if the Assembly does not succeed in gaining the rights to introduce legislation and to select members of the Commissions or the power of budgetary control, the federalists are convinced that the votes of the European peoples

---

* These are the Political Committee, the External Trade Committee, the Committee on Agriculture, the Social Committee, the Internal Market Committee, the Economic and Financial Committee, the Committee on Cooperation with the Development Countries, the Committee on Transport, the Energy Committee, the Research and Cultural Affairs Committee, the Health Protection Committee, the Administration and Budgets Committee, and the Legal Committee. EPA, *Annuaire-Manuel 1961–1962*, pp. 94–101. Each *Annuaire-Manuel* contains a lengthy account of the activities of these committees.

will enable the Parliament to increase its powers in practice if not in theory. They hope that after the elections the Assembly will be in a sufficiently strong position to be able to ask the Commissions to accept the majority decisions of its debates as a basis for putting forward their proposals to the Council.[86]

If the Assembly has so far failed to acquire any real influence over the EEC decision-making process, if its role here seems to be largely a potential for the future, there remains the very striking development of internal consensus that is revealed in its system of political groups. We have suggested that participation in the activities of the central institutions would facilitate the development of a "European" consensus whose effects would be felt at both the national and the Community levels. Such a development would strengthen the position of the institutions even though they lacked the competency to wield power directly. It would indicate that cleavages of opinion were occurring on other than national lines, or that national interests were being subordinated to some notion of a Community interest. The role played by political groups in the Assembly confirms that these processes are under way.

The Assembly is organized not on the basis of nationality, but according to political affiliation. There are three political groups—the Christian-Democrats, the Socialists, and the Liberals (with affiliates)—each with its own officers, secretariat, caucus rooms, library, and so on. The political groups meet far more frequently than the national delegations (which have no official status), and act as nominating and electing agents for the Assembly's officers.[87] They caucus regularly during debates and before votes, and always try to arrive at a group position, which is then presented by an official spokesman in the formal debate. The political groups of the EPA are distributed as follows:[88]

	Christian-Democrats	Socialist	Liberals & Affiliates	Totals
Italy	27	3	5	35*
France	3	5	28	36
Germany	21	12	3	36
Netherlands	7	5	2	14
Luxembourg	3	2	1	6
Belgium	6	6	2	14
Totals	67	33	41	141

Personal stands are also taken, but a considerable effort is made to deemphasize purely national points of view. As Kapteyn observed of the Common Assembly,

* One Italian seat unfilled.

Obviously, this development did not mean that national considerations no longer played a part in the forming of opinions. It is not surprising, therefore, that each national group had certain favourite questions which the members repeatedly brought before the Assembly. Not only national, but also some regional and party interests were advocated. It is a sign of the atmosphere prevailing, however, that the delegates often apologised for doing so. The reaction of group colleagues was quick to follow if one of their members went too far.[89]

These groups are seen by their members as the precursors of "European" political parties. They work diligently in caucus to hammer out common positions, which are reached on the basis of mutual compromise,[90] and to which the members of the group are expected to adhere during the debate. Over the years there has been a marked *rapprochement* of national party views. As Haas points out:

Doctrinal consensus has developed significantly. . . . Largely as a result of the increased opportunities to criticize meaningfully and continuously the activities of a true administrative agency, the Socialist deputies of six nationalities began to function as a supranational politicial party, showing a consistent record of successful internal compromise, deference to each other's wishes, alternating leadership, and willingness to de-emphasize issues on which a unanimously endorsed doctrine proved unobtainable. . . . The group . . . of Christian-Democratic deputies shows less doctrinal unity but functions smoothly as a general support for any "European" policy. . . . The Liberal group shows no such unity and is rarely cohesive on concrete policy issues. Nevertheless, all three groups have developed into a permanent parliamentary elite conversant with the problems of integration and respected as such in their home legislatures.[91]

Procedural and substantive consensus is likely to continue to develop. The very nature of the Assembly's functions would seem to assure this. If the Assembly is to expand its influence in EEC policy-making, it must operate in terms of the new realities. The governments of the Six are engaged in a process whereby powers of decision are being shared or delegated to central institutions committed to a search for "European" solutions to common problems. As Kapteyn observed about the Common Assembly, "The democratic control of such a . . . policy by the Assembly only had any meaning if, in principle, it also had the same conception, all the more so in view of the fact that the national interest had a natural and a powerful defender in the Council of Ministers. In judging a policy based on the *general* welfare as its chief aim, the Assembly had to make this criterion the point of departure if a successful discussion was to be made possible."[92]

However, if these parliamentary groupings are to develop into real

European political parties, their activities will have to be coordinated with those of electoral parties organized on European and not national lines.[93] This will come only with the introduction of direct popular elections for the Assembly. Only the most tentative steps in the direction of electoral parties have been taken so far, namely by the Nouvelles Equipes Internationales (NEI), the Europe-wide association of Christian-Democratic parties, and by the Socialist Movement for a United States of Europe (MSEUE), the organization representing the Socialist parties.[94]

THE ECONOMIC AND SOCIAL COMMITTEE

The ESC to date has not played a significant role in EEC decision-making.[95] Its status is purely advisory, the Member States maintain strict control over appointments, the Council must approve its Rules of Procedure by unanimity, and, with relatively minor exceptions, it cannot meet on its own initiative. This is not to prejudge its possible long-range significance, however. Such significance would depend, first, on its being able to achieve a real influence over the policies of those institutions that are directly involved in the decision-making process, and, second, on whether or not participation in the Committee led its members to develop some sort of "European" consensus whose effects would extend back to the national context, thus activating interest group elites and contributing to the spill-over process.

The 101 members of the ESC are drawn from major interest groups in the Member States and are roughly divided into one-third trade unions, one-third business, commerce, and industry, and one-third "general interests" (including representatives of the liberal professions, engineers, etc.).[96] By March 1961, the ESC had held 14 plenary sessions and had formulated twelve opinions concerning the EEC.[97] These opinions were prepared in Specialized Sections and then submitted to plenary session for final approval. Specialized Sections exist for agriculture, economic questions, transport, social questions, activities of the nonsalaried and service professions, and overseas countries and territories.[98] The bulk of the work of preparation, as well as the reconciliation of positions, goes on in the Specialized Sections and any working groups that they might set up, and the plenary session normally accepts their reports. The preparation of these opinions has taken an average of four and a half months (ranging from one and a half months to eight months),[99] and has been taken very seriously by the participants. Although majority voting is provided for in the Rules of Procedure, the normal practice of the ESC has been to try to draft opinions that could receive unanimous or almost unanimous approval. Most votes taken have been by a very large majority and only with abstentions, not negative votes.[100] This quest for compromise may have salutary effects so far as internal consensus is concerned, but it has consistently made for extremely general opinions. Such opinions have been taken into consideration by the Council and the Commission when it was convenient for them to do so. The Commission has made considerable efforts to establish good relations with the ESC and to enlist its support for Commission proposals. To this end they have asked the Committee for opinions in several instances in which the Treaty does not require it.[101] Should the ESC consistently support Commission proposals, and should this support be reflected back to the behavior of national interest groups toward their respective governments, the influence of the ESC might increase. It is too early, however, to make a prediction about this.

On the basis of the experience of the similarly constituted Consultative Committee of the ECSC,[102] and on that of economic and social councils in other countries (Weimar Germany, France, and Belgium),[103] we would expect that interest groups wishing to influence Community decision-making will find the ESC too rigid, too comprehensive, and too heterogeneous. These groups will doubtless seek direct access to decision-making centers at the Community and national level, and their participation in the debates of the ESC may well become perfunctory. This would also suggest that groups which lacked possibilities of access at either the national or Community level might seek to overcome this through participation in the ESC. As Haas noted with regard to the Consultative Committee, "Interest lagged in direct proportion as the business representatives realized that they could gain access to the High Authority through orthodox lobbying channels and that the High Authority was not disposed to pay close attention to their deliberations in any case."[104]

It appears that differences of opinion in the ESC do not follow national lines, but have developed according to the interest represented. The Rules of Procedure permit the formation of "groups based on the various economic and social groupings."[105] Three groups have been formed representing employers, workers, and "various interests," each group seeking to coordinate the positions of its members in working parties, Specialized Sections, and plenary sessions. The degree of coordination varies greatly, being, as one might expect, practically nonexistent in the "various interests" group. The trade union organizations existing at the level of the Six—the European Organization of the ICCTU (International Confederation of Christian Trade Unions), the European Secretariat of the ICFTU (International Confederation of Free Trade Unions), and the UNICE (the Union of Industries of the European Community)—are closely associated with the efforts to coordinate the activities of their respective groups.

The activities of the farmers' representatives in the ESC are coordinated by a regionally organized interest group, COPA (Committee of Agricultural Organizations of the European Economic Community). COPA has channeled the great majority of its efforts through the ESC, and the final opinion voted by the plenary session on the Commission's proposals for a common agricultural policy largely represents the COPA view. Moreover, the farmers' representatives have developed a definite pattern of mutual consultation and compromise in an attempt to win trade union support against the representatives of industry. As participants in the proceedings of the ESC testify, the constant meeting together, the preparation of reports, and the exchange of ideas constitute a marked feature of integration:

The national points of view discernible during the examination of this or that problem are generally dropped in favor of a "European decision" when the moment comes to seek a common formula embodying the group's point of view. . . . Quite as important perhaps as its consultative role is the fact that it represents a forum for discussion by the circles directly concerned in the measures enacted by the Councils and the Commissions. The Committee is the sole organ within which organized interests can collaborate on an institutional basis. . . . This tempers purely interested points of view and contributes greatly to the formation of a feeling for Europe in the executive bodies of influential organizations. Under the influence of the constant discussions between the representatives of the economic and social sectors, the Committee members not only get to know the problems of other countries and categories and become accustomed to thinking in terms of European economic criteria: the insight thus acquired affects the attitudes of the categories represented.[106]

It is not clear, however, whether this sort of compromising in Brussels has had any significant effect on the activities of the constituent groups at the national level. Such an effect would depend to a great extent upon the influence wielded by the representative of a given group in the policy-making of that group. If interest-group leaders of major importance are consistently involved, significant long-range effects will probably occur;* but if the participants are for the most part technical experts or minor officials, a minimal "two-way" effect seems more likely.

* In 1961–62 approximately three-quarters of the delegates to the ESC were Presidents or Secretaries-General of national federations. Zellentin, p. 23.

NONOFFICIAL DECISION-MAKERS

ECONOMIC INTEGRATION will lead to political integration only if it involves matters of immediate concern to *significant elites,* i.e., if it involves some marked change in the conditions of their environment. This principle has already been established with respect to political elites, and we have seen how the Treaty of Rome has affected the governmental decision-makers of the six Member States: how the distinction between foreign policy and domestic policy has begun to break down, and how a Community view has begun to develop. A similar change is taking place among socio-economic elites, and the purpose of this chapter is to describe and analyze the extent to which economic interest groups have restructured their expectations and their activities in response to the changed conditions of their environment.

We expect to find two major patterns of reaction: on the one hand, measures of adjustment taken by firms, or groups of firms, to adapt to the changes in competitive conditions brought on by the institution of a Common Market, and, on the other hand, changes in political organization and tactics to adjust to the fact that new decision-making centers are being created. Developments in both these areas have far exceeded expectations.

MEASURES OF ADJUSTMENT

At the level of the firm, the Common Market has been accepted as an imminent reality. The main preoccupation of most firms, large and small, in all sectors of the economy and in each Member State, is with programs of rationalization and investment designed to prepare for the coming of the Common Market.[1] Its impact is revealed in two major trends: first, in the internal policy of firms, and, second, in structural changes affecting the relationship between firms.[2]

Internal Policy

The purpose of the first set of reactions was to prepare for the coming of the Common Market by improving competitive positions and lowering costs by means of a rationalization of production methods, a redistribution of work, increased specialization, etc. There is a new urgency in the area of technical research and an ever-increasing concern with the training of staff, especially in modern management techniques and in marketing.[3] Several new schools of business administration (patterned after the Harvard Business School) have been set up for the specific purpose of training "European" executives. Business and commercial groups have shown great interest in the question of harmonizing laws concerning incorporation and the rights of companies. Because this is a long-range affair at best, research has been concentrated upon the possibility of creating a new type of company, constituted in such a way that it could be incorporated under identical terms in each of the six countries. The Commission has also shown interest in this area.[4]

Elaborate preparations are being made in anticipation of increased exchanges of products among the Six. According to one observer:

Business firms are establishing commercial networks of agents, distributors, and concessionaires in the Community, which, if not yet active, are making preparations for the future conquest of markets. The newspapers in each of the Community countries are filled with publicity concerning products manufactured elsewhere in the Community. All of this is new because exporting firms were never sure in the past whether they were going to get import permits from neighboring countries or not. Now they have an almost absolute guarantee that the import policy of the other countries of the Six will become more and more liberal as time goes on. Consequently they are prospecting markets and organizing outlets to an extent which they would never have considered a short while ago.[5]

Investment programs are being undertaken to build plant and equipment designed for a large market of 170 million. New factories and subsidiaries are being opened, often in other countries of the Community.[6]

Commercial publicity uses the Common Market as a sales argument, stressing sales of products from the other Common Market countries, or using the argument that the Common Market requires rationalization to sell equipment goods.[7] An interesting example is the sales campaign of the Brussels department store "A l'Innovation," in which hundreds of products from the other Common Market countries were sold at the prices that would prevail if all duties had disappeared in intra-Community trade.[8]

Banks and other credit institutions have set up special services to advise businesses about the problems and opportunities of the Common Market. Numerous syndicates, such as the "Syndicat Euralliance"[9] and the "Syndicat Européen d'Études et de Financement" (Eurosyndicat),[10] have been formed by banks in several countries so as to pool information and market research facilities, and to ensure collaboration in the area of investments. Individual banks have made great efforts to increase their capital reserves for investments both within the Six and in the Overseas Territories.[11] A large number of investment societies have been set up, both at the level of the Six and in each country, specifically for the purpose of financing economic expansion in the Common Market.[12] Alongside this expansion of investment from within the Community, there is a marked increase of American investment in the Six. Taking advantage of the Community's rapid rate of growth and of the fact that trade restrictions are likely soon to disappear, American firms are opening subsidiaries or building factories at an ever-increasing rate. According to a study of the Chase Manhattan Bank, of 326 American enterprises opened in Western Europe between 1958 and mid-1960, 267 were in the Common Market and these especially in the chemical and mechanical construction industries.[13]

Structural Changes

Two related structural transformations have taken place. First, there has been a greatly accelerated rate of mergers and concentrations between firms at the national level.[14] Newspapers, trade journals, and publications like *Agence Europe* regularly publish long lists of such agreements, and examples galore might be cited. No statistics, however, are available on their relative incidence, nor is it known to what extent they may involve restrictions on trade such as price-fixing or market-sharing.[15]

Second, the Common Market has also given rise to an ever-expanding network of various kinds of agreements between firms of the several EEC countries: for the coordination or specialization of production, for the utilization of common sales organizations, for the creation of joint affiliates or new enterprises, and for the exchange of patents and technical information.[16]

POLITICAL ORGANIZATION AND TACTICS

In terms of political activity, economic interest groups have continued to rely for the most part on traditionally developed channels of access to national policy-making centers. However, the volume of their contacts with administrators and parliamentarians has greatly increased in direct relation to the extent to which their vital interests have been affected by provisions of the Treaty.[17] At the same time, however, there has been widespread awareness that the establishment of the EEC and its central institutional system poses new problems of access, that more and more decisions would be taken in the context of a new decision-making system. Accordingly, national interest groups have sought to organize at the level of the EEC, to develop regularized contacts with their opposite numbers in the other Member States, and to seek access to the new decision-making centers. As the Commission points out, "one of the most striking signs that the various branches of the economy have become 'Europe-minded' and that the markets of the six countries are becoming increasingly interlocked has been the proliferation of professional, industrial, agricultural, commercial and crafts associations in the countries since the Treaty of Rome was signed."[18]

By late 1961, there were 222 regionally organized economic interest groups, all but a handful of which had been created since 1958. This did not include the several groupings among the so-called "liberal professions."[19] The distribution is as follows:

Industry	89	(excluding industries dealing with food and drink)
Commerce	42	(excluding trade in agricultural products)
Handicrafts	6	(including two groups related to industry and two related to trade)
Agriculture	82	(including trade in agricultural products and organizations of agricultural workers)
Trade Unions	2	(excluding a large number of specialized groups)
Banking	1	
Total	222	

It is not possible here to analyze all these groups in detail. They vary in character from groups meeting for sporadic round-table discussions, or exchanges of view, to legally constituted associations with formal statutes and permanent secretariats. They may be "peak" associations representing national confederations of industry (UNICE, Union of Industries of the European Community), of trade (COCCEE, Committee of Commercial Organizations in the Countries of the EEC), of farmers (COPA, Committee of Agricultural Organizations of the EEC), of trade unions (European Regional Organization of the ICCTU, the International Conference of Christian Trade Unions, and the European Secretariat of the ICFTU, the International Confederation of Free Trade Unions), of artisans (the Committee of Handicraft Associations in the Six Countries of the EEC), of consumer cooperatives (the Committee of National

Organizations of Consumer Cooperatives in the Common Market), or of bankers (the Banking Federation of the European Community). Or they may group together associations of special industries (mining, foodstuffs, beverages, textiles, shoes, clothing, wood, leather, paper, rubber, chemical products, nonferrous metals, foundries, mechanical and electrical equipment, construction, and electric power), or of trade in the same products, or of workers in the various professional internationals.[20] Agriculture is the most extensively organized, with 82 groups formed at the EEC level: nine organizations of farmers, six of agricultural cooperatives, 36 in agricultural foodstuffs industries, 27 in trade in agricultural products, three organizations of workers, and one organization of consumer cooperatives.[21]

These organizations may have large, highly competent secretariats with extensive budgets, or they may maintain only a part-time secretary-general; they range from organizations which can act independently and even take decisions that are binding on their natural constituent federations or confederations, to organizations which only collect and transmit information. Their stated purposes or goals are similar: to establish a liaison between groups representing a given sector in the several countries of the EEC, to promote the interests of their particular sector before the institutions of the EEC (Commission, Council, Assembly, Permanent Representatives, ESC), to do this by trying to achieve common positions on as wide a range of issues as possible, to exchange information and make technical studies of problems faced by the sector at the European level, to develop centralized statistical and documentary services, and so on.

We have already seen that the Commission has encouraged the development of these groups, actively fostering it, in fact, in the case of agriculture.[22] Contacts take place on an irregular basis, at large-scale meetings or round tables. One such meeting is described as follows:

In the industrial sector, a first exploratory meeting between the officials of the Commission's staff and those of the European federations representing the various branches and those of the UNICE took place on 20 December 1960. This meeting was devoted to the study of problems related to the achievements and the prospects of the Common Market, to the development of internal Community trade, to the external relations of the Community and to tax questions, as well as to the problems raised by competition. . . . Exploratory meetings have taken place with the trade organizations of the textile industry. Among the problems raised the accent has been placed by the trade organizations on the disturbances in the market deriving from the abnormal conditions of competition in certain non-member countries. . . . As far as crafts and small industry are concerned . . . discussions bear on all the questions concerning the work of craftsmen and, in particular, policy, statistics and the right of establishment in this field.[23]

Many of these groups channel a large proportion of their energies through the Economic and Social Committee, depending on whether or not it is currently occupied with an issue affecting their interests. This has been particularly true of the trade unions' and farmers' organizations in regard to the debates over a common agricultural policy. Efforts have also been made, with apparently indifferent success, to contact the Permanent Representatives and the Council;[24] accordingly, with regard to the institutions representing the governments, most contacts take place through regularized channels at the national level. In such cases the common position of the regional group, if one has been reached, will be conveyed to the national Ministers by representatives of the respective national member groups.

The sheer number of these groups and the scope of their activities are significant indications of the extent to which economic interest groups have been "activated." We have here a parallel development to that already traced at the level of national administrators: thousands of interest-group leaders from the six Common Market countries are traveling to Brussels, are getting to know each other, are often engaged in a process of trying to reach a compromise and take common positions. A regional interest-group bureaucracy is being created, which already shows signs of developing a distinct vested interest in increasing its attributes vis-à-vis the national constituent groups. Nevertheless, these regional groups will be of limited significance for political integration unless participation in them comes to represent a fundamental restructuring of expectations and tactics. To what extent have collective needs at the regional level taken priority over national differences? Do the necessities of "international lobbying" force compromises of initial positions? Do interest group officials become more "Europe-minded"? Is all agreement between national groups purely tactical or do groups seek to work out agreements on basic principles? Are conflicts solved on the basis of the "lowest common denominator," "splitting the difference," or "upgrading common interests"? To what extent are the regional groups given actual powers of initiative or decision?

No definitive answers can be given to such questions at this point. Most of these groups have been in existence for only a few years. The vital interests of relatively few are as yet directly affected by decisions of the Community institutions.

Preliminary indications reveal that as a general rule national considerations continue to shape the character of participation in these regional interest groups. Common positions are reached when interests coincide, but otherwise decision-making is of the lowest-common-denominator type, with final agreement rarely exceeding what the least cooperative participant is willing to grant. Meetings of such groups resemble the classical diplomatic conference between formally instructed delegates of sovereign entities. We would thus expect that the narrower the interests of a given group, the more likely it would be to develop a significant cohesion at the regional level. For example, the jute producers of the EEC are strongly united around their mutual interest in excluding imports of jute from Pakistan.[25] Nevertheless, these groups are undeniably a significant expression of a political adjustment to a new situation and a *de facto* acceptance of that situation. As Haas concluded in reference to regionally organized groups in the coal and steel industries, "while they have not made homogeneous groups of their affiliates, they nevertheless represent the political adjustment to a regional governmental agency which is accepted as given, from whom favours must be asked and advantages extracted, or whose policies must be opposed 'en bloc.' "[26]

Thus, such an organization as UNICE (Union of Industries of the European Community), made up of the peak industrial confederations in each country, has been established in order "to create, maintain, and develop . . . the spirit and the bonds of solidarity; to stimulate the working out of an industrial policy in a European spirit.[27] Similarly, the aim of the Banking Federation of the European Community is "joint action by the banking associations to facilitate attaining the European aims fixed by the Treaty of Rome in the field of banking activities."[28] The existence of these groups with permanent staffs, as well as the greatly increased number of interactions between interest-group leaders in a given sector, has led to the gradual development of at least a preliminary procedural consensus. And, as Haas points out, "if a procedural consensus prevails we may expect the members to be more responsive to one another than to non-members. Even if they cannot agree on the substance of any policy, their mutual responsiveness enables them to debate any issue and to view this assembly as a forum for frank discussion and continuous communication."[29] Thus the members of UNICE undertake to keep the Secretary-General of the organization informed and to consult with each other prior to taking a position before any of the institutions of the Community.[30] They do this in the common realization that if they present conflicting positions, the EEC institutions would "have the choice of picking from the bouquet of positions presented the most agreeable one."[31]

Such a procedural consensus may already exist and have institutional expression. This is the case with the two trade union associations which, in addition to a tradition of internationalism, were already organized at the level of the Six to deal with the ECSC.[32] Both have reorganized to accommodate the creation of the two new Communities (the EEC and Euratom).[33] However, the resulting organizations have not been based on, nor given rise to, any wide-ranging substantive consensus. Neither the European Organization of the ICCTU nor the European Secretariat of the ICFTU has been given any significant powers of initiative or decision, and they serve as little more than liaison bureaus. As the Secretary-General of the latter organization observed:

It is, moreover, very difficult to ask our governments to give up certain sovereign rights to European authorities when we ourselves continue to preserve our national trade union rights to such a degree that one can speak only of trade union collaboration but in no way of trade union integration. . . . We find ourselves faced with the choice of losing on the European level what we have won at the national level as regards rights of consultation and of co-determination, or of leading our movement as a directing element in the battle for a free, prosperous, and united Europe.[34]

Nevertheless, a procedural consensus is well-developed in these two organizations, and the regional secretariats are actively engaged in seeking to maximize the amount of substantive consensus, thus creating the potential for a higher level of conflict resolution.

One can expect that over time the necessity for lobbying will force groups to emphasize collective needs rather than national differences. Such a development can be expected as the central institutions of the EEC become more active, as the types of actions taken involve the harmonization of legislation and the formulation of common policies (rather than the negative process of eliminating barriers to trade), and as given groups become aware that their interests can no longer be adequately served at the national level alone. This can already be seen in the agricultural sector, which is the most highly organized. The Commission had been engaged actively since mid-1958 in the elaboration of its proposals for a common agricultural policy, envisaging the ultimate establishment of a single market and a single agricultural policy for the six countries. All groups involved in agriculture—whether producers, distributors, workers, or consumers—stand to gain or lose a great deal, and have actively sought to influence the content of these proposals. Practically all the groups involved agree that there should be a common agricultural policy, but all are concerned that it approximate their particular needs and desires as far as possible. Already one can detect a growing feeling of solidarity among the farmers' organizations of the EEC (organized in COPA) as a result of their long efforts to achieve a maximum common position and to influence the Commission. COPA's decision to concentrate on trying to influence the ESC's opinion on the Commission's agricultural proposals has forced them to negotiate intensively inside the organization and to compromise with the trade union members in opposition to business and industrial interests:

Both farmers' and farm workers' organisations have devoted attention to the work of the Community's Economic and Social Committee and its agricultural section. Many of the representatives attending COPA have also attended the meetings of the Agricultural Section, either as official representatives or as "technical advisers" (who are permitted to speak but not to vote). Through their participation in COPA, as well as through their earlier participation in the European Confederation of Agriculture and in the International Federation of Agricultural Producers, the representatives of farmers' organisations have acquired considerable solidarity. Over the draft proposals of the Commission, for example, they arrived at an agreement among themselves on the general lines of the advice to be given by the ESC to the Commission and to the Council of Ministers. After a compromise had been reached in the agricultural section between the farmers' groups and the trade union group, the resulting statement was accepted, with only a few amendments, by the full ESC by 72 votes to 19 (mainly by industrial representatives) abstentions. . . . This advice, although very general and vague, was mainly in support of the Commission's draft proposals and reflected little of the criticisms of those proposals heard so frequently among the member countries of the Community.[35]

As a result of these activities, and in anticipation of the future, COPA has recently reorganized in an effort to effect closer collaboration and set up a stronger central authority.

A President and a Praesidium (one representative from each country) have been established to flank the COPA Assembly and to provide the cohesion necessary to strengthen the organization's voice before the Commission and in the Economic and Social Committee. The Praesidium disposes of a certain amount of political initiative, although major decisions still require unanimity.[36] The first President is Edmund Rehwinkel, influential head of the Deutsche Bauernverband (DBV). It seems clear that these organizational changes represent a recognition that the interests of agriculture can be adequately defended only by giving up a certain amount of national autonomy.

Interesting also is COPA's success in establishing itself as the spokesman for the interests of all agricultural producers. Most of the organizations at the regional level that are grouped according to product (beets, hops, wine, etc.) have agreed to participate in COPA Assembly meetings and to submit their position papers to COPA before sending them to the Commission. Although the *substantive* consensus achieved to date by COPA is quite modest, a potentially significant procedural consensus is developing rapidly. The meetings of the Assembly involve a frank and relaxed exchange of views and seem to manifest a genuine desire to reach a maximum of agreement. Of some interest was COPA's position on acceleration. The DBV was unalterably opposed to acceleration, whereas it was supported by the others. Yet under the presidency of Rehwinkel a compromise solution was found, which stated that "COPA does not oppose the principle of acceleration in spite of the particular difficulties it presents for agriculture."[37]

Of greater importance is the declaration of October 13, 1960, in which COPA expressed apprehension lest progress on a common agricultural policy be delayed or called into question by de Gaulle's notion of an "Europe des patries." The organization renewed its support for a "European" solution to the agricultural problem: "COPA feels that the elaboration of a common agricultural policy cannot be effected on the basis of a lowest common denominator of existing national policies, but that we must develop a policy which is adapted to *new common circumstances* and which at the same time assures tangible results to agricultural producers."[38]

That this process of meeting together to hammer out common policies has what we have called latent effects (the development of multiple perspectives, personal friendships, a camaraderie of expertise) is readily attested to by COPA members. Such consistent COPA participants as Edmund Rehwinkel of the DBV, Constant Boon of the Belgian Boerenbond, Luigi Anchisi of the Italian Confederazione Nazionale Coltivatori Diretti, Georges Bréart of the Assemblée Permanente des Présidents des Chambres d'Agriculture (France), and Albert Genin and Pierre Hallé of the Fédération Nationale des Syndicats d'Exploitants Agricoles (France) are all influential in their respective agricultural organizations. We may expect therefore that the organizational experiences at the regional level will affect national policy-making. As progress is made toward a common agricultural policy, this process will be accelerated. The Consultative Committees which were set up in 1962, when the first concrete measures of the common agricultural policy came into force, and which consist of representatives of agricultural producers and of labor and commerce, will probably impose upon these groups the need for still further internal coordination.

THE DECISION-MAKING PROCESS
IN THE EEC

PERCEPTIONS OF INTEGRATION

IT IS CLEAR that a complex decision-making machinery is evolving within the EEC, a machinery that cannot readily be categorized as either national or communitarian. The Six are becoming increasingly linked in many functional contexts and at many levels through the activities of national and Community politicians, parliamentarians, high civil servants, and interest-group leaders. This process is equally marked at the level of the internal policies of firms and in the relationships being established between firms. Some of the manifest and latent implications of these phenomena for political integration have already been suggested. No definitive judgment of the integrative impact of the EEC can be ventured, however, until we observe this system in action. Has the Commission been able to operate as a real catalyst in producing unity among the Six? Do the governments habitually seek to resolve basic conflicts of interest by mutual accommodation? Are pressures generated which endow the Community with an expansive potential and which limit the independent policy alternatives open to the Member States?

The following case studies, illustrating several decision sequences, have been chosen because they were central to the early life of the EEC. Each of them involves basic conflicts of interest. Strong, and often divergent, positions were taken by governments, parties, and interest groups, as well as by Community officials, bringing to the surface the tensions and potentialities inherent in the pattern of motivations which led to the negotiation and ratification of the Treaty, and upon which future developments depend. The measure of "success" achieved in each case reveals some fundamental aspects of the integrative process in the EEC.

We have noted earlier that the Treaty of Rome was ratified as the result of a combination of convergent expectations. Measures of integration are sought or supported by governments, groups, and elites for distinctly different reasons. Consequently, "Europeanism" continues to be a mixture of frequently opposing aspirations. This is, of course, a fundamental characteristic of politics in any pluralistic setting. As Haas points out, "the dominant fragmentation of ideologies and groups [in Europe] . . . explains why support for integration must continue to rely on convergence and cannot go forward on the basis of generally accepted propositions. The nature of pluralism militates against their ever being accepted by all simultaneously."[1]

Haas has developed a typology of aspirations as follows: (1) *Long-run positive expectations:* elites develop comprehensive programs that can be realized only in the framework of further integration. (2) *Short-run positive expectations:* elites desire to make use of integrative measures to establish a single goal or measure. (3) *Short-run negative expectations:* elites oppose a specific policy or measure without opposition to integration in general. And (4) *Long-run negative expectations:* elites oppose integration as a matter of principle. "Unlike groups opposed to supranationalism in essence but reconciled to work with it if only to block its progress, elites possessing negative long-range expectations will use their influence with national authorities to bring about withdrawal from supranational bodies and block the creation of new ones."[2]

One of the outstanding developments since the signing of the EEC Treaty in 1957 has been the *apparent* disappearance of opposition to the principle of integration. With the exception of the Communists, who have viewed the EEC as another capitalist plot, there is no major voice to oppose integration as such. The idea of "integration" seems to have taken on a status of sanctity analogous to that of such concepts as "democracy." Of course, this surface unanimity conceals the fact that integration is conceived of in widely divergent and often contradictory ways. It ought to be remembered, too, that up to now economic conditions have been highly favorable, and the EEC has had mostly salutary effects on the governments, groups, and elites concerned. But the general approval of the EEC does suggest that almost all those involved have begun to define their interests and expectations as in some way related to it. Given this apparent unity, it might be useful to develop a typology of *positive expectations* toward integration, a typology that will differentiate more clearly between the goals that different governments, groups, or elites seek to maximize. We can identify the following conceptions of integration as revealed in EEC experience:

1. *Integration as political unification.* The political unification of Europe is desired as an end in itself for a variety of ideological or tactical reasons, or is considered a necessary precondition to any far-reaching eco-

nomic goals. A maximum of central institutional development and central policy-making is also championed as an end in itself.

2. *Integration as economic unification.* The preoccupation is with the maximization of long-range economic and welfare goals, a process that is possible only through far-reaching unification of economies. Central institutions and central policies will be supported if these appear necessary, as long as access to these new decision-making centers is retained.

3. *Integration as economic and political cooperation.* It is recognized that long- or short-range goals cannot be achieved solely on the basis of the economic or political resources of the nation-state (as in No. 2). But these goals continue to be defined in terms of the nation-state. Hence, central institutions are not encouraged, although tactical support or acquiescence may be given under special circumstances.

4. *Integration as free trade.* Integration is defined in essentially negative terms: namely, as a process whereby barriers to the free exchange of goods and services are eliminated. This implies hostility to Europe-wide planning and to "dirigistic" central institutions.

In each of the cases that follow we shall try to demonstrate the several ways in which these often competing goals have been the basis of the EEC's expansive potential, how they have led to further integration through the operation of the spill-over principle. The way in which conflicts are resolved will also be considered. Does the accommodation follow the pattern of the lowest common denominator, or of splitting the difference, or of upgrading common interests? Do the central institutions participate creatively? Are they able to set limits within which agreement is achieved, or do they actually define the terms of the agreement?

In reality the four cases to be examined constitute one large case study involving a highly complex over-all concession pattern. The acceleration sequence, the negotiations to complete the common external tariff, and the complicated process of preparing a common agricultural policy are intricately interwoven, and all were fundamentally influenced by the state of the Community's relations with the outside world. The problems posed by the Community's external relations have consumed an enormous amount of time and energy. Commission officials and negotiators of the Six have been engaged constantly in complex and interminable negotiations that actually began before the Treaty was signed and that are still continuing, somewhat modified, today. Three broad sets of problems have been involved: relations with the signatories of the General Agreement on Tariffs and Trade (GATT); negotiations for membership in, or association with, the Community; and relations with the members of the former OEEC. Let us briefly examine each of these sets of negotiations.

All members of the EEC are signatories of GATT, which imposes the general rule of nondiscrimination and the obligation to extend most-favored-nation treatment to all other signatories. Article 24 of GATT permits the formation of customs unions and free trade areas, the plans for which must be submitted to the organization for approval. The Rome Treaty was severely criticized in GATT sessions in 1957 and 1958, and the Member States and the EEC institutions were constantly in a defensive posture. Before the signing of the Treaty and the introduction of the customs union, there were four tariffs (Benelux, Italy, France, and Germany). Each had accorded concessions under GATT, and now these had to be modified, renegotiated, and translated into new concessions in view of the common external tariff. A very involved series of negotiations ensued.

The second set of negotiations was no less complicated. A number of countries opened negotiations with the EEC, either for association or for full membership. Official discussions were begun with Greece and Turkey about possible association, and whereas the talks with Turkey came to nothing, those with Greece led to an agreement that was signed on March 30, 1961. This took the form of a customs union between Greece and the Community. Greece will be given time to prepare, but will eventually adopt the common external tariff of the Community. In 1961, Britain, along with Ireland, Norway, and Denmark, applied for full membership in the EEC. The ensuing negotiations, which continued throughout 1961 and 1962, and which were finally cut off so abruptly and dramatically by de Gaulle, are beyond the scope of this study.

The third important problem in external relations concerned negotiations with the other members of the OEEC. Nondiscrimination had been a guiding principle of the OEEC in the trading policies of the members with each other. The decision of six of these Member States to form a Common Market and an Economic Community could but mean that although barriers would be lowered between the Member States, an outside tariff would be maintained that would discriminate, or differentiate, against the other members of the OEEC. As soon as it became clear that the Six were serious about the Common Market project, the other members of the OEEC, led by the United Kingdom, tabled a project for a free trade area to cover all seventeen countries. The choice of a free trade area as a vehicle was imposed by the GATT rules, which prohibited new tariff preferences except customs unions and free trade areas. Negotiations were initiated as early as July 1956, were continued in the spring of 1957, were taken up again in October of that year, and were finally suspended in December 1958. This suspension was soon followed by the creation of the European Free Trade Association (EFTA—Norway, Sweden, Denmark, Switzerland, Austria, Portugal, Britain) and the emergence of the problem of the Six and the Seven.

This third series of negotiations was of central political significance because it put under stress the convergence of expectations that accounted for the ratification of the EEC Treaty, and because it conditioned all the other activities of the Community. Many of the difficulties encountered by the Community in its relations with the OEEC countries, and many of the difficulties experienced in the cases to be considered, as well as in the original Treaty negotiations, derived from differences in the structure of foreign trade in the Six countries, and the differential dependence of their economies upon foreign trade. Before we analyze the negotiations themselves, therefore, let us briefly examine this general background.[3]

THE COMMERCIAL PROBLEM

The Benelux countries have had their own customs union since 1950. Their general level of tariff protection has been very low, although there are fairly high duties on some manufactured goods. These countries are poor in raw materials and have traditionally depended on foreign commerce. Germany, since the war, has freed its economy from controls and has a relatively low level of tariff. A highly dynamic policy of world-wide commercial expansion has been followed, and Germany has a very favorable balance of payments and growing exchange reserves. Foreign commerce contributed the smallest share of national income in Italy, although a considerable expansion occurred after the war. Italy was considered a high-tariff country. France, a comparatively self-sufficient country, has been traditionally protectionist and because of chronic balance of payments difficulties maintained high tariffs and rigid import quotas (see Table 1). Foreign commerce was comparatively unimportant for both Italy and France in the postwar years, as is shown in Table 2.

TABLE 1.—AVERAGE DUTIES IN FORCE
(Arithmetical average)

	Benelux	France	Germany[a]	Italy
Foodstuffs, beverages, tobacco	10%	20–25%	15%	20%
Crude materials	75% imports exempt, remainder 6%	45% exempt, remainder 5–7%	60% exempt, remainder 3–4%	exempt, except for a few products
Semimanufactured products	5–7%	15%	8–10%	20–25%
Finished goods	10–15%	20%	15%	20–25%

SOURCE: EEC Commission, *Report on the Economic Situation* (September 1958), p. 100.
a Many German duties remain suspended, so that actual incidence is considerably less.

TABLE 2.—PERCENTAGE SHARE OF EXPORTS OF GOODS AND SERVICES
IN THE GROSS NATIONAL PRODUCT

	Imports	Exports
Germany (1957)	24.8	29.4
Belgium (1954)	35.2	35.5
France (1957)	18.2	15.9
Italy (1957)	18.6	17.7
Netherlands (1957)	61.4	59.1
Luxembourg (1956)	89.0	99.5

SOURCE: Compiled from EEC Commission, *Report on the Economic Situation*, p. 111.

Table 2 demonstrates the striking variations in the extent to which the Member States depended upon foreign commerce and gives a relatively accurate index of the stake each had in maintaining a liberal commercial policy. Clearly, Benelux and Germany stood to lose a great deal should import prices be increased at the same time that export markets were threat-

TABLE 3.—DISTRIBUTION OF WORKING POPULATION BY SECTOR (1956)

	Agriculture	Industry	Services
Germany	17.9	47.8	34.3
Saar	14.2	57.5	28.3
Belgium	10.3	49.0	40.7
France	26.6	37.8	35.6
Italy	39.8	28.8	31.4
Luxembourg	22.8	43.4	33.8
Netherlands	12.4	42.9	44.7

SOURCE: EEC Commission, *Report on the Economic Situation*, p. 62.

TABLE 4.—ORIGIN OF GNP BY SECTOR (1955–56)

	Agriculture	Industry	Services
Germany	9	51	40
Belgium	7	47	46
France	15	41	44
Italy	22	42	36
Luxembourg	9	54	37
Netherlands	11	44	45

SOURCE: EEC Commission, *Report on the Economic Situation*, p. 34.

ened by rival trading groups like the EFTA. Tables 3 and 4 illustrate the relative importance of agriculture, industry, and services in the various national economies. Of particular note is the importance of services for Belgium, the Netherlands, and France. In the case of France and to some extent Belgium, this reflects the great importance of tourism. In the Netherlands, it reflects the role of transportation and commerce, and the part played by the great port of Rotterdam (also Antwerp for Belgium).

Table 5 shows the prominence of various groups of products in the general structure of foreign trade.

Table 6 indicates the geographical distribution of exports and imports. We can see that slightly more of Germany's exports go to the other OEEC countries than to the EEC, and that a full 70.8 per cent of her exports go outside of the Six. We would therefore expect a great deal of concern in Germany about commercial relations with the other European countries. The figures for Italy are similar but less significant in this context because of the relative unimportance of foreign trade in Italy's economy (Table 2). Note also that well over 50 per cent of France's exports go to regions covered by the EEC Treaty (including the Overseas Territories), and that only 16.4 per cent go to the rest of Europe. Though exports to the other OEEC countries are important for Benelux, especially for the Netherlands, this fact is counterbalanced by their high dependence on intra-EEC trade.

Table 7, when read in conjunction with Table 5, gives a fairly clear indication of which economic sectors are likely to be most concerned about the problem of the commercial relations of the EEC with the other European countries and with the world at large. We see, for example, that approximately three-fourths of the exports of equipment and of chemicals and manufactured goods, which represent 27 per cent and 61 per cent, respectively, of Germany's total exports, go outside the EEC, and that the other European countries alone represent a more important market for

TABLE 5.—PERCENTAGE SHARE OF MAIN GROUPS OF PRODUCTS IN OVER-ALL IMPORTS AND EXPORTS (1956–57)

	Germany		France		Italy		Bel.-Lux.		Netherlands	
	Imp.	Exp.	Imp.	Exp.	Imp.	Exp.	Imp.	Exp.	Imp.	Exp.
Food, etc.	28	2	25	16	17	23	15	4	14	28
Crude materials and fats..	30	3	27	9	33	5	24	8	15	9
Energy, lubricants	12	7	18	8	21	8	11	6	17	14
Machinery and transportation equipment	6	27	11	18	11	23	20	11	20	15
Chemicals and manufactured goods	24	61	19	49	18	41	30	71	34	34

SOURCE: Compiled from EEC Commission, *Report on the Economic Situation*, pp. 87–88.

TABLE 6.—IMPORTS AND EXPORTS ACCORDING TO ORIGIN AND
DESTINATION (1957)

	Germany Imp.	Germany Exp.	Belgium-Luxembourg Imp.	Belgium-Luxembourg Exp.	France Imp.	France Exp.	Italy Imp.	Italy Exp.	Netherlands Imp.	Netherlands Exp.
EEC	23.5	29.2	43.5	46.0	21.4	25.2	21.6	24.9	41.2	41.6
Rest of OEEC	20.4	29.4	15.8	17.4	10.2	16.4	18.3	26.9	15.7	25.5
Overseas territories of the country	—	—	5.5	4.4	17.5	27.0	—	—	0.6	1.8
Overseas territories of other EEC countries	1.7	0.8	0.5	0.6	0.8	0.3	1.4	1.5	0.8	1.2
Other sterling area..	9.8	9.1	8.3	6.2	16.4	4.2	15.4	9.0	6.6	7.5
Dollar area	26.6	13.2	16.0	12.7	17.1	8.1	22.7	15.6	20.4	8.8
Rest of world	17.8	18.3	10.4	12.6	16.7	18.5	20.5	22.0	14.8	13.7

SOURCE: Compiled from EEC Commission, *Report on the Economic Situation*, pp. 123–32.

TABLE 7.—IMPORTS AND EXPORTS ACCORDING TO ORIGIN AND DESTINATION
OF GROUPS OF PRODUCTS (1957)

	Food, etc. Imp.	Food, etc. Exp.	Crude mat. and fats Imp.	Crude mat. and fats Exp.	Energy and lubricants Imp.	Energy and lubricants Exp.	Machinery and transport equipment Imp.	Machinery and transport equipment Exp.	Chemicals and manufactured goods Imp.	Chemicals and manufactured goods Exp.
1. Germany										
EEC	25.9	33.6	9.3	48.9	16.5	63.4	29.0	26.3	40.9	24.9
Rest of OEEC	16.1	31.7	19.3	28.9	3.1	26.4	42.5	29.7	29.6	29.7
Overseas territories of the country	—	—	—	—	—	—	—	—	—	—
Overseas territories of other EEC countries	1.0	1.0	3.2	0.4	3.5	0.0	0.0	0.8	0.2	1.0
Other sterling area..	8.5	5.8	17.7	3.8	11.3	0.2	0.0	10.9	3.2	9.4
Dollar area	26.5	12.5	28.2	7.2	51.1	0.7	27.4	14.1	12.9	14.9
Rest of world	22.0	15.3	22.3	11.7	14.6	9.2	1.0	18.4	13.2	20.1
2. Belgium-Luxembourg (BLEU) Economic Union										
EEC	39.7	56.3	25.6	60.7	40.5	71.1	59.6	53.1	50.6	40.4
Rest of OEEC	7.5	16.0	13.1	19.0	3.7	26.7	23.1	10.9	22.1	17.5
Overseas territories of the country	2.3	7.8	8.5	0.8	0.0	0.3	0.1	10.5	9.7	3.9
Overseas territories of other EEC countries	0.3	1.9	0.8	0.3	1.9	0.1	0.0	0.6	0.0	0.5
Other sterling area..	4.1	4.8	21.6	1.9	12.6	0.5	0.0	6.0	2.9	7.3
Dollar area	25.3	3.1	16.6	5.0	21.7	—	16.3	6.8	9.5	16.3
Rest of world	21.0	10.1	13.8	12.3	19.6	1.2	0.8	12.1	5.2	14.0

Table 7.—*Continued*

	Food, etc.		Crude mat. and fats		Energy and lubricants		Machinery and transport equipment		Chemicals and manufactured goods	
	Imp.	Exp.	Imp.	Exp.	Imp.	Exp.	Imp.	Exp.	Imp.	Exp.
3. France										
EEC	7.9	25.5	5.3	59.4	22.1	37.3	46.3	16.9	46.7	21.1
Rest of OEEC	5.7	20.4	8.8	20.4	2.3	20.8	21.9	12.3	19.8	15.6
Overseas territories of the country	55.0	33.4	16.1	6.6	0.2	19.7	0.2	31.8	5.1	27.8
Overseas territories of other EEC countries	0.1	0.3	1.1	0.0	0.3	0.3	0.0	0.4	2.2	0.3
Other sterling area..	1.1	2.7	31.3	0.4	32.6	3.9	—	5.9	2.9	4.8
Dollar area	6.5	6.7	13.5	3.8	27.5	0.1	30.5	11.1	14.8	9.1
Rest of world	23.8	11.0	23.9	9.3	15.0	17.9	0.8	21.7	8.5	21.3
4. Italy										
EEC	12.7	37.7	12.4	32.6	10.0	9.2	49.6	20.5	39.9	22.0
Rest of OEEC	26.0	33.2	16.6	26.5	0.9	54.8	24.9	19.9	30.1	22.4
Overseas territories of the country	—	—	—	—	—	—	—	—	—	—
Overseas territories of other EEC countries	3.7	1.0	1.3	0.2	0.8	7.3	0.0	0.5	1.5	1.5
Other sterling area..	10.4	8.1	26.9	17.3	29.6	0.3	24.5	20.7	16.2	19.5
Rest of world	38.2	16.0	17.5	20.0	35.5	22.1	0.8	30.3	8.6	21.2
5. Netherlands										
EEC	14.6	49.1	13.8	53.6	16.0	34.7	60.6	32.9	67.3	39.1
Rest of OEEC	9.0	22.7	16.8	21.2	4.0	46.6	25.4	23.1	18.3	21.2
Overseas territories of the country	0.2	1.4	0.3	0.4	2.9	3.1	0.0	2.3	0.0	1.7
Overseas territories of other EEC countries	2.7	1.6	2.4	0.6	—	0.5	0.0	1.0	0.1	1.4
Other sterling area..	5.5	8.0	9.5	1.1	20.5	3.0	0.1	9.2	1.1	9.8
Dollar area	34.3	8.7	23.7	9.8	39.0	0.3	13.0	12.0	7.6	10.7
Rest of world	30.7	8.5	33.6	13.3	17.6	11.8	0.9	19.6	5.5	16.2

SOURCE: Compiled from EEC Commission, *Report on the Economic Situation*, pp. 123–32.

German manufacturers than the EEC. These same sets of products represent 11 per cent and 71 per cent, respectively, of BLEU exports, but 63.6 per cent and 44.3 per cent go to the EEC and the Overseas Territories. Consequently a trading split or a deflection of trade would not have as great an impact. The most striking fact about the structure of French foreign commerce is the importance of her former overseas dependencies. While 20.4 per cent of agricultural exports go to the other OEEC countries, the EEC area accounts for 59 per cent. Agricultural products have an importance in Italian exports that is second only to their prominence in the Netherlands (23 per cent as against 28 per cent). The OEEC countries represent a valuable market, taking 33.2 per cent of exports (37.17 per cent for the EEC). But in the other product groups, trade to the rest of the world (especially the U.S. and Latin America) is more important than that to the other OEEC countries. Agricultural products (mainly transformation products like ham, butter, and cheese) make up 28 per cent of the value of the Netherlands' exports. Almost 50 per cent of these go to the EEC (chiefly Germany), but 22.7 per cent go to the OEEC area (chiefly the U.K.). The OEEC area trade is of major importance in the other product groups as well, although except for energy products the EEC market is considerably larger.

In short, then, we can expect the greatest internal pressures in favor of a special trading association between the EEC and the other European countries to come from the following sectors: Belgian and Dutch commerce and transportation, machinery industries in Germany and the Netherlands, chemicals and manufactured goods in Germany and the Netherlands, and agriculture in Italy and the Netherlands.

THE FREE TRADE AREA

WHAT WAS the over-all impact on the EEC of the negotiations for a free trade area? Was the issue centrifugal or centripetal?[1] In an attempt to answer these questions, we shall first examine the divergent positions that existed (and that persist) among the Six, singling out the sources of support for, and opposition to, the idea of a free trade area. We shall then analyze the process whereby a common EEC position was finally achieved. In view of the importance of these issues, and the fact that such widely divergent positions were held, we might have expected some sort of stalemate, with a slackening of integration and a weakening of the central institutions and of central policy-making. This did not occur. The Commission stepped into the negotiations, gradually expanded its role, and offered its own compromise which, although vigorously attacked at first, was ultimately accepted as the Community doctrine. In addition, the timetable of the Rome Treaty was speeded up and the general tempo of integration accelerated. We shall try to account for these developments.

A detailed chronology of important events in the free trade area negotiations is given in Appendix B (pp. 313–15). The intimate relationship between these negotiations and the other case studies is also indicated. The negotiations can be divided somewhat arbitrarily into three stages:

From July 1956 to November 1958. The stage of multilateral negotiations within the OEEC framework. An interministerial committee, the Maudling Committee, was established in October 1957 for the purpose of negotiating a free trade area treaty. These negotiations broke down in November 1958, largely because of the opposition of the French government.

From November 1958 to January 1960. A period of relative disengagement. The Commission was invited to take over the task of trying to reach a solution to the free trade area impasse, and submitted two sets of proposals. The EFTA was created at British initiative. The EEC moved toward internal consolidation, and the Rome Treaty timetable was accelerated. Direct American participation began.

From January 1960 to the end of 1960. The idea of a free trade area now definitely dead. The OEEC was replaced by the Organization for Economic Cooperation and Development (OECD), which, with the United States and Canada as full members, had a broader basis. Trade discussions were *generalized* in the Committee of Twenty-One (which included all the members of the OECD). Mounting pressures developed in the United Kingdom for formal adhesion to the EEC.

We can achieve no real understanding of the positions taken by the various governments of the Six in the free trade area negotiations unless we identify not only the views of top policy-makers, but also those of interest groups and political party leaders. National positions may not always clearly reflect those taken by interest groups and parties, but they must always take them into account. Furthermore, in the EEC context, groups and parties can and do function politically and influence decision-making in the larger Community setting, both through the EPA and the ESC and through the lobbying efforts of regionally organized groups.

In the following discussion we shall try to focus on the perceived relationship between the free trade area issue and over-all expectations regarding integration. Was the free trade area seen as likely to threaten or reinforce the advantages expected from the EEC?

FRANCE

Although the French were not alone in entertaining serious reservations about a free trade area, an agreement in principle on some sort of association between the Six and the OEEC countries might have been possible by the end of 1958 had the French been willing to negotiate.[2] The French were therefore roundly scored by the British press and government,[3] and within the Six as well,[4] for having precipitated the breakdown in the Maudling Committee negotiations. Not that this was the result of a sudden contrary decision on the part of the government. Right from the start, and throughout a number of political changes, including a revolution and the accession to power of General de Gaulle, French governments have scarcely wavered from their opposition to a free trade area as conceived by the United Kingdom. Indeed, the French had already made their position clear during the negotiation of the Rome Treaty, when it was apparent that they had little interest in the free trade area as a device for promoting trade.

Nevertheless, the political attraction of some sort of link with the United Kingdom, and the fact that its partners in the Six attached so much importance to such an association, made the government willing to participate in the negotiations.[5] However, at the first meeting of the Maudling Committee in November 1957, Maurice Faure set forth the essentials of the French position. The free trade area agreement could not be limited to a mere dismantling of tariffs and quotas, but must include most of the safeguards, harmonization provisions, escape clauses, etc., that the French had insisted on in the Rome Treaty.[6] On the problem of origins, i.e., the existence of different external tariffs in a free trade area, Faure indicated that only a common external tariff, with very few exceptions, would be acceptable to France. Roughly the same position was taken regarding commercial policy: the French did not see how the participating countries could retain full autonomy in this sphere.

Furthermore, M. Faure felt that unless the provisions of the Treaty of Association between the Six and the other OEEC countries were roughly similar to those in the Treaty of Rome, the trade advantages accruing to the "associated" countries would have to be different and more limited than those enjoyed by members of the Community. Otherwise it would be difficult to explain to the French people why the "advantages" of the Treaty of Rome should be made available to those who would not accept the "obligations."[7]

In March 1958 the French unofficially circulated counterproposals among their EEC partners. The main points of the French memo were these: (1) that the enlargement of markets ought to be associated with a certain degree of common policy, (2) that a global solution was impossible and that a "sector" approach, involving a series of industrial agreements and special arrangements, would be more appropriate, (3) that the rhythm of liberalization must be subordinated to that of the harmonization of social charges, (4) that agriculture must be included, and that an agricultural accord must "respect the existing equilibrium."[8]

The French delaying tactics were consistent with the general *immobilisme* of the Fourth Republic. The French obviously did not want an association of the kind that was being negotiated and yet did not dare to incur the odium of wrecking the negotiations. The easiest course was to play for time.

In June 1958, time ran out for the Fourth Republic, and de Gaulle came to power. For several months there was no change in position or in delaying tactics; understandably, de Gaulle was unwilling to address himself to the unpopular issue of a free trade area until he had received endorsement for his constitutional reforms and a clear mandate in the elections.[9] At the October session of the Maudling Committee the same French objections were restated. It was obvious that an impasse had been reached and that "the only hope of progress lay in a political decision by General de Gaulle."[10]

This decision was forthcoming at the conclusion of the next Maudling Committee session in mid-November. It was stated by Jacques Soustelle: "It is not possible to create a free trade area as wished by the British, that is with free trade between the Common Market and the rest of the OEEC but without a single external tariff barrier round the seventeen countries, and without harmonization in the economic and social spheres."[11]

De Gaulle doubtless shared the suspicions of the French negotiators "that the British were up to their old game of destroying 'Europe,' seeking through the device of the free trade area to deprive cooperation among the Six of any real meaning."[12] The British could logically anticipate that France would either give in to their position, or so alienate the other five countries as to weaken the Community. De Gaulle's vision of reviving French power and prestige, his desire for a reform of NATO, his plans for the future of French Africa, his wish to see the Franco-German *rapprochement* continued, all came to bear on the decision about the free trade area and the Common Market. Already in late 1958 we can see the stirrings of his ambition to play the role of *primus inter pares* on the Continent—a desire that in the summer of 1959 was to lead to the proposals for a political secretariat and organized political cooperation among the Six. Moreover, the great majority of high civil servants, whose influence certainly has not diminished under de Gaulle, were opposed to the plan for a free trade area. For many of them the EEC was a method of compensating for the risks inherent in a policy oriented to the French-African community. And to a few, by opening up the French economy to the fresh winds of international competition, it represented a way of strengthening the economy and of freeing the country from the control of pressure groups.[13] These advantages, it was felt, would be diluted in the larger grouping of the OEEC.

The de Gaulle government was more openly opposed to the plan for a free trade area than its predecessors. Nothing had occurred to eliminate the reasons for France's long-standing objections to the plan, and new political reasons had emerged. France consistently resisted attempts by the Benelux countries and Germany to minimize the effects on the other OEEC countries of the first Common Market liberalization measures. By April 1959 the French were openly questioning the objective of seeking any form of wider European association. They apparently would not accept on any condition at all the total disappearance of customs protection and of restrictions in trade toward the OEEC as a whole.[14] They welcomed acceleration of the EEC timetable, and proposed in November 1959 that this include taking a first step toward establishing the common external tariff, thus increasing the difference in treatment between Community countries and the other European countries.

France's goal at the Paris Conference in January 1960 was to rule out once and for all the possibility of a multilateral European trading agreement.[15] Government spokesmen maintained consistently that nothing must interfere with the progress of the Common Market, such as its "dissolution" into a free trade area. French officials welcomed the U.S. proposals initiated in mid-1959 as further support for a non-OEEC solution. They emphasized that the only way a solution to European trading problems would be found was for the Community to practice a liberal policy, which would be possible only as it developed its solidarity and strength.[16] Progress toward integration should first of all be manifested in the attitude of the Member States toward third countries and underdeveloped countries. Parallel to this economic integration there must be a political integration (or cooperation), and to this end de Gaulle proposed periodic meetings of the Heads of State of the Six, with the eventual goal of coordinating their policies on matters of foreign, military, and cultural affairs. It is not surprising that these proposals elicited mixed feelings among France's EEC partners, who perceived that they were not unrelated to de Gaulle's views on NATO.

French economic groups achieved a rare unanimity in their complete opposition to the free trade area proposals, in which none of them could see any economic benefits. The Common Market offered the advantages of a common external tariff and a common commercial policy, harmonization of social and economic charges, coordination of social and economic policies, and access to Community funds and probably mutual aid, advantages that would not be enjoyed with a free trade area. Conversely, the free trade area was opposed because it extended the advantages of a common market to all the OEEC countries, thereby reducing the special benefits to the Six, and because it seemed the British would have the most to gain from this arrangement. Even before the Rome Treaty was signed, the Conseil National du Patronat Français (CNPF) observed that there was a fundamental contradiction between the establishment of a strong European economy and the concomitant pursuit of a policy of free trade toward third countries: "A certain degree of protectionism seems necessary at the start in order to permit the establishment and consolidation of this new unity, for only in this way can it obtain the power of negotiation that will later enable it to propose a reciprocal reduction of tariffs to the other world economic groupings."[17]

In September 1957, the President of the CNPF, Georges Villiers, de-

clared that the free trade area was incompatible with the establishment of
the Common Market. In November, in a resolution to the President of the
Council, the CNPF announced the unanimous opposition of all its associated professional groups in industry and commerce to the free trade area.
Similar positions were taken by the Chambre Syndicale de la Sidérurgie
Française, the Union des Industries Chimiques, the Union des Industries
Textiles, the Union Industrielle des Fabriques de Papiers et Cartons, and
others.[18] In mid-February 1958, the Conseil Economique unanimously rejected the free trade area, concluding "that from a strictly economic point
of view the proposed free trade area would involve grave risks for the
French economy; that it would compromise the establishment and the development of the EEC. . . . in these circumstances this solution is not acceptable."[19]

It is probably true that much of French industry accepted the Common
Market out of fear of the free trade area, but once the Common Market was
a *fait accompli,* and after the financial and economic reforms of December
1958, French industry rapidly discovered that its fears about the Common
Market had been exaggerated, and it could quite successfully compete with
its EEC partners. Rather than decreasing their opposition to the free trade
area, this led them to support, if not to originate, the whole acceleration
movement, and to become (as did the French government) champions of
the unity and cohesion of the Six. The French had no interest in sharing
their new continental markets with the other OEEC countries, or of further
opening up their overseas territories to the larger Community, hence the
mass conversion to the EEC. As Villiers commented:

How could one believe that the economic integration of the Six countries could
be pursued if the Six were to join a larger system whose sole aim was tariff
disarmament? We know that the creation of a free trade area would irremediably involve the destruction of the Common Market and that . . . the free
trade area itself would be doomed to failure because of the impossibility of
putting into competition economies with different structures, disparate economic social systems, and divergent policies.[20]

French business spokesmen began more and more to reproach the other
EEC countries for being insufficiently "European." According to one businessman, "France's partners interpret the Common Market as if it were a
free trade area. They apply all that is likely to favor the liberty of their
commerce, but refuse to make efforts of common discipline such as the
harmonization of fiscal matters, of commercial relations with regard to third
countries, or of social security systems."[21] Business circles argued that
France had accepted the Common Market to reinforce the weakened old
Continent, by extending the idea of the nation to the frontiers of Europe.

She had lowered her tariff barriers to her EEC partners, and had accepted a far lower external tariff. For the others, in contrast, especially the Dutch and the Germans, the Common Market meant only a policy of free trade. In their eyes the Common Market was not a goal in itself, but merely a step toward western free trade.[22]

Similar conclusions held for groups representing other sectors of the economy. The Confédération Nationale des Petites et Moyennes Entreprises (PME) hesitantly accepted the Common Market, but vigorously opposed the free trade area.[23] Three major agricultural groups, the Assemblée Permanente des Présidents des Chambres d'Agriculture (APPCA), the Confédération Générale d'Agriculture (CGA), and the Fédération Nationale des Syndicats d'Exploitants Agricoles (FNSEA), opposed the idea of a free trade area from the start. Many of the gains they saw in the Common Market would be watered down in the larger grouping. Closer relations should be nourished within the Community, and a common agricultural policy must be developed, and this would all be compromised if a free trade area were instituted.[24] In Community discussions on the common agricultural policy, it has been notably the French agricultural groups that have demanded a clear preference for EEC-produced goods. France is the most important agricultural country in the Six, with lower-than-average prices, and thus stands to gain the most from a protected market. This has led French agriculture, as it has French industry, to support most suggestions for strengthening Community cohesion, such as the acceleration proposals.[25]

French trade unions were not as unequivocally opposed to the free trade area, although they shared many of the same protectionist fears as their employers. The Confédération Générale du Travail (CGT) was against both the free trade area and the Common Market, but its opposition to the former was the stronger. The Confédération Générale des Cadres (CGC) wavered between its desire to maintain close relations with the United Kingdom and its doubt that there would be any benefit to France. The Confédération Française des Travailleurs Chrétiens (CFTC) and the Confédération Générale du Travail-Force Ouvriers (FO) held that although the free trade area was politically desirable, it was not acceptable as then formulated. Their position was very close to that of the French government: "That while the Common Market would bring harmonization in Europe, and some benefits for France, the free trade area would only have meant more severe competition."[26] Hence, any free trade area would have to include measures of social harmonization, and the members would all have to share such burdens as contributions to an investment bank, as well as certain commitments to full employment and to worker readaptation programs.[27]

French parliamentarians, although perhaps more sensitive to the political gains inherent in the participation of the United Kingdom, raised most of the same arguments against the free trade area as their countrymen in the government and in organized groups. The 1957 report of the Committee for Foreign Affairs of the National Assembly (the Savary Report) pointed out that in a free trade area the participation of EEC countries could bring about far greater disparities than those which the Treaty of Rome had sought to neutralize (for example, the accession of countries with very advanced or very retarded economies and different systems of social legislation). The report also pointed out quite frankly that in a free trade area France would have far less influence than she could expect to have in the Common Market.[28] Here, again, concrete objections to a free trade area outweighed the less well-defined political gains.

After the advent of de Gaulle, the opposition parties were preoccupied with criticizing the de Gaulle–Debré conceptions of an "Europe des patries," and with defending and promoting maximalist integration programs. They supported direct elections for the EPA, increased harmonization of commercial policy, acceleration, and coordinated aid to the underdeveloped areas. These are all goals that are perforce limited to the framework of the Six, and their achievement has the inevitable consequence of consolidating the identity of the EEC and of confirming its separation from the United Kingdom and the other OEEC countries.[29] The opposition parties were concerned more with the relations between the EEC and Africa than with those between the Six and the Seven. Moreover, they were particularly sensitive to the possibility that the Common Market would be dissolved in a free trade area, a development that would forfeit all the benefits of economic and political integration.[30] In their view, the political goals of the EEC far outweighed the purely commercial advantages that might accrue in a free trade area. They felt rather typically that if the European Communities have been formed without the United Kingdom, it is because the U.K. has always refused to accept the goals of integration and, what is more, has tried to undermine these goals at every opportunity.[31]

UNR (Union pour la Nouvelle République) deputies echoed the Gaullist position. They underlined France's adherence to European unification, citing such French proposals as acceleration and a political secretariat. UNR spokesmen opposed pressures for a liberal trade policy for the EEC, arguing that the Common Market would not be realized if the EEC practiced too liberal a policy and if the common external tariff were too low. If the same advantages were granted to third countries as are granted to the Six, what advantages would accrue from membership in the Six? France's partners were accused by the UNR of dragging their feet and of not being sufficiently devoted to the building of Europe.[32] In a vigorous defense of de Gaulle's proposals for a political secretariat, Christian de la Malène, speaking before the EPA, denied that France could be accused of opposing the unity of the Six:

She has done more for Europe than any other country. She made a devaluation in order to enter the Common Market, thus renouncing the use of safeguard clauses. She proposed measures of acceleration that were severe for her economy. She accepted a common external tariff lower than that foreseen in the Treaty. She has also accepted too liberal a policy on the part of the EEC Commission, a policy that places the heaviest burdens on France. And finally it was France who resisted those who wanted to dissolve the Common Market in a free trade area in order to please the English.[33]

GERMANY

Bonn spoke with two voices on the free trade area, as on most integration issues. Adenauer and the group around him continued to favor any actions that would advance the cause of integration and that would keep France moving toward it. He refused to make an issue of the free trade area negotiations, much as he did with regard to the Saar crisis.[34] Ludwig Erhard, on the other hand, carried on a tireless, and often overt, campaign in favor of the free trade area, a policy that further exacerbated his relations with "der Alte."

The German negotiators of the Rome Treaty were apparently under instructions from Adenauer to give first importance to the political aspects of the treaties (especially French adherence), and were less outspoken on the free trade issue (as well as on many others) than one might have expected from the general state of German opinion at the time.[35] The press criticized the negotiators for making so little progress toward the creation of a free trade area, and several speakers in the Bundestag debate on the ratification of the Treaties expressed similar opinions. Heinrich von Brentano, the Foreign Minister, replied to such arguments by urging that "we should do now what is possible, and that is the realization of the Economic Community." He noted further that in his opinion the conversations on the free trade area would cease if the Common Market were to fail.[36]

Shortly after the breakdown of the multilateral Maudling negotiations in November 1958, de Gaulle and Adenauer met at Bad Kreuznach at the former's request to discuss the situation.

The Bad Kreuznach meeting between Dr. Adenauer and General de Gaulle on 26 November was regarded in "European" circles as an event of first importance, both because it dramatised the intention of the French to proceed with the implementation of the Treaty of Rome, and because it underlined, once again, the German willingness to support the French and to give priority to the Treaty of Rome despite considerable pressure from German industry to reverse the priorities and put agreement on the free trade area first.[37]

This position was maintained throughout 1959 and 1960. In his speeches, Adenauer constantly referred to the Common Market as the "political core"[38] and as something that must not in any way be weakened because of EEC-EFTA differences.[39] Thus, while favoring the idea of reaching some sort of multilateral agreement or accommodation with the other OEEC countries, Adenauer supported all measures that tended to strengthen the EEC and especially those initiated by the Commission, such as acceleration.[40]

Britain's effort to enlist German support against France in the early negotiations seems to have created considerable distrust of British motives in Bonn. For the British, "Dr. Adenauer's determination to give Franco-German relations pride of place clearly set a limit beyond which it was not prudent to count on German support and a less obvious limit beyond which it was unwise to go in soliciting it."[41] Macmillan's visit to Moscow in spring 1959 elicited a good deal of resentment in both France and Germany, and Adenauer is reported to have declared that the British should learn that they could no longer lead on the Continent, for Germany and France were the leaders now. The logical policy for any German Chancellor would appear to have been to rely chiefly on France regarding the British and the Summit, and to be willing to make concessions to the French as a result. This is what Chancellor Adenauer has done.

The reported remarks of Macmillan in Washington in March 1960, in which he compared the current situation to that prevailing 150 years before when Britain frustrated Napoleon's Continental plans, did little to allay doubts, resentments, or suspicions.

The views that prevailed in the Economics Ministry, which reflected those of the great bulk of German industry and a large proportion of the press, were but a corollary of the general position taken by Erhard to the Europe of the Six since the early 1950's. The free trade area issue in fact summarized and epitomized all his doubts about European integration. In 1957 he wrote:

> Such a European integration, with as its first aim a customs union, appears to be morally, economically and politically justified only if this community in turn does not itself trigger off new differences and tensions. This means that the trading policy of the customs union as far as the outside world is concerned must be handled liberally, and that there must be no discrimination against third countries.

One must point to the highly important British proposals in the early autumn of 1956 to widen the Common Market area of the six Messina countries to that of the free trade zone. I understand only too well London's view that a tariff wall protecting the smaller European Common Market from the rest of the world could not be in the general European interest.[42]

If the "Common Market" does not adopt a clearly liberal trade policy towards other economic areas, we are threatened with a return to other ideological conceptions of a truly unhappy past, viz., the splitting of the world into so-called big blocs which breathe the selfish spirit of economic inbreeding and which sharpen the conflicts within the free world.[43]

The fact that the likelihood of a "split" would also involve distinct commercial disadvantages for Germany served to reinforce this fundamentally ideological position. Erhard does not oppose the Common Market in principle and is always at great pains to defend his reputation as a "European." He has opposed, however, all moves to enlarge the role of the Commission, and to accelerate the timetable of the Treaty of Rome.[44] He also appears to share the view frequently expressed in the German press that a Bonn-London bridge might be a valuable substitute for the Bonn-Paris axis, in view of de Gaulle's nationalism.[45] In a speech at the Hannover fair on April 25, 1960, he is reported as saying, "We can't buy the friendship of France by renouncing our relations with other countries."[46]

In an article entitled "What Is to Become of Europe?" published at the end of 1960, Erhard vigorously restated all his major points: *

One is not necessarily a "bad European" if one refuses to abide by the highly subjective fantasies of those who want only to think in terms of the "Six." Although it should have become sufficiently clear by now that despite a faithful implementation of the Treaty, . . . this integration of a "Little Europe" is unable, particularly from the political point of view, to solve either the European problem as a whole or that of the Atlantic Community, I should like to point out again for the sake of the record that no thought of such a limitation was godmother at the cradle of the Rome Treaties.[47]

After taking personal credit for having delayed the acceleration decision by six months, Erhard unleashed a strong attack on the Commission, which, "without any instruction to do so," had stated that it considered a multilateral solution inopportune. "We in Germany never thought of integration in this way. What is taking place has no longer anything in common with the promised liberal policy toward outsiders."[48] He went on to maintain that the only sensible solution was a multilateral association, empha-

---

* So vigorously, indeed, that the French government expressed its formal concern to Bonn, as a result of which the German government officially stated that Erhard's statement was personal and in no way engaged the Federal Republic. *Revue du Marché Commun*, No. 32.

sizing that "here I do not speak for myself only, but am happy to enjoy the united support of the whole German economy."[49]

Undeniably, a large proportion of German industry and commerce supported this position. The Common Market was seen by many as an ephemeral construction, bound to give way sooner or later, and the example of the United States was often cited to show that a large internal market is not enough to assure continuous economic expansion. Given the fact that, for most industries, exports to the Seven are as large as, or larger than, to the Six, it is not surprising that the dual vision of a widening split in Europe and the more rapid realization of the Common Market with the imminent introduction of the common external tariff evoked anxiety.[50] Not only could German industry look forward to reprisals from the EFTA, but it could expect a rise in prices paid for raw materials, etc., as a result of the gradual *rapprochement* toward the common external tariff.[51]

In its annual report for 1958–59, the Bundesverband der Deutschen Industrie (BDI) affirmed its support for the EEC and the Franco-German entente. The report stressed, however, that an association based solely on the Rome Treaty could not lead to real integration, and that "unfortunately the hopes for which there seemed grounds at the beginning of the year, of seeing a speeding up of the process of European integration, have been disappointed, and today there is a growing threat that Western Europe will be divided into two economic blocs."[52] This position is widely representative and was expressed frequently by Fritz Berg, President of the BDI. It is similar to some of the views of Alwin Münchmeyer, representing the Deutsche Industrie und Handelstag, who proposed negotiations with the EFTA based on the following principles: (1) they must tend toward progressive customs disarmament for all of Europe; (2) the customs autonomy of each separate country of the EEC would not be maintained except for countries outside Europe; (3) in the event of difficulties, customs disarmament could be limited in the first phase to products for which proof of origin is easy to establish; (4) for countries with insufficiently developed economies, and for all countries in the case of agriculture, special conventions aimed at the progressive elimination of commercial barriers could be negotiated.[53]

It follows that the attitude of the bulk of German industry, as expressed in such statements and in the industrial press at large, would be hostile to the Commission's initiatives and to the project for acceleration, insofar as acceleration threatened to make agreement with the EFTA less likely (especially the projected first step toward the common external tariff).[54] According to one report, "German industry has accepted the EEC for political reasons. Economic considerations require that an understanding with the EFTA not be frustrated. That is the danger inherent in acceleration of the

EEC."[55] Practically all press comment supported Erhard in his opposition to acceleration and applauded his efforts to require serious prior negotiations at the ministerial level between the EEC and the EFTA.[56] Scarcely a day went by without new proposals and urgings for a "bridge" between the EEC and the EFTA.[57] German businessmen were said to be unable to plan their future investments because of their doubts about future trading partners. [58] It is fair to conclude that there were many in Germany who were prepared "to sacrifice some of the more uncertain goals of the 'Europeans' to a wide, but looser, arrangement with British participation."[59] As Fritz Berg said, "German industry does not consider it in its interest to lock itself up in the little circle of the Common Market, for this would only result in holding back integration."[60]

The Deutscher Gewerkschaftsbund (DGB) shared many of the views of German industry and commerce about the dangers inherent in a split in Europe. That they had a certain identity of interest in maintaining trade expansion is obvious. The DGB favored the original free trade area, seeing it as a check on the Six's becoming too closed to the outside world.[61] The doubts of the DGB about the free circulation of labor, the harmonization of welfare benefits, and the association of the overseas territories tended to give it fewer reservations about a wider European grouping than most trade unions in the Six.[62] It did regard it as essential, however,

that as time goes on, any wider association should become more and more closely associated with the Common Market, so that European economic unification can come about gradually, and harmoniously. It has kept both projects in mind because it believes that one does not exclude the other, but is complementary to it. . . . It firmly believes that the close harmonization of a Common Market and a wider scheme can be a powerful instrument for bringing about higher employment levels, higher living standards and higher social security benefits.[63]

Being generally favorable to integration and the EEC, the DGB continued to support efforts to increase the cohesion of the Six through such measures as acceleration. And since its goals involved strengthening the EEC institutions, it was unlikely to remain in favor of a larger association if this entailed any risk to gains already made.

The Deutscher Bauernverband (DBV) did not take an active part in the free trade area question. It did, however, favor those portions of the Commission's agricultural proposals that provided protection against agricultural imports from outside by the imposition of a tax or charge on raw materials. And it called for a tax on transformed products in order to offset the advantages that third countries had in the world market.[64]

In the Bundestag debate on the ratification of the Rome Treaty, all

parties favored the institution of a free trade area. The Bund der Heimat-
vertriebenen und Entrechteten (BHE) and the Freie Deutsche Partei
(FDP) both voted against the Treaty, ostensibly because a free trade area
agreement did not come into force at the same time. Artur Stegner, spokesman for the BHE, predicted that an economic and political split in free
Europe would result from the EEC, so that the Community would not serve
the main goal of his party, namely, reunification. Heinrich Deist and
Karl Mommer, speaking for the Sozialdemokratische Partei Deutschlands
(SPD) stated that the realization of the free trade area was a decisive prior
condition to the proper functioning of the Common Market. Hans Furler
and Fritz Hellwig, for the Christlich-Demokratische Union (CDU/CSU),
also favored a free trade area, but emphasized the EEC as the necessary
basis without which the proposal for a free trade area would never have
been made. CDU speakers pointed out the obstacles to such an association
in view of the radically different national interests involved.[65] At the conclusion of the debate, the SPD and the CDU-Liberals both presented resolutions calling on the Federal Government to pursue energetically an association with other countries in the form of a free trade area.[66]

On October 2, 1958, the Bundestag passed a unanimous resolution
underlining again the importance of concluding a treaty for a free trade
area and calling on the government to make even greater efforts in this
direction.[67] Since then, however, party positions have diverged markedly.
The CDU in general followed the policies represented by Adenauer, von
Brentano, and Franz Etzel, placing priority on the development of the
Community of the Six and on the Franco-German rapprochement, and rejecting the accusation that the EEC was precipitating a split in Europe.[68]
They consistently supported the Commission in the EPA. The FDP, which
was closely associated with industrialists and Protestant anti-Adenauer
groups (and some former Nazis), continued to demand that further efforts
be expended to build a bridge between the Six and the Seven, and rejected
all measures tending to widen the split, such as acceleration.[69]

The SPD held fast to its position that an agreement with the other
European countries should be of first priority. The continuing goal of
reunification and the preference for association with the successful Socialist parties in the U.K., Scandinavia, and Austria led the SPD to oppose
Commission initiatives on the free trade area and the acceleration proposals. Erich Ollenhauer noted in late 1959 that although the SPD was
pleased that good relations existed between France and Germany, it was
not prepared to see a Continental Europe of the Six constituted at the price
of Germany's friendship with the other European countries. The SPD had
approved the Treaty only on the condition that the EEC be complemented
by a free trade area. "The collaboration of the Six, which must be extended to those European countries not members of the EEC, rests on an

economic basis. We must not concentrate our efforts on the single idea that it is necessary to act in the sense of a political community of the Six by the intermediary of the EEC."[70] SPD deputies Hellmut Kalbitzer and Willi Birkelbach repeatedly attacked the policies of the Commission, accusing it of introducing the acceleration proposals for the sole purpose of sabotaging any collaboration with the other countries of Europe. They declared that if this economic split persisted, it would inevitably lead to a political split, heavy with consequences for the free world.[71]

BENELUX

The governments of these three small countries have been among the most consistent and dedicated supporters of economic and political integration; recall that the Messina *rélance* was inspired by the Benelux Memorandum of 1955. During the long negotiations on the Rome Treaty they were the principal advocates of strong Community institutions, low external tariffs, and a liberal economic policy, including especially a liberal trading policy toward third countries. Animated by a fairly close identity of interests with regard to commercial policy, the Benelux countries were consistent and persistent advocates of a free trade area. In order to maximize their influence they sought to coordinate their views as much as possible, usually presenting a uniform Benelux position. The Dutch were particularly unhappy about the lack of progress in the free trade area negotiations, as they had been about the many concessions granted the French in the drafting of the Treaty, whereas the Belgians, with higher prices and wages and a less efficient agriculture, were more inclined to compromise. The events of 1958–60 widened this gap, and resulted in the relative isolation of the Dutch government.

After the breakdown of the Maudling Committee negotiations, the Benelux countries repeatedly sought to soften the impact on the other OEEC countries of the tariff and quota changes the Six were instituting between themselves. In November 1958 they presented a joint memorandum declaring that a split between the Six and the other OEEC countries had to be avoided so that the adjournment of negotiations might be only "a pause for reflection."[72] In discussions among the Six, Benelux consistently favored proposals that tended to minimize the differentiation between the Six and the others, and that sought to reaffirm that the ultimate goal was a "free market" of the seventeen OEEC countries.[73] They were critical of the Commission for not working for such a multilateral solution. The Belgian Foreign Minister, Pierre Wigny, was the formal initiator of the proposals to accelerate the realization of the Common Market, but he tied his proposals to a reopening of serious negotiations with the Seven.

The Benelux common front began to show signs of strain late in 1959.

The Belgians reluctantly accepted the impossibility of reaching an agreement on a multilateral association, given the wide divergence of views among the Six. Wigny obviously gave pride of place to the kind of political integration represented by the EEC and was unwilling to jeopardize this goal or see progress toward it slowed down. Purely commercial considerations counted for more in the Ministry of Foreign Trade, Minister Jacques van Offelen accepting acceleration only reluctantly. Still, the political goal remained pre-eminent here, too, as the following statement shows: "Above and beyond trade and national interest, we must consider the supreme political aim of uniting Europe. The Union of the Six marks the end of a long history of misunderstanding and suffering."[74]

Belgian industry overcame its initial mixed reaction to the Rome Treaty, and accepted it as a necessity and an opportunity. The position of industrial groups on the free trade area inched closer and closer to that of the French Patronat, although initially they favored its simultaneous introduction with the Common Market. By 1958 they were urging "caution" in the free trade area negotiations.[75] When van Offelen offered another Memorandum in the name of Benelux in November 1959, calling for a "free market" of greater Europe and the extension of tariff reductions,[76] the Fédération des Industries Belges (FIB) reacted vigorously. The FIB declared that Belgian industry could not accept an extension of tariff reductions without getting guarantees on the irrevocability of commitments. They argued that the Benelux proposals made it difficult, if not impossible, to plan new investments. Several conditions were listed under which the FIB would accept an association: (1) the free trade area must not endanger the functioning and integrity of the EEC; (2) it must be acceptable to all EEC members; (3) the principle of the harmonization of external tariffs and trade policy must be admitted on the basis of such an area; and (4) the principle of the irreversible nature of the process of integration must be admitted so that industry could establish its investment program.[77]

Of the two trade union federations, the socialist Fédération Générale des Travailleurs Belges (FGTB) was more broadly in favor of a free trade area agreement. They thought it would strengthen the EEC and lead toward greater European unity. They suggested that social harmonization was as essential for a free trade area as for the EEC, and that this should take account of wage scales, social charges, and additional state benefits. Furthermore, coordination of monetary policy (especially regarding exchange rates) was considered essential to prevent constant use of escape clauses.[78]

The Catholic Confédération des Syndicats Chrétiens (CSC) did not have much to say on the issue. Its President, August Cool, spoke favorably of the free trade area in very general terms in 1957.[79] But the CSC, like all Catholic trade unions, was pre-eminently concerned with the Europe of the Six, and Cool warned against losing the social advantages of integration of the Six to a free trade area.[80]

Belgian agricultural groups, the most important of which is the Boerenbond, do not appear to have taken a significant role in the free trade area debates except to demand the inclusion of special provisions for agriculture. Belgian agricultural policies are generally protectionist, even as regards their Benelux neighbors, and the Boerenbond vigorously defended these policies.[81] Belgian agriculture is quite concerned about its competitive position in the EEC, not to speak of a possible larger association.

At the ratification of the Rome Treaty by the Belgian parliament there was a generally favorable reception to the idea of a free trade area, both because of the resulting expansion of liberalization, and because this is a way to get British participation. Objections were raised to the exclusion of agriculture and to the generally vague nature of the U.K. propositions. Senator Fernand Dehousse (Socialist), Pierre Wigny and Corneille Mertens in the Chamber, and Senator Paul Struye (all Christian-Democrats) stipulated that the countries of any free trade area would have to assume some risks and responsibilities if they expected to share in the customs and commercial advantages of the Common Market, and that care must be taken to ensure that the secondary objective of a free trade area did not distract from the primary objective, which was the strengthening of the Community of the Six.[82]

This order of priority was maintained, and while insisting on some sort of association, the Liberal and Christian-Democrat majority agreed in early 1960 that the solution to the problem of the relations between the Six and the Seven should be sought in an "Atlantic" context, and could not be limited to the European countries. The opposition Socialists, on the other hand, objected to those aspects of the acceleration proposals that they thought would make an agreement between the Six and the Seven more difficult (i.e., the early approximations to the common external tariff).[83]

The Luxembourg government and parties (except for the Communists), while always having supported the idea of a free trade area, shared the view that this must not be allowed to interfere with the establishment and functioning of the Common Market.[84] Because of Luxembourg's full economic union with Belgium, the positions of the major interest groups were essentially identical.

In the Netherlands, on the other hand, there seemed to be a significant difference of opinion between the policy of the government, especially of Foreign Minister Joseph Luns, and the parliament, although a feeling of disenchantment with the EEC was fairly widespread. Whereas the Dutch parties have been characterized by almost unanimous support for political integration and strong central institutions,[85] the government has held some doubts about too extensive an emphasis on "Little Europe."[86] In a parliamentary debate in December 1958 there were angry recriminations between the pro-EEC majority and Luns, who was reproached for being pro-British.[87] Certainly there is widespread support in the Netherlands for a Six-Seven bridge. The Dutch were consistently the most critical of the concessions made to France during the negotiations on the Treaty, and here again it was French intransigence that prevented a free trade area agreement. The Dutch in many ways felt a closer affinity with the United Kingdom and Scandinavia than with France and Germany—for political as well as commercial reasons. They threw in their lot with the Little Europe countries, but also felt they must remain the Continent's open window to the rest of the world. Because of their general dependence on exports, especially in agricultural products (for which grains must be imported at low tariffs), and on commercial services, they were willing to accept the higher tariffs, and hence higher production costs, in the EEC, but only on the understanding that this would be supplemented by the creation of a free trade area.

Consequently the Dutch were bitterly critical of the trend in the fall of 1959 and afterwards to forgo the search for a multilateral solution.[88] They did not accept the argument that a larger association would threaten either U.S. interests or the integrity of the EEC. The Dutch attitude became even stiffer when the free trade area and acceleration issues became tangled, and particularly when it was proposed that an accelerated movement toward the common external tariff be made.[89] The Dutch counterproposal, the Luns Plan, contemplated the extension of future tariff reductions by both the Six and the Seven to all countries with which they had most-favored-nation commitments, and a 20 per cent reduction in the level of the common external tariff. Many in the Six felt that this proposal went too far and threatened the integrity of the Community.[90] With the Luns Plan the Dutch went beyond a Benelux alternative, which would have merely affirmed a readiness to negotiate with the Seven on reciprocal tariff reductions so as to avoid differences of treatment.

Throughout 1960 the Dutch became more and more convinced that they were getting the worst of all possible worlds. They acquiesced in the acceleration decisions although their minimal demands were not completely met. The de Gaulle initiatives in the summer of 1960 for increased political cooperation among the Six and a political secretariat convinced them that the French, having used the Community to block the free trade area, were now trying to substitute a Franco-German alliance for a true Community.[91] The isolation of the Dutch seemed complete when at the Summit

Conference of the Six in February 1961 they refused to agree to a permanent organ for political consultations unless the British were included. After the meeting, Luns said: "Holland believes that a new Europe must be built on the idea of integration. However, the Paris plans would only result in splitting Europe into two hostile blocks."[92] Another source quotes him as saying: "If we want to continue on the basis of integration and supranationality, then let us remain as we are, for England is not ready to follow us. But nothing that has been presented to us here prevents English participation, and I don't see why we should deprive ourselves of this when it is so important for our future in Europe as well as in Africa that we align our position with that of Great Britain."[93] Note that, in contrast to much German opinion, the Dutch are not opposed to further integration in the EEC. The Dutch alternative proposals for political consultation called for representation of the three executives (the Commission of the EEC, Euratom, and the High Authority) in the political consultations, and for an annual report to be submitted to the EPA.[94]

Most of the objections raised by Dutch commercial and industrial circles to the EEC Treaty had stemmed from their conviction that the Treaty was not providing for a sufficiently free common market. In addition, they feared that the common tariff toward third countries would not only make a free trade area agreement difficult, but also raise all Dutch prices.[95] Commercial groups, especially in inland shipping and the port of Rotterdam, were far from enthusiastic about the Treaty.[96] They continued to push the hardest for a multilateral accord between the Six and the Seven, holding that such an agreement was more important than accelerating the Common Market.[97] They stated their views as follows:

In absolute contradiction with its objectives as defined in the preamble to the Rome Treaty, the EEC has realized a disintegration in Europe. . . . The shortening of the transition period should be subordinated to the creation of this association [of other European countries]. . . . The Netherlands must take the initiative. And if, despite all efforts, this idea is not accepted by our EEC partners, the Netherlands must not renew her error of 1957; also, when the convention for shortening the transition period is signed, [the Netherlands] must make formal reservations in order that this association see the light of day.[98]

Dutch industrialists also opposed acceleration "as long as some states had not yet met their commitments."[99]

The attitude of noncommercial groups was not so strong, and in December 1959 the seven associations of workers and employers (comprising most of Dutch industry) addressed a letter to the Minister of Economic

Affairs insisting that the Dutch government accept the Commission's proposals (opposed by Luns at Strasbourg) as a point of departure. The letter recognized that Six-Seven negotiations made little sense given the wide divergences of opinion among the Six.[100] Industrialists continued to favor an agreement based on a free trade area, but seem to have accepted that this was growing more and more unlikely. The 1960 Annual Report of the Verbond van Nederlandsche Werkgevers noted that the failure of the free trade area negotiations "is in conflict with what is to be regarded in general as desirable for our country. One iron curtain is already quite adequate for Europe."[101] Whereas a big free trade area was still an acceptable possibility, the problem of trade diversion, solved in the EFTA with complex origin rules, would now create more problems for the Netherlands, which formerly had a low tariff but would have much higher duties in the EEC framework. The Report regretted that the Commission had not given a clearer lead in the Six-Seven problem, but pointed out that since "within the Six a unanimous political determination to achieve an economic association with the Seven is lacking, . . . there remains, alas, no other way open than to remove, by an 'over-all solution,' points of friction arising between the EEC and the EFTA."[102] The Dutch government was called upon to do its best to mitigate the effects of the economic division between the Six and the Seven.

All three trade union federations—the Netherlands Socialist Trade Union Federation (NVV, Socialist), the National Confederation of Christian Workers (CNV, Protestant), and the Confederation of Catholic Workers (KAB, Roman Catholic)—supported the original free trade area proposals as a necessary complement to the EEC. There was considerable anxiety lest the high common external tariff (high compared to the Dutch tariff) should stifle Dutch trade with the outside world. But in a free trade area some tariff harmonization was necessary, agriculture would definitely have to be included, and all the members should contribute to the Social Fund and the Investment Bank. Under no conditions could the integrity of the EEC be questioned.[103]

Although the Netherlands has at least three major agricultural groups for both producers and workers, the only authoritative voice for agriculture is the semipublic Landbouwschap. It argued strongly for the inclusion of agriculture in the original free trade area and for strong institutional provisions for agricultural questions. With the rupture of these negotiations and the creation of the EFTA, the Landbouwschap began to press the government for a speedy resumption of negotiations leading to an agreement, because the preferences that Denmark had now gained on the U.K. market were an obvious threat to Dutch exports.[104] The Dutch were also concerned about maintaining the supply of the low-cost cereal imports that were so important to their transformation industry. If the cost of these raw materials were to go up, their competitive position both in the EEC and outside would suffer.[105]

During the ratification debates in the Second Chamber the general attitude of parliamentarians toward the free trade area was cautious. Pieter Blaisse (Catholic People's Party) called attention to the need for harmonizing commercial policy. Gerard Nederhorst (Socialist) emphasized the great difficulty of reaching a free trade area agreement. He noted that the Socialist group disapproved of abandoning powers when no new opportunities were offered to compensate for them. The free trade area would be rendered meaningless without any regulation of services, capital movements, transport, or cartels, and without adequately endowed institutions. Similar considerations were raised in the First Chamber. Emanuel Sassen (Catholic People's Party) called for controls on competitive conditions, and urged in addition that the Commission be given the mandate to speak for all Six countries in the negotiations. Paulus Kapteyn (Socialist) strongly supported the free trade area as a guarantee that the EEC would practice a liberal commercial policy toward the outside world.

The strongly pro–European orientation of all the Dutch parties was credited with forcing Luns to give in on the acceleration issue. The Socialists, especially Jonkheer van der Goes van Naters, criticized the "distinctly anti-European attitude of Luns's advisers." But the Liberals increased their attacks on a Europe limited to the Six,[106] and there was disappointment among even the most enthusiastically pro-European members of the Dutch contingent in the EPA when, late in 1959, it appeared that the idea of a multilateral association was being ignored. As van der Goes van Naters remarked, "The Dutch are sincere Europeans but do not make the task more difficult for us." He went on to urge that "steps be taken to prevent the little countries of the Community from being forced to abandon their collaboration and their community spirit. It is always maintained that an enlarged, multilateral European association is favored, but nothing is ever done about it."[107]

ITALY

Italy favored a wider European trading association in principle, but shared most of the French objections to the particular proposals put forth.[108] Italy's protectionist tendencies and the unevenly developed nature of her economy placed her closest to the French in economic outlook. The basic attitude of the government to integration has not changed since Giuseppe Pella proposed a General Common Market to the OEEC in 1950. In reacting to the Benelux Common Market initiatives in 1955, the Italian government argued for the greatest possible amount of economic integration, with emphasis on a European labor policy, European adaptation funds, European investment funds, and freedom of movement for workers.[109]

The imperatives of such continuing problems as unemployment and the need to protect certain industrial and agricultural producers have to a large extent shaped the government's attitude. As early as 1957, the Italian representative to the Maudling Committee introduced demands for provisions for the free circulation of labor. [110] The free trade area offered no solution to these problems, whereas the Common Market did.[111] The Italians also favored some system of economic aid for the modernization of their industries.[112] Further, they were particularly concerned with the problem of the deflections of trade that would result from the tariff disparities in the type of free trade area desired by the British. In March 1958 the Italian delegate to the Maudling Committee, Guido Carli, tried to break the deadlock between the French and the British with a proposal involving compensatory taxes.[113] The Italians agreed with the French, however, in their general assessment of the need for some real solution for the problem of "origin."[114]

In summarizing the negotiations for a free trade area before the Chamber of Deputies, Mario Martinelli, Minister of Foreign Trade, noted the profound differences of conception between the EEC and the proposed free trade area, the former encouraging a general economic integration, and the latter resting on purely commercial considerations and permitting the participating countries to retain complete autonomy in commercial policy. He concluded that a multilateral agreement as desired by the United Kingdom was not possible under these conditions.[115]

The political and ideological content of the Rome Treaty always appealed to the Italians; the plan for a free trade area was interpreted as no more than an economic or commercial venture, and often as only a convenient maneuver on the part of the British.[116] It was declared Italian policy, however, to encourage collaboration between the United Kingdom and the EEC,[117] and the Italian government often saw itself in this objective position of mediation between France and the United Kingdom.[118]

Italy's industrialists seem largely converted to the basic idea of the EEC, but had reservations about the free trade area. The Confederation of Industry (Confindustria) attributed the failure of the Maudling Committee negotiations to the desire of the United Kingdom and the others to keep complete liberty over their tariff policy toward the outside, while at the same time benefiting from tariff abolition between the Six. An agreement was to be desired, but not regardless of cost, and countries should not be allowed to benefit from a widening market without assuming the responsibilities involved.[119] This position was reiterated in the 1960 Annual Report. The EFTA seemed to be no more than a second-best solution, entirely lacking in political drive, whereas the EEC was far too important to be watered down in any free trade area without a common external tariff and policy harmonization. Some kind of broad agreement was still desirable, but only if efforts to torpedo the EEC were made to stop.[120]

The two non-Communist trade union organizations took roughly the same position. In 1958 the Confederazione Italiana dei Sindicati di Lavoro (CISL) submitted to the Italian government a memorandum envisaging the free trade area as a first step toward the formal accession of other countries to the EEC. A free trade area must in no way endanger the EEC, and therefore should meet three conditions: the EEC must be permitted to develop Community economic and financial policies so as to enable it to act as a unit in negotiations; the free trade area should have supranational institutions so as to be able to promote trade development, to guarantee employment levels, and to ensure policy coordination; and there should be a general undertaking concerning the level of employment.[121] The Unione Italiana di Lavoro (UIL) took about the same position, favoring the free trade area because it was seen as a step toward wider economic and political integration, but calling for provisions for full employment, social harmonization, public investment funds, free movement of labor, etc.[122] The Confederazione Generale Italiana di Lavoro (CGIL), consisting of Communists and Nenni Socialists, made no formal statement, but its officials saw the free trade area as less dangerous than the EEC. In a larger association there would be less opportunity for an international alliance of capital, because British employers would counterbalance the Germans, and the British trade unions would buttress labor strength against monopolistic industrialists seeking to exploit the Common Market.[123]

Of the agricultural groups, Paolo Bonomi's Confederazione Nazionale Coltivatori Dirreti is the most important. Its attitude to the free trade area was in general cold. Bonomi's group is made up of small farmers, who deal with such products as grapes, fruit, and vegetables. The EEC is important to them, since it guarantees access to the valuable German market.[124]

There appears to have been no important debate over the free trade area in the Italian parliament at the time of the ratification of the Rome Treaty. Such debates as have occurred since have confirmed the continuing general support of all Italian political parties for wider agreements, but also their insistence upon efforts to strengthen the cohesion of the EEC (i.e., acceleration measures).[125]

CONCLUSIONS

In this chapter we have seen how the plan for a free trade area put under stress the convergence of values and goals that accounted for support or acceptance of the Treaty of Rome. The worst fears of those who accepted the EEC as a first step in a progressive freeing of trade were realized, and many came to consider the EEC a threat rather than a potential source of advantage. For others whose motivations were perhaps more complex, the question of a free trade area created powerful cross-pressures and forced difficult decisions. It is not surprising that the Six had trouble in achieving a common position. The French were uninterested at best, and, as we have tried to demonstrate, consistently maintained an attitude that was incompatible with, if not hostile to, the free trade area as proposed by the United Kingdom and as discussed in the Maudling Committee. Furthermore, those who favored some sort of free trade area were not in agreement on their objectives. As Miriam Camps points out.

To some the problem was to establish an arrangement between the Six and the other OEEC countries that would preserve and strengthen the amount of co-operation that had developed since the war, but to do so without weakening the Treaty of Rome or prejudicing the development of the maximum amount of unity among the Six. To others it was to create a broad European economic arrangement that would be almost as far-reaching as the Treaty of Rome. To others the problem was to create a trading arrangement among the seventeen countries that was non-discriminatory within the area and eventually transitional to a broader multi-lateral trading system. Thus, for some, the overriding consideration was the integrity of the Treaty of Rome. For others the primary concern was to achieve as much economic integration as possible for the group as a whole. While for others the first consideration was non-discrimination in trade within the OEEC area. In the eyes of some, economic union of the Six was an urgent need and an eventual federation a feasible goal. In the eyes of others these aspirations were will-o'-the-wisps that hard-headed people ignored.[126]

It remains now to trace the steps whereby a common Community position was finally achieved. How was it possible to develop such a policy at anything but the lowest level of accommodation? What accounts for the continued efforts to do so? What role was played by the Commission and with what effect?

A COMMUNITY DOCTRINE

UNTIL THE END of December 1958 and the collapse of the Maudling Committee negotiations, all efforts to achieve a common position for the Six were carried on in intergovernmental committees. The Commission, although it gradually expanded the scope of its participation, was necessarily in a secondary role, since the free trade area negotiations had been going on in the OEEC for almost a year before the Commission was constituted. At the time of the signing of the Rome Treaty on March 25, 1957, the Ministers of the Six set up an Interim Committee, which was to perform certain tasks of preparation and coordination until the Treaty came into force and until the common institutions were set up. This committee was made up of the heads of delegation to the Intergovernmental Conference, the conference that had prepared the final draft of the Rome Treaty. Among their assigned tasks was "the coordination of the attitude of the six governments in other international organizations."[1]

Until the fall of 1957, the committee concentrated on preparing the position of the Six in view of the GATT debates, i.e., preparing official notes, etc.[2] In July the French government proposed that the Six meet to discuss the problems of creating a free trade area."[3] Working groups were set up, and in October the Interim Committee held its first meeting to try to lay down the general principles to be followed. The Six affirmed their desire to achieve a free trade area agreement and declared their determination to preserve the integrity of the Rome Treaty. It was agreed, however, that a free trade area based solely on the elimination of customs duties and quotas was not acceptable. There would have to be some real integration: namely, the coordination or harmonization of commercial policy and of the conditions of production, and the provision of adequate safeguards. Furthermore, solutions would have to be found for the problems posed by agriculture and the relationship between the United Kingdom and the Commonwealth. Differences among the Six persisted with reference to the problem of origin and that of the harmonization of social legislation.[4] The Interim Committee also prepared the dossier for the ministerial meetings of the Six that preceded the Maudling sessions.[5]

When the Treaty came into force, the Interim Committee was replaced by the Permanent Representatives Committee,[6] which took over the tasks of coordinating the national policies and of preparing the Maudling meetings.[7] The French counterproposals, circulated in a memorandum in March, became the basis for the discussions of the Permanent Representatives.[8] In late March 1958, a temporary group of experts, presided over by Roger Ockrent, the chief of the Belgian delegation to the OEEC, was set up in the Permanent Representatives Committee and charged with preparing the common position of the Community for the next session of the Maudling Committee.[9] The work of reconciliation went on through March into April, when a first paper was submitted to the EEC Council of Ministers. No real progress had been made, however, since France had been plunged into crisis by the Algerian revolt. The work of the Ockrent Committee continued through the summer, but was limited to technical matters. Another report was presented to the Council of Ministers at Venice at the end of September, by which time some progress had been made, although the major issues remained open, e.g., the scope of and procedure for safeguard clauses, the powers of free trade area institutions and voting procedures, how to proceed from one stage to another, imperial preference, and harmonization.[10]

Another Council meeting was held in Brussels on October 7 and 8, and agreement was finally reached in a Community memorandum (known as the Ockrent Report), which was submitted to the Council of Ministers on October 17.[11] The main points made in this memorandum were: (1) the OEEC countries must accept the principle that the differences in treatment arising from the Treaty of Rome were valid and nondiscriminatory; (2) there must be explicit recognition that any treaty of association could not impede the implementation of the Treaty of Rome; (3) the fact that there would be no common external tariff and no common trade policy would raise such problems as the deflection of trade and the transfer of activities, and these must be resolved not by general rules, but by means of sector studies of the main branches of economic activity; (4) the Member States of such a free trade area should coordinate their trade policies in regard to third countries (a common trade policy should not be regarded as an objective) so that competition between firms would not be distorted; and (5) if a Member State felt that the import system applied by another state to third countries would distort competition, the institutions would examine the system and make recommendations, the state that believed itself injured being permitted to have recourse to safeguard measures in the interim.[12]

Although the Ockrent Report was put forth as the collective view of the Six, the French delegate to the Maudling Committee went beyond this position, raising the question of the extent to which a common commercial policy was required and the amount of freedom that members would have to change their external tariffs. It was thus revealed that the Six were still not fully in agreement. This was confirmed in November, when the French government announced it had decided that it was not possible to create the free trade area as conceived by the United Kingdom. Although the announcement did not represent a new development in French policy (this position had been held for over a year), it did seem to many of France's partners to be a repudiation of the Ockrent Report. Nor were the other members of the EEC consulted before the announcement was made. It was widely felt in the Six (especially in Benelux and Germany) that the French had not negotiated in good faith, since the position taken was in contradiction with the very point of departure of the whole negotiation.[13]

The EEC Council of Ministers met in Brussels on December 3 and 4 to consider what action was now to be taken. The Benelux countries had proposed a plan to their EEC partners for softening the impact of the tariff and quota changes due to come into force on January 1, 1959. Certain provisional arrangements were to be made so as to prevent a clear break and allow more time to negotiate a definitive agreement. This plan called for extending the first 10 per cent tariff reduction to all GATT members, and for a reciprocal extension of the 20 per cent quota increases.[14] The bulk of the Benelux proposals were incorporated in the decision taken by the Council, although the obligation to establish quotas for all products at 3 per cent of national income where small or null quotas existed was not extended to non-EEC countries. The Council also agreed to request the Commission to prepare a report on what kind of common position the Member States could take on the general problem of a broader association.[15]

As already noted, up to this point the Commission had played a secondary role in formulating a common position for the Six. Not that it had been inactive or unwilling to expand its participation. The Treaty did not make clear what the Commission's role should be if a negotiation was begun before the Treaty came into force. The Interim Committee had developed the doctrine that the free trade area discussions were to be regarded not as an accord with third states, but as an association of other countries to the Community, and by this interpretation the discussions fell under Article 238, which does not specify who is to do the negotiating. The Permanent Representatives declared in January 1958 that the participation of the Commission "would be pragmatic and would be developed empirically." The Commission accepted this role at the time since it had neither staff, nor a clear position of its own.

The problem for the Commission was to determine the extent to which it could adopt an independent position in opposition to that of a Member State. The High Authority of the ECSC negotiated for the Six in the Maudling Committee, but did so on the basis of a mandate from the Council arrived at by unanimity. These matters were the subject of study within the Commission, and in March, before the EPA, Walter Hallstein for the first time defined the Commission's point of view regarding the free trade area. The Commission, while convinced of the need for an association with the other OEEC countries, considered that the present conception of the free trade area needed drastic modification. Lack of a common external tariff and limitation to a removal of trade barriers were the chief points that would have to be adjusted. Furthermore, the problem was not to link up the markets of the seventeen OEEC countries, but rather to "associate" the other OEEC countries with the existing common market of the Six in such a way as to leave the Community unaltered.[16] The governments promised to take note of the Commission's ideas, but observed that it was "up to the governments" to carry on the negotiations; the Commission was merely to "assist" them.[17]

At this point, however, the Commission decided to stop playing a subordinate role and to take the initiative. In June, therefore, it proposed that provisional steps be taken in case no agreement on the free trade area had been reached by the end of the year. The chief recommendation was for the reciprocal application among all OEEC countries of the same tariff reductions as were to take effect within the Community.[18]

By this time the Commission had defined its role very clearly:

The European Commission deems that its duty is to *achieve a compromise* between the divergent positions which emerge manifesting themselves not only between the Member States but also between these States and the eleven other states of the OEEC. The Commission will be guided by its first duty, which is *to watch over the general interest of the Community as a whole.* In adopting this attitude it will be able to appreciate more objectively the particular problems which pre-occupy each of the six Member States. On the other hand it must advocate a form of association which will not impede the realization of the Community and the execution of its essential tasks. In order to accomplish this, the Commission believes *it will have to play an increasingly large role* in the negotiations.[19]

Throughout the deliberations of the Ockrent Committee, the Commission continued to make its views known. Several notes were sent to the Permanent Representatives to underline the dangers that certain solutions entailed for the realization of the Common Market.[20] In August the Commission decided to prepare a document designed to reconcile the positions still at issue in the Ockrent Committee and to submit this at the Venice meeting of the Council of Ministers.[21] At the Venice meeting, the Commission was asked to work out detailed proposals on two points in the forthcoming Ockrent Report: on the question of institutions and on special sector studies. The Commission's proposals on institutions were in part incorporated into the Ockrent Report; the special sector studies were under way when the Maudling Committee negotiations were adjourned.[22]

At this juncture the Commission again took the initiative:

The European Commission decided that its President and the chairman of the External Relations Group should visit the Heads of Government of the Member States in order to hear their views and to study with them any measures that might be taken.

Following these talks, the President of the European Commission was in a position to state the unanimous opinion that an interim solution must be sought in view of the date line of January; negotiations for a final solution could then be resumed later, after careful preparation.[23]

This was probably a tactical move. As has been pointed out, "For some time the 'Europeans' had felt that the Commission should be charged with negotiating on behalf of the Six; the suspension of the Maudling Committee seemed to many to offer the opportunity to renew negotiations on a different basis."[24]

It is interesting to note that up to this point the position taken by the Commission on the free trade area was closest to that of France and Italy, although for different reasons. For the Commission the most important thing was to see that a free trade area agreement in no way prejudiced the future development of the EEC. According to the Commission's own statement, every care should be taken "lest the envisaged association prevent the Community from carrying out its mission in the manner laid down in the Treaty of Rome. From the viewpoint of the Commission there can indeed be no question of association which would impede the development of a more stable organization as a step on the way to more important results."[25] This accounts also for the Commission's insistence all along that the principle of differentiation of treatment be accepted by the OEEC countries. The British had sought to avoid this and to force continuation of the principle of nondiscrimination among the OEEC countries. The French, above all, were determined to make it clear that a new situation had been created and to force the OEEC to accept differentiation of treatment.[26] This close identity of view between the Commission and the French was again evident in January 1959, when the British counterproposals to the interim steps taken by the Six in December were discussed within the Community. The British had objected particularly vehemently to the fact that the 3 per cent quotas would be available only to Treaty of Rome countries, and proposed that the benefits of this arrangement be extended to all OEEC countries on the basis of reciprocity. Miriam Camps comments:

In one sense this was an ingenious proposal since it would not have cost the Six anything, that is, they would not be freeing any greater volume of goods but would simply be letting more countries compete for the same quota. . . . However, by accepting the British proposal the most obvious and important difference in treatment between a Treaty of Rome country and an OEEC country would have been eliminated, and a firm precedent of OEEC-wide non-discrimination would have been created.[27]

At French insistence, consideration of the British proposal was put off until January. When the discussion was taken up, the French argued that the Six should tell the OEEC that it was not possible to extend the 3 per cent rule. The Italians agreed, but were in favor of proposing alternative solutions. The Benelux countries and Germany were opposed to the French position. They made no secret of the fact that it would be to their economic advantage to accept the British proposal. The Commission had always opposed the extension of the interim agreement to quotas, being concerned above all with safeguarding the individuality and special character of the Community, and took essentially the same position as the French and Italians.[28] There were many in "European" circles who agreed that it would be preferable to postpone the free trade area negotiations. This would permit the Treaty of Rome to become more fully accepted and the institutions better organized, and would allay the fears of those who felt the EEC would become lost in a looser and larger federation if the EEC institutions had not had time to acquire power and permanence in a separate context.

THE FIRST MEMORANDUM OF THE COMMISSION

In December 1958, the Council of Ministers passed the following resolution:

Anxious to continue the efforts to establish a multilateral association between the European Economic Community and the other states of the Organization for European Economic Co-operation, and recognizing that the difficulties which have come to light during the negotiations call for fresh studies and fresh contacts, the Council requests the Commission to undertake, in the light of the work already done or now in hand, a detailed examination of the problems and of the possibilities of resolving them. In accomplishing this duty the Commission will maintain constant contact with the six Member Governments of the European Economic Community.

The Council requests the Commission to submit a report by 1 March 1959 on what kind of common position could be taken up by the Member States.

The Council, when it has approved this report, will decide on the procedure to be followed. One possibility that may be considered is that the Commission should make official contact with other Governments in order to discuss the problem with them.[29]

The terms of the resolution are of special interest because they reaffirm the desire of the Six to reach an association agreement with the other OEEC countries and request the Commission to prepare a joint Community position *to that end*. However, the memorandum the Commission submitted on February 26, 1959, accepted the impossibility of reaching an agreement and suggested a policy to deal with this situation instead.

The Commission began by recalling that it had always had serious doubts about the chances of success of the free trade area negotiations, given the heterogeneity of the seventeen states and their varied interests.[30] Furthermore, there was a basic incompatibility of conception between the Six and the other OEEC countries.

For the eleven European states outside the Community there should be no difference of treatment between the Member States and the other members of OEEC. No difference can be made between the seventeen members either in the field of tariffs or in the field of quotas. Any measure that can lead to such differences is called "discrimination" and condemned out of hand.

For their part the Member States of the Community consider that by establishing their Community, by agreeing to certain efforts and certain sacrifices in order to bring this Community into being, by accepting new disciplines and specific burdens, they have constituted an association which gives them the right to treat each other in a manner which is different from that adopted towards non-member states. . . .

It is not surprising that such fundamental differences in conception should have led the negotiations into an impasse.[31]

The Commission also observed that all these normal difficulties were exacerbated by the fact that the whole question had come up before the Community had become established. This had made it difficult for the Community to act. "It is also difficult for the Community not to be concerned over anything which might harm its development, which might even prove to be a threat to its existence."[32]

In the Commission's view, none of the outstanding problems had been resolved. It had not been possible to find a compromise between a free trade area of the classical type, which the Six rejected as impossible, and a customs union, which the others were not prepared to accept. The search for such a compromise should go on, but the Six could not in the meantime commit themselves to any abolition of obstacles to trade within the OEEC framework, since their OEEC partners had not accepted the prior conditions for this. Without a specific commitment on the part of all OEEC countries, the rules of GATT required that any advantages granted must be extended to other contracting parties. Furthermore, the world-wide responsibilities of the Community must be taken into account, for the problems raised by the introduction of the EEC could not be confined to Europe. The relationship of the EEC with its OEEC partners, therefore, was really only one facet of the general problem of the external relations of the Community.

This being so, it is important for the Community, if it wishes to avoid being drawn into dispersed but cumulative negotiations, haphazard in their development, and incalculable in their overall results, which would take no account of the particular requirements of the Common Market, to undertake simultaneously the study of its economic relations with the Eleven and with non-member countries as a whole.[33]

The Commission went on to sketch out the broad outlines of this approach, emphasizing the liberal orientation of the Community, the need for close cooperation with the United States, and a program of coordinated assistance for underdeveloped countries.

In view of these factors:

The Commission believes . . . that for the immediate future a pragmatic approach to the difficulties might be more advisable and would better answer the actual facts of the situation.

Apart from seeking a permanent solution, it is now necessary to decide what in practice can be done during the next three or four years and within the framework of the organizations which already exist in Paris and Geneva, in the endeavor to follow a liberal policy of bringing the quota and customs systems of the Treaty of Rome and the remaining Eleven into line.

The Commission is convinced that it is now possible to define and to put into practice plans for a period of several years of living side by side, while at the same time seeking for solutions of a more definitive character.[34]

The Commission's chief suggestions for practical action were these: (1) the OEEC countries should automatically enlarge by 20 per cent the quotas still in force between them, without globalization and without application of the 3 per cent rule; (2) the EEC might open tariff quotas to OEEC countries in case of hardship; (3) negotiations could be opened at the level of the OEEC for a reduction of customs duties on products figuring particularly in intra-European trade; and (4) tariff differences should be reduced in the course of the forthcoming Dillon negotiations in GATT.[35]

It is clear that the Commission was basically opposed to a wider European association on the lines of a free trade area. But because of the considerable support for such an arrangement within the Six it would have been unacceptable to all but the French had the Commission written off the idea. Hence, the First Memorandum made a point of including general statements in support of the OEEC and the desirability of participation in a larger Europe. The continuous thread in the Commission's thinking on this matter was the conviction that the creation of a free trade area at this time would have imperiled the existence of the Community. To merge, or "dissolve," the Community into a larger organization when its common external tariff was not yet in force and its commercial policy not yet made in common, would yield too much to centrifugal forces. The Commission's attitude concerning the possibility of solving the problems raised by a free trade area had hardened perceptibly since the publication of its First General Report, an indication that fears of "dissolution" had not been assuaged.[36] In the eyes of the Commission a free trade area was acceptable only under certain conditions: (1) the free play of competition must not be hindered by restrictive practices, state aids, etc.; (2) there must be provisions for the free movement of workers, for the liberalization of services, and for increased trade in agricultural products; (3) there must be adequate coordination of policy relating to economic trends; (4) there must be a concerted and active development policy; and (5) there must be no appreciable distortion in competitive conditions as a result of diversities in the external tariffs and trade policies of the Member States.

The memorandum claimed further that the problems posed by different external tariffs could not be solved either by systems of definition and verification of origin of products or by systems of compensatory taxes.[37] The conclusions drawn from this are interesting:

If a very strict system of control of origin is rejected, there remain in point of fact only two entirely satisfactory systems of multilateral trade without customs duties or quotas: *the customs union* (or more exactly, the economic union) which secures for all participants the same conditions of supply, and *world free trade*, which ensures this same equality. Any intermediary system is necessarily imperfect. This means that a free trade area is acceptable only to the extent that it is fitted into a setting of increasing liberalization of world trade and abandons any idea of strengthening European economic solidarity in the strict sense of the word, or approximates to the type of the customs union.[38]

As early as mid-January the Commission had revealed the principles that were guiding its work. In a speech to the European Parliamentary Assembly on January 13, 1959, President Hallstein vigorously rejected the accusations of protectionism and *dirigisme* leveled at the Community. He similarly refuted the widespread argument that all the difficulties resulted from French intransigence (if not bad faith). It was the other eleven members of the OEEC who were creating a real discrimination when they asked to benefit from the advantages of the Community without making any of the sacrifices. It was not the Community that had fixed membership at Six, but the other nonmembers. How could the Six cause a split in Europe when it was the Common Market that was erasing thousands of kilometers of frontier from the map? In reference to the free trade area, Hallstein described it as a pure abstraction, incapable of realization. Complete customs and quota dismantling could not be achieved unless accompanied by jointly imposed discipline in all other spheres of economic and social life. This had been confirmed during the negotiations on the Rome Treaty.[39]

Commissioner Rey, in the same forum, spoke of the proposals the Commission was then preparing, and announced that the solutions offered would set the problem in its proper world context, rather than in a purely European one. He suggested that the Maudling Committee had had too restricted a view of its task in imagining that the only question to be settled was the relationship of the Community to the OEEC countries. "We shall propose to the Governments and to our partners a framework which does of course *leave a place* for European policy, but in a larger context, on a scale befitting our responsibilities.[40]

Essentially what the Commission sought to do in its First Memorandum was to demonstrate that the free trade area was a cul-de-sac. It was not possible, however, to suggest where to go from here, given the widely divergent views among the Six. Therefore the Commission's proposals were limited to trying to change the terms within which the conflict was being waged.

The Commission finds that the great ideological battle on discrimination has assumed a quasi-theological character, with each party clinging to its views for such fundamental reasons that it has become almost impervious to the arguments of the other.

Consequently the Commission considers that in present circumstances it would be wise to seek some terrain other than that of doctrinal quarrels. In a perhaps less ambitious but more pragmatic manner, a practical compromise must be found which will allow the two parties to live together.[41]

It was acknowledged freely that this First Memorandum amounted only to a preliminary reply to the Ministers and that the opinions expressed would have to be studied more thoroughly. The Commission asked to be given the opportunity to continue its work "in close contact with Government representatives."

In the course of these exchanges of views it would doubtless be possible to work out in detail the common position of the Member States of the Community on the basis of the various suggestions contained in this Report, both in the matter of long-term solutions and in that of the measures to be undertaken immediately.[42]

REACTIONS TO THE FIRST MEMORANDUM

The Commission could hardly have been surprised that its memorandum was not given a very friendly reception by the Community governments. The positions of Germany and Benelux were well known. Commission members had toured all the capitals in January to exchange views, and had also visited London in February.[43] The general reaction of all who favored a wider agreement was highly critical, the Commission being reproached for having failed to carry out its mandate as stated in the Council resolution. Only the French government supported the Commission's memorandum. In fact, Maurice Couve de Murville, the Foreign Minister, proposed entrusting the Commission with making contact with the governments of the other OEEC countries on the basis of the contents of its report and then reporting back to the Council. The other governments all emphasized that a European solution must be found for tariff reductions, and that in order not to violate GATT rules this required entering into a formal commitment to bring about a multilateral association. This suggestion was of course contrary to the Commission's idea of putting off an automatic mechanism for tariff reductions between the OEEC countries for three or four years.[44]

Erhard, the German Minister of Economic Affairs, was the most critical of all. He stated that since the Commission had not carried out its mandate, it would be necessary to start the work over again, with the memorandum serving merely as a starting point. He made it clear that he still considered a free trade area could be achieved if the will to do so existed.

The Italians expressed their approval of the world view taken by the Commission, especially in the light of the "unjustified attacks" that had been made against the Community. Nevertheless, Foreign Minister Pella felt that the proposals did not take adequate account of "political considerations." He made several specific suggestions, which amounted in effect to taking up where the Maudling Committee talks had broken off. The Italians still felt that the Carli Plan of compensatory taxes could be the basis of an agreement on a customs union among the OEEC countries.* As an

---

* Italy also proposed the coordination of commercial and agricultural policies, the harmonization of social and fiscal legislation, and the freeing of manpower movements.

alternative, should this prove impracticable, they suggested a customs union limited to the most important goods in intra-European trade.[45]

The Belgian Minister of Foreign Trade, van Offelen, speaking for Benelux, also thought that tariff harmonization should be part of any plan. He accepted the Commission's proposal for quota extensions, but wanted to include small or null quotas, too (the 3 per cent rule). He proposed that a comparative study be undertaken of the customs tariffs of the various countries, as well as of the common external tariff of the Community, to determine the differences and discover for which products there were the biggest discrepancies. This suggestion would put off a solution for a year or so, and thus make it possible to get away from theoretical discussions and to approach the problem concretely.[46]

The Council was unable to reach a decision on the Commission's memorandum and instead of accepting it simply "took note" of it, at the same time reaffirming its desire to achieve a multilateral association between the OEEC and the EEC.

The Council takes note of the memorandum submitted by the Commission of the European Economic Community in implementation of the instructions given by the Council to the Commission at the session of 3 December 1958, and in particular of the proposals contained in that memorandum;

thanks the Commission for the work accomplished in studying the problems raised by the creation of a European Economic Association;

reaffirms its determination to pursue the efforts for the creation of a multilateral association between the EEC and the other countries of the OEEC and desires that the conditions necessary for its realization may be established at an early date;

is anxious in this spirit henceforward to strengthen the solidarity existing between the countries of the OEEC and thus to prepare the foundations for a closer association;

requests the Governments Members of the EEC to inform the Commission before 15 April 1959 of their comments on the memorandum and of their proposals;

instructs a special committee composed of representatives of the Governments of the Member States and of members of the Commission—one of the latter to be chairman—to study these comments and proposals and to report to the Council.[47]

Thus was created a new body—a special committee consisting of representatives of the governments and of members of the Commission—appointed by the Council and instructed to study the Commission's memorandum and any comments or suggestions that the governments made on it (these were to be submitted before April 15, 1959). The chairmanship of the committee was entrusted to the Commission, and it became known as the Rey Committee (after Commissioner Rey, who was President of the

External Relations Group). It was the first of several mixed committees set up between the Commission and the governments to handle special problems. There is no provision in the Treaty for such committees—in fact, as we have seen, many have felt that it was contrary to the spirit of the Treaty, since it seemed to violate the Commission's independence. We have argued, however, that it represents an institutionalization of the close collaboration between the government representatives and the Commission, a collaboration that has characterized the EEC institutional system. The Rey Committee took over the task of preparing a common position for the Community with regard to a wider European arrangement; its terms of reference were later extended to all questions of trade policy.

The Rey Committee met for the first time on April 30, 1959, and subsequently in May, June, and July.* Its deliberations revealed that the Member States were even further apart than before. The differences among the Six were no longer about the type of free trade association or the timing of it, but rather about whether or not a large tariff-free area of all the OEEC countries was desirable at all. The French and some of the Commissioners felt that the free convertibility of currencies, as well as the extent of economic recovery since the war, obviated the need for a "Europe of the Seventeen."[48] The German and Benelux governments, on the other hand, were extremely critical of the failure to provide for any automatic mechanism for the reduction of tariffs at the European level. In April, the Benelux governments submitted a proposal calling for a formal commitment by the Six and the other OEEC countries to the establishment of a "free market." Under the terms of the proposal, it would not be necessary to settle the form this free market might take, whether free trade area or some kind of customs union along the lines of Italian suggestions. All discussions of principle would be abandoned and the tariffs of the Eleven (the other OEEC countries) compared systematically with the common external tariff. In the meantime, the Six would extend to all European countries the same tariff reductions as they applied among themselves.

Reactions to this proposal were varied. The French refused to accept any commitment until all features of the agreement were known.[49] The Germans were in favor of a commitment to "come down to zero" with respect to customs duties and quotas within the European framework.[50] Italy had in effect committed herself to such an adjustment, on condition that

* The Committee was made up of Rey (Chairman); Marjolin, Petrilli, and von der Groeben (Commission); Müller-Armack (Germany); Baron Snoy et d'Oppuers (Belgium); Wormser (France); Cattani (Italy); Borschette (Luxembourg); and van der Beugel (Netherlands). Cattani and Borschette were also their countries' Permanent Representatives to the Community. EEC Commission, *Bulletin*, No. 2 (1959), p. 22.

the third countries agreed to give up free administration of their external tariffs. France, however, was unwilling to accept the total disappearance of customs protection on trade toward the OEEC as a whole under any condition at all.[51]

By the time the Rey Committee reconvened in September the Commission had decided to take a new initiative.

Despite the redoubling of efforts since the First Memorandum of the Commission was submitted and work was begun by the Special Committee, . . . it has so far proved impossible to reach unanimity within the Community on the way in which these problems are to be solved. The resulting situation is unsatisfactory, if only on the psychological plane.

The failure to define the future relations between the EEC and its European neighbors is producing a sense of uncertainty in industrial and commercial circles. . . . Disquiet has been increased by public controversy, and the result has been disharmony, not to say tension, in the relations between the Community and its commercial partners in Europe, and even within the Community itself. . . .

For these reasons the Commission wishes to recommend a pragmatic and gradual way out of the present impasse. Rather than bow to the alternative of "all or nothing," the Commission considers that an attempt should be made to reach agreement among the six governments on a programme which, though not meeting all the wishes of each of them, does not require any one of them to sacrifice basic positions which they are not prepared—at the moment—to abandon.[52]

In the Second Memorandum there is no endorsement whatsoever of a wider European arrangement. In fact, the memorandum stresses that recent experience has confirmed the Commission's conviction that a solution is to be found only in the context of the progressive economic policy the Community intends to pursue toward the world at large. Three levels of action were contemplated:[53]

1. *Measures to narrow the differences between the tariff and quota arrangements operating on trade within the Community and with other countries.* These included an offer to extend to the other OEEC members, and to all GATT members, the next 20 per cent increases in quotas, as well as a declaration that the Community proposed eventually to abolish *all* quotas on industrial goods. Null and small quotas could also be included. With regard to tariffs, the Commission proposed a reaffirmation of the liberal intentions of the Community and its willingness to take part in GATT tariff negotiations. Proof of this was to be provided by a statement declaring the Community's readiness to offer still further substantial reductions, condi-

tional upon reciprocity. Finally, the Community would extend to third countries those tariff reductions to be made in July 1960, subject to the condition that the resulting rates did not fall below the level of the common external tariff.

2. *Measures to deal with particular European problems.* The creation of a "contact committee" was proposed. Such a committee, to consist of spokesmen of the Community and of other European states, would examine trade flows, determine where difficulties were likely to appear, and suggest remedies. The Community should also declare its willingness to open tariff quotas.

3. *Measures to strengthen economic cooperation between the Community, the United Kingdom, and the United States.* The Commission suggested that regular consultations be held with the United States and the United Kingdom concerning aid to underdeveloped countries and a concerted policy on economic trends.

These specific proposals have been noted in some detail because they show that although the Commission's position on a European settlement had hardened, a considerable effort had been made to take into consideration the demands of those Member States conducting a significant trade with the OEEC countries. The Commission was at pains to map out a liberal trade policy and to combine this with proposals for strengthening the Community and for speeding up its realization. In explaining its proposals to the EPA in late September, Hallstein argued that the Commission was not in principle opposed to a wider European association, but that under present conditions definitive proposals would be of no significance because the governments were not in agreement.[54] Rey, answering to the debate, listed several new factors that the Commission had had to take into consideration: the creation of the European Free Trade Association, the new balance of payments position of the United States, the fact that theoretical discussions between the Six had not yielded positive results, and the increased importance of relations with underdeveloped countries. Given these new factors, the Commission had the *duty* to take the initiative because the Community could no longer afford the luxury of being without a definite trade policy.[55]

Fundamental to the Commission's position was the decision taken in the second half of 1959 to give first priority to making the Community irreversible, a process that would be hindered if wider negotiations were to take place.[56]

Hardly less important was the great stress placed by the Commission on the need to avoid intensifying the U.S. balance of payments problem by creating an even larger preferential trading area in Europe. As Mrs. Camps points out, however, this concern was not motivated solely by an appreciation of American willingness in the past to accept discrimination, or by a recognition that protectionist forces in the U.S. would increase if American goods were discriminated against; it also seems probable "that one element in the Commission's concern for the U.S. balance of payments position was the judgment that by playing on this theme it might gain U.S. support in withstanding pressure for an early resumption of negotiations for a Europe-wide arrangement."[57]

REACTIONS TO THE SECOND MEMORANDUM

The debates in the EPA and the Rey Committee highlight the compromise character of the Commission's proposals. The proposals were criticized by the Germans and Benelux for being too timid and by the French for going too far. The Dutch were the most critical, claiming that the Second Memorandum did not pave the way for a multilateral association of the OEEC countries, for it did not eliminate the differences between the Six and these countries.[58] The Dutch also wanted to be free to extend all tariff reductions to other countries, rather than merely those that resulted in tariffs at or above the level of the common external tariff.[59] On the other hand, the French objected that the Commission was giving away all the advantages of the Rome Treaty in order to avoid the charge of protectionism. By committing themselves to such measures as harmonization, which was awkward and derogated their sovereignty, the partners of the Community had sacrificed much in order to create a free market; why should they offer the same advantages to third countries without asking anything from them?[60] If third countries were granted these same advantages, it would be difficult to expect Member States to observe the rules and limitations of the Rome Treaty, which they accepted as the counterpart of tariff and quota disarmament.[61]

Nevertheless, at its session of October 19, the Rey Committee decided to take the Second Memorandum as the *basis* of its report to the Council of Ministers. The Council would be presented with formal proposals based upon the memorandum and upon the government's comments on it. There was no identity of views in the Committee, but everybody had apparently come to recognize that the choice was not between limited, practical steps and the setting up of a wider association, but between such measures and *immobilisme*.[62]

Still greater pressures for adopting the Commission's approach came as the result of the growing support within the Community for accelerating the introduction of the Common Market.[63] These ideas had been developing during the summer, and the Commission picked them up in its Second Memorandum; its comment was similar to the statement it had made in 1958:

The strengthening of the Community is not only an internal objective for the [Community], but the very condition of its ability to carry out a liberal policy towards the outside world.

The Community would therefore state that it is in this spirit and with this object in view that it is taking measures to speed up its integration, to shorten the working out of the common commercial policy and the strengthening of its monetary solidarity.[64]

The Belgian Foreign Minister, Pierre Wigny, had circulated recommendations for acceleration in September, and these were presented to the Council of Ministers in October. The idea was accepted in principle, and the Commission was instructed to submit specific proposals, which it did at the end of February 1960.[65] Although the Wigny Plan made it quite clear that the strengthening of the Community and the shortening of the transitional period should go hand in hand with progress toward setting up a Europe-wide area of free trade, the introduction of this issue reinforced not only the position of the Commission but also the general proposition that pride of place should be given to consolidating the EEC.

The French tried to take advantage of this development at the November session of the Rey Committee. The purpose of the session was to agree on the final form of the report to be presented to the Council. The French accepted the Benelux proposals for accelerating the Common Market, but suggested combining this with a requirement that the first step be taken in bringing the common external tariff into operation. They argued that the extension of the first 10 per cent tariff reductions to third countries in December 1958 had in effect been a speeding up of the approximation to the level of the common external tariff. If the extension were repeated this year, as the Commission proposed, it would create a serious disequilibrium in the process of instituting the common external tariff because only the high-tariff countries would continue to make approximations. The French delegate was in favor of making larger reductions on July 1, 1960, than foreseen in the Treaty, but at the same time low-tariff countries should increase their tariffs toward third countries and thus also begin to align themselves with the common external tariff. The proposal thus had a definite "Community aspect," but certainly did not help the Committee in its task of finding ways to ease the fears of third countries. It would, on the contrary, have the opposite result of increasing the differentiation between the EEC system and that applied to the rest of the world.[66]

Partly because of these new proposals, the Rey Committee could come to no agreement on tariff questions. The following conclusions, however, were reached: (1) that it was impossible to propose final solutions because there was no unanimity among the Six and because the time did not "seem ripe" for new negotiations; (2) that under these circumstances the Six should make a new "gesture" to avoid too big a difference between the EEC and other countries by extending, within limits, the benefits of the next customs reductions and quota enlargements that they were to make among themselves; and (3) that since tariff reductions could not be limited to the OEEC but must be extended to GATT, a "contact committee" should be set up to keep in mind the question of European solidarity.[67]

Of considerable impact, also, had been the official endorsement by the U.S. Under-Secretary of State, C. Douglas Dillon, of the Commission's Second Memorandum. This was interpreted as indicating U.S. support for the thesis that the European trading problem should be resolved on a global, rather than a regional, basis.[68]

On November 23, 1959, the Council met to consider the report of the Rey Committee, which was, as we have seen, based upon the Second Memorandum of the Commission. With regard to tariffs, where agreement had been impossible, the report did no more than present the four alternative proposals, namely, those made by the Commission, Benelux, the Netherlands, and France. The Rey Committee in fact *prepared* the meeting of the Council, thus performing the function usually carried out by the Permanent Representatives. Actual intergovernmental negotiating was carried on, positions taken, commitments accepted, and points settled. Only those questions that had eluded solution were taken up by the Council in any detail. This is especially interesting when we recall that the Commission had provided not only the chairmanship and secretariat of this committee, but also the only real initiatives with any chance of acceptance.

As might have been expected, the Dutch Foreign Minister, Luns, took the strongest stand in the Council debate. He remarked that the Commission's memoranda and the work of the Rey Committee had fallen far short of Dutch hopes, that there had been no real discussion of how to achieve a wider European agreement, and that the constructive proposals of "some countries" in this area had not been taken sufficiently into account. The technical problems could be overcome (as they had been in drafting the Rome Treaty) if only the will to do so existed. He rejected the arguments of the Commission and the French that the Common Market would be in danger of dissolution in a free trade area, and that such an association would be contrary to the interests of the United States. He proposed that the EEC should offer to extend to all GATT countries the tariff reductions the Six were to apply on July 1, 1960 (the EFTA should do the same), and that the EEC should make a 20 per cent reduction in its common external tariff. Reciprocal reductions would be "hoped for" from the non-European members of GATT. Finally, he wanted to extend quota enlargements on agricultural products and to enter into negotiations on agricultural tariffs.

The Commission had proposed extending the tariff cuts, but had specified that the ensuing reductions should not result in tariffs inferior to those in the common external tariff. The Benelux position, presented by Wigny, was not so far-reaching as that of Luns and merely called for a commitment to take up talks with the EFTA with a view to mutual tariff reductions. Couve de Murville, in presenting the French proposals for accelerating the approximation of both high- and low-tariff countries to the common external tariff, stressed the liberal intentions of the French (and the Community) toward third countries, but argued that this did not mean one should make concessions without getting something in return; and here the French government favored a decision only on the quota provisions, leaving all mention of tariffs, a contact committee, underdeveloped countries, GATT, etc., for further discussion.

In the ensuing debate, the Commission's proposals were given strong support by the Italian delegate, Cattani, who felt that the other alternatives were all open to question and should be studied further. Similarly, the German State Secretary, Müller-Armack, thought the Commission's proposal was the best compromise for the moment. Germany, however, remained attached to the idea of a wider association, albeit for the future. The French proposals were welcomed, as were the Dutch. Müller-Armack felt that a compromise between these two approaches—i.e., an acceleration toward the common external tariff, but reduced by 20 per cent—would be acceptable to the low-tariff countries, and pledged Germany to present proposals on the subject. Wigny indicated that Belgium would be willing to accept much of the French proposals, even though this would involve a considerable sacrifice. Furthermore, he accepted the proposition that the Community could be more liberal if its internal development were accelerated, although he did favor some special gestures toward the other OEEC countries.

Thus neither the French nor the Dutch were in favor of the position of the Commission. In the course of the debate, however, both gave in to the arguments of the German and Italian delegates. As a result, the Commission's original tariff offer was accepted, although at French insistence it was reworded in the conditional tense; i.e., the Member States *may* extend the tariff reductions, etc. It was also agreed that any reductions made could not bring tariffs below the level of the common external tariff. The proposals of the Netherlands, Benelux, and France were to be studied further by the Rey Committee, whose mandate was thus extended. On quotas the Council went further than the Commission and extended quota enlargements to all GATT members without need for reciprocity. Otherwise the proposals made in the Second Memorandum were retained as the policy of the Community. As Pella, President of the Council, said to the EPA, "The Council is convinced that these measures take into consideration the inter-

ests of the various Member States of the Community and that they constitute the best solution that could be found under present circumstances."[69]

These compromise measures were apparently as much as could be done
for the time being. As Mrs. Camps comments:

There were many pressures within the Six working in the same direction [in
favor of a wider European trade area]: most of German industry, the German
Ministry of Economic Affairs (but not the Foreign Ministry), the Dutch Government, and quite a number of the parliamentarians and civil servants in all
of the Six countries, save France. But these forces within the Community were
not strong enough to overcome the continued resistance of the French Government and industry, and of the Commission, M. Monnet and those other "Europeans" in positions of importance in all the six countries—of whom Dr. Adenauer was the most important—who were convinced that, for the present, an
over-riding priority should be given to the development of the Community.[70]

The strategy of postponing European multilateral trade negotiations
was assured of success in December 1959, when the United States became
decisively involved. At American initiative a Special Economic Conference of representatives from the Six, the Seven, the other OEEC countries,
the United States, and Canada was called. Among the reasons for the U.S.
decision to take a more active role in the European trade conflict was the
fear that a political deterioration would result from the animosity between
the two European economic groups, a situation that would inevitably
weaken NATO. It was clear, however, that the United States was not disposed to support the Seven and to urge a renewal of Europe-wide negotiations. On the contrary, the U.S. had always strongly supported the consolidation of the integration of the Six—ECSC, Euratom, EEC—and was therefore sympathetic to the argument of the "Europeans" that nothing should
be allowed to interfere with this. The awareness of the fact that both European trading groups were discriminatory against American trade increased
as the U.S. balance of payments position deteriorated further in the second
half of 1959. The EFTA had no political overtones to offset its economic
disadvantages and was therefore rather coolly received. Added to these
purely European considerations was the growing interest in making a new
attempt to strengthen economic cooperation among the countries of the
entire Atlantic area, especially in regard to coordinating aid to underdeveloped areas. This was affirmed by Dillon, U.S. Under-Secretary of State,
when he opened the conference. Still, the main purpose to be served was
to engage both the Six and the Seven in a new joint enterprise, hoping thereby to sidetrack the idea of a larger European free trade area.[71]

In this respect, U.S. goals were practically identical with those of the

Commission and of other "Europeans." In fact the decision to call the conference was taken after an extended series of visits by Dillon to the several European capitals and to the Commission (not to mention discussions with Jean Monnet). The conference met in Paris on January 12 and 13, 1960.* Decisions were taken on three proposals introduced by the United States. It was decided to appoint a working group of four "wise men" to study how the OEEC could be reorganized so as to allow the United States and Canada to join, and so as to broaden the scope of its activities accordingly. A working group was set up to study the problem of aid to underdeveloped areas—the Development Assistance Group—representing Belgium, Canada, the United States, France, Italy, Portugal, Germany, the United Kingdom, and the Commission. Japan was subsequently invited to join. With respect to trade problems, the following statement was made:

Considering the need to examine, as a matter of priority, the relationship between the EEC and the EFTA, with due regard to the commercial interests of third countries and the principles and obligations of the GATT; [the Conference] decides to propose to the twenty Governments that they constitute themselves, together with the EEC, a committee with power to: (1) establish one or more informal working groups for the consideration of these problems without infringing the competence of the existing international institutions such as the GATT or the OEEC; . . . .[72]

It is striking to note the continuity between the U.S. proposals at the Paris Conference (and the decisions taken) and the general suggestions contained in the two Commission memoranda. In the Paris discussions, too, there was "an apparent identity of interest between the Six and the U.S., and a disposition on the part of the Six to sit back and let Mr. Dillon argue their case. . . . It was clear that neither the Six nor the U.S. shared the sense of urgency of the Seven with respect to the trade problem and that the U.S., in particular, wanted time to explore informally the kind of interim accommodation that might be made between the two groups."[73]

It should be pointed out that the Committee on Trade Problems, or the Committee of Twenty-One as it came to be called,† did not resemble the Maudling Committee. Its mandate was vague, but it is clear that it was not to occupy itself solely or principally with finding a *rapprochement* between all the OEEC members. Its membership also included the United States, Canada, and the Commission, and special provision was made for the par-

* It was, in point of fact, one of three interrelated meetings: the Special Economic Conference met on January 12 and 13, and reported to the Conference of Twenty-One, representing all the OEEC countries, the United States, Canada, and the Commission. On January 15, the same 21 delegates met as the OEEC Council.

† Uniformly on the Continent, but in the United Kingdom one saw references to the Committee of Twenty, an obvious reluctance to accept the full and equal participation of the Commission.

ticipation of a GATT representative. The Committee held its first meeting at the end of March 1960, the chief purpose of which was to have been agreement on tariff actions to be taken by the Six and Seven on July 1, 1960. However, the Commission had presented its definitive proposals for the acceleration of the Common Market on March 10, and nobody was prepared to negotiate until acceleration was decided upon. The strategy of the EEC was, in the words of Commissioner Rey, "to keep silent in a harmonized manner."[74] This "harmonization" was carried on in the Rey Committee, whose mandate had been expanded by the Council of Ministers to cover all the questions of trade policy discussed at the meetings of the Committee of Twenty-One, and which was thus charged with preparing the EEC positions for each meeting.[75]

THE ACCELERATION DECISION
AND RELATIONS WITH THIRD COUNTRIES

The acceleration sequence is examined in detail in Chapter 9, and we shall restrict ourselves here to those aspects of special relevance to the problem at hand. The proposals of the Commission were designed to grant some portion of the demands of each of the Six, while at the same time appealing to the United States and holding the door open to an interim agreement with the EFTA. They incorporated major portions of the proposals made by France and the Netherlands in November 1959, in that accelerated steps were taken on quota and tariff disarmament among the Six, including a first step in the approximation of national tariffs, both low and high, to the common external tariff, but to a common external tariff reduced by 20 per cent.

There was much opposition to these proposals within the Six, especially from Germany and the Netherlands, based essentially on the fact that not only would prices go up as a result of higher tariffs, but the gap between the Six and the Seven would be irremediably widened. There was also considerable opposition from members of the EPA. The force of these internal dissents was muffled, however, by the violent reaction of the United Kingdom and the other members of the EFTA, who hinted that the Six were making an "unfriendly move" and exercised what pressure they could to defeat the acceleration proposal or at least to have it postponed. Prime Minister Macmillan's remarks made in Washington, D.C., in late March*

---

* According to a report published in the *Washington Post*, Macmillan emphasized the dangers arising from the economic split in Europe. Should the split continue, Britain would have no choice but to lead another peripheral coalition as it had done in Napoleon's day. Britain might also have to impose dollar import restrictions and withdraw British troops from Germany.[76]

fully confirmed the fears of those who had always mistrusted British motives regarding the free trade area and made acceleration practically a certainty. The Council of Ministers met on May 10–12, 1960, and adopted a decision on acceleration that accepted the major part of the Commission's proposals.[77]

The decisions are in direct line with those taken in November 1959, in that they emphasize the Community's thesis that the stronger the Community is, the more liberal its external policies can be. The Council decision, as regards third countries, reaffirmed the Community's intention to eliminate all quotas on imports of industrial goods as soon as possible, reciprocity not being required. The Six agreed to make their first approximations to the common external tariff a year ahead of schedule, but the level of rates in the common external tariff was to be lowered by 20 per cent.[78] Member States of the EEC were also free to extend to third countries, subject to reciprocity, any reductions that would not bring the level below that of the common external tariff. The 20 per cent cut in the common external tariff was provisional, however, and would be consolidated only if adequate reciprocity were received. Negotiations on the consolidation of the 20 per cent cut were to be carried on in the general GATT negotiations due to begin in 1961.

During the debates, Erhard and Luns had argued that the time before the application of the acceleration measures should be spent seeking a *modus vivendi* with the Seven on tariffs. They proposed that direct talks at the ministerial level be undertaken at once (these would have excluded the Commission). Whereas Erhard did not stipulate that acceleration should be dependent upon the successful outcome of such negotiations, the Dutch proposal did imply this.[79] The other governments were unwilling to accept either of these positions, however. Even Wigny thought this would be a poor negotiating tactic, since the British had not shown themselves prepared to depart from their game of "wait and see." The compromise formula finally adopted was to invite the EFTA to discuss mutual commercial problems in the framework of the existing Committee on Trade Problems (the Committee of Twenty-One). The decision was officially communicated to the EFTA by the President of the Council, who declared that it was the intention of the EEC "to see the commercial problems arising from the existence of the European Economic Community and the EFTA settled in a spirit of friendly cooperation and by liberal practices on both sides. . . . the natural setting for these negotiations would be the Committee on Trade Problems."[80] This offer was accepted by the EFTA. As Mrs. Camp observes, "Rather optimistically, they deliberately interpreted the "declaration of intent" in the broadest possible way and read into it a willingness to negotiate on the longer term problem that corresponded more closely with the desire of some of the Six than it did with their agreed position."[81]

By the time the Committee of Twenty-One reconvened on June 9 and 10, it was evident that the Six were not ready to talk about long-term measures, and that there was little disagreement among them on the general positions to take during the session. In prior meetings of the Rey Committee, the Six had agreed on several specific proposals,[82] the bulk of which were accepted by the Committee of Twenty-One. It was agreed to establish a study group, which would be open to all members of the full committee and which would be given the following tasks:

(a) to examine the ways in which reciprocal tariff concessions could be achieved. . . .

(b) to analyse the data collected by the Secretary of the Committee on Trade Problems . . . with a view to defining those products of the various Member countries in respect of which particular trade difficulties might arise, and seeking appropriate solutions in accordance with the rules of GATT. . . .

(c) . . . to continue to watch the development of currents of trade and to endeavor to find appropriate ways and means for the removal, in accordance with the rules of GATT, of particular difficulties which might be encountered.[83]

Note that the Study Group is in effect the Contact Committee as proposed by the Commission in its Second Memorandum.[84]

CONCLUSIONS

In terms of political integration as we have defined it, the most interesting aspect of these negotiations is the striking role the Commission succeeded in playing. Little more than a year after the publication of the Commission's First Memorandum, all the members of the EEC had come to accept the proposals sketched out therein and later expanded in the Second Memorandum. This confirms our expectation that the ability of any of the Six to make policy autonomously will be substantially limited, at least when some of the basic gains expected from the undertaking are threatened. The Maudling Committee negotiations had revealed that the Six were unable to achieve a solution to the problem of a free trade area by which all could abide, but, at the same time, that they were unwilling to negotiate without one. The only way out of this difficulty was to give the task of elaborating a solution to the organization that represented the interests of the Community as a whole, namely, the Commission. Once this was done, the dynamics of the situation were such that the Commission's proposals were hard to turn down. Community loyalties were severely strained, particularly in the Netherlands and Germany, but very few groups or individuals were really willing to risk the integrity of the EEC, and when the chips were down, all parties compromised their initial positions.

The Commission's success was due primarily to its ability to emphasize the interests of the Community as a whole and to convince "waverers" that the very integrity of the Community was at stake. In Germany and the Benelux countries, those who favored reaching some kind of agreement with the British were forced to re-evaluate the short-run gains they expected from a free trade area against the possibility of losing the more important objectives of a far-reaching integration.

The Commission certainly did not limit itself to making proposals that the governments wanted to hear. We have traced the steps by which it gained the initiative in the free trade area affair, making a series of proposals based on its own definition of the situation. And we have seen how it went about building up an *ad hoc* coalition in support of these proposals, a coalition that comprised, on the one hand, the "Europeans," whose major preoccupation was with the political unity of the Six, and, on the other, the French. The French and the Commission, although for different reasons, saw eye to eye on the main end to be achieved: namely, the establishment of the Community as an economic and political entity. Theirs was a marriage of convenience. The French, who are generally opposed to any proposals tending to enlarge the scope of the Commission's activities or to increase its authority, were in this case obliged to do just that in order to achieve their goal—the final rejection of the whole idea of a free trade area.

The Commission had already decided in 1958 that the free trade area posed a potential threat to the fragile unity of the EEC. Its main goals in the free trade area negotiations were to "take the sting out of attacks, to grasp the initiative in creating conditions for cooperation with non-member states in a spirit of mutual confidence, in other words to practice a dynamic external policy, to establish its liberal character and to make its content increasingly clear, and so to make the personality of the Community stand out against a world setting."[85] The Commission restated these aims in its two memoranda, declaring that it sought to *"change the very climate* of the discussions by concentrating on the study of concrete problems rather than on discussions of theory . . . [and] *to adapt the external policy of the Community to the new realities* of the world economy, particularly to the changing commercial and financial relations between Europe and America."[86]

By mid-1960 the Commission had achieved all of these goals. The idea of a free trade area had been set aside, probably for good. The Community had been strengthened and was committed to an increasingly liberal economic policy. The Commission's own role was ensured by its continued chairmanship of the Rey Committee and by the expanded mandate given to that committee. The Commission had been among the first to suggest the importance of a new economic relationship between the United States and Europe, setting in motion a series of events culminating in the establishment of the new OECD. Ultimately, even the Commission's solution for the Six-Seven problem was accepted (the idea of a "contact committee") with the establishment of the special Study Group of the Committee of Twenty-One.

What was the over-all effect of the free trade area issue on the Community? Miriam Camps writes that it was an unfortunate first issue, that it was divisive because it accentuated national differences, and that it hindered the development of Community policies.[87] But our analysis has demonstrated that the role of the central institutions and of central policies was increased. Furthermore, the Six took major steps to accelerate the implementation of the Treaty, as well as to coordinate their economic and political policies. Conflict in this case seems to have strengthened rather than weakened the original bonds of unity.[88] The ultimate solution achieved belongs to the category of "upgrading common interests" because it forcefully demonstrated to the Six the extent of their growing interdependence. This is the essence of spill-over. The ability of any of the Six to achieve major policy goals is dependent upon the attainment by the others of their policy goals. In such a situation the role of the central institutions in helping to define the terms of the final agreement is crucial.

ACCELERATION

On May 12, 1960, the Council of Ministers, acting as an intergovernmental conference of the Member States, agreed to implement the Treaty of Rome more rapidly than called for in the timetable, thus accelerating progress toward a Common Market. The Commission described this decision as "the *fundamental political and economic fact* in the history of the Common Market since the signing of the Treaty of Rome. The speed-up decision indeed showed that progress over the last two years has been such that a timetable which was considered reasonable in 1957 appears out-dated in 1960."[1] The broad lines of the acceleration can be seen in the chart on the next page.

The proposal to move toward a Common Market gradually, in three stages of four years each, with all kinds of escape clauses, safeguards, and contingency provisions that could extend the transition period to fifteen years, was advanced in the Treaty negotiations by the French government, supported by the Italians, and the idea was readily accepted by the others. Both France and Italy have long-standing protectionist traditions and were anxious to provide for maximum protection for their internal economies so as to cushion the shock of adjustment to the Common Market.[2] Even so, there were loud outcries from French industry that twelve to fifteen years was not long enough, that more time would be needed to prepare to meet German competition.[3] Many of the writers who were commenting on the Treaty in 1957 and 1958 were quite pessimistic about achieving the goals set down, and all emphasized the scope of the escape clauses available to governments that wished to avoid their specific obligations. Yet less than eighteen months after the Treaty came into force, pressures began to be

SUMMARY OF THE ACCELERATION DECISION

	Original treaty	Acceleration decision
Cuts in tariffs:	Dec. 31, 1958...........10%	Dec. 31, 1958.......10%
	July 1, 1960...........10%	July 1, 1960.......10%
	Dec. 31, 1961...........10%	Dec. 31, 1960.......10–20%[a]
	End 1st stage...........30%	End 1st stage.......40–50%[a]
Quotas:	Ordinary quotas to be enlarged at rate of 20% per year. Small or nil quotas to achieve 20% of national production by end of transition period.	All quotas on industrial goods to be abolished by Dec. 31, 1961.
Intro-duction of common ex-ternal tariff:	First approximation on Dec. 31, 1961.	First approximation on Dec. 31, 1960.
		Common external tariff level provisionally reduced by 20%.

[a] The Member States were to decide by June 30, 1961, whether these reductions were to be 10 per cent or 20 per cent, and 40 per cent or 50 per cent, respectively. But owing to the difficulties over agriculture, agreement was not reached until May 1962, and it was not until July 1, 1962, that the total tariff reduction of 50 per cent was put into force.

exerted to shorten this painfully negotiated timetable. These pressures culminated in the decision of May 12, 1960.

Let us try to analyze this decision, to account for these pressures, and to assess their significance for political integration. What positive expectations would be served by an acceleration of the Common Market? How were these often competing expectations translated into a positive decision? What functions did the several Community institutions perform in the sequence?

THE ORIGINS OF THE IDEA

The decision to accelerate the Common Market timetable came as part of the general quickening of tempo of EEC activities that became evident in the second half of 1959. This was not limited to matters requiring action under the Treaty, such as List G or the common agricultural policy, but involved an extension of consultation and cooperation to financial and monetary policy and to foreign affairs. Regular quarterly meetings of the finance ministers of the Six began in July 1959, and the foreign ministers held their first political consultation in November 1959.[4]

As the Commission pointed out in its formal proposals on acceleration:

The introduction of the common market is due to take place by progressive steps fixed in the light of the situation existing at the time the Treaty was signed. This gradual process was based on a given initial situation in the fields of internal economic policy and of commercial policy. However, economic circumstances have changed and the forecasts made at the time are now seen to have been pessimistic. It would therefore be legitimate, in the light of the experience gained in the first phase, to revise the forecasts and to adopt the stages of European economic integration to a changed situation. This follows from the recognition of two facts: the results obtained in the last two years are in advance of the time-table of the Treaty; and the present favorable situation offers an opportunity to complete and confirm the partial acceleration which has already taken place. The principle of gradual implementation is not in question; it is the pace which today seems too slow, because the factors which set the pace have changed.[5]

Four major factors, all pointing toward acceleration, were singled out as accounting for the change in the situation: an increasingly favorable rate and pattern of economic development, a rapid *rapprochement* of the economic policies followed by the Member States, the need to give the Community a real unity and a real personality in a world context, and the surprisingly favorable reactions of business circles to the Common Market.[6]

1. The prosperous state of the European economy was probably the greatest factor favoring acceleration. It seems true that "economic expansion, as well as being one of the primary objectives of economic integration, is almost a pre-condition for it."[7] The balance of payments situation of all the Member States had continued to improve since the signing of the Treaty, and the financial situation was stable. Industrial production had increased by 7 per cent in 1959, almost double the growth rate of 1958.

2. Since the Treaty was signed, the Member States had greatly reduced the differences between their internal and external economic policies. In financial and monetary matters, the studies and reports of the Monetary Committee had had a salutary effect on the developing coordination among responsible officials in the six countries, especially regarding exchange policy. A Business Cycle Committee (mixed governmental and Commission) had been set up to develop Community consultation in this area. Regular meetings of technical ministers responsible for finance, labor, agriculture, transport, etc., indicated the growing cohesion and cooperation at all levels among the Six. The commercial policies of the Six also had come closer into line; all had achieved a high level of liberalization toward third countries, whereas only two years before some still exercised strict controls over imports. The introduction of full convertibility at the end of 1958 was probably the key achievement. Furthermore, primarily because of external pressures, the common external tariff was being completed two years ahead of time.[8]

3. The pressure being exerted on the Community from the other mem-

bers of the OEEC had caused many in the Community to affirm the importance of demonstrating the reality of the EEC. Only a concrete manifestation of this reality and unity would convince outside countries (and some groups in the Six) that the situation had really been changed and that there was no possibility of going back.

4. Business circles, after initial reactions ranging from cautious support to outright hostility, had accepted the Common Market as a *fait accompli* and jumped in with almost breathtaking speed to form a network of agreements within the Six. An acceleration of the realization of the Common Market, far from exceeding the pace desired by business groups, would only catch up with the pace they had already set. As one observer remarked, "The dynamic intensity with which big and small business in all six countries has adapted its thinking and its plans to the visions of a Common Market has already given it far more reality than one might have expected from the tentative provisions of the Rome Treaty."[9]

It is this last factor that will interest us most, for it was from business circles that much of the political pressure for acceleration originated. According to Eric Stein, "One of the most interesting and unexpected later developments has been the demand by industrial groups in the Community that the transitional period be shortened. These groups have accepted the Common Market, have made their investment plans on the basis of a large market and now wish that large market to come into being as quickly as possible."[10] This is all the more remarkable when we recall that these were the same groups who had fought the hardest to lengthen the transition period and ring it around with a multitude of escape clauses. Stein, seeking to explain the change, writes:

One reason may be that they have concluded that their earlier fears of competition were groundless. Another reason which may be suggested, if one chooses to be cynical, is that industrialists have now made restrictive arrangements with their potential competitors in the other Member States of the Community which will prevent competition. . . . It is certainly true that there has been a wave of industrial mergers and agreements for cooperation and specialization across national frontiers in the Community in anticipation of the larger market.[11]

It is impossible to determine to what extent these "anticipations" are actually restrictive, but they have a very real significance.*

That some fears of the Common Market were soon proven groundless was especially true in France. "French industry," it was reported, "has

---

* Community officials fear that many may be restrictive and are trying to speed up completion of a Community "antitrust" law to deal with them. A first Community Regulation on competition came into force on March 13, 1962. For details see EEC Commission, *General Report 1962*, pp. 73–79.

taken to the Common Market as a duck to water."[12] The fear that their prices were too high and their methods poor was exaggerated, and the French soon discovered that they could compete quite effectively in the Common Market, as is confirmed by the figures on the development of intra-Community trade between 1958 and 1959.

TRADE WITHIN THE COMMUNITY, 1959

(Per cent change as compared with 1958)

Exporting countries	Importing countries					Exports to EEC
	Germany	France	Italy	Netherlands	BLEU	
Germany	—	+13.1	+20.4	+13.5	+4.7	+13.0
France	+37.7	—	+65.6	+39.8	+19.2	+35.9
Italy	+28.5	+34.5	—	+11.6	+20.1	+27.2
Netherlands	+25.1	+24.5	+10.1	—	+10.4	+18.6
BLEU	+26.1	−10.5	+20.4	+11.7	—	+10.8
Imports from EEC	+29.8	+11.0	+29.3	+15.3	+10.9	+19.0

SOURCE: Compiled from EEC Commission, *General Report 1960*, p. 135.

We see that France increased her exports to her Common Market partners by 35.9 per cent, whereas imports were up by only 11 per cent. The Pinay-Rueff "Truth and Austerity" economic reforms of 1958–59, by devaluing the franc and liberalizing trade, had greatly improved the competitive position of French industry and are generally given most of the credit for France's successful entry into the Common Market.[13]

In his speech to the EPA on acceleration, President Hallstein pointed out that the spectacular expansion in intra-Community trade since the signing of the Treaty could not be explained entirely, or even mostly, by reductions in tariff levels, because these reductions had been rather modest and had been extended to third countries anyway.* It should rather be explained in terms of an anticipation of the Common Market on the part of economic groups. Having accepted the Common Market as inevitable (if not desirable), businessmen had to begin to plan for the future as if it were a reality. This recognition and planning have involved several sorts of activity, the result of which is a significant amount of market interpenetration long before tariff and quota barriers have disappeared.

We have already dealt at some length with the developing pattern of business activities and the striking incidence of new professional associations organized at the Community level for political activity. Individual firms and groups of firms have accepted the Common Market as a reality

* Germany, because of tariff reductions carried out in 1957, had not had to reduce her tariffs at all, and yet imports to Germany were up 29.8 per cent.

and have begun to make their plans with a market of 170 millions in view. Consequently, thousands of trading agreements, mergers, commercial and financial links, and license agreements have been concluded. Once these are formed, the firms concerned want to get the full benefit from an enlarged market as soon as possible: "A company that decides to open a subsidiary in another country because it will be able to sell at a profit when the tariff is reduced or eliminated clearly has a strong interest in having the tariff reduced as quickly as possible."[14]

Given this acceptance of the Common Market as imminent reality, and this pattern of transnational links, it becomes evident that it is not only unnecessary to have such a long transition period, but also potentially dangerous. How can you plan a program of investments for a market that will not come into existence for ten to twelve years? What if the present economic prosperity should be interrupted? If we are going to integrate, let's do it as quickly as possible, for "uncertainty is bad for business."[15] In a very real way the Common Market had now created its own vested interests. Its existence gave rise to positive expectations whose realization required a more rapid pace for integration. As will be seen, however, not all economic sectors in all EEC countries were equally affected.

By the summer of 1959, reports began to appear in the press about the possibility of speeding up the establishment of the Common Market.* One of the earliest, it seems, was that of Léon Bekaert, President of the FIB and the UNICE. He was reported on June 2 to have argued before the Chamber of Commerce of Courtrai for reducing the length of the transitional period. His argument at this time was that U.S. investment was increasing in the Common Market area, but that it was in France that the best opportunities would exist because the French would have the highest tariff protection throughout the transitional period. This gap, existing right from the start, would thus favor France in the Common Market, and if the Common Market took too long being established, there was a serious danger that American industry would settle in France and remain there.[16]

In July the *Bulletin* of the French Patronat published an article commenting on the arguments "one hears from certain foreign economic circles" about speeding up the Common Market and noting that they did not lack value. The Patronat pointed out that tariff reductions were probably easier to take early in the game, especially since economic conditions were so favorable in all the Member States. If tariff reductions were to induce producers to adjust to new conditions, then the sooner they were applied, the better. Further, it would have happy results for the external

---

* People in the Benelux countries had maintained for some time, on the basis of their own experience, that trade liberalization could be realized more rapidly than foreseen by the Treaty.

relations of the Community, since it would facilitate relations with GATT and tell the British once and for all that the Community was a real entity. Foreign industrialists would also be encouraged to invest in the Common Market. But customs and quota disarmament would be dangerous and useless unless efforts were first made to speed up the harmonization of competitive conditions, including the coordination of commercial policy toward third countries, the harmonization of wages and social charges, the suppression of restrictions on the right of establishment, and the rapprochement of legislation. The article concluded: "The Common Market was conceived as an operation of economic integration and not as a simple juxtaposition of markets that would continue to be controlled by national economic policies."[17]

The idea that the development of the Common Market should be speeded up so that it would be irreversible also became current in "European" circles. The Commission, it will be recalled, had always stressed the importance of solidarity, and had been especially afraid of the possibility that the Community might be dissolved in a free trade area if it were not permitted to develop further by itself. Continued external pressure, the favorable economic situation, the evolution in business thinking, Adenauer's decision to retain the Chancellorship, the favorable attitude of the de Gaulle government toward the EEC, all contributed to a deliberate decision on the part of the "Europeans" to attempt to quicken the pace of integration.[18] According to the Commission, "From the middle of 1959 it was clear that economic conditions and *political opportuneness* justified—and perhaps required—speedier implementation of the Treaty of Rome with, perhaps, a shortening of the transition period."[19]

Belgian Foreign Minister Wigny, a dedicated supporter of political and economic integration, began a series of discussions with his counterparts for the purpose of "formulating a series of suggestions and hypotheses for alternative orientations to be given to the future activity of the Six." During the summer he met with Pella, Couve de Murville, and de Gaulle, as well as with Jean Monnet, who was developing his ideas on the fusion of the executives and the direct election of the EPA.[20] On the basis of these meetings, Wigny drew up a draft plan for "relaunching the European idea," gathering together most of the ideas that were "in the air," including the various proposals for acceleration. He circulated this among his colleagues in early September, and on the basis of their views drew up a final draft that was adopted as the official position of the Belgian government on October 9, and subsequently submitted to the Permanent Representatives and the Council of Ministers of the EEC.[21]

The possibility of speeding up the realization of the Common Market had also been studied within the Commission, whose Second Memorandum on the free trade area issue had already officially invited the governments to adopt measures with a view to speeding up integration and shortening the length of the stages envisaged in the Treaty.

THE WIGNY PLAN AND THE FRENCH COUNTERPROPOSALS

As indicated earlier, the proposals that Wigny put before the Foreign Ministers of the EEC amounted to much more than a new timetable, being in fact an attempt to relaunch the whole Common Market idea. The text of the plan was forty pages long, much of which consisted of explanations of the motives behind this new initiative. In particular, Wigny stressed that speeding up the Common Market was not a protectionist move, but rather that its aim was to make relations with the rest of the world easier (a point that had been consistently made by the Commission). When the plan was presented to the Permanent Representatives, the Belgian representative also called for an early resumption of OEEC-wide talks. The concrete proposals in the Wigny plan called for the following measures:[22]

Institutional reinforcement. (1) The Rome Treaty's provisions for a European Assembly elected by universal suffrage should be adopted as soon as possible, or there should be at least a moral commitment to give the Assembly a greater role. (2) An interexecutive committee of two members each from the High Authority, the Euratom Commission, and the EEC Commission should meet regularly to discuss such subjects as transport, energy, and social policy. Wigny had originally favored a merger of the three executives into one (as Monnet was proposing), but dropped this idea after talks with his colleagues. (3) The meetings of technical Ministers (Agriculture, Transport, Finance, etc.) that had hitherto taken place *ad hoc* should be institutionalized. According to Wigny, there was a political danger in the fact that these meetings took place outside of the framework of the Council. (4) The Council should make a final decision on the seat of the institutions as rapidly as possible, Brussels having been designated only the provisional capital of the EEC pending a final decision by the six governments.

Speeding up the realization of the Common Market. (1) The governments should formally commit themselves to waive the right to ask for an extension of the first stage. (2) The next two stages would then be reduced to two years each, so that the transition period would end in 1965.

Cooperation in the monetary and financial spheres. (1) The possibilities for mutual assistance in case of balance of payments difficulties should be strengthened, particularly the possibilities for granting limited credits to the state in difficulty. (2) Every effort should be made to align the fiscal and budgetary systems of the Six, and a European monetary unit should be institutionalized and made general by using it for accounting purposes. (3) The liberalization of capital movements should result in a real common money market so that better use of the existing credit reserves could be made. (4) A common organization for financing and insuring exports should be set up, bills of exchange of one country should be negotiable in other countries and in public and semipublic financial organizations, and national guarantee commissions should organize mutual insurance systems.

Political collaboration. Periodic meetings of Foreign Ministers could be held for the purpose of comparing the foreign policies of the Six from the point of view of information and discussion. These meetings must not involve obligations or interfere with the wider collaboration inside NATO and the Western European Union (WEU).

Cultural rapprochement. The Member States should multilateralize all the bilateral cultural agreements and harmonize the provisions permitting students to go from a university in one country to a university in another country.

Aid to underdeveloped countries. (1) An active policy of joint aid should be set up to provide, not for gifts, but for loans, technical assistance, and the stabilization of raw material prices. (2) Relations between the countries giving assistance and those receiving it should be arranged on the basis of area groupings so as to avoid any appearance of direct dependence.

With the exception of the proposals on aid to underdeveloped areas,* the Foreign Ministers took no action on the Wigny Plan at their session of October 31, 1959, postponing discussion until the November session so that the governments could prepare their positions. In accordance with Community practice, intensive work was undertaken by the Permanent Representatives Committee and the Commission on the problems raised by the Wigny Plan. Discussions tended to separate the extra-Treaty collaboration called for by Wigny (monetary and financial policies, cultural relations, scientific research, etc.) from the proposals for speeding up the Common Market and strengthening its institutions.

As we have noted, the Commission had been studying the possibilities of acceleration for some time. The trend of these studies was revealed in a speech made by Commissioner Lambert Schaus on September 23, 1959, before the EPA. He pointed out that whereas it was legally possible to speed up the rate of tariff and quota disarmament, as well as the rate at which the

---

* An *ad hoc* committee was set up consisting of representatives from the three executives and from the Permanent Representatives to make a preparatory study.

common external tariff was established,[23] it was extremely complicated to shorten the stages as a whole.

If we shorten the stages, the acceleration will not be limited to the tariff and quota fields alone, but the entire mechanism that is connected with the stages will be shortened as well. . . . There is also a political side to the question, since the vote in the Council of Ministers is regulated differently according to the stages. If at the beginning unanimity is generally required, the majority becomes the rule in the stages to follow. Will the Member States agree to speed up this rhythm also? . . . In certain fields the stages are provided for to carry out the aims of the Treaty. Agriculture is a typical example. Can we now shorten the realization of a common agricultural policy? Or if not, would it be possible to shorten the stages in general, but making exceptions for some spheres? . . . There is another essential question, and this concerns the passage from the first to the second stage . . . certain conditions have to be fulfilled . . . and the extension of the first can be requested. The question arises whether it is possible to consider shortening the second and third stages before it is certain that none of the Six will ask for an extension of the first.[24]

Hence, in the detailed examination of the Wigny Plan inside the Community institutions, the Commission came to favor accelerating the first stage, by setting bigger objectives for each step in tariff and quota disarmament, rather than formally shortening the timetable as a whole, as Wigny proposed.

This was similar to the position being taken by the French. Shortly after the introduction of the Wigny Plan, the Finance Minister, Antoine Pinay, observed:

It is neither possible nor desirable to make long-term commitments such as shortening the second and third transitional stages, but the proposal to accelerate tariff reductions in the first period seems advisable, on condition that the relationship between tariff reductions and the coordination clauses of the Treaty is respected. That is why the application of the future common external tariff should be hastened, harmonization of legislation pushed, and the elaboration of the common agricultural and trade policies expedited. Furthermore, substantial and rapid steps toward the complete amalgamation of markets will lead to better coordination of political and financial policies.[25]

On November 17, at a session of the Rey Committee, the French made a formal proposal that the tariff reduction scheduled for January 1, 1962, be brought forward to July 1, 1960 (thus making a 20 per cent reduction), and that the first step be taken to bring the common external tariff into effect.[26] The Ministers of the Six were now for the first time confronted with a specific and practical proposal for acceleration, although one that was limited in scope.

At the November session of the Council, the Foreign Ministers met to consider the Wigny Plan. The situation, however, had been fundamentally changed by the French proposals, and it was decided to instruct the Commission to study the various alternatives, especially between "linear" acceleration—reduction of the length of one or more stages to extend to all fields—and "selective" acceleration—one or more phases in one or more fields. By January 18, 1960, the Commission was to submit practical proposals to the Council.[27] That the Commission was given this task is itself significant. It also demonstrates that the Commission continues to play a role at the broadest political level and that this is accepted as a fact by the Member States. This belies the hypothesis that the Commission is a technical body pure and simple.

THE COMMISSION'S PROPOSALS ON ACCELERATION

The task before the Commission was to find some formula for achieving a maximum acceleration that would be acceptable to all the Member States. Upon being given the task of making specific proposals the Commission began an intensive series of studies directed and coordinated by François Ortoli, General Director of the Internal Market Directorate, and designed to inform the Commission on the following questions:

(a) The possible consequences, both for the realization of the Treaty's objectives and for the internal economy of each Community country, of a decision to speed up implementation.

(b) The conditions in which the timetable and momentum of the Treaty could be substantially modified without endangering its balance.

(c) The possible repercussions in the external relations of the Community of a speed-up in the implementation of the Treaty.[28]

The Commission held several special meetings in January and February of 1960 to examine the dossier prepared by the various departments. Following the now familiar pattern, the Commission was in constant contact with the Permanent Representatives and the national administrations for the purpose of obtaining information on the difficulties envisaged and the reasons for anxiety in each country.[29] President Hallstein and other members of the Commission also made extensive visits to the national capitals of the Six to compare views and to determine "the limits of the possible" with regard to acceleration. Because of the complexity and importance of the issue, the Commission was not able to submit its proposals until February 26, 1960, instead of January 18 as originally scheduled.

Although there was much support for the general idea of acceleration, many widely divergent goals and interests were involved. "Europeans" in all the Member States favored acceleration because they thought it would strengthen the institutions of the Community, make the Common Market irreversible, and hasten the day when Europe would achieve some kind of federal or confederal political system. For many of them this political goal had come to involve clearly differentiating the EEC from the free trade area as proposed by the United Kingdom. Yet, one of the main ideas in Wigny's Plan was that acceleration should be undertaken with a view to resuming talks with the British,[30] a theme that was echoed by the Dutch and by the Germans (especially Erhard).

The French government and much of French industry were in general hostile to, or uninterested in, the political goals of integration, but favored acceleration as a means to establish the break between the EEC and the OEEC countries, and to bury the free trade area once and for all, thus ensuring the continuation of French ascendancy in the Common Market (or at least the ascendancy of the Bonn-Paris axis). Thus whereas "Europeans" wanted to obtain commitments to extend the role of the Community institutions (direct elections, fusion of the executives), to give up the possibility of extending the first stage of the transition period, and to cut the last two stages in half, the French stressed intergovernmental consultations, pragmatic steps in the first stage, and no actual commitments to shorten the transition period.

French industry, and to some extent Belgian industry, favored acceleration chiefly for its ability to protect their preferential position in the Six, whereas German and Dutch industry approved of it if it would make a larger European market more realizable. The Benelux countries wanted to speed up the elimination of internal barriers to trade, but in general did not want to accelerate the rest of the Treaty, and certainly not the rate at which the common external tariff was to be applied. The low-tariff countries, Benelux and Germany, strongly disliked the idea of increasing their tariffs as a matter of principle, and also felt it would lead to higher prices and at the same time hurt their export position. For the French and Italians, however, speeding up the establishment of the common external tariff was the *sine qua non* of any acceleration agreement. The Dutch government was formally committed to working for a lower level for the common external tariff,[31] a position favored also by the German and Belgian governments, but an anathema to Belgian, Italian, and French industry, as well as to the French and Italian governments. France and Italy wanted acceleration of the whole treaty with all its safeguards, especially the provisions concerning the harmonization or coordination of commercial and social policy and those concerning competitive conditions, a position that the Germans found hard to accept. Finally, the Dutch and French insisted that the provisions on agriculture also be accelerated, whereas the Italians and Germans did not want any acceleration in agriculture at all.[32]

To a certain extent, then, the support that existed for acceleration of the Treaty was the result of converging expectations, "aims based on a reasoning pattern peculiar to a given national group but sufficiently similar in aim to result in support for integrative proposals."[33] So far as the Commission was concerned, however, it was confronted with diametrically opposed plans that seemed to be mutually exclusive. The crucial factor was that most (if not all) of the groups and governments involved were determined to maximize their goals within the "rules of the game" of the EEC.

To recapitulate, it will be recalled that two major acceleration proposals had been offered. The French proposal, made before the Rey Committee on November 17, 1959, and the only really specific proposal, called for a "selective," or "trade cycle," method of acceleration: i.e., bringing forward or speeding up the realization of some of the provisions of the Treaty. The Wigny Plan, on the other hand, presented in October of 1959, favored a "linear" or "organic" acceleration in which there would be an across-the-board speed-up in the implementation of the entire Treaty. This latter approach had the advantage of putting off as long as possible the commitment that its supporters dreaded the most: having to raise their tariff levels to that of the common external tariff. The French countered by asserting that the time to accelerate was when times were good, for who could say what they might be several years hence. They therefore proposed to speed up the rate of tariff disarmament within the Six, but made it a condition that the low-tariff countries agree to advance the date on which they would begin to raise their tariffs to the level of the common external tariff. "France makes the point, with some logic, that unless this is done the high-tariff countries would be doing all the accelerating, whereas if its proposals were followed a balanced move towards the real meaning of a customs union would be taken ahead of time. The French think the cohesion of the Six would be demonstrated and their bargaining power strengthened."[34]

As we have seen, the Commission's ideas had been developing along lines similar to those of the French, although the Commission's goals were not the same as those of the de Gaulle government. Doubtless, a majority of the Commission favored the political goals of the Wigny Plan and would have liked to achieve an actual formal shortening of the transition period. But given the legal and political difficulties alluded to in Schaus's speech, and the position being taken by the French government, such goals appeared chimerical.

The Commission also took the position that acceleration should be carried out in the first stage as well as in the two subsequent stages. According to our thesis, the determining factor in acceleration was the pressure from business circles, and they wanted action now. These groups were anxious to establish the irreversibility of the Common Market, for they had made their choice and were drawing up their plans in the light of the EEC market. The Commission felt that the important thing was to get acceleration going as soon as possible, especially since it could be assumed that, given such a start, the whole operation would continue to move at an increasing pace. For economic reasons it would be extremely difficult to decide to shorten the second and third stages without at the same time speeding up some of the terms of the first. If, for example, customs reductions among the Six amounted to only 30 per cent at the end of 1962, it would be very hard to achieve the remaining 70 per cent reduction in only four years.

In the Commission's view, therefore, the way to proceed was to try to combine the "organic" and the selective approaches to acceleration. Some of the provisions of the Treaty would be speeded up in the first stage to take advantage of the situation and set the scene for reducing the length of the second and third stages.[35] Such a reduction is clearly possible under the terms of the Treaty: "The second and third stages may not be extended or curtailed except pursuant to a decision of the Council acting by means of a unanimous vote on a proposal of the Commission."[36] But, as Hallstein pointed out in his speech on acceleration before the EPA, it was not *prudent* to propose an actual shortening of the second and third stages at this time. He was careful to add, however, that "we did not abstain from doing so because we were opposed to such an abridgment, which is foreseen in particular in the Wigny Plan; on the contrary, the reason for our reserve should rather be sought in our 'sense of moderation.' "[37]

In its recommendations to the Council, the Commission divided its detailed proposals for acceleration into two parts: "(a) For those portions of the Treaty which are subject to a time-table, the speed-up will essentially consist in the more rapid introduction of the customs union. (b) In the other fields, where it is not possible to measure the speed-up, the Member States would have to affirm their awareness of the problems which arise and take further steps to maintain the unity of the Treaty."[38] The recommendations were as follows:

1. Quotas on industrial goods between the Member States should be abolished before December 31, 1961. This could be extended on condition of reciprocity to nonmember countries. Member States would draw up with the Commission a program for eliminating discrimination with regard to supplies and market outlets, a situation that resulted from the existence of state commercial monopolies. Trade in agricultural products was to be increased in ways to be worked out as the common agricultural policy was established.

2. Customs duties between Member States should be reduced by 50 per cent instead of 30 per cent during the first stage, which would be accomplished by setting the two internal tariff cuts due on July 1, 1960, and December 31, 1961, at 20 per cent each instead of 10 per cent.

3. So as to avoid deflections of trade, the common external tariff should be introduced on July 1, 1960, instead of December 31, 1961. This would be done on the basis of the common external tariff reduced by 20 per cent, this representing an advance suspension of duties pending the results of the tariff negotiations in GATT, at which reciprocity would be requested. The question of extending to GATT members the tariff reductions that the Member States were to grant each other on July 1, 1960, could be discussed at the same time.

4. In areas for which no timetable has been laid down in the Treaty, the Member States should agree to speed up their activities in order to work out common policies *pari passu* with the implementation of tariff and quota disarmament and the introduction of the common external tariff. The Commission suggested that a speed-up should be effected in the following areas:

(a) In social policy, joint studies should be undertaken on the problems of vocational training and the training of technicians. Member States should try to ensure by the end of 1960 the application of the principle of equal pay for men and women. (b) On commercial policy, Member States should systematically coordinate trade negotiations with nonmember states, including a more rapid unification of liberalization measures toward nonmember states, and, in important cases involving considerable deflection of trade, Member States should agree to open the first joint negotiations under Article 113. (c) On agricultural policy, the Commission noted that the acceleration of the customs union, which mostly concerned the industrial sector, should be rounded off by speedy action on the proposals it had already presented to the Council. (d) Member States should undertake thorough harmonization or coordination of their statistical systems within two years in order to facilitate comparative studies. (e) Member States should abolish the barriers to trade resulting from discrepancies in the regulations applied on such subjects as health, hygiene, and industrial safety.[39]

Nowhere in these proposals do we find the recommendation that Member States should not be allowed to ask for an extension of the first stage, or that the following stages should be shortened. The nearest we get to such a suggestion is this statement: "The Commission would nevertheless express its *conviction* that the provisions enacted in accordance with its proposals would make it possible, at the end of the fourth year of operation of the Treaty, to shorten the second and third stages under the conditions laid down in Article 8. The Commission *reserves* the *right* to propose such shortening in due course."[40]

The Commission considered these proposals were the best that could be attained under the circumstances. They "were an ingenious attempt to achieve acceleration while satisfying conflicting interests among the Six."[41] For "Europeans" they held out the possibility of achieving a very real acceleration which, even if it was not all that could be hoped for, would still be a gesture of enormous psychological importance. Most of the original French proposals were retained: accelerated tariff reductions among the Six and, most important, an earlier start on the common external tariff. The common external tariff, however, was to be reduced by 20 per cent, which was what the Dutch had suggested and was also favored by the Belgians and Germans. The interests of the low-tariff countries were served by the possibility foreseen in the recommendation that the internal tariff and quota disarmament be extended to the GATT countries. And, finally, the Commission laid great emphasis on "the EEC's mission as champion of liberalism in its dealing with the outside world."

The advocates of a speed-up believe that if the Community is established rapidly it will be able to apply a liberal and bold common policy to the best advantage. . . . It cannot be denied that the existence of the Community has given a powerful impulse to the vigorous growth of economic relationships in the world during the last fifteen months: the extension of convertibility, the considerable reduction of import restrictions, the new world tariff conference, the meeting of the "21." . . . The sooner economic integration is a fact, the more the commercial policy of the Common Market will of necessity be dynamic, open and liberal.[42]

It has been pointed out that the acceleration proposals did not entail any shortening of the transition period, although this is seen as a future possibility. The Treaty does not provide for shortening the first stage or for obtaining from the Member States a commitment not to ask for its extension. Several governments, most consistently the French, were unwilling to undertake any serious discussions at this time about shortening the second and third stages. Not only would this involve unknown contingencies so far as economic conditions were concerned, but it would also affect the voting procedures of the Council of Ministers. All that was possible, then, if an acceleration were to be achieved, was to increase the targets set up in the Treaty for the first stage. According to the Treaty, this could be done by a decision of the Community institutions as regards the tariff and quota timetables.[43] But it appeared that no Community decision could oblige a Member State to advance the date of the first approximation to the common external tariff, which was fixed for the end of the fourth year of the transition period and was not formally linked directly to the stages. This, however, could be accomplished under the Treaty by means of an intergovernmental agreement.[44] The proposed 20 per cent reduction in the level of the common external tariff could also be subsumed under the Treaty, although this was challenged by many.[45]

The Commission would probably have preferred the acceleration decisions to have taken the form of a decision by the Council as a Community institution, to the extent that this was possible; but it appeared that France, in particular, preferred that they be in the form of an agreement between the governments. This was necessary, as we have noted, in order to advance the first approximation to the common external tariff, but the Treaty also provided for the possibility of tariff and quota acceleration by the same means.[46] Consequently, the Commission's recommendations, though submitted to the Council of Ministers, concern actions that could be taken by the Member States. Thus the final decision on acceleration was taken by "the Representatives of the Governments of the Member States of the EEC meeting in the Council." This procedure was perhaps best suited to the legal complexities of the situation, as well as being the quickest and least complicated course (which appealed to the Commission); but it should be pointed out that such an agreement is not binding *under the Treaty*, and that a Member State could not be brought before the Court of Justice for failure to comply.

The Commission concluded its recommendations by observing:

It is clear that other suggestions might have been made and a different presentation of the problems adopted. However, the Commission considers that its proposals correspond to the two objectives which in the present circumstances the Member States seem bound to pursue: to profit from favorable economic conditions by moving ahead as rapidly as possible on the road of integration and to launch the maximum possible number of study and planning operations in those fields where acceleration cannot be brought about simply by altering a time-table laid down in the Treaty.[47]

The Commission's aim was to find a solution which would be acceptable to all the Member States (or which none would dare to block), and which, at the same time, would be the best-suited to achieve the Community's long-range goals. The final proposal was designed to "cure the inhibitions and hesitations which, here and there, still stand in the way of conversion to the new facts of life, and it will thus strengthen the process of expansion in which our economy is at present engaged."[48] In explaining this purpose to the EPA, Hallstein said:

We like to say that this Community is a dynamic entity. But being dynamic does not mean being automatic. The establishment of the Community did not set in motion a machine that will move forward toward its goal without any help from us. What is dynamic about it is rather that the changes demanded by this work call every day and every hour for fresh decisions on our part. This means that the will that produced the decision to sign the Treaty must be constantly reinforced, constantly reaffirmed.[49]

These words reflect the Commission's determination to continue to press for maximum economic and political integration with all the means at its disposal, and not to limit itself to a simple execution of the specific tasks imposed by the Treaty. Hallstein emphasized that the Commission was making proposals on acceleration not only because it had been requested to do so by the Foreign Ministers, or because the Council had declared itself in favor of acceleration, but because under the Treaty it was duty-bound to do so.[50] He pointed out, moreover, that the Commission had the power to make further proposals in the future on its own initiative, since it was required by the Treaty to keep the question of speedier implementation constantly under review. The Treaty posed the possibility of acceleration for the customs union provisions and did not set down a strict timetable for the rest, leaving it to the institutions of the Community to decide on their timing. Since the possibility was provided for in the Treaty, and the institutions were given the authority to effect it, an obligation was imposed on the institutions to make use of this authority. It must be exercised in the proper manner:

in the spirit of the total mission entrusted by the Treaty to the institutions of the Community, in the spirit of the objectives of the Treaty. This is the perspective that has guided the Commission. It is incumbent upon it, under the Treaty, to ensure the application of the Treaty. This means that it has the obligation—I repeat, the obligation, not the right—to ensure that each of the provisions of the Treaty is put to whatever use best serves the interests of the Community, its existence, its solidarity, its functioning, and its development. [The Commission] ought to take into account not only the timetable of the Treaty (when it fixes one), but also the possibility of an acceleration.[51]

THE PREPARATION OF THE ACCELERATION DECISION

As might have been expected, hardly anybody was very pleased with the Commission's recommendations. Each Member State had got some major demand included, but each was also required to give up another demand in return. But the Member States could not escape the fact that these represented *the* authoritative proposals, and if there were going to be an acceleration decision at all, it would be along these lines. The Member States and the Council had accepted the principle of acceleration in November 1959, and had entrusted the Commission with devising compromise proposals precisely because they could come to no agreement among themselves. The Commission's proposals were designed to give as much satisfaction to these national and group demands as was necessary to achieve acceptance (or create great reluctance to reject), while at the same time assuring progress toward Community goals, most particularly that of making the Community truly irreversible. The important thing was to achieve some sort of acceleration at once so as to take advantage of the propitious economic situation. The details were less important than the fact of the gesture. Acceleration was presented by the Commission as a sort of manifest necessity: failure to accelerate would be a sign of grave weakness and would encourage opponents of the EEC, both within the Six and outside, to continue their delaying tactics. Only by accelerating the implementation of the Treaty could the Six reaffirm their political will to go on with the integration of their economies.

This argument found a widely favorable reception in "European" circles. Perhaps the strongest support for the Commission's recommendations came from Wigny himself. In an address before the EPA, he affirmed that this was above all a political question, and that the details of the acceleration were less important.

You are discussing acceleration. That word is not strong enough. In my opinion, you are discussing the very existence of our Community. All the conditions exist for speeding up the opening of the Common Market. . . . How guilty we would be if we were to let this moment pass! . . . Aren't you afraid that by not deciding now to integrate more rapidly, you will compromise the existence of the Community in eighteen months? . . . We must give proof of our will. It must be absolutely clear that above all we want the Community with all its institutions, [and] its external tariff which assures its internal cohesion. . . .

This Assembly must therefore . . . say to the Governments that the time has come not only to accelerate, but to confirm our Community.[52]

Many parliamentarians were not entirely convinced, however. The special concern of the Netherlands and Germany over the effect of acceleration on the Community's relations with nonmember countries was reflected in the debate that followed.[53] Several CDU members warned against the political dangers for Western unity if the split between Europe's two groups were widened, but all concurred in the statement of Josef Illerhaus (CDU, Germany), who gave the full support of the CDU to the Commission's proposals, which would be a "tangible proof of European solidarity." SPD members Kalbitzer and H. Schmidt were especially critical of the Commission for, in effect, presenting third countries with a *fait accompli* and for not making any real effort to negotiate an agreement with them. Kalbitzer was against any unilateral acceleration of the EEC. In his view, the Europe of the Six was too small; everything possible should be done to bring about a wider European organization. Many French parliamentarians, on the other hand, thought the Commission had gone too far in its overtures to third countries.[54]

The other major criticism of the Commission was that its recommendations were not far-reaching enough. All the speakers pointed out the lack of balance in proposing to accelerate only the customs union provisions of the Treaty. The Socialists stressed acceleration in the social sphere, the Dutch wanted more precise proposals for agriculture and transport, and so on. These preoccupations were evident in the resolution finally voted by the Assembly.* This welcomed the initiative taken by the Commission, but went on to make the following requests:

[The Assembly *asks*] that the EEC Commission, the Council of Ministers, and the Governments speed up the simultaneous and harmonious application of measures for the establishment of common policies in the spheres of agriculture, financial and economic affairs, and transport;

hopes that the EEC Commission's recommendations be completed so as to give social questions, whose importance is increasing with the speeding up of economic integration, the place that is theirs, and so as to improve the provisions for the European Social Fund;

insists that customs disarmament toward third countries be carried out on the basis of reciprocity, and that the acceleration procedure take into consideration the special economy of the underdeveloped countries associated with the EEC;

asks the EEC Commission to submit to the Assembly as soon as possible concrete and effective proposals, taking into account the above-mentioned considerations.[55]

The Commission's proposals were sent to the Council and to the governments on February 26, 1960. The process of achieving a final decision began on March 10, when the Council met for a first exchange of views. The Council again declared itself unanimously in favor of the principle of acceleration, although admitting that some differences still existed regarding method. The Permanent Representatives and the Rey Committee were charged with further study of the plan, the latter from the point of view of its effects on the Community's relations with third countries. The Council agreed to discuss the matter further in May.[56] The task of these two committees was to negotiate agreement among the Six and *the Commission*, so far as this was possible at this level. Such agreement would be incor-

---

* This was a compromise resolution presented by all three groups. In the final vote there was only one vote against, Christian de la Malène (UNR, France), and two absentions, Jean Filliol (Liberal, France) and Jean-Eric Bousch (UNR, France). Several SPD members left the hall before the vote was taken, however.

porated in a draft decision to be presented to the Council at its May session, and where no agreement was possible, alternatives would be presented. The Commission, by its Presidency of the Rey Committee, its active participation in the Permanent Representatives, and its constant proselytizing activities in favor of acceleration throughout the Community, played an active role in this process of preparation.

The Permanent Representatives and the Rey Committee had had preliminary exchanges of view early in March, and began active discussions in the last week of that month. Several meetings were held in April, and a joint meeting of the two committees was held on May 6 to examine all outstanding questions and to agree on a draft decision to be sent to the Council. The Commission was closely associated with the work of both committees and, in fact, drew up the draft decision that was considered in the joint session. The positions taken by the governments during these sessions reflected the diversity of their goals as well as the balance of economic and political forces in the Community.

The most heated and extensive debates on acceleration took place in Germany and the Netherlands. The great majority of economic interest groups in these two countries had accepted the EEC somewhat reluctantly and on the condition that a larger free trade area would soon be created. To the extent that this goal now seemed threatened, acceleration was opposed. In both countries, however, political considerations ultimately prevailed: in the Netherlands, owing to pressure exerted by a highly pro-"European" parliament on a somewhat hostile Foreign Minister, and in Germany because of Adenauer, the Foreign Office, and a majority of the CDU/CSU. Neither the French nor the Italians liked the proposal that the common external tariff be reduced, but there was never serious doubt that they would agree to some compromise solution. The French Patronat had been among the first to urge acceleration, parliamentary opinion in both countries was strongly pro-"European," and the two governments were in principle in favor of acceleration—the Italians because they were basically committed to political and economic integration, and the French because this was the price they were willing to pay in order to consolidate their position in the EEC. Only the Belgian government and Belgian industry wholeheartedly endorsed the Commission's proposals. The FIB declared that they were a balanced compromise between the divergent interests of the Six, a compromise that would strengthen the Community, without, however, requiring the low-tariff countries to raise their tariffs very much.[57]

Two months of negotiations in the Permanent Representatives and the Rey Committee revealed that basic differences existed on the following points in the Commission's proposals: (1) the date of application of the specific measures of acceleration, (2) the nature of the proposed 20 per cent reduction in the common external tariff, (3) the extent of the internal reduction to be achieved by the end of the first stage, (4) acceleration of the other sectors of the Treaty (common policies, etc.), and (5) acceleration in agriculture.

The Date of Application of Specific Measures

The Commission's proposal that the first alignment to the common external tariff be taken on July 1, 1960, was supported by France, Italy, and Belgium, but elicited violent opposition from German Minister of Economic Affairs Erhard, who was backed by German industry. The position of the Dutch government, as well as Dutch industry and trade, was similar.[58] The Germans and the Dutch feared this would have unfavorable repercussions on the competitive position of their exporting industries and that it would further widen the gap between the Six and the Seven.[59] The Dutch government, however, decided to give general support to acceleration on the condition that the EFTA should not react too negatively, that the 20 per cent reduction in the common external tariff be immediate and definitive and not subject to reciprocity, and that acceleration of the customs union provisions be accompanied by effective measures to eliminate existing limitations in the free access to markets in the Member States.[60] Adenauer pronounced himself firmly in favor of acceleration in a joint declaration with President Eisenhower in Washington in March. Foreign Minister von Brentano and Finance Minister Etzel had also welcomed the Commission's proposals.[61] Erhard criticized these expressions of approval and came out strongly against speeding up the Common Market at all, expressing the view that things were going too fast as it was,[62] and in effect agreeing with German industrial circles, who were advocating *extending* the transition period so as to gain time for EEC-EFTA negotiations.[63] The Ministry of Economic Affairs released statistics that claimed to prove that acceleration would result in a 45 per cent increase in the average duties of the Federal Republic on imports from third countries (from 2.59 per cent to 3.46 per cent). It was argued that such an increase would be dangerous for Germany, for it would slow up imports and might provoke a price rise. "The Federal Government, which came out in favor of acceleration while Herr Erhard was absent owing to illness, will have to take these facts into consideration when it makes a final decision."[64]

A battle of statistics ensued between the German Ministry of Economic Affairs and the Commission. The Commission pointed out that different conclusions could be drawn if one did not select one's figures so carefully, and issued a "corrected" version indicating that any rise in German prices would be compensated for by increased internal reductions in the EEC.[65] The German Finance Minister, Etzel, also challenged Erhard's figures with a set of his own and reaffirmed his support for acceleration. It was announced that the official position of the German government remained that which was expressed in the Eisenhower-Adenauer release.[66] Erhard and the industrialists, however, were not alone in their opposition to acceleration. The FDP and a number of SPD Bundestag members were also hostile, again mainly because acceleration would probably mean a final break with the plan for a free trade area.[67]

The stage was set for another clash between Erhard and Adenauer.[68] Seemingly, however, Erhard's arguments, the adverse reaction among the EFTA, and the strong opposition of the industrialists impressed Adenauer, and when the German Cabinet met on April 5, no final decision was reached. The acceleration proposals were welcomed "in principle," and the government committed itself to do everything in its power to achieve the economic and political objectives of the EEC, and also to ensure that all possibilities for satisfactory free foreign trade, especially with the countries of the EFTA, had been exhausted. It was decided to give the matter further study, and a special committee consisting of Erhard, von Brentano, Etzel, and Schwarz (Minister of Agriculture) was appointed for this purpose.[69] Erhard had won time, for it was widely accepted that the original timetable of the Commission's proposals could not now be kept. (October 1, 1960, or January 1, 1961, were suggested as probable dates.) But he was obliged to protest his loyalty to the political and economic objectives of the EEC, reserving objections only on aspects of the acceleration plan.[70]

A compromise position was finally adopted by the Cabinet in late April, according to which Germany would accept acceleration under certain conditions: (1) there must be serious negotiations at the ministerial level between the EEC and the EFTA prior to the implementation of the acceleration plan; (2) the date of implementation was to be January 1, 1961, instead of July 1, 1960; (3) agriculture was to be exempted from acceleration; (4) the common external tariff was to be definitively reduced by 20 per cent, with possible additional cuts in GATT; (5) only 50 per cent of the earlier German tariff cuts were to be rescinded; and (6) the German tariff level was to be raised to the EEC level in steps of only 22.5 per cent at a time, instead of the 30 per cent proposed in the acceleration plan.[71]

Although this compromise solution met some of Erhard's demands, it revealed that Adenauer and the "Europeans" had carried the day against the massed weight of interest group opinion, the hostility of the opposition parties, and the best efforts of the Ministry of Economic Affairs. On May 5, a debate was held in the Bundestag on European policy in general and on the government's position on acceleration, and its effects on relations with third countries, in particular. Erhard committed the government to do everything in its power to bring about a *rapprochement* with the EFTA before implementing the acceleration proposals. He combined this with an attack on the Commission, arguing that it should not be permitted to negotiate on behalf of the Governments. Strong support was given to acceleration by the CDU/CSU group, and special stress was placed on the importance of accelerating the introduction of the common external tariff. The SPD declared itself fundamentally opposed to the formation of economic blocs, and alleged that the Commission's acceleration proposals, and the position being taken by the German Federal Government, were endangering economic and political relations with the rest of Europe. The SPD welcomed the six-month postponement of acceleration as an opportunity to prevent an economic war in Europe.[72]

The six months' delay was not of basic significance, since it was already evident that the mere technicalities of instituting tariff changes in line with the common external tariff could not be completed before October 1, 1960, at the earliest. Hallstein was actively engaged in the German discussions and reportedly even took part in some of the Cabinet debates. Moreover, both he and other Commission members spoke frequently to German business groups in defense of the acceleration proposals. It must be noted that the anti-acceleration forces had been considerably weakened by the active support given by the U.S. government to the Commission and especially by the violence (ought one to say intemperance?) of reactions from the United Kingdom and the EFTA. The EFTA declared the acceleration proposals to be a deliberately unfriendly move, and openly campaigned for their rejection. In late March, Macmillan went to Washington supposedly to discuss questions relating to the coming Summit Meeting. He also had talks with the Under-Secretary of State for Economic Affairs, Dillon, in which he expressed his fears about the economic split in Europe. The substance of these remarks was leaked to the press and, although denied in part by the British, evoked immediate and violent reaction on the Continent. Macmillan had reportedly declared that if the split in Europe continued, Britain would have no choice but to lead another peripheral coalition as she had done in the days of Napoleon. He also warned that the economic effects of the split might force the British to reimpose dollar import restrictions and reduce British troops in Germany.[73]

Under the circumstances it is not surprising that Adenauer and most Germans should have considered France and the United States to be their most dependable allies at the forthcoming Summit Meeting; and both the United States and France were urging that the acceleration be approved.

The British attack was considered unwarranted by all factions in Germany, as elsewhere in the Six.[74] It strengthened the pro-integration forces by placing emphasis on the political aspects of integration and giving prominence to the Commission's arguments. That Britain's real goal was to block economic and political integration was considered to be thus revealed.[75] Striking indication of this was given by the reactions in the EPA, which was debating the acceleration proposals at the time of Macmillan's remarks. The Commission's proposals had been rather severely criticized, especially by the Dutch and the German parliamentarians on the grounds that they would result in a deterioration of relations with the United Kingdom and the other EFTA countries.[76] This was forgotten in the wake of Macmillan's declarations, and the Assembly passed a resolution welcoming the Commission's initiative with only one negative vote.

The Proposed 20 Per Cent Reduction in the Common External Tariff

The Commission proposed that the level of the common external tariff be provisionally reduced by 20 per cent, which would represent an advance suspension pending reciprocal reductions from third countries. Only the Belgians accepted this proposal without reservation. We have already seen that the Dutch and German governments had both committed themselves to demanding this reduction be made definitive and not subject to reciprocity. The Dutch made this a condition for accepting acceleration. However, the opposition of French business and industry to any reduction of the common external tariff was just as vehement as that of their German and Dutch counterparts had been to accelerating the procedure for aligning national duties to it.[77] The French government declared that it was forced to respect the fears of French industrial circles, for whom the 20 per cent reduction in the common external tariff would be very dangerous. Such a unilateral move, combined with the proposed extension of internal tariff and quota reductions to GATT countries, would result in destroying the concept of the customs union, a concept that necessarily implies discrimination toward third countries. The French pointed out that if the Germans found it difficult to absorb an increase of 0.87 per cent in the average cost of imports, the French economy would be even harder pressed to adapt itself to a reduction that was far more extreme.[78] They did not exclude the possibility that they would accept *some* reduction in the common external tariff, but the low-tariff countries would have to accept an earlier application of the common external tariff. The Italians took essentially the same position, arguing that they could not accept more than a provisional 10 per cent reduction.[79]

The Extent of the Internal Reduction

There was no objection to making an extra 10 per cent cut on internal tariffs as between the Six, but once again only the Belgian (and Luxembourg) government supported the Commission's proposal that the Six commit themselves to achieving a 50 per cent reduction in internal tariffs by the end of the first stage. This would have been achieved by formally increasing the 10 per cent reduction scheduled for January 1, 1962, to 20 per cent. The French were the most firmly opposed, claiming that a further reduction of this order would have to be paralleled by a second step toward the common external tariff.[80]

Acceleration of the Other Sectors of the Treaty

The Commission was criticized by all six governments, as well as by agriculture, labor, and business, for having limited its concrete proposals to the customs union provisions of the Treaty. The French, in particular, had always stressed that the equilibrium of the Treaty must be maintained, so that if the customs union were speeded up, all the safeguard devices should be accelerated as well. The French Patronat (CNPF) had demanded, as conditions of acceleration, the equalization of men's and women's wages and overtime pay, the coordination of import policies toward Eastern Europe, the adoption of Community antidumping legislation, etc.[81] The government pointed out that it was impossible for France to accept such sweeping and rapid customs reductions as those proposed by the Commission without any precise undertakings from the other governments concerning the harmonization of national policies provided for in the second and third stages. The Italians, and Socialists in all Six countries, wanted to see acceleration in the following spheres: in social policy (the free circulation of workers, the equalization of working conditions, expansion of the activities of the Social Fund, and social security for seasonal workers), in the freedom of establishment and of services, and in the harmonization of state aids to exports.

So strong and widespread were demands for acceleration in these other areas of the Treaty that the Permanent Representatives drew up a list of problems on which the Commission was asked to clarify and expand its proposals.[82] The Commission agreed to do this, and undertook work on three new chapters dealing with agriculture, social questions, and imports from overseas territories. Proposals had been drawn up by the end of April, but the Commission decided not to introduce them in spite of pressure from all sides to do so. They argued that recent contacts with the various governments had revealed that positions were so divergent as to make agreement impossible at the next Council session. The Commission considered it crucial that the basic decision to accelerate be taken at once and promised to submit a full set of proposals covering the economic union aspects of the Treaty when it was "opportune" to do so.[83]

Acceleration in Agriculture

Right from the beginning the Dutch made the inclusion of agriculture a condition for accepting acceleration.[84] Dutch agricultural organizations had used all their influence to argue that trade in agriculture ought to be freed to the same extent as it had been in industrial goods, and they received almost unanimous support within the Netherlands.[85] The Germans, who had been reticent on this point all along, finally took the position that there should be no acceleration in agriculture.[86] The Germans had not, in fact, been applying the quota changes required by the Treaty to agricultural products. They argued that until a common agricultural policy were adopted, the existing controls could not be lifted.[87]

The effect of German policies was to restrict the access of Dutch agricultural products to the German market, thereby reserving access for the Scandinavian countries, especially Denmark. The Germans hoped in this way to protect their own export markets in these countries. The Dutch were determined to put an end to this situation, since their only chance of making up for the losses they might incur on the British market as a result of the establishment of the EFTA lay in increasing exports to Germany. The Commission gave up presenting special proposals for agriculture because these would only have delayed action, and instead worked hard to bring about a compromise between the Germans and the Dutch. The Commission managed to persuade the Dutch to restrict their demands for the time being to an increase in the liberalization of trade; but, right up to the Council session in early May, the Germans refused to consider any acceleration in agriculture, and would not even negotiate seriously.[88] Consequently, when the Council met on May 10 to try to reach a final decision on acceleration, relations between the Netherlands and Germany were somewhat embittered.

ACCELERATION AND THE COUNCIL OF MINISTERS

The May 1960 meeting of the Council held in Luxembourg was given enormous advance publicity as a turning point in the history of the Community.[89] The Commission's recommendations had evoked lively debate within the Community and a vigorous reaction from nonmember countries. The Commission and "Europeans" in all six Member States had continued to stress the political and symbolic importance of acceleration, and did all they could to marshal support throughout the Community. Members of the Commission spoke before groups of industrialists, toured the capitals, and gave press conferences. A "round table" between the Commission and the trade unions of the Six was organized in order to mobilize labor support behind acceleration.[90] The Monnet Committee was actively engaged in promoting acceleration, especially in Germany and the Netherlands, where resistance was the greatest. The cause was further helped by the dramatic expressions of opposition from the United Kingdom and the EFTA. Macmillan's remarks, coming as they did just before the Summit, could have had no other effect than to throw Adenauer and de Gaulle together. Acceleration had taken on even more political meaning than it had been invested with by the "Europeans."

That the Member States considered the May session important was clear from the number of high officials in attendance. Germany was represented by Erhard, Etzel, and von Brentano, Ministers of Economic Affairs, Finance, and Foreign Affairs, respectively, and by Under-Secretaries of State Albert von Scherpenberg and Alfred Müller-Armack. Foreign Minister Pierre Wigny and Minister of Economic Affairs Jacques van der Schueren represented Belgium; Foreign Minister Maurice Couve de Murville and Finance Minister Wilfrid Baumgartner, France; Minister of Industry and Commerce Emilio Colombo, and Under-Secretary of State Carlo Russo, Italy; Foreign Minister Joseph Luns, Minister of Economic Affairs J. W. de Pous, and Minister of Agriculture G. M. Marijnen, the Netherlands; and Prime Minister Pierre Werner, Minister of Economic Affairs Paul Elvinger, and Foreign Minister Eugène Schaus, Luxembourg. The Commission was also represented, President Hallstein and Vice-President Mansholt, in particular, taking an active part in the debates.

The work of accommodation and negotiation that had already taken place in the preceding two months made it possible to achieve rapid agreement on the bulk of the Commission's recommendations. But with regard to the actions to be taken toward third countries, namely the EFTA, and on the question of extending acceleration to agriculture, the debates were long and arduous. Agriculture proved the most difficult and for a time threatened to ruin the whole negotiation, since the Member States had agreed that no decision on any detail was binding until all points had been settled. A compromise on agriculture was finally reached, but only after the Ministers had remained in session until 4 A.M. on the night of May 10-11 and had held an extra session on the 12th that lasted until after midnight.

Agreement was reached without difficulty on the following matters:*

The date of application of acceleration. The other Member States accepted the proposal of the Germans and the Dutch that the acceleration should be put off until December 31, 1960, although in slightly attenuated wording: viz., the necessary measures were to be taken *at the latest* on December 31, 1960. Thus the extra 10 per cent decrease in tariffs between Member States was to be achieved by the end of the year, as well as the first steps toward the common external tariff, reduced by 20 per cent.

The extent of the internal tariff reductions. Wigny was not able to win

---

* There had never been any difficulty with the Commission's proposal that all quotas on intra-Community trade should be abolished by December 31, 1961, and it was readily accepted by the Council. The intention to remove quotas on industrial goods from third countries was reaffirmed, but no time limit established.

over the French (who were supported by Italy, Germany, and the Netherlands) to the proposition that a commitment should now be made to achieve a total reduction of 50 per cent by the end of the first stage. It was agreed that the Council would decide by June 30, 1961, *at the latest*, whether the reduction due on December 31, 1961, should be more than the 10 per cent set down in the Treaty. But the implication was apparently that this would be the case, unless the economic situation made it impossible.

Acceleration of the other sectors of the Treaty. A declaration was adopted in which the Council confirmed its intention to proceed as quickly as possible with a more rapid implementation in all sectors of economic integration. Special emphasis was put on measures in the social field, especially the vocational training of workers and their freedom of movement, the application of social security provisions, and equal pay for men and women. Also specifically noted were competition, transport, the right of establishment, and the economic development of associated overseas countries and territories. The Commission was asked to submit concrete proposals on all these matters within three months.

The difficulties began when the Ministers came to discuss the nature of the 20 per cent reduction in the common external tariff, for this involved diametrically opposed positions and the whole problem of relations with the EFTA. It had already been decided that the common external tariff was to be reduced by 20 per cent, and it was now a question of deciding whether this reduction would be made definitively or provisionally. The Germans and the Dutch had maintained all along that they would accept an accelerated approximation to the common external tariff only if it were definitively reduced by 20 per cent; the French and the Italians, on the other hand, were firmly against this, considering a 20 per cent reduction too great, regardless of whether it was conditional or definitive. They were joined by Belgium in proposing that no definite percentage should be mentioned, and that all or part of the reduction should be consolidated on the basis of reciprocity granted. Wigny and van der Schueren actively intervened to try to win over the Dutch and the Germans, pointing out that Belgium was also a low-tariff country and as anxious as they that the Common Market should practice a liberal policy toward third countries. But one did not start a negotiation by giving away one's trump card. Unilateral concessions were not going to ease Europe's trading problems; only a requirement of reciprocity would force third countries, too, to practice a liberal commercial policy. The Dutch-German demand was then modified so that half of the 20 per cent would be considered definitive with no counterpart from third countries required, while the other 10 per cent could be withdrawn by the Council on a proposal from the Commission.

In the compromise finally arrived at, the principle favored by the French, Italians, and Belgians was retained, and all tariff reductions benefiting nonmember states were declared to be provisional. However, Member States would be entitled to extend national reductions to all countries against reciprocity, so long as this did not result in cuts below the common external tariff (not reduced by 20 per cent). The Community would decide at the tariff negotiations to be held in GATT whether the 20 per cent reduction would be wholly or partially consolidated. But the Dutch and Germans obtained agreement to a protocol laying down in detail the procedure for such a consolidation, which was not published in the decision, but was included in the minutes of the Council.[91] By its terms, unanimous approval of the Council would be necessary either to withdraw or to consolidate the entire 20 per cent reduction. If such agreement did not prevail, and as long as the Council did not decide otherwise, only half of the reduction would be consolidated.

The French and Italians, while accepting the principle of a reduction in the common external tariff, sought to exclude from such provisions the products on List G, for which the tariff levels had just been determined after long negotiation. Both governments were under heavy pressure from domestic interest groups not to agree to another reduction in these rates so soon after their determination. The Belgians, Dutch, and Germans, however, maintained that List G was an integral part of the common external tariff, and that it was neither economically nor juridically possible to exclude it from the terms of the general agreement. This principle was finally retained, but it was agreed that for particularly sensitive products on List G, Member States could *request the Commission* to permit them to effect the first approximation to the common external tariff on the basis of the level agreed to and not reduced by 20 per cent.[92]

The Dutch and the Germans had publicly proclaimed that they were demanding the six-month delay in acceleration so as to make possible new contacts with the United Kingdom and the EFTA. Their concern over the 20 per cent reduction in the common external tariff was similarly motivated. Accordingly, Erhard now proposed that the Six should forthwith invite the EFTA countries to open direct political negotiations at the ministerial level.* The Germans did not insist that a favorable outcome of such talks be a condition for going ahead with acceleration, their aim being simply to resume talks in a framework outside that of the Committee of Twenty-One. The Dutch also submitted a proposal, but one that made acceleration dependent on an agreement with the Seven. The debate on these proposals

---

* Erhard had announced his intention to do so in the Bundestag debate of May 4. One of his chief aims was to exclude the Commission from such negotiations.

lasted three hours, with the Dutch and Germans holding out for Six-Seven negotiations. They were opposed by Belgium, Luxembourg, and France, all of whom stressed the interests of the United States and Canada in any negotiation. The Germans finally gave in, and Luns, finding himself isolated and accused of being the British Trojan horse in the Common Market, was forced to accept the compromise suggestion of Couve de Murville. A letter was to be sent to the EFTA suggesting that talks be held in the Committee of Twenty-One on European trade problems. A "declaration of intention" was appended to the decision, in which the Community reaffirmed its determination to pursue a liberal economic policy that would take the anxieties of the other European countries into account. The Community declared itself willing to open active negotiations with the members of the EFTA in the Committee of Twenty-One, with the goal of achieving the reciprocal reduction of trade barriers, and of maintaining and increasing the traditional trade among the European countries. Recognition of the EEC as a customs union must be the starting point of any negotiation, however.

Up to this point, the negotiations had been characterized by a mutual sensitivity to the particular problems and demands of the various Member States, and a willingness to compromise initial positions. This pattern seemed to break down when it came to the problem of agriculture. As mentioned, the dispute between the Netherlands and Germany over agriculture was of long standing. The Germans had not been applying the provisions of the Treaty, especially as regards quotas on agricultural produce from the Netherlands.* This can be explained not only by the desire to protect German export markets, but—perhaps more important— by the heavy pressure exercised on the government by agricultural interest groups as represented by the DBV. With parliamentary elections due in the fall of 1961, it was even harder for Adenauer to oppose this well-organized and strategically important body. The DBV maintained that there could be no liberalization of agricultural trade (let alone acceleration) until the common agricultural policy had been instituted and some approximation of production costs effected. Accordingly, at a meeting of the German cabinet in April, it was decided to exclude agriculture from acceleration.

Dutch agriculture was efficiently organized and profited from low duties on the secondary cereals used in the transformation of animal products— ham, butter, etc. Some of the traditional export markets of the Dutch,

---

* It must be added that there was a tacit understanding among all but the Netherlands to delay putting agricultural measures into effect until the common agricultural policy was instituted. This understanding had now begun to damage Dutch interests too much.

notably the United Kingdom, were threatened by the creation of the EFTA, and new EEC outlets were crucial. The Landbouwschap demanded that the government make it a *sine qua non* that agriculture be included in any acceleration agreement. This had been the official Dutch position since March.*

All attempts on the part of the Commission to ease the situation before the Council session began had failed. Luns officially announced at the start of the ministerial meetings that the Netherlands was determined to get something (especially an enlargement of quotas) in agriculture, and that all agreements reached were contingent on this. Erhard as firmly declared that Germany was determined to grant nothing in this sphere. France and Italy supported the German position to some extent, maintaining that no acceleration could be made in agriculture until some progress had been made on the common agricultural policy. So stubbornly did Erhard cling to his original position that many people wondered whether he was using agriculture as a pretext to block acceleration. Separate meetings of experts and other officials went on all during the afternoon and evening of May 10, recalling the toughest negotiations on the Rome Treaty. The German delegation held a special meeting and were exhorted by telephone calls from Adenauer to work out some solution so as to avoid a breakdown. A private meeting of the Council and the Commission was held in the evening, but still no solution was reached.

The task of drawing up a compromise agreement was finally handed over to a working party headed by Mansholt, the Commission member responsible for agriculture, and the discussions continued into the early hours of May 11. The Germans declared themselves prepared to grant tariff and quota concessions to the Netherlands on condition that they be tied to the common agricultural policy. The Dutch demurred, noting that this would take years and that they were determined to have something in 1960. The French then proposed that the working party should draw up a preamble declaring that the institution of any specific decisions on agriculture was dependent on *some progress* being made in the development of a common agricultural policy. The Dutch finally accepted this condition, but only if the decision on such progress were taken by a two-thirds majority vote. The Germans were now isolated, and it was clearly up to Adenauer to make a

---

* The intensity with which organized agriculture expressed its views on this occasion seems to have stemmed partly from the importance of the issue, but also from an understanding of the strong negotiating position of the Dutch government at this stage. With a veto power on many decisions of the Council of Ministers (a power that it would not have had at a later stage in the development of the EEC), the Dutch government was in a position to exact considerable concessions from other countries in exchange for its support.

political decision or allow acceleration to fail. A start on concrete proposals was also made, providing for an additional reduction of 5 per cent in tariffs on agricultural products (to a total of 25 per cent at the end of 1960 rather than 20 per cent).

A special session of the Council was then scheduled for May 12 in Brussels. Meanwhile, intensive discussions went on in Bonn between Adenauer and von Brentano. These resulted in new instructions, and the German representatives, Müller-Armack and von Scherpenberg, came to the special session with a considerably larger margin of maneuver. Germany now agreed that the principle of acceleration be partially extended to agriculture under certain conditions, but nobody was able to decide how the existence of these conditions was to be determined. Neither the Netherlands nor Germany was willing to grant the other a veto—Germany wanted the decision to be by unanimity, and the Netherlands insisted on two-thirds. A way out of this impasse seemed to be offered by a suggestion from Hallstein that the decision be left indirectly to the Commission. The general outline of an agreement on the concrete provisions to be applied was also completed.

The final decisions on agriculture were taken in a private session attended by fourteen people—two from each Member State and two from the Commission—which lasted from 6 P.M. to shortly after midnight. The chief concrete provisions were as follows (all to go into effect on January 1, 1961). First, for nonliberalized agricultural products an additional tariff reduction of 5 per cent was to be made.* And, second, the approximation to the common external tariff would not apply to agricultural products; global quotas were to be increased annually, normal quotas by 20 per cent annually, and small or nil quotas to a total of 5.2 per cent of national production in 1961.†

But more important are the terms of the "preamble" that precedes these specific proposals. It was agreed, first of all, that the measures provided for in the Treaty relating to the liberalization of agricultural trade and not yet implemented should be put into effect by the end of the year, a polite way of inviting the Germans to stop violating the Treaty. Work on the common agricultural policy was to be speeded up, a timetable being established: final proposals from the Commission before June 30, a first general

* This concession is not very important at the present stage, since most agricultural products are controlled by quotas.

† For products for which global quotas have not been opened and for products for which no long-term contracts have been entered into, the Member States are required to permit imports equal to the average imports for three years before the Treaty came into force, increased by 10 per cent each year to the end of the first stage.

discussion by the Council before July 31, and the creation of a special committee to prepare the Council's decision, as well as a first report from this committee, before October 15. The Council was to hold one or more sessions before the end of the year to work out a first solution on the Community level for the problems caused by different competitive conditions in agriculture. The progress on this point was to be reviewed by the Council and the Commission, also before the end of the year, and the *Commission* was charged with drafting such proposals *"as may be necessary* for the execution or revision of the concrete provisions" agreed upon. These proposals could be amended only by unanimity, but were to be adopted by a qualified majority vote.

Although the Dutch Foreign Minister, Luns, expressed great disappointment about not having obtained more concessions from the Germans, there was general satisfaction, even elation, with the final compromise. Agriculture was generally recognized to be the most difficult problem the Common Market had to face, hence even this modest progress took on great significance. The specific concessions granted the Dutch may have been meager, but one should note that the Germans did accept the principle of extending acceleration to agriculture, and that they probably gave up as much the Dutch. Luns accused the Germans of completely lacking a Community spirit in the negotiations.* He complained that the Netherlands would be the chief loser, for the additional tariff reductions were only for nonliberalized products, and the concessions obtained only covered 1961, with no commitments for subsequent years. He said that the Netherlands had accepted the compromise out of Community feeling and owing to the enormous political pressure exerted in the Community in favor of acceleration.[93] Dutch agricultural groups were less critical than Luns, observing that at least their minimal demands had been met. The Dutch press in general expressed considerable satisfaction that the Netherlands had been able to achieve this result, even though it had stood almost alone.[94]

Much of the credit for the final compromise belongs to the Commission members, who participated in all phases of the negotiation and proposed crucial compromise solutions. Particularly notable was the role of Mansholt as head of the working group that prepared the final agreement and the preamble. The solutions eventually arrived at, to which Mansholt persuaded the Dutch to agree, isolated the Germans and forced a change of instructions from Bonn. When it came down to the point of jeopardizing the whole acceleration agreement, neither side was willing to bear the responsibility for failure. In the agricultural debate, as throughout the ses-

---

* This is perhaps an accurate assessment, but a somewhat paradoxical one, given the fact that on most issues in the Council sessions the Germans and Dutch had cooperated closely, supporting each other's positions.

sions, the Belgians showed themselves to have the most Community spirit. On agriculture they were supported by the French, who, though originally opposed to accelerated steps in agriculture, were willing to give some satisfaction to the Dutch in order to get agreement. Moreover, they were responsible for introducing the important preamble that formed the basis for the final agreement.

The consequences of the crisis over agriculture are interesting. Agreement was finally reached only on the condition that work on the common agricultural policy be accelerated as well. All the Member States were put under pressure to achieve some concrete results by the end of 1960, lest the acceleration might still be compromised. Germany and the Netherlands, however, could not agree on voting procedures for determining whether sufficient progress had been made to go on with acceleration; the decision was therefore left indirectly to the Commission, which was asked to present formal proposals on this question.

The Council of Ministers, after seventeen hours of debate on December 20-21, 1960, finally adopted the Commission's proposals and agreed that enough progress had been made to finalize the acceleration decisions in agriculture. It was again a matter of German resistance being eventually broken down by pressure from the other Member States. This decision will be treated in more detail in Chapter 11.*

CONCLUSIONS

We have seen that acceleration is primarily an example in the operation of the spill-over principle. It met the positive aspirations of the following groups: businessmen, who, having accepted the inevitability of the Common Market, and having begun to adopt measures of adjustment, had set in motion planning programs that could not be stretched ahead for the full transition period; "Europeans"—in the Commission, in the EPA, and in the Governments—who saw acceleration as a way to strengthen the central institutions and make the Community irreversible; those whose chief interest was in long-range economic unification and who welcomed any accelerated progress; and those who saw acceleration as a means of finally terminating all talk of a free trade area. Spill-over does not require that all governments,

---

* That agriculture continued to be a divisive issue was revealed by the recurrence of the German-Dutch conflict in mid-1961. The Council of Ministers was unable to reach a decision on applying the second 10 per cent reduction in internal tariffs. The Dutch refused because no further concessions in agriculture were forthcoming. Agreement on the second reduction was not possible until after the basic decisions on a common agricultural policy had been taken in January 1962. The full acceleration was finally instituted in July 1, 1962.

groups, and parties favor a given step for the same reasons; it requires only that a convergence of interests exists, concrete and extensive enough to enable a coalition to be constructed, and powerful enough to make opponents of the general goal reluctant to bring about its frustration. Nowhere could this be more strikingly demonstrated than in the acceleration decision, a point that is emphasized in the Commission's own statement: "As the preparation of the decisions clearly brought out, an acceleration of the Treaty is fraught with many difficulties. It is therefore all the more remarkable, not only that on 12 May there should have been unanimous agreement in the Council on the procedure laid before it, but also that the principle of a gesture of such great political and economic moment was never seriously contested."[95]

Our analysis has shown that although there was a convergence of support for some kind of acceleration, a decision would not have been achieved without the Commission. The inability of the governments to agree on a precise formula forced them to delegate the task of formulation to the Commission. None was willing to accept the possibility of a deadlock.

The ensuing negotiations illustrated in a striking manner the mediating and brokerage functions of the Commission. Throughout the two months of preparation and during the marathon sessions of the Council and the various working groups, the Commission continued to play an active role in many ways: campaigning for the adoption of its proposals, representing the Community interest, offering compromises when this seemed necessary, agreeing to modifications in its own recommendations—in effect, sharing the responsibility and the decision-making powers. The final decision thus came as a result of the close cooperation between the Member States, the Council, the Commission, the Rey Committee, and the Permanent Representatives. As President Hallstein observed, just after the acceleration decision had been finally approved:

The debate was extremely difficult, but the conclusion was one of complete agreement both between the Governments and between the Council as a whole and the Commission. It should in fact be stressed that all the modifications that were made in the Commission's original recommendations had been approved by the Commission. Community feelings have gained the day over individual sentiments and interests, even perfectly justifiable and defensible interests. With this decision the Community has withstood the most difficult test. This has a double value: it signifies, on the one hand, the irreversible strengthening of the Community and, on the other, the Community's increased ability to follow a liberal and open policy toward third countries.[96]

Hallstein's words express the general satisfaction of the Commission with the results achieved. The substance of the Commission's proposals had been accepted. Although acceleration was to be delayed by six months, this involved no sacrifice on the basic principle, for it was universally accepted that the sheer technical task of approximating the national tariffs to the common external tariff would have forced a delay anyway. Not only had the Commission's specific recommendations been substantially approved, but it had also been given the authority to submit further acceleration recommendations covering the rest of the Treaty. Thus it retained the advantage of initiative.

As subsequent events have demonstrated, it has been very difficult for the governments to avoid going on with further accelerated moves. Speeding up only the customs union provisions of the Treaty had been opposed by all the Member States. All had made additional, often conflicting, demands. The Commission maneuvered in the situation so as to make the most of its own role. Since there was enough support for the principle that some acceleration should be effected at once, it was able to put off making specific recommendations on the rest of the Treaty. This acceleration was now achieved, and if the Member States were to avoid economic and political difficulties, they would have to reach further compromises on the new recommendations of the Commission. French business insisted that steps leading to the harmonization of social charges be accelerated, Socialists and trade unions in all countries demanded an acceleration in the field of social policy, and Dutch and French agriculture called for a more rapid introduction of a common agricultural policy. Hence this partial acceleration of the Treaty gave rise to more keenly felt expectations, many of which made themselves felt in the 1961–62 crises over the passage to the second stage of the transition period and the institution of the common agricultural policy (see Chapters 11 and 12 for details).

As we have seen, during the final negotiations of the Council, disagreements between Member States could be settled only by means of compromises that gave the Commission, as the representative of the Community interest, added competence. To the two instances regarding agriculture, we should add that of the List G applications. Here the Commission was given the authority to *grant or deny* applications for exemptions of List G products from the general 20 per cent reduction in the common external tariff.

It seems clear that the accommodation pattern here belongs to the category of "upgrading common interests." Obviously a number of specific bargains were struck of the "splitting-the-difference" type, but the over-all decision represents a solution at a higher level, in which the common interest of all parties has been maximized. The Commission was clearly the catalyst in this process, precipitating agreement both by setting limits within which accommodation was reached and by defining the actual terms of the contract.

That the Ministers stayed in session until four in the morning on one occasion and until after midnight on another confirms the fact that all the participants recognized the absolute necessity for reaching an agreement. The Commission's proposals met the needs of such a wide range of interests and had been so dramatized by the press, especially following the opposition from the EFTA "out-group," that nobody was willing to accept responsibility for a failure. The Ministers' deliberations were characterized by a sensitivity to each others' needs and a willingness to compromise, except for the German attitude on agriculture. The Germans gave in only after they became convinced there was no alternative if the rest of the acceleration decision were to be saved. Each Member State sought to gain the maximum advantage from the decision, but each was forced to make concessions in favor of a compromise agreement, and in so doing to resist the pressures of important interest groups. The French and Italians accepted the principle of a 20 per cent reduction in the common external tariff in spite of strong objections from industrial federations in both countries. Similarly, they abandoned their demands that the other provisions of the Treaty be accelerated at the same time as the customs union. In exchange, the Germans and Dutch accepted accelerated implementation of the common external tariff in spite of opposition from practically all economic interests in both countries and from the Minister of Economic Affairs in Germany and the Foreign Minister in the Netherlands. The Germans and Dutch in turn obtained French acquiescence to a new overture to the EFTA countries, and to definite steps toward a liberal Community trade policy (at least a 10 per cent consolidation of the provisional 20 per cent reduction in the common external tariff).

Reactions in the various Member States to the Council's decision ranged from exultant enthusiasm to sober satisfaction. It was greeted jubilantly in France and Belgium with large headlines: "Good Agreement for Europe and France" (*Figaro*); "Green Light for European Economic Integration" (*Aurore*); "Definitive Victory for the Common Market" (*Paris-Presse*); and "The Six Have Negotiated the Decisive Stage" (*Le Soir*). The Patronat Français also welcomed the decision, describing it as vitally important for French industry, since it constituted a definitive commitment to go on with European economic integration; furthermore, it would eliminate the doubts and hesitations of some of their partners.[97] The general emphasis in these reactions was on the significance of the decision for the external relations of the Community,[98] an emphasis that attests to the importance of external pressures at the Luxembourg-Brussels meetings. The French Finance Minister, Baumgartner, announced that "the acceleration measures are in line with French interests. . . . The world now knows that the Six are resolved to maintain, strengthen, and accelerate the Community."[99]

The German reaction was more restrained, but there was general satisfaction with the compromise achieved. "After a battle it is usual to ask who won and who went down, but this case is no occasion for either laurels or consolation."[100] Everybody had made concessions. This was the price of setting acceleration into motion.[101] Besides obtaining a six months' delay, Germany had the satisfaction of knowing that she had helped to increase European solidarity and to promote a more liberal trade policy for the Community. Typical of Dutch opinion was the observation that the minimum demands of the Netherlands had been met, not because the justice of these demands was accepted, but because the negotiators realized that otherwise the Dutch would reject the whole acceleration plan.[102]

THE COMMON EXTERNAL TARIFF AND LIST G

ONE OF THE defining characteristics of a customs union like that of the EEC, the characteristic that sets it apart from a free trade area, is the existence of a common external tariff toward the outside world. It is the fundamental instrument of the trade and external policies of the Community. But how was its level to be determined? Benelux and Germany had relatively low levels of tariffs, whereas France and Italy were high-tariff countries. In deciding on a level for the common external tariff, the Member States were bound by GATT, which stipulates that the general rate of customs duties in a customs union cannot be higher than the rate previously in force in the countries constituting the union.[1] The general solution agreed upon was that the level would be at the arithmetical average of the duties applied in the four customs areas of the Community.[2]

For a number of products, however, it was decided that the level of customs duties would not be fixed at the arithmetical average, but by negotiation between the Member States. These products are enumerated in special lists appended to the Treaty, and the duties for most of them were settled by agreement before the Treaty was signed.[3] No agreement, however, was reached on seventy customs positions, and these were placed in List G. Each Member State was furthermore authorized to add other products to this list, up to the limit of 2 per cent of the total value of its imports from third countries (1956 as base year).[4] Negotiations on List G were to be set in motion by the Member States before the end of the second year of the first stage and concluded by the end of the first stage. If agreement was not reached within this limit, the Council, on a proposal of the Commission, was to fix the duties, by unanimity until the end of the second stage, and by qualified majority thereafter.[5]

The technical problems involved in calculating the arithmetical averages were to be settled within two years after the entry into force of the

Treaty; and any adjustments required in order to ensure the internal harmony of the common external tariff with respect to the degree of processing undergone by various products were to be completed by the end of the first stage.[6] Thus the common external tariff was to be completed by the end of the first stage of the transition period in order that the first approximations to it of the various national tariffs could be made.

However, it soon became obvious that the tariff would be needed much earlier. The reasons for this were as follows. (1) The Community was already engaged in, or about to be engaged in, three major sets of negotiations within GATT, and it would be extremely awkward not to have a completed common external tariff to use as a basis for discussion.* (2) The Community had been subject to very severe attacks in GATT and had constantly to defend itself against charges of protectionism. Much of this rancor was due to uncertainties about the level of the common external tariff, since the products on List G are of considerable importance in world commerce. (3) The Council of Ministers had decided in December 1958 that, *within the limits of the common external tariff,* the reductions of customs duties provided for in the Treaty should be extended to nonmember states enjoying the m-f-n (most-favored-nation) treatment. (4) It was felt that completion of the common external tariff would affirm the unity of the Six, particularly in view of the relations with the Outer Seven. And (5) the prospect of acceleration made the preparation of the tariff more urgent.

In response to these pressures, both the technical work involved in consolidating the four tariff schedules into one and the intergovernmental negotiations on List G were accelerated. All this work culminated on February 13, 1960, when the Council approved that part of the draft tariff based on the arithmetical average, and on March 2, 1960, when an agreement was signed fixing the duties in List G.† The completion of the common external tariff almost two years ahead of schedule represents one of the less spectacular, and yet most important, successes of the EEC. As Giuseppe Caron, Vice-President of the EEC, observed, "The common external tariff of the EEC is not only a very important technical document, it also confirms the political will of the Six countries to continue on the road they have

---

* The three sets of negotiations: renegotiation of the consolidated duties, negotiations on the general incidence of the common external tariff, and the Dillon negotiations.

† The tariff was thereby 97 per cent completed. The remaining positions presented special technical problems: the introduction of special duties; adjustments under Article 21, paragraph 1; and the determination of the extent to which certain duties declared by Member States to be of a fiscal nature were protective. In addition, four headings of petroleum products in List G remained unsettled. EEC Commission, *General Report 1960*, p. 237.

traced toward their complete economic integration. . . . This success proves in a tangible way. . . . the possibility of solving concretely all the problems the Common Market presents on the technical level when the political will of the Member States is there.[7]

The EEC thus differentiated itself clearly from a free trade area, affirming its vitality and "proclaiming with solemnity that the Common Market was neither dead nor dying."[8] According to one report, "Without a highly developed community spirit, agreement on the controversial items of List G would not have been possible."[9] The European Commission could hereafter negotiate in GATT in the name of the Six and on the basis of the common external tariff, thus presenting the Community as a nonprotectionist entity. Thus were assuaged the widespread fears that the Common Market was in danger of losing its unique character owing to British demands for a free trade area, demands that had received a sympathetic hearing in Germany and Benelux. The common external tariff was now set; the duties were in a fixed relation to each other, and they could not be changed except by the unanimous approval of the Council.[10] The significance of all this was increased by the agreement on acceleration. It will be recalled that in May 1960 the Member States agreed to make the first approximation to the common external tariff on January 1, 1961, instead of one year later as provided for in the Treaty. They also agreed that the level of the common external tariff, just completed after strenuous negotiations, should be lowered by 20 per cent, subject to a degree of reciprocity.

There were substantially two kinds of problems involved in completing the common external tariff, and these were dealt with in separate negotiations: technical (the consolidation of tariff schedules) and political (List G). Although we shall concentrate on the latter in the analysis that follows, a few remarks about the technical negotiations are in order since they, too, have a significance for political integration.

It is not a simple thing to consolidate several tariff schedules into one.[11] First, a comparison of national tariff schedules must be made so as to define the bases upon which the averages are to be calculated. In one country a duty will be levied on cars by weight, and in another according to the number of cylinders. The simple juxtaposition of the four schedules resulted in the elaboration of a list comprising just under 20,000 positions (an average tariff may have 5,000). Second, a single, manageable tariff schedule must be evolved from all these positions and must be based on a common nomenclature. Third, a "table of concordance" between the headings of the Community and the national schedules must be created so that calculation of the arithmetical average will be possible. This also provides a basis for determining which tariffs each Member State will have to increase or decrease in the course of the successive stages. It leads, moreover, to further problems because some states apply specific duties, and others ad valorem duties. Finally, an equilibrium must be established within the completed schedule to take account of the degree to which various goods have been finished (raw materials should have a lower tariff than semimanufactured goods, and so on).

These tasks were undertaken by the Interim Committee at the end of 1957 and transferred to the Commission in early 1958.[12] Groups of experts drawn from the national administrations were set to the work of juxtaposition, harmonization of nomenclature, and subsequent contraction. Preliminary drafts were established by the experts and the Commission, and then submitted to the various customs administrations for comment. These comments were examined by the Commission staff and then by a mixed committee of economics and customs experts delegated by the Member States and possessing powers of decision sufficient to overcome most difficulties. It was on the work of these committees that the Commission based its final proposals, which were subsequently presented to the Council and approved.[13]

The common external tariff consists of a relatively modest 2,893 lines or positions (the Italian tariff contained 7,618). It has made an immediate impact on the national tariff schedules because of the accelerated alignment of the national rates to it. Thus the new French Customs Tariff, issued at the end of December 1960, was based on the nomenclature adopted for the common external tariff. It contained three columns of rates: (1) that of the ultimate common external tariff of the EEC; (2) the national duties now applicable to third countries, as approximated not only to the common external tariff according to Article 23, but to the acceleration decision of May 12, 1960; and (3) the duties then applied to EEC exchanges, which were 70 per cent to 80 per cent of those applied to third countries.[14]

The procedure followed in this negotiation was characteristic of the Community pattern. Decisions are made as the result of a sometimes tortuous process of prior consultation, meetings of experts at various levels, and the continual participation of the Commission. Hundreds of meetings are held; thousands of national experts are involved in a process of Community decision-making. The services of the Commission normally take the initiative, presenting a Community point of view and offering compromises when agreement between the experts is impossible. When agreement fails at the level of the experts, the negotiations are moved to the level of the Ministers or bureau chiefs, who have the authority to depart somewhat from instructions.

Thus we see that in a very real sense the common external tariff of the EEC was "made in Brussels." Since the first approximation toward it had been taken, its level could not be changed except by mutual agreement of the Six, and therefore future tariff legislation will also be made in Brussels. The effect of a customs union is to eliminate the possibility of a national commercial policy. But this does not imply a supranational policy formulated by a higher authority. Decision-making is shared with the other Member States and with the organizations representing the Community as a whole. A customs union also elicits reactions and fears from the outside world, which, in the case of the EEC, have forced the Member States to accelerate their pace in numerous ways. This speeding up has been possible largely because of the expanded roles granted to the institutions of the Community. Only the institutions representing the "general interest" are in a position to mediate between the national viewpoints effectively. It is more and more obvious that although the Treaty does not require a common commercial policy to be adopted until the end of the transition period, events will demand its adoption long before that. Thus the role of central decision-making will be again expanded.

THE LIST G NEGOTIATIONS

The agreement on List G, two years ahead of the most optimistic schedule, has far greater political significance. Here is a list of products on which the differences of opinion between the Member States were sufficiently lively to have defied all attempts to overcome them before the signing of the Treaty. The differences between the Member States on these products represent in microcosm the general problem faced by a customs union of high- and low-tariff countries, a problem that has strained the "European" loyalties of many individuals and groups.

The negotiations on List G were considered so sensitive that care was taken to keep them entirely in government hands. Hence, whereas the Commission and Council were assigned the task of fixing the arithmetical average in the common external tariff, "the duties applicable to the products in List G shall be fixed by means of negotiation between the Member States."[15] Not even by the Council acting alone by unanimity! The Commission was not entrusted with making a report or a recommendation, much less a proposal, but was limited to taking "all appropriate steps in order that such negotiations shall be *undertaken* before the end of the second year after the date of the entry into force of this Treaty and concluded before the end of the first stage."[16]

THE CONTENTS OF LIST G

Ouin summarizes the problem as follows:

The conflict among the Member States concerning List G exemplifies a more general problem which the Community as a whole faces. If the Community is to be a world commercial power capable of exporting at competitive prices, its industries must procure raw materials at the most advantageous prices, which is to say, at world market prices. If these prices are to be increased by heavy duties the export position of the interested industries will be worsened. If, on the other hand, the Community protects the raw materials it produces with high tariffs it will encourage their exploitation even though they can only be sold at higher than world prices, and it will run the risk of developing tendencies toward autarky.[17]

There are 70 headings in List G, covering products representing 15.7 per cent of the EEC imports from nonmember countries in 1957 and having a total value of $2,671 million.[18] Three-quarters of these products are raw materials on which certain countries of the Community apply very high duties and others very low ones. Those states applying high duties do so because the cost of their production is very high compared to the world price. A lower duty would force a cessation of production, accompanied by serious economic, financial, and social repercussions.[19] A high duty, on the other hand, would force the transforming industries of countries having a very low or nil tariff to procure raw materials at higher than world prices, thus crippling their competitive posture.

Some products (aircraft and aircraft engines) were put on the list because it was thought that the arithmetical average was too high; but the general rule was that items were placed on the list because a country wanted special protection for an industry that was important to it but unable to face competition. The country most involved was Italy, which has 12,000 workers in its sulfur industry, 10,000 in silk, 9,000 in the lead and zinc mines in already depressed Calabria, and substantial numbers engaged in the production of cork, bromine, iodine, and a few other goods. France wanted special protection for aluminum, cork, bromine, wine, petroleum products, machine tools, and wood pulp. Germany and Benelux, as importers of most of these goods, could be counted on to fight for low duties, although Belgium wanted protection for its automobile assembly industry, and Germany for glass pearls, engines, and a few other items.[20]

Despite the difficulties involved, agreement was reached in a surprisingly short time. And notwithstanding the special care taken to keep the negotiations in the hands of the Governments, the Commission came to play an increasingly large role in the negotiations, and the decision-making pattern did not differ significantly from the prevailing Community style. How can we account for this?[21]

THE ROLE OF THE COMMISSION

Instead of waiting until the end of 1959, and rather than limit itself to the minimal role implied in the Treaty, the Commission took the initiative in calling for negotiations at the end of 1958, presented the dossiers, proposed the negotiating procedures, chaired the major negotiating committee, made specific proposals on duties, and in general represented a Community pressure forcing conciliation and action.

Already in 1958 the Commission was engaged in preparing the negotiations on List G. The First General Report notes that "this work must be done with scrupulous care. It requires a whole series of economic and statistical studies and the preparation of a 'negotiation file' which will have to be transmitted to each Member State. It is only after this work is well under way that a meeting to compare viewpoints will serve a useful purpose."[22] In December the Commission decided to speed up work on the whole common external tariff,[23] and the first meeting with national experts was called for the end of January 1959. At this meeting the Commission presented the dossier it had prepared, noting that it would be "opportune for the Governments to have at their disposal a complete over-all picture of the position of these products from a Community point of view."[24] The Commission had also prepared a draft questionnaire, to which the national administrations were to be asked to reply, indicating volume of exports, imports, production, consumption, future prospects, etc., with respect to each product on the list. The Commission suggested further that since this would take time, and since some of the products were on the list for other economic reasons, such products might be exempted and intergovernmental negotiations set in motion immediately. All Governments agreed and were to submit to the Commission a list of such products by February 25, 1959.[25]

The Commission also proposed a general procedure for negotiation, which was accepted by the Governments at the subsequent meeting of the expert group.[26] Three Working Parties, presided over by representatives of the Member States, and a Central Group, presided over by the Commission, were set up. The Working Parties were (1) to determine for which products speed-up negotiations could be envisaged; (2) to formulate for the Central Group, for each product, proposals on the duty to be applied, or to inform it of disagreements; and (3) to study disputed cases on the basis of new instructions from the Central Group. The Working Parties were also to make periodic reports to the Central Group.[27] The Central Group was charged with coordinating and directing the work of the Working Parties, with negotiating customs duties on the basis of the proposals or information supplied by the Working Parties, with examining cases in dispute and if necessary referring them back to the Working Parties, and, finally, with recording at the end of the negotiations the agreements or disagreements reached. The Commission was to chair the Central Group "as a neutral element," on the understanding that the responsibility for the negotiations and the decisions rested entirely with the national governments.[28] A precise mandate, however, was not elaborated, since it was considered wiser to allow the Commission to be guided by experience.[29] The Commission was also involved in another way. Since it was to make proposals at the end of the first stage concerning products for which no agreement had been reached in the intergovernmental negotiations, the experts suggested that in cases of disagreement the files should be submitted to the Commission at once for study.[30]

However, after two months of arduous negotiation in the Working Parties, almost no progress had been made. By the end of May not a single proposal on a specific duty had been made to the Central Group. The Commission observed that List G involved very difficult questions, as was confirmed by the fact that the Treaty gave four years for a solution, but that over and above the work of the experts the Governments should give some evidence of their desire to reach agreement. A good first gesture would be to refrain from adding any more products to List G, no matter what the pressure from the industries concerned.[31] It will be recalled that the Treaty provides for the addition of products to List G up to the limit of 2 per cent of the total value of imports from third countries. Discussions had been under way all year on what products to add, and when such a second list (List G II, as it came to be known) should be closed. The Commission pointed out that agreement on List G was taking long enough as it was, and that if the Governments really wanted to accelerate the completion of the common external tariff, some sacrifices would have to be made.

The negotiations continued throughout June, with the Commission's representative, François Ortoli (who was chairman of the Central Group), continuing to push for rapid solutions. By the end of the month he was calling for a time limit on the technical negotiations, arguing that agreement on the technical plane was obviously not possible for most of the products, and that only political negotiations at the ministerial level, involving reciprocal concessions, would be likely to succeed.[32] By mid-July, when the negotiations were adjourned for the summer, agreement had been reached on a few products, but achievements in general were minimal, and all possible difficulties had appeared.[33]

When the technical negotiations resumed in September, the Commission tried to conclude this stage as rapidly as possible in order to move negotiations to a higher level. An attempt was made to get a greater power of decision for the experts, and it was proposed that when high duties were involved, and when differences between the Member States were not great, the experts should have the right to adopt levels not more than 10 per cent away from their instructions.[34] This, however, could be no more than a palliative, since the Member States were still far from solutions on a majority of the List G products, most of which involved other than technical or commercial questions. For many agricultural products, agreement proved difficult because the common agricultural policy of the Community was not yet fixed, or because trade in that product was by government monopoly (e.g., alcohol). Also, as mentioned, there were conflicts between producers and consumers when uneconomic production was supported for social reasons. And, finally, there were a number of goods whose production within the Community certain members wished to foster (French aluminum, Belgian auto parts, French paper pulp, and fats and tropical woods in the Overseas Territories).[35]

At the October session of the Council of Ministers, the Commission reported the difficulties being encountered and pointed out that the Working Parties and Central Group did not have the necessary powers to settle political and social problems. It suggested further that the technical work be concentrated on drawing up an exact picture of the situation, and that each country should examine the position it could assume in the interests of the other countries, thus passing from a national to a Community outlook. The Council adopted this suggestion. These positions and solutions were to be set forth by mid-November, and a special Ministerial Meeting was to be held to provide for negotiation on reciprocal concessions. The Commission also stressed the need for giving up List G II, but although there was much support in the Council, no decision was made.[36] France and Italy were reported as being ready to give up making additions, but Germany, and especially the Netherlands, were very reticent, and had already submitted their lists. The Dutch list raised some basic problems about the common external tariff as a whole, bringing up again the question of fixed duties on derivative products.[37]

The Commission and the Central Group favored setting up a special group to have competence to propose general economic solutions for certain products. Difficulties arose over the fact that such a competence would exceed the powers of the Central Group. Ultimately, however, an *ad hoc* working party was set up under the Economic and Financial Affairs Department of the Commission. The products in question were cork, sulfur, silk, lead, and zinc. The group's mandate was to define the prospects on the national and world markets of the products; to examine whether and to what extent the products could become competitive; to indicate the solutions suggested and the solutions preferred by the group; and to determine the costs of modernization or reconversion if that seemed necessary. This "economic group" was to report to the Central Group.[38]

The Central Group met in November to draw up a concluding report on the technical negotiations for the Ministerial Meeting. Great efforts were made to reach agreement on as many products as possible. The problem of List G II defied solution, and by late October this second list had exceeded the original list in length. By November 18, however, 93 of the 114 products on List G II had been otherwise settled, and the Commission insisted the Governments show their good will by withdrawing the rest.[39]

The report of the Central Group submitted by Ortoli revealed that agreement had been reached among the experts on 29 of the 70 positions on List G (31 per cent of the volume). The remaining problems were analyzed, and Ortoli said that the Commission was prepared to make proposals for their solution should the Ministers consider this necessary.[40]

THE MINISTERIAL MEETINGS

Between December 1, 1959, and the final agreement in Rome on March 2, 1960, there were four Ministerial Meetings devoted to List G. The Commission, acting within the Central Group and in cooperation with the Permanent Representatives, continued to play the role of initiator and ultimately of broker.

At the first session, December 1–3, the Commission urged that the positions be discussed by groups of products, rather than in the order they appeared on the list. This grouping, thoughtfully prepared by the Commission, ordered the products according to the ease with which solutions could be achieved. This technique maximized the feeling of accomplishment and good will, while at the same time increasing the pressure to solve the "few" problems that remained. Thus the 29 positions settled by the experts were immediately confirmed. A second group was made up of products for which relatively small differences existed, and the Ministers assigned the experts the task of "going next door" for a few hours and preparing concrete proposals on an arithmetical basis. The more difficult problems were the subject of serious negotiation. As the bargaining began, it became obvious that there was a reluctance to give in on one product when the levels on other products were also in doubt. Consequently, it was decided that no results were final until the whole list was determined.[41] An additional eleven positions were agreed upon at this meeting, and considerable progress was made on the rest. The Central Group and the Permanent Representatives were given the mandate to prepare the next meeting just before Christmas. Active negotiations went on in the interim, and pressure was applied on the national administrations by the Permanent Representatives for a greater flexibility.[42]

Ministerial Meetings from December 19 to 21 ran into difficulties, but agreement on cork (the Netherlands and Germany gave in), as well as on aircraft and wines, was reached in private meetings that excluded officials and doubtless involved hard bargaining. The third session, from February 12 to 15, settled all but six positions.[43] In preparing for the fourth meeting, the Central Group and the Permanent Representatives drew up a draft agreement, which was finally signed, along with numerous protocols, on March 2, 1960. Here again most of the sessions were private and the bargaining hard.

The final result reveals that all Member States made substantial concessions from their original demands. France and Italy accepted lower duties for industrial products, Germany accepted higher duties for food products and raw materials, and the Benelux countries higher duties on almost everything. Numerous special arrangements were made. The Italian market for lead, zinc, sulfur, and iodine was isolated for six years. Differential duties were levied according to the use to which a product was to be put (fats for other than food purposes, salts for industrial purposes, etc.). Frequently recourse was made to tariff quotas,[44] i.e., duties were set fairly high and then provisions made for one or several countries to import a given amount at lower or nil tariff (aluminum, paper pulp, some agricultural products, etc.).[45] Hence it is difficult to determine the commercial significance of the final agreement, or the extent to which problems were merely accommodated. Nevertheless, the Member States' "successful compromises in this sensitive area indicate their political determination to proceed with the establishment of the Common Market."[46]

We have stressed the role of the Commission because it was the active initiator of this successful series of negotiations, despite a minimal formal role. During the Ministerial Meetings it continued to play an active part and to represent the Community interest as a whole. The success of the negotiations in such record time was widely attributed to the energy of the Commission's representative on the Central Group, François Ortoli. Agreement, however, could hardly have been reached without the positive will of the Member States. That the Commission was able to take the initiative, to perform its brokerage and mediating functions, and to cajole the Member States to agreement shows that the will to agree, to continue with the Common Market, was present. The atmosphere of the Ministerial Meetings was excellent. Member States were willing to resist pressures from special interests in order to keep the negotiations moving, especially with respect to List G II. The Ministers met in long sessions until late at night to reach agreement, exhibiting considerable sensitivity to each other's problems. No government took absolute positions. The pattern revealed in the negotiations clearly fits the generalizations already made regarding integration and confirms the engagement of the Member States.

CONCLUSIONS

We have thus seen that the decision-making process involved in the List G negotiations did not differ markedly from the general Community pattern, in spite of the fact that the formal provisions of the Treaty called for a different procedure. This confirms our thesis that a Community decision-making pattern is developing in response to special situations, a pattern that is relatively independent of the provisions of the Treaty. This pattern brings together the representatives of the Community interest (the Commission) and those of the Member States (experts, Ministers, Council) in a continuous problem-solving operation. It is clear that although final policy-making powers reside with the Member States in Council, the Commission plays a most significant role. If an accommodation is to be achieved in which common interests are upgraded, these interests must have an active institutional embodiment. In this case we have seen that the Commission has actively expanded its role: it initiated proceedings, kept them moving ahead, and intervened with procedural and substantive proposals, presenting the dossier from a Community point of view. It is surely not too much to say that agreement would not have been achieved without the Commission's intervention. The Member States acquiesced in the enlarged role of the Commission mainly because they had no choice if a solution, and a quick one, were to be achieved. Commitment to form a customs union forces agreement to construct an external tariff and to develop a common commercial policy. As we have seen, the completion of the common external tariff was made difficult by the lack of a common agricultural policy. Conversely, the successful termination of the List G negotiations increased the need for more rapid action in this field, too. This internal dynamic invariably results in increasing the scope of central decision-making.

The nature of the EEC decision-making pattern has a further consequence: the involvement of thousands of national civil servants is in itself a significant factor. List G is a fine example of this. Participants in these negotiations testify to the increased understanding of mutual problems and to the sense of sharing in a common enterprise that result from meeting together over an extended period of time.

Given the importance of the items on List G (and those proposed for List G II), it is not surprising that all the governments were under severe pressure from the organizations representing the interests concerned. As the negotiations progressed and the role being played by the Commission evolved, a change took place. The Commission, and especially Ortoli, now became the focal point of group activity, the intensity of which increased as the negotiations proceeded. There was also closer contact between the Commission and interest groups organized at the level of the Six.[47]

We have seen, then, that the List G negotiations served an integrative function. This is not to say that the case has a unique significance, but merely that it demonstrates some of the processes at work as the Member States and the Community institutions proceed to apply the provisions of the Rome Treaty and to work toward an economic union. In the words of one of the participants in the negotiations: "On the occasion of its first battle the Community has carried off a victory; let us hope that this is only the first step in a long series that will culminate finally in the integration of Europe."[48]

XI

PREPARING A
COMMON AGRICULTURAL POLICY

"THE COMMON MARKET shall extend to agriculture and trade in agricultural products. . . . The functioning and development of the Common Market in respect of agricultural products shall be accompanied by the establishment of a common agricultural policy among the Member States."[1] Thus did the Six commit themselves to creating a common set of policies in agriculture. The commitment is a large one, since it implies the disappearance of strictly national agricultural policies. The Treaty itself, however, states merely that a common agricultural policy should have the following objectives: to increase agricultural productivity, to ensure a fair standard of living for the agricultural population, to stabilize markets and guarantee regular supplies, and to ensure reasonable prices for consumers.[2] Due account is to be taken of the particular character of agricultural activities, of the need for making adjustments gradually, and of the fact that agriculture is closely linked to other sectors of the economy.[3] Enunciation of the policy measures and specific rules needed to implement these general goals is left to the central institutions of the Community.

We are thus brought to that aspect of the Treaty of Rome that has elicited perhaps the most comment, namely its generality, its nature as a "traité cadre" or framework treaty. Here the Community institutions have the power to *legislate* for the Community as a whole, without being required to refer back to the national parliaments. The progress made in agriculture will be of definitive importance for the integrative potential of the EEC. It represents the Community's first effort to develop a common policy in a major economic sphere. Such common policies are central to the successful implementation of the broader goal of economic union as well as to the efficient operation of the customs union.

The unique problems of agriculture in general, as well as the widely divergent policies pursued by each of the Member States, made the agricultural sector the most difficult of all in which to achieve a common policy. And yet it was impossible to exclude agriculture from the Common Market. To leave it outside was politically unthinkable for the Netherlands, Italy, and France, in whose trade balances agricultural exports weigh heavily. The following figures show the percentage share of agricultural products in over-all exports of each country in 1956:[4]

Belgium-Luxembourg	5.4%
Germany	3.2
Netherlands	35.3
France	15.5
Italy	24.0

Even beyond this, the exclusion of agriculture from the Treaty would probably have caused serious wage and production problems. As Deniau points out, "It would have been out of the question for industry to be entirely liberalized and subjected to greater competition while agricultural prices could be kept at quite different levels."[5] A free market for agricultural products was not envisaged; rather it was decided to effect a *common organization* of the agricultural markets of the Six. The institutions of the Community were given the choice of establishing common rules of competition, a compulsory coordination of national market organizations, or a single European market organization designed to supersede separate national organizations altogether.[6]

We shall now turn to the actual process by which the Community institutions began to develop the common agricultural policy. What roles were assigned to the several institutions? How were these defined and exercised in practice? What were the objectives of each of the Six in respect of the common agricultural policy? What was the reaction of agricultural and other interest groups? What progress has been made to date, and how can we account for it? And have our expectations regarding spillover and conflict resolution been fulfilled? Before trying to answer these questions, however, let us briefly examine the general situation that confronted the Six at the outset of the negotiations.

THE SPECIAL PROBLEMS OF AGRICULTURE

The EEC was fully aware that agriculture posed special problems. In the Commission's words, "Although agriculture is . . . put on the same plane as the other sectors of economic activity, it is nevertheless true that, owing to its traditional situation and the conditions characteristic for farming and for agricultural work, agriculture must find its own method of integration into the common market."[7] Agriculture is a declining sector in the Six, as it is in most industrial countries. The level of agricultural income has not kept pace with that in other sectors of the economy. Moreover, the share of agricultural income in total national income is markedly lower than the proportions of people working in agriculture would lead one to expect. The following figures show the position of agriculture in the respective economies of the six countries:[8]

	% of total working population in agriculture	% of GNP derived from agriculture
Germany	17.9	8.4
Belgium	10.3	7.2
France	26.6	16.0
Italy	39.8	21.2
Luxembourg	22.8	9.0
Netherlands	12.4	10.9

This lag in agricultural income is due to two sets of factors: first, the relatively low productivity of agriculture resulting from such structural deficiencies as too many small holdings and the fragmentation of farms, the lack of available capital, and the poor mobility of agricultural manpower; and, second, the inelasticity of demand for agricultural products and the unfavorable relationship between the prices received for agricultural products and those paid by the farmer for his means of production.

The structural weaknesses of agriculture have proved very difficult to remedy, largely owing to a strong peasant tradition in much of Europe. According to the Commission, "In the course of many centuries the history of Europe has moulded the structure of agriculture into the manifold forms and types of farming activity found today in rural areas from the North Sea to the Mediterranean. These reflect not only the differing natural conditions and economic factors but all the intellectual currents and the social and political forces which have contributed to their formation."[9] Farms are divided into units too small for the efficient use of machinery and fertilizers. There is an excessive scattering of holdings; an individual farmer may till a number of tiny plots at some distance from each other. Farm buildings, which are often out of date and in poor repair, are frequently located at a considerable distance from the fields. Road networks are generally inadequate.[10] Small farmers are unable to raise capital for improving their holdings, and many are either unaware of technical innovations or unwilling to make use of them. Although there has been a movement off the land toward the cities and industrial employment, this has not been sufficient to improve the relative position of agricultural income. Many small farmers and peasants continue to cling to holdings that yield them a bare subsistence.[11]

The inelasticity of demand for agricultural products, combined with the instability of agricultural prices, is a characteristic problem of agriculture everywhere:

As incomes rise, expenditure on food also rises in absolute terms, but generally a smaller proportion goes to buying food and a larger proportion is spent on household equipment, motoring, more expensive holidays, et cetera. Moreover, an increasing part of this expenditure on foodstuffs tends to be spent on the processing and distribution of the products and a decreasing part on the products themselves. These tendencies mean that as national income rises, an increasing part of it goes to the people who manufacture goods and provide services, and a decreasing part to those who produce foodstuffs.[12]

At the same time, there has been a steady rise in the price of the things the farmer must buy. Furthermore, his income is subject to extreme fluctuations because of the tendency of agricultural prices to vary widely from season to season. He is uniquely dependent upon the weather, which might destroy his crops one year and yield such lavish results the next that the prices he receives are substantially depressed. He has little control over the agricultural market, which comes closest to approximating the classical model of many small producers making independent decisions.[13]

For these reasons, as well as their substantial electoral strength, farmers have been able to make claims on their governments for state intervention. These interventions may be classified as follows: (1) policies designed to improve agricultural structures (the amalgamation of small holdings, land development programs, the construction of roads, expanded use of electricity in rural areas, etc.); (2) policies designed to improve productivity (credit and investment assistance, and education and technical advice); and (3) policies designed to exercise some control over agricultural markets (control of imports, export subsidies, state trading, minimum prices, support prices, etc.). The pattern of such intervention within the Six varies widely according to particular national characteristics: whether a country is a net importer or exporter of agricultural products, whether yield, output, price level, and income are high or low, and what the relative importance of different products is. Important variations are introduced also by differences in political and social systems, so that within each country agricultural groups have developed particular constituency relationships with political parties and with the government and bureaucracy.[14]

POSITION AND CHARACTERISTICS OF AGRICULTURE
IN THE ECONOMY (1956)

	Foreign trade (% total trade)		Yield			
	Imports	Exports	Wheat (cwt. per acre)	Milk (gal. per cow)	Agric. produc'n per active person[a]	Relative income in agriculture[b]
Belgium and Luxembourg ..	17.5	5.4	24	810	300	58–54
Germany	35.0	3.2	20	640	290	56
Netherlands	19.2	35.3	28	840	340	76
France	30.4	15.5	16	460	190	57
Italy	20.8	24.0	13	380	80	38

SOURCE: The figures for foreign trade have been obtained from EEC Commission, *Recueil*, p. 134, and those for yield from *Agricultural Policy in the EEC*, p. 8.

[a] Calculated in "grain equivalent"–hundredweights per year.

[b] Income per active person in agriculture as percentage of income per active person in other sectors.

Belgium, Luxembourg, and Germany are predominantly industrial countries and large net importers of agricultural products. They have a high-cost peasant agriculture with a relatively high level of productivity. All three pursue policies of market intervention. In Belgium there is an Agricultural Fund whose task it is to administer credits and subsidies in support of *target prices* for wheat, milk, butter, pork, and eggs (an average price is stated as a seasonal objective and the governmental agency intervenes to aid in its realization by purchasing, selling, or stocking). Luxembourg has fixed prices for feed-grains, milk, butter, beef, and pork. Germany has a system of price supports for cereals and feeding stuffs, sugar, milk and milk products, fats, cattle, and meats. These are established and administered by Import and Stabilization Boards, which regulate market supplies by stockpiling domestic production and by controlling imports. Imports are also subject to quotas and tariffs.

France is the chief agricultural producer among the Six, accounting for close to 40 per cent of the EEC production. The following figures show the percentage shares of the Six in gross EEC agricultural production (1956):[15]

Belgium-Luxembourg 4.9%
Germany 23.0
Netherlands 6.4
France 39.4
Italy 26.3

France has an elaborate marketing scheme: single marketing agencies that buy wheat, barley, and rye from the producer at government-fixed prices, and that administer price supports for butter, beef, and pork; a system of fixed prices for corn and rice; a target price for milk; and state purchase of beet sugar and alcohol. Tropical and semitropical agricultural products from her former overseas territories are given a highly preferential place on the French market, which they will continue to enjoy in the EEC. France maintains high tariffs against agricultural imports (25 per cent for butter, 35 per cent for meat, and 110 per cent for sugar), and also a system of quotas and state trading. Exports are encouraged by various types of governmental subsidies.

The Netherlands has the highest level of agricultural productivity and the best relative income level. It is the only EEC country with a significant net export of agricultural products. Agriculture is quite modern and highly organized. Dutch prices are low, and the government maintains a strict control through semiofficial marketing boards that establish and administer minimum, fixed or guaranteed prices for most products. Milk and meat production constitutes a big proportion of total output and requires the importation of large amounts of wheat and feed-grains at low world-prices, a position that brings the Dutch into conflict both with exporters of grain within the Community (France) and with farmers in other countries who must pay high domestic prices. There is also a system of export subsidies for selected products.

Italy represents the opposite extreme—the lowest productivity and income level in the EEC, a situation that is particularly marked in the South. Direct government intervention is limited to a few products—wheat, rice, and sugar beets—for which there are fixed prices for the compulsory delivery of a set portion of the crop. There are semiofficial marketing cooperatives for wheat, feed-grains, milk products, wine, and olive oil. Imports of wheat and wheat flour are subject to state-purchasing; and high tariffs are also imposed (30 per cent for wheat, beef, mutton, and butter, and 105 per cent for sugar).

These divergent patterns attest to the severe difficulties that were to be expected when the EEC institutions sought to merge the separate systems of agricultural support into a single policy. Furthermore, the development of a common policy presupposes a common price level. But agricultural prices varied greatly among the Six, and approximation would be hard. Agricultural groups in Germany, Luxembourg, and Italy could be expected to resist a decrease in the prices they received. Similarly, industry and labor in the Netherlands and France, which had comparatively low prices, would object to the likely increase in labor costs and the cost of living. Governmental policies of price and wage controls such as were in force in the Netherlands and France would also be affected.

DIFFERENCES IN PRICE SHOWN BY THE CHIEF AGRICULTURAL
PRODUCTS IN THE MEMBER STATES OF THE EEC 1958–59
(Arithmetical average = 100)

	Germany	France	Italy	Belgium	Luxem-bourg	Nether-lands
Wheat	109.4	74.9	109.1	100.4	123.3	83.0
Rye	116.7	71.0	101.7	87.1	138.9	84.7
Barley	134.6	76.6	93.4	105.1	98.9	91.4
Oats	121.2	83.6	84.3	100.3	110.5	100.1
Sugar beets ...	122.3	81.5	103.9	92.8	—	99.1
Milk	101.6	92.1	98.7	94.3	116.1	97.8
Cattle	101.3	87.8	113.7	89.5	105.9	101.8
Pigs	110.0	93.7	105.7	84.9	115.3	90.4
Eggs	109.4	89.8	113.1	94.5	119.9	73.2

SOURCE: EEC Commission, *Proposals*, Part I, p. 21.

Thus, in undertaking to legislate for a common agricultural policy, the EEC was venturing in an area that posed unique problems, problems, moreover, that had eluded successful governmental regulation in practically all industrial countries:

The measures of support adopted by most countries have helped to raise their own farmers' incomes and to protect them from price fluctuations, but while the problem of low agricultural incomes remains to be fully solved, national policies have created or have aggravated other difficulties. Expansion of output by means of price incentives encourages high-cost production, reflected in high food prices or in taxation to finance agricultural subsidies, and has led in many cases to a decrease in trade both within Western Europe and between Western Europe and overseas exporters.[16]

Each of the Six had developed agricultural policies to suit the characteristics of its own agriculture and its own over-all economic policies. Establishment of a common agricultural policy required the setting aside of established policies and relationships. For agricultural interest groups, as well as governments, this presented serious difficulties.

AGRICULTURAL INTEREST GROUPS IN THE SIX

In each country, agricultural interest groups have achieved comparatively stable relationships with government agencies, and have established lines of access to the seats of political power that are at least adequate for the "defense" of their interests. Added difficulties arise from the fact that in many of these countries, as throughout Europe, the American bias against "pressure group politics" is not shared, the relationships between interest groups and the government bureaucracy and between interest groups and political parties being quite close and formalized. Interest-group leaders may hold high posts in political parties and sit in the parliament. Interest groups frequently participate directly in the making and execution of public law and assume a semipublic character. These organic links with government, and the general orientation to political action, reflect claims to special treatment based in part, at least, on rights accorded the "estates" during feudal and preconstitutional periods.

While such constituency relationships and such lines of access have generally not sufficed to fulfill the expectations of agriculture, there is some doubt whether national groups will be willing eventually to give them up, and to construct new relationships at the EEC level in the anticipation of greater benefits from a common agricultural policy. Furthermore, political studies have revealed that agricultural groups are in general emotionally nationalistic in their politics.[17] In Western Europe they have been important sources of support for authoritarian parties that appeal to exclusively national symbols and reject supranational values altogether.

Some indication of the political strength of agricultural interest groups can be derived from the following figures on the working population in agriculture (1956):[18]

	Number of Farm Workers	% Total Working Population
Germany	4,296,000	17.9
Belgium	350,000	10.3
France	5,040,000	26.6
Italy	7,300,000	39.8
Luxembourg	33,000	22.8
Netherlands	509,000	12.4

And the following chart summarizes some additional features of farmer participation in politics. Although the relevant literature on agricultural interest groups is spotty, certain generalizations may be ventured. The best organized are the Dutch.[19] More than 60 per cent of agricultural producers are members of one of three confessionally defined groups: the Katholieke Nederlandse Boeren-en Tuindersbond (KNBTB), the Nederlandse Christelijke Boeren-en Tuindersbond (NCBTB), and the Koninklijk Nederlands Landbouwcomité (KNLC). Although religious differences have been important enough to thwart the creation of a single national organization, or of national organizations on a product basis, the three have always functioned in close cooperation. For purposes of coordinating their political activities outside the Netherlands they have set up a single committee (the Internationaal Sekretariaat der Drie Centrale Landbouworganisaties).

THE PARTICIPATION OF AGRICULTURAL GROUPS IN POLITICS

Party affiliation	Main interest groups

BELGIUM

Majority Catholic (PSC)

Belgische Boerenbond (Cath-Flem)

Alliance Agricole Belge (Cath-Walloon)

Fédération Nationale des Unions Professionnelles Agricoles Belges (nonconfessional-Walloon)

GERMANY

CDU .... 55%   Deutscher Bauernverband e.V. (DBV)

SPD 10%

FDP and DP 24%

FRANCE

Farmers

Assemblée Permanente des Présidents des Chambres d'Agriculture (APPCA) (semi-governmental)

MRP 20%

Modérés 31%

RGR .... 28%   Confédération Nationale de la Mutualité de la Coopération et du Crédit Agricole (CNMCCA) (co-ops)

RPF 18%

Fédération Nationale des Syndicats d'Exploitants Agricoles (FNSEA)

ITALY

Agricultural laborers

Confederazione Nazionale Coltivatori Diretti (small farmers)

PCI 26%

PSI .... 15%   Confagricoltura (large landowners)

DC 21%

Federazione Italiana dei Consorzi Agrari (co-ops)

Landowners and managers

PCI 11%

PSI 5%

DC 30%

THE PARTICIPATION OF AGRICULTURAL GROUPS IN POLITICS—*Continued*

Party affiliation	Main interest groups
	LUXEMBOURG
Majority Catholic (Ch-Dem)	Centrale Paysanne Luxembourgeoise
	THE NETHERLANDS
Catholic 48%	Katholieke Nederlandse Boeren-en Tuinders-bond (KNBTB) (Catholic)
Protestant 16%	Nederlandse Christelijke Boeren-en Tuinders-bond (NCBTB) (Protestant)
Nonconfessional 36%	Koninklijk Nederlands Lanbouwcomité (KNLC) (nonconfessional)

SOURCES: The figures for Germany were obtained from Heidenheimer, p. 77; those for France and Italy from LaPalombara, "Political Party Systems," pp. 141–42; and those for the Netherlands from Robinson, pp. 53–54.

The relationship between the farmers' organizations and the Dutch government is formalized in the Netherlands' unique semicorporative system of public industrial organizations.[20] The three farmers' organizations are joined with three organizations representing agricultural workers in a public body known as Landbouwschap. "As a public industrial organization, the Landbouwschap is an organization in which membership is compulsory for all those engaged in agriculture. Both farmers and farm workers are bound by its regulations, whether they belong to one of the six private organizations or not, and are unable to withdraw as long as they work in agriculture."[21] The task of the Landbouwschap is to defend the interests of agriculture in the economic and social field, and to advise the government on request or on its own initiative. It also has autonomous legislative power with regard to standards of purity and quality, the regulation of production, storage and land cultivation, conditions of employment, and the rationalization of production.[22] It is regarded by the Dutch government as the authoritative voice of agriculture and has developed extremely close relationships with the Ministry of Agriculture. Access is thus permanently assured. But, as Robinson points out, this has often meant that the Ministry of Agriculture has used these channels of access from organized agriculture to the government in order to gain support for its policies.[23]

In Germany the relationships among organized interests, the civil service, and political parties are especially close. Officials move more or less freely from positions in one organization to positions in another, or may hold them concurrently. German farmers constitute reputedly the most strongly organized economic sector in the country.[24] The Deutscher Bauernverband (DVB), with 1.3 million members, represents 77 per cent of all independent farmers. It has devoted itself primarily to protecting Germany's high-cost agriculture against imports from the outside, especially from the Netherlands.[25] German farmers have thus succeeded in extracting from the government a system of price supports that yields them the highest price level in Europe. In 1960, when there was much talk in West Germany of budgetary retrenchment, they obtained an agricultural aid plan calling for the expenditure of 1.5 billion DM.[26]

Although the committees of the Bundestag do not take testimony from economic groups or hold public hearings, German political parties typically nominate interest group representatives as their candidates, thus giving them opportunities for influencing policy directly in caucus or in committee. The DVB has close ties with the CDU, 18 per cent of all CDU members being directly associated with farming interests;[27] and of the 29 deputies on the Committee of Nutrition, Agriculture, and Forestry of the second Bundestag, 20 were agriculturists or officials of interest groups in these areas.[28] The President of the DVB, Edmund Rehwinkel, has direct access to Chancellor Adenauer and has demonstrated his political influence on the government's agricultural policies on many occasions.

In Belgium, the Catholic-Flemish Boerenbond is by far the most important agricultural group. It is closely associated with the Christian-Social Party (PSC) and represents the interests of agriculture in numerous official advisory agencies. It provides a wide range of services for the farmer— credit facilities, insurance, banking, technical assistance and education— and also operates food-processing plants and purchasing and marketing cooperatives.[29]

Of the three major agricultural groups in Italy, Paolo Bonomi's Confederazione Nazionale Coltivatori Diretti is the most vocal, the best organized, and the most influential.[30] Confagricoltura, representing the great landowners of the South (Latifundia), used to be the dominant power in agriculture, but was supplanted by the Coltivatori Diretti, which emerged after World War II under the sponsorship of the Christian Democratic Party. The Coltivatori Diretti draws its strength from the largest sector of Italian agriculture, the small independent peasants and tenant farmers, especially the growers of wine, vegetables, and fruit. Bonomi is one of the few Italian interest-group leaders who frankly describes his organization as a pressure group. He is also the leading figure in the Federazione Italiana dei Consorzi Agrari, a national federation of cooperatives with semiofficial status. Its functions extend to credit, education, and the export of agricultural commodities.[31] Bonomi is a member of the central committee and the executive bureau of the Christian Democratic Party. He claims to wield enormous power, boasting that 62 Christian Democratic deputies (of 273 in the third legislature, 1958–63) owed their election to him.[32] According to Kogan,

> He can bargain with other factions in his own party to throw his support to right, left, or center, depending on who will pay his asking price. His organization controls the system of grain collections and prices through its control over the state collecting agencies, Federconsorzi, his influence in the party directorate, and in the Ministry of Agriculture. Bonomi men are planted in the ministry's bureaucracy, and he exercises a strong influence over the nomination of the Minister of Agriculture.
>
> The Coltivatori Diretti has a monopoly on the sale to farmers of agricultural machinery built by FIAT and fertilizers produced by ENI and Montecatini, the huge chemical combine. Bonomi can use his influence and bloc of deputies to support the claims on public policy of his business friends, as an accommodation and as a means of log-rolling.[33]

The political, economic, and social fractionalization that is so characteristic of French life is clearly reflected in the organization of groups representing agriculture.[34] France is a country of small family farms; it has been estimated that up to six million farmers either own their farms or work on a family farm.[35] Yet the claim of the most important of the several agricultural groups, the FNSEA (Fédération Nationale des Syndicats d'Exploitants Agricoles), to represent 700,000 farmers is probably exaggerated.[36] The FNSEA is a national federation bringing together departmental federations and nationally organized associations specialized by product. These "vertical" organizations are often more important politically than the "horizontal" FNSEA itself. Chief among them are the beet growers,[37] wheat farmers, winegrowers, and tobacco growers.[38] Agricultural groups have close constituency relationships both with the French parliament, through the APA (Amicale Parlementaire Agricole), and with the administration, through the APPCA (Assemblée Permanente des Présidents des Chambres d'Agriculture), and various specialized consultative committees.[39] However, with the decline of parliament and of party influence under de Gaulle's Fifth Republic, all interest groups have had to depend more and more on direct contacts with the cabinet and the administration, and on attempts to defend their interests by negotiating ordinances or decrees.[40] Recently, more spectacular tactics have also been employed. According to one report, "The FNSEA has resorted to direct action such as calling mass meetings, barricading national highways, and participating in other demonstrations meant to focus the attention of the government and the public on the truly difficult plight of French agriculture."[41]

It appears, however, that there is a considerable gulf between the French farmer and the groups claiming to represent him. Certainly these groups have no decisive influence over the attitudes or actions of the individual farmer. All agricultural groups have great difficulty with their finances, the French farmer being notoriously unwilling to contribute to organizations that bring him no immediate material advantage.* The APPCA, a semiofficial advisory body, is financed by the state, as is, in effect, the CNMCCA (Confédération Nationale de la Mutualité de la Coopération et du Crédit Agricole), another group of considerable importance. The "vertical" groups deduct from state taxes and from the proceeds of the cooperative sale of produce. The FNSEA has fallen back upon the financial support of the large, wealthy farmers (mostly in the northeast Paris basin), and is therefore more responsive to their views. This is recognized by the small farmer and heightens his distrust of his "mouthpieces" in Paris. "The big agriculturists are on one side and the state is on the other, but the small farmer in whose name everybody speaks stays at home paying nothing."[42]

The small farmer in France, perhaps more than anywhere else, has firmly resisted the logic of the industrial revolution, glorifying the virtues of rural life in a sort of "messianisme paysan," and defending the cult of the small and the marginal.[43] He views the steady decline of agriculture in the economy as the consequence of a plot between the administration and big business, and believes that the "technocrats" deliberately keep prices depressed in order to maintain a low level of industrial wages and at the same time drive the farmer off his land into industry. This attitude has nourished general resentment and has frequently given rise to violent political demonstrations against the government (and sometimes against agricultural interest groups as well).[44] It is an attitude, however, that typifies the individual farmer rather than the interest-group leaders, who are beginning to accept the need for a major transformation in French agriculture.

Agriculture in the six countries stands at the threshold of a new day. In practical terms most farmers have much to gain. But the transition implies not only major economic changes, but the transformation of traditional social and political patterns as well. The migration from farm to city will doubtless continue, and at an accelerated rate. New ways of doing old and familiar things will have to be accepted. But much will depend upon the willingness and ability of interest-group leaders to adapt to the situation,

---

* Mendras, pp. 741–42. In the period of scarcity following World War II, the Gaullist group, the Confédération Générale d'Agriculture (now extinct) was the official, and sole, distributor of certain scarce consumer goods, notably rubber boots; and it had one and a half million dues-paying members. The day that boots went on sale at regular commercial outlets, the paying of dues stopped.

upon whether the Bonomis and Rehwinkels will be prepared to relinquish old ties and to seek new sources of influence.

According to the Treaty, "the Member states shall gradually develop the common agricultural policy during the transitional period and shall establish it not later than at the end of that period."[45] During the transitional period, trade in agricultural products was to be liberalized at the same rate as in other sectors; that is, tariffs and quotas among the Six would be progressively eliminated.* Until such time as the common agricultural policy had been agreed upon and a common organization of agricultural markets had been instituted, various special protective devices were authorized. Should the progressive abolition of tariffs and quotas result in hardship to agricultural producers, a Member State might institute a system of minimum import prices in their place.[46] Under such a system, imports of a given product whose price was below the minimum level might be suspended or made conditional on the price being raised. An effort was made to prevent abuse of this provision. Minimum prices were not to be used in such a way as to obstruct the expansion of trade in agricultural products. Furthermore, the Council, acting unanimously on a proposal of the Commission, was to lay down objective criteria for fixing such prices.[47] When the prices were decided upon, they would have to be applied by the Member States. If prices established by a Member State did not conform to the criteria, the Council, acting by a qualified majority vote on a proposal of the Commission, could *correct* the decision. The same procedure could be applied, from the beginning of the third stage, to change the prices established unilaterally by a Member State for those products for which it was impossible to agree on objective criteria. At the end of the transition period, the Council, acting by a majority of nine votes on a proposal of the Commission, would decide what to do with those minimum prices still in force.

Another device to be used until national market organizations were replaced by some form of common organization was the conclusion of long-term contracts between exporting and importing Member States.[48] These contracts were designed to provide for an increase in the previous average volume of trade, as well as to effect an alignment of prices.[49]

Clearly, minimum prices and long-term contracts were temporary de-

---

* Except that the Treaty's provisions on competition would in general not apply to agricultural production; i.e., states may grant subsidies and other kinds of aids. Article 42.

vices that were to be superseded gradually as the common agricultural policy was developed and set in motion. We turn now to the procedures by which this policy was to be formulated.[50] The Commission was assigned the central role of formulation. Within two years after the Treaty had come into force, it was to present concrete proposals to the Council for developing and implementing the common agricultural policy. Preliminary policy direction was to be provided by a special agricultural conference of the Member States, which the Commission was enjoined to convene as soon as the Treaty came into effect.* The Commission also was required to consult the Economic and Social Committee. The Council, after it had consulted the Assembly, would act on these proposals by issuing the appropriate recommendations, regulations, directives, or decisions. Such action required unanimity during the first two stages, and a qualified majority vote thereafter. This procedure applied to all aspects of the proposed policy, although a Member State that objected to the institution of a common market organization for a given product, but had been outvoted, could insist upon certain guarantees for its producers.[51]

A CHRONOLOGY OF EVENTS

The several institutions of the EEC will develop the common agricultural policy step by step during the transition period. It is still too early to predict its final form or full content. But we are not concerned so much with the substantive content of the common agricultural policy as with the institutional and political setting within which it is being developed. And here it is possible to advance some conclusions about the over-all implications for political integration.

At this point, therefore, let us pause a moment to take our bearings. The following steps toward the common agricultural policy had been taken by January 1962, and will form the basis of the analysis that follows in this chapter and in Chapter 12:

1. The Agricultural Conference specified in the Treaty was held at Stresa in July 1958.

2. The Commission completed a draft of its general proposals, which was submitted to the ESC for an opinion in November 1959.

3. From March 1958 to December 1959, the European Parliamentary Assembly tried to influence these proposals through committee work and plenary debate. In March 1960, the EPA adopted eight reports on the Commission's draft proposals.

---

* It will be recalled that the Treaty was silent about the specific provisions of the common agricultural policy.

4. The ESC issued an opinion on the general provisions of the Commission's proposals in May 1960, and on the product-by-product proposals in June 1960.

5. A deadlock over agriculture developed during the Council of Ministers' debates on acceleration in May 1960. Acceleration was agreed to, including a partial acceleration in agriculture, but only on condition that work on the common agricultural policy be speeded up, in particular a first Community solution to deal with "distortions" of competition. A detailed timetable was drawn up, and it was agreed that the Council would meet at the end of the year to decide if sufficient progress had been made in establishing a common agricultural policy to permit the acceleration to go into effect.

6. The Commission accordingly submitted its definitive proposals at the end of June.

7. In July, the Council met to consider these proposals and created the Special Committee on Agriculture, giving it a continuing mandate to prepare future Council decisions on agriculture.

8. In October, the EPA held a lively, and frequently critical, debate on the Commission's final proposals.

9. As a result of discussion and negotiation between the Commission and the Special Committee on Agriculture, the Council was able to approve a resolution on the basic principles of the common agricultural policy in November.

10. In December 1960, the Council accepted the substance of the Commission's proposals for a system of levies to be applied to intra-Community trade and to trade with third countries. The Commission was called upon to submit during 1961 draft regulations applying the levy system to a series of products. A specific timetable was set. As a result of these decisions, it was agreed that sufficient progress had been made to permit the acceleration decision to take final effect.

11. In January 1961, the EPA gave an opinion on competition in agriculture and passed a resolution on the application of the levy system to trade in agriculture.

12. The Commission, working closely with the Special Committee on Agriculture, completed, and sent to the Council, draft regulations for cereals and pork at the end of May 1961, and for eggs, poultry, fruit, vegetables, and wine at the end of July.

13. The EPA adopted four opinions on these draft regulations at its October session.

14. The ESC's Agricultural Section prepared reports on the regulations and sent them to the Commission in December.

15. On January 14, 1962, after more than 200 hours of intensive nego-

tiation, the Council adopted a series of regulations giving legal effect to the levy system and instituting a common market organization for a number of products. Other important decisions were also taken. The regulations are fully binding and applicable in all Member States of the Community. The levy system took effect on July 1, 1962, and from that date agriculture formally ceased to be a subject of purely national administration and control.

THE ROLE OF THE COMMISSION: PREPARATION AND INITIATION

As we have noted, the Commission has important advantages in EEC policy-making by virtue of its rights of initiative and its nonnational character. This is clearly seen in the efforts to work out a common agricultural policy, both at the time of the writing of the Treaty and again at the Stresa Conference. For although the Six were in substantial agreement that the problems of agriculture could be resolved only in the context of over-all economic integration through joint or Community policies, they were unable to agree about the specific form such policies should take. This was most apparent at the Stresa Conference, a conference that was marked by the highly cooperative attitude assumed by all parties; yet the differences remained. As one participant put it, "A genuine desire for cooperation prevailed throughout the conference. Each country, of course, is still preoccupied by its own problems."[52]

It is not surprising, therefore, that the final resolution of the Stresa Conference does no more than outline general principles. In its operative section, Part III, the following points are made:

1. Agriculture must be regarded as an integral part of the economy and as an essential factor in social life.

2. The implementation of the Treaty must lead naturally to a progressive expansion of trade within the Community; . . . account must be taken of the need to maintain . . . links with non-member countries . . . [and to provide] safeguards against unfair external competition.

3. Close correlation must be established between policy on structural adaptation and market policy; . . .

4. A balance must be sought between production and potential outlets . . .

5. The efforts thus made to increase productivity should render possible the application of a price policy which will avoid overproduction while enabling goods to remain or to become competitive . . .

6. The elimination of subsidies which run counter to the spirit of the Treaty must be regarded as essential.

7. The development of production and demand in the associated countries and territories should be taken into account . . .

8. The improvement in the structure of agriculture should enable capital

and labour to secure and maintain earnings comparable with those . . . in other sectors . . .

9. In view of the importance of the family structure of European agriculture . . . it would be proper to use all possible means to increase the economic and competitive capacity of family undertakings. An occupational readaptation of available agricultural labour and a more intensive industrialization of rural areas would make possible a progressive solution of the problems of marginal undertakings.[53]

The details are left to the Commission, the Working Parties at the Conference in general limiting themselves to indicating the areas of their disagreement and to spelling out the problems that the Commission would have to solve.[54] They requested the Commission to undertake special studies in a number of areas,[55] drew its attention to the *urgency* of making proposals for a common organization of markets, and pointed out the special importance of achieving an approximation of prices for basic products, of increasing the supply of capital to agriculture, and of harmonizing social, commercial, and economic legislation. The importance of "maintaining close and continuous cooperation with governments and non-governmental organizations" was also stressed.[56] It was thus left to the Commission to formulate specific proposals that might be acceptable to all. In fact, it was implicitly recognized that this was the only way in which a common policy could be achieved.

What objectives, then, did the Commission seek in agriculture? How were these reconciled with other and opposing points of view, and how were they translated into the form of concrete proposals?

In commenting on the Stresa negotiations, the Commission observed that the main achievement of the Conference had been to make clear "that a satisfactory, and above all a permanent, solution can no longer be found within the framework of single states nor by means of economic policies confined to the national plane. The choice between national solutions and joint solutions is a thing of the past."[57] The Commission went on to stress that courage would be needed "to seek new solutions which will go beyond those limited to the national framework." These must be worked out in "close cooperation with the Governments, the Council, the Assembly, the Economic and Social Committee, and the professional organizations." Such solutions, however, could not "be the simple outcome of a struggle between the various interest groups." An entirely new concept of agricultural policy must be developed, involving new habits of thought and action, and a fresh perspective. An agricultural policy must serve the interests of the Community as well as the interests of agriculture.[58]

According to the Commission, one of the chief problems would be to create "an organic equilibrium between production and the market for the products." The situation was summarized as follows:

In the past, attempts to increase agricultural incomes have been based on the too one-sided principle of increasing production. True, this has led to a marked increase of productivity per worker, especially as there was simultaneous decrease of the number of persons occupied in agriculture. However, the increase in production has led to new difficulties on the markets. In view of the fact that production of the major products is increasing more vigorously than consumption, surpluses are appearing on the various markets.[59]

In spite of the obvious difficulties, a common price policy must be developed, with an approximation of the prices of basic agricultural products as its starting point. Furthermore, "Some member countries are at present exporters of products produced on a large scale and it is in the interest of the Community to maintain and develop these exports. A flourishing export depends, however, on competitive prices; *the lowering of production costs* is therefore an essential factor."[60] Finally, the Commission considered that structural reform on a European scale was the best single instrument for improving the situation of agriculture, for it was largely differences in agricultural structures that accounted for production cost differentials. Agriculture must be enabled "to partake in the accelerated rhythm of industrial development in the Community."[61]

Throughout 1958 and 1959 the Commission's General Directorate for Agriculture, under the leadership of Commission Vice-President Sicco Mansholt (former Dutch Minister of Agriculture), was engaged in preparing the Commission's proposals. Throughout this period, close working relationships were maintained with governmental and nongovernmental experts drawn from the Member States, in addition to which Mansholt and the six Ministers of Agriculture held meetings at intervals of from two to four weeks. Of special importance from the Commission's point of view were the close contacts maintained with interest groups (perhaps the result of Mansholt's influence, since interest groups play so prominent a part in the Dutch system). The Commission had been convinced from the start that an integration of agricultural interest groups was a prerequisite to progress in the integration of agricultural policies. Consequently, it encouraged the formation of groups at the Community level, by giving such groups preferential access, and by doing its utmost to involve representatives of agricultural interests in Community affairs. It invited the various agricultural groups to send observers to the Stresa Conference, and representatives of eleven organizations attended.[62] Since then, largely because of the ease with which they have obtained a hearing from the Commission, these Community-level groups have proliferated, and there are now at least eighty of them.

All through this preparatory period, the Commission held periodic briefings with agricultural producers, agricultural workers, and representatives of various agricultural industries. Its practice was to submit working papers to these groups, mainly to COPA (Comité des Organisations Professionelles Agricoles), which represents the interests of agricultural producers, for their comment and discussion.[63] The working papers were also circulated to the Agriculture Committee of the EPA, which was holding concurrent hearings, and to the Agriculture Section of the ESC. In addition, the Commission participated in preliminary agricultural debates held by the EPA in October of 1958, and in January, April, and June of 1959. It took care, however, to preserve its full freedom of maneuver, resisting all efforts by the EPA to exercise prior control over the content of Commission proposals.[64]

In order to meet the two-year deadline set down in the Treaty, the Commission submitted a set of draft proposals to the ESC on November 7, 1959, and to the Council on December 11, 1959. There had been considerable disagreement within the Commission, and the consequent delay had made it impossible to consult the ESC in any realistic sense.[65] Hence, in submitting its draft, the Commission reserved the right to alter its proposals on the basis of the ESC opinion, if this were forthcoming by spring 1960,[66] and presumably also on the basis of EPA debates and governmental and interest-group comments. The Commission's definitive proposals were submitted to the Council on June 30, 1960.

In the following summary of these proposals, our objectives will be twofold: to relate policy content to the general political and economic goals of the Commission, and to assess the integrative potential of the proposals in terms of the roles envisaged for the central institutions of the EEC.[67]

In its analysis of the general situation of agriculture in the Six, the Commission continued to emphasize the need to achieve a healthier balance between supply and demand. For such products as cereals (especially wheat), sugar, pork, and potatoes, the problem was particularly acute. Moreover, the systems of market and price protection upon which most of the Member States relied tended to make matters worse. As the Commission noted, "Since it has recently become apparent that excessive support for prices and markets easily leads to overproduction, it is easy to see the limitations of price policy as a means of under-pinning incomes."[68] According to the Commission, structural policy, market policy, trade policy, and social policy for agriculture must be closely linked:

Structural policy must help to reduce and approximate costs in the agriculture of the six countries and to guide production rationally in the light of market trends. Market policy must take into account the need for improving agricultural productivity and to this end be based on the conditions found in economically viable enterprises of adequate productivity. Commercial policy . . . must contribute to the success of the market policy by stabilizing trade. . . . at the same time it forms part of the general commercial policy, which is directed to the harmonious growth of world trade. It is of great importance . . . that the competitive capacity of agricultural enterprises should be improved . . .

Social policy . . . must contribute . . . to improving the living and working conditions of the farm population and bringing these conditions closer to the level obtaining in other comparable occupational categories.[69]

Only with regard to structural and market policy were specific proposals formulated. The Commission observed that the first step in structural reform must be to coordinate the measures being taken by the individual states. The Commission would make an annual report to the Council on progress made, and would submit proposals for guiding and harmonizing national policies. It argued that "every proposal, every action, taken in the field of agriculture at Community level must be based upon an objective judgment of the situation. . . . Knowledge of this situation is based mainly on an exhaustive review. . . . Such a review can only be really efficient if it is made periodically. . . . For this purpose, the Member States are to inform the Commission regularly of their projects and of the results obtained."[70] Also on the basis of its report, the Commission would make recommendations for further action, as well as suggesting how much financial assistance individual states should offer in their domestic systems. Several of the Member States had repeatedly deferred structural reform, thereby seriously threatening the balanced development of agriculture. Continuous collaboration would be maintained between the Commission and those national officials responsible for structural policy. In addition, "a Committee will be set up which will enable the Commission to consult the producers', traders' or industrial organizations concerned on the problems involved. . . . The organizations at Community level which group farmers, agricultural workers and other branches of activity interested in the improvement of agricultural structure will be represented on this Committee."[71]

In each of these areas the responsibility for implementation is left to the States. The Commission also proposed the establishment of a European Fund for Structural Improvement in Agriculture, financed by means of the general Community budget and administered by the Commission. Grants would be made on application, and would be awarded chiefly with a view to subsidizing lower interest rates or extending the redemption of credits. In order to qualify, projects must meet certain criteria designed to assure their consistency with the common agricultural policy of the Community. The Commission suggested that the sum of 192 million Belgian francs (3.84 million dollars) be made available for the first year.

The most far-reaching proposals were made with regard to market policy. They covered the following products, which account for 80 to 90 per cent of the agricultural production of the Six: wheat, coarse grains (feed-grains), sugar, dairy produce, beef, veal, pork, poultry, eggs, fruit, vegetables, and wine. The measures required to bring about a common market, "in which trade will be carried on in conditions similar to those existing in a domestic market," would differ from product to product, and accordingly three systems of market policy were envisioned:

1. For certain products (wheat, coarse grains, sugar, and dairy produce), the policies followed by the Member States varied greatly because of special problems and a high degree of state intervention. Therefore, "in the common-market phase it is not possible merely to coordinate domestic systems which differ so widely or to adopt any one of them unchanged for application to the market as a whole. The aim must be to arrive at a new form of organization, selecting its elements from the various existing forms and wherever possible enlisting the assistance of the market organizations of the various countries."[72] For these products, European Offices, acting on directives from the Commission, would be established to administer systems of target and intervention prices, to make support purchases on the internal market, and to provide external protection by means of variable levies and import certificates. They were also to supervise market trends, furnish basic statistical data, execute decisions of the Commission, and coordinate the activities of national market organizations. Target prices designed to maintain a stable income for producers were to be proposed each year by the Commission, and would take effect unless the Council decided otherwise, unanimously and within a specified time limit. The criteria for fixing these target prices would be established by a qualified majority vote of the Council on a proposal of the Commission. The European Offices would enter the market when prices fell below this level and make support purchases at an "intervention price." (This would vary from product to product, but would be in the region of 5 per cent to 7 per cent below the target price.)

Import regulations would also be established and administered by the Commission and the European Offices. Import duties were to be replaced by a system of variable levies established by the Commission on the basis of the differences between the target price and the world price. Because of variations in the methods of international trading, a supplementary system of import certificates for supervising imports would be employed. These licenses, valid for three months, would normally be issued on demand. However,

If imports increase to such an extent or occur on such a scale or in such conditions as to cause or threaten to cause serious injury to Community producers the Commission will decide . . . to suspend the issue of import certificates until there is no further injury or threat of injury. A case in point is where the market price reaches the level of the intervention price, when the Grain Office will be obliged to intervene in the internal market on a substantial scale.[73]

The operations of these European Offices were to be financed by stabilization funds, which would be grouped in a European Agricultural Guidance and Guarantee Fund administered by the Commission. The various funds were to be financed somewhat differently by means of combinations of import levies, governmental contributions, contributions by the producers, and other resources to be determined later.

The proposals also called for the creation of Consultative Committees for each product, to include representatives of the Community-level organizations of farmers, traders in agricultural produce, workers in the agricultural and foodstuffs industries, and consumers. A number of Directors' Committees was also called for, "consisting of persons playing a leading part in the establishment of the marketing organizations in the Community countries. . . . [They] are to help the Commission in working out its policy, and they will also ensure effective coordination between the various national bureaux."[74]

2. For a second group of products (beef, veal, pork, poultry, and eggs), the main instrument of market support was to be protection against imports. For beef and veal this would consist of a fairly high customs duty, and for pork, poultry, and eggs, a reduced duty plus variable levies set by the Commission. Additional protection could be afforded by minimum import prices. Should the import price plus duty fall below this level, a levy might be applied. The Commission would establish this minimum price, which would stand unless changed by a unanimous vote in the Council. There was also to be a system of export subsidies based on the differences between internal and world prices. European Offices were to be created for these products, too, although their functions would be less extensive than the functions of those already discussed. They would lay down the technical procedures for imports and exports, perform other duties of implementation, and above all "reinforce" the coordination of national policies. Necessary financing would be accomplished by stabilization funds. Consultative Committees and Directors' Committees were also called for.

3. Finally, for fruit, vegetables, and wine, no European Offices were envisaged, and market organization would be based on restrictions on the marketing of products falling below certain standards of quality. For fruit and vegetables, a common external tariff would provide external protection, and no import levies or stabilization funds were proposed. Since control of quality would be administered centrally, national services would have to be coordinated; and this task was to be performed, under the authority of

the Commission, by a committee composed of the heads of the services responsible for quality control, plant health, and so on. National market information services would also be coordinated under the Commission. The common standards would be established by a qualified majority vote of the Council on a proposal from the Commission. For wine, the Commission would put forward a long-term plan for the adjustment of production to demand, this plan to be adopted by a qualified majority in the Council. Short-term support for wine storage, export, or distillation was also provided. A stabilization fund for wine would finance these efforts.

In order to assess both the effects of the common agricultural policy and the general situation of agriculture, the Commission would prepare an annual report covering developments in productivity, producer prices, means of production, consumer prices, and processing and distribution margins. Annual surveys of short-term market developments would be issued as well. "Efforts will be made at the same time to give an indication of the price policy to be expected. Together with the Annual Reports, these surveys will make it possible to adjust policy in the field of production and market organization."[75] The Commission further recommended that the Member States should start to make the necessary adjustments at once, so that the bulk of the unified market provisions might be instituted after a six-year transitional period.* A precise timetable was provided for the creation of the European Offices, the Consultative Committees, and the Directors' Committees for each product; and concrete proposals were made covering the approximation of prices, common rules of competition, the harmonization of legislation, increases in intra-Community trade, and common trade policy toward third countries.

The Commission recommended immediate action not only on an approximation of national agricultural prices, but also on intra-Community trade. It proposed that the Member States should proceed at once to replace customs duties and quotas on intra-Community trade with a system of levies. These were to be introduced at specified intervals and would be based on the price differentials between importing and exporting countries. In order to stimulate trade, the levies would be gradually reduced, and would disappear entirely when a common price level had been achieved. Levies were also intended to replace minimum prices as a protective device.

With regard to commercial policy, the Commission proposed that the Member States undertake the following: to inform the Commission of all bilateral and multilateral trade agreements; to refrain from taking any steps in these fields without consulting the Commission and the other Member States; to arrange that all trade obligations would either expire

---

* Four years for beef, ten for wine.

The Commission's Proposed Price Adjustments

(In DM per 100 kilos)

	Wheat	Feeding barley	Maize	Sugar
Belgium	—	—	—	—
France	+1.0	+1.0	−1.0	+0.5
Germany	−1.0	−1.0	—	−2.0
Italy	−1.0	—	−1.0	−2.0
Luxembourg	−1.5	—	—	—
Netherlands	+0.5	—	—	+1.0

SOURCE: *Agriculture, the Commonwealth, and EEC*, p. 17.

by the end of the transition period or be adapted to the common agricultural policy; and refrain from consolidating tariffs or imports on products subject to a Community organization without first consulting the Commission and the other Member States.

It is clear from this summary that the Commission kept certain aims to the front: to concentrate on structural reform and modernization rather than market policy; to maintain a relatively low price level for the Community in order to prevent overproduction and to protect the interests of the consumer; to encourage specialization, and thereby to avoid pressures for making the Community self-sufficient in agriculture; and to evolve a system which would offer a degree of Community preference, but which would still be relatively liberal toward imports from third countries. It is also clear that the implementation of these measures would greatly expand the role of the central institutions of the EEC, and especially of the Commission itself. A complex body of European Offices, Consultative Committees, and Directors' Committees had been proposed. Their institution could not fail to bring about a rapid reorientation in the activities of government agencies and interest groups. Government officials concerned with agriculture would no longer administer national programs. Interest groups would be unable to rely on national activities to affect the levels of price support. New sources of technical and financial assistance would open up. The potential for political integration, as we have described the process, was truly enormous.

THE ROLE OF THE COMMISSION: NEGOTIATION AND BROKERAGE

As we have seen in the other case studies, the Commission's functions are not limited to making proposals that are then acted upon by the Council. The Commission takes an active part at all levels and stages of decision-making. It is an advocate, seeking constantly to build support for its policies or to play opponents off against each other. It also steps in and offers compromise solutions when the Member States are unable to agree.

All these activities were much in evidence during the acceleration discussions and especially in the debates in the Council of Ministers in May 1960 (see Chapter 9). It will be recalled that the Netherlands had refused to accept a general acceleration unless some liberalization was also achieved in agriculture. The Germans, with considerable support from the other Member States, refused to consider liberalization until a common agricultural policy had been instituted. The Commission made a crucial contribution to the final compromise, according to which substantial progress would have to be made on the common agricultural policy before the end of the year in order for the acceleration agreement to be confirmed. Of particular concern was Germany's insistence, as a condition for agreeing to acceleration, that some progress be made toward the equalization of competitive conditions in the Community, a demand implying a renunciation by her partners of all export aids and differential prices for basic agricultural products. Thus the Member States were forced to confront the problems of agriculture at a relatively early stage, and in relation to other goals.

There could hardly be a clearer example of spill-over. If an accelerated trade liberalization were to be achieved, and the pressures behind acceleration were strong, work on the common agricultural policy would have to be speeded up, a situation inevitably involving an expansion of the role of the center. Once again the inability of the Member States to agree, combined with irresistible pressures for an agreement to be reached rapidly, gave the Commission a crucial advantage in EEC decision-making. Deadlock simplified the task, since it increased the receptivity of the Member States to whatever measures and compromises the Commission might eventually suggest. It is clear that in the case of agriculture preliminary discussion and maneuvering for position would have gone on much longer had it not been for the crisis over acceleration in agricultural trade.

In the acceleration agreement, the Commission was enjoined to submit its definitive proposals by June 30, 1960. It did so, and on July 19–20 the Ministers of Agriculture met in the Council for a first exchange of views. The May agreement had required the creation of a special committee to prepare the decisions of the Council, and a first report from this committee before the middle of October. The Special Committee on Agriculture was duly created, although it took some time for the Six to agree on its organization. Four countries favored giving the chairmanship to Commission Vice-President Mansholt, with the secretariat also being provided by the Commission (as in the Rey Committee). The Germans and the Belgians, however, opposed this, and it was decided that the chairmanship would rotate among the members on the same basis as in the Council, and that the secretariat would be under the authority of the Council Secretariat.[76] The Committee was to consist of high-level civil servants and experts representing all the interested Ministries. This composition was apparently designed to broaden the discussions on the common agricultural policy and to prevent the Ministries of Agriculture from dominating the negotiations. It was widely felt that no progress would be made if it were left to the Ministers of Agriculture, who represented only the interests of their agricultural constituents. It is interesting to note that only one of the six delegations to the Special Committee was headed by a representative of the Ministry of Agriculture.[77]

The Special Committee was charged with carrying out all preliminary discussions and negotiations, and with preparing the Council's decisions regarding agricultural questions. It was to continue in existence even after the principles of the common agricultural policy had been approved, being entrusted with the task of examining all the necessary implementing rules and decisions.[78] It represents a permanent institutional innovation of a type with which we are already familiar. It is formally an extension of the Council, but it is already clear that the initiative in its discussions lies with the Commission, which continues to "present the dossier." The Commission also acts as a preparatory and executory organ of the Committee, even though the secretariat is formally provided by the Council. The Commission was requested to prepare special reports, to present detailed measures for implementing proposals already made, and to convoke and direct working parties of national experts.[79]

Intensive study and negotiations were carried on by the Commission and the Special Committee from September through December of 1960, in order to meet the end-of-the-year deadline. As a result, the Member States succeeded in reaching three important decisions in the Council of Ministers. The first was made in November, when the Council approved the first written report of the Special Committee on the basic principles of the common agricultural policy. The second and third were both reached in December, when the Council accepted the substance of the Commission's proposal for a system of variable levies to be applied on intra-Community trade and on trade with third countries; and when it noted that sufficient progress had been made in working out the common agricultural policy to permit the application of acceleration to agriculture.

It had been evident since the July session of the Council that the Member States held widely divergent views on the Commission's proposals, and the discussions in the Special Committee bore this out (see pp. 266–69). Nevertheless, some progress was made under the prodding of the Commis-

sion and the stimulus of the end-of-the-year deadline. The ten-point declaration of basic principles adopted by the Council in mid-November contained some points of interest, but much of it was very general and of
relatively minor significance, merely echoing what had already been agreed
to at Stresa.[80] It noted that the common market for agriculture implied a
common price level (as yet undetermined), that a means must be found
to bring national prices to this level, and that all measures taken at the
national level should be designed to facilitate this approximation. The
common market organizations must guarantee the producers a level of employment and a standard of living equal to those provided by the national
market organizations that they replaced. It was also agreed that the establishment of the Common Market should be accompanied by the establishment of a common trade policy that would assure a Community preference.
In addition, Community solutions to the problem of distortions of competition would have to be worked into the common agricultural policy during
the transitional period. Finally, all agreed to the necessity for coordinating
national policies.

The chief task of the Special Committee, in accordance with the acceleration decision, was to try to reach a first "Community solution" to the difficulties arising from the existence of different competitive conditions within
the Community. Each delegation was to submit a list of "sensitive" products for the consideration of the Committee. In fact it was German reluctance to allow an agricultural liberalization that posed the problem. Germany insisted that trade could not be liberalized until France, Benelux,
and Italy gave up certain production and export subsidies which, it was
claimed, falsified competitive conditions within the Community; and the
Germans accordingly presented a list of products said to be affected by such
distortions.[81]

At its second meeting, the Special Committee decided to take as a point
of departure the Commission's proposals for a system of levies to be applied
during the transition period to intra-Community trade and to trade with
third countries. The Commission had been called upon to supply details
about how the system would work—how the levies would be calculated,
how long they would be valid, and so on. As a result of discussions in the
Committee, the principle of levies had been accepted by all the Member
States. This agreement was included in the Committee's November report
and was approved by the Council. It was noted that the levy system was a
"valid proposal" and could in some cases facilitate the transition to the
Common Market stage. It also constituted "a Community solution" to some
of the problems arising out of differing competitive conditions. The levies
applied to intra-Community trade were to be reduced gradually to zero, but
this was subject to progress being made in establishing a common price

level and abolishing all direct or indirect export aids. Numerous difficulties remained, however. The Commission, Italy, and the Netherlands maintained that the levies ought to imply a rejection of quotas and minimum prices on Community trade. France, Belgium, Luxembourg, and especially Germany were loath to give up these additional protective devices. The Germans questioned the adequacy of the levy system with regard to third countries. Other problems included settling who was to impose the levy and to whom the product of the levy would go.[82]

At this point, on December 6, the Commission took the initiative by submitting new proposals in the form of a draft Council resolution on the levy system. In this draft the Commission suggested that it present specific proposals on the levy, to be applied for pork by March 31, 1961, and to be followed soon after by proposals for grain, sugar, eggs, and poultry. The Commission further suggested that it be the one to impose the levy, the product of which would be distributed between the producer and consumer countries. The Commission's draft also provided that no other measures of protection apart from safeguard clauses would be employed within the Community, and that the levies themselves would be eliminated by the end of the transitional period.[83]

The Commission's draft was amended in the Special Committee and then sent to the Council, where, after a strenuous debate, a resolution was accepted incorporating its main features. The resolution stated that the Council had reached agreement on the following points:

1. For a certain number of products, to be defined, a system of levies shall be set up both for trade between member countries and third countries and for the trade of member countries between themselves.

2. The basis for these levies shall be the difference between the price in the importing country and the price in the exporting country. For processed goods for which the levies are applied the difference between the raw material prices shall be taken as the basis, subject to possible additional temporary levies as and when appropriate.

3. The intra-Community levies shall be progressively reduced until they are abolished. This progressive decrease shall be carried out in relation on the one hand to the evolution towards the common price level, and on the other to the progressive elimination of measures leading to distortions of competition between member States.

4. The proceeds of the intra-Community levies *shall go to the importing member State*.

As regards the *transitional period*, the proceeds of the extra-Community levies shall go to the importing member State, subject to progressive grants either from these proceeds, or of ordinary contributions, equitably shared, towards the *financing of joint activities* in connection with joint organisation of agricultural markets necessitated by the development of the common agricultural policy and unanimously decided upon by the Council on the basis of proposals from the Commission.

5. The *system of intra-Community levies shall take priority in its application* over any measures of protection provided for in the Treaty.

Any decision by the Council instituting intra-Community levies will also have to settle what is to be done concerning protective measures such as quantitative restrictions, or minimum prices.

6. The application of intra-Community levies should also involve modifications of internal provisions concerning market organisation.

7. The levies imposed on trade between member countries on the one hand and on trade with third countries on the other should be so inter-related that the member States benefit on the Community market from the advantages provided for in the Treaty in the field of commercial policy.

8. Such levy systems should apply in the first place to *cereals, sugar, pork, and eggs and poultry*.

The Commission shall present proposals to the Council before May 31st 1961 for pork and cereals, and by July 31st 1961 for sugar, eggs and poultry.

The levies decided upon following the proposals mentioned in the present article should thus be applied in the 1961–62 farm year.[84]

Note that the Council's decision called for a *more specific calendar* for the presentation of levy proposals than had the Commission's draft. The Special Committee had suggested that proposals be made for grain, as well as pork, by May 31, and the Council had adopted this suggestion. In fact, in the Council debates, the French had demanded that proposals be made also for the other products by that date. The Commission's plea for more time was responsible for the final timetable.

The most difficult point was the incompatibility of the levy system with other means of protection. The Dutch again locked horns with the Belgians and Germans, and it was only owing to the mediatory efforts of the French and the Commission that a compromise was finally reached. The principle that the internal levies ought to take priority over all other protective devices was accepted, but the Council would decide case by case, as the Commission submitted specific proposals, if minimum prices or quotas might be justifiable.

This still left the basic problem of "competitive distortions," the levy system being merely a temporary tool to make up for competitive inequalities. It did not go to the heart of the problem raised by the Germans, since it dealt only with symptoms and not the disease. In September, Germany submitted a list of affected products, indicating the measures it considered necessary to remove distortions. France, Belgium, and the Netherlands were asked to eliminate their export subsidies on draft animals, animals for slaughter, meat, and lard. The Netherlands was asked to remove its production and export subsidies for dairy products, and France and Belgium their export subsidies on dairy products. France and Italy were asked to give up the rebates they paid to exporters of flowers, fruit, and vegetables. Germany also asked for the application of compensatory taxes under Articles 46 and 226 of the Treaty for grain, honey sweeteners, and fruit preparations.[85] These demands were discussed by the Special Committee, as well as by a series of governmental working parties presided over by the Commission. The other Member States observed that the use of export subsidies and other aids was also a common practice in third countries that exported agricultural products to Germany, namely Denmark, Poland, Spain, Tunisia, and Morocco. Should such aids be removed within the Community, third countries would receive a competitive advantage on the German market. Germany declared itself willing to envisage compensation payments with regard to third countries in the event of trade diversions, but this kind of *a posteriori* measure was unacceptable to the rest.[86]

Once again the Commission took the initiative by submitting to the Council a series of special proposals designed to meet the German objections.[87] The most important were as follows: (1) a draft of a first Council Regulation on the extent to which the Treaty's rules of competition should apply to production and trade in agricultural products; (2) a statement of the conclusions reached by the Commission on the German list, along with a declaration of readiness to fix countervailing charges (under Article 46) for some products imported into Germany; (3) a declaration of the Commission's intention to make recommendations to the Member States for the supervision and regulation of certain export aids in the meat, fruit, and vegetable sectors; (4) a declaration of the Commission's intention to begin at once to draw up an inventory of existing aids and to submit relevant proposals to the Member States; and (5) a recommendation that the Council immediately institute Directors' Committees for grain, sugar, dairy products, livestock, meats, eggs, poultry, fruit, vegetables, and wine, as called for in the Commission's proposals on a common agricultural policy. These committees would consist of one member per country, would be presided over by the Commission, and would advise the Commission on all matters concerning the setting-up and functioning of the market organizations, and on the proper measures to be taken to eliminate competitive distortions.

In response to the Commission's proposals and under pressure from her partners, Germany whittled down her list of demands to three points. Agreement was reached on these points in the December 19–20 meeting of the Council.[88] Italy agreed to eliminate immediately the preferential transport rates granted to exporters of fruit and vegetables to Germany. It was agreed that no new export aids would be introduced for lard, and

Germany accepted the Commission's position that a final solution would come under the common organization for the pork market. A compensatory tax was to be applied to powdered and condensed milk and to honey sweeteners, but this would have to be accompanied by the application of special measures so that third countries would not be given an advantage. Added to these concessions to German demands was the commitment, already undertaken in the decision on levies, that the other Member States would eliminate all existing export aids by the end of the transitional period. The Council also called upon the Commission to draw up its inventory of export aids with all possible speed. The Commission's draft on rules of competition was transmitted to the EPA for a formal opinion, and to the Special Committee for preliminary negotiations.

Thanks to the Commission's active negotiation and brokerage, the Council was able to agree on December 20, after some seventeen hours of debate, that the progress made was sufficient to permit the acceleration in agriculture to be implemented.* This happy ending to the acceleration story allowed still another set of obligations to be put in force more rapidly with regard to the common agricultural policy. The fears and uncertainties of the Member States about competitive inequalities were assuaged, partly, at least, by the Commission's offer to submit concrete proposals on the levy system within a few months. Germany gave up many of her demands in response to the several proposals of the Commission for accelerated action, including the suggestion that the Directors' Committees called for in the Commission's general proposals be set up immediately to advise the Commission on problems of market organization and competition.

The Commission worked intensively to complete draft regulations instituting a levy system and a common market organization for grain and pork by May 31, and for sugar, eggs, and poultry by July 31, as specified in the Council's December resolution. Work was also begun on most of the remainder of the Commission's general proposals. Collaboration with the Special Committee on Agriculture, which met several days a month throughout the year, was close. The Commission used the Special Committee as a forum, presenting progress reports and, where necessary, changing its proposals to meet particular national objections. Working groups of national experts for each product were convened under the Commission. The Commission also continued to consult with other interested parties, and the final versions of its draft regulations represented its

---

* Germany had requested that acceleration for wine be put off. However, a Commission proposal to revise the acceleration decision regarding increased quotas for the import of wine into Germany failed to obtain the necessary qualified majority and was rejected.

judgment as to the maximum that might be achieved given the existing situation. This is not to say that *all* national objections were met in the draft regulations, but only that the Commission had acted "with due regard to the discussions . . . in the Council and its Special Committee on Agriculture."[89]

The draft regulations for grain, pork, poultry, and eggs were submitted to the Council on schedule, and then promptly sent back to the Special Committee, which was to "prepare" Council decisions before the end of the year. The same pattern of negotiation—consultation between the Commission and the Special Committee, backed up by study groups and working parties of national experts, and by Commission progress reports—was begun again. But this time the work was based on a definitive text, which was strenuously defended by the Commission and its allies among the national delegations. It also took place in a context of intensified pressure for concrete agreement. The French, faced with increasing domestic unrest on the farm and mounting agricultural surpluses, were making it clear that they would not even consider moving from the first to the second stage of the transition period[90] unless the common agricultural policy were put into motion.[91] They were joined by the Dutch, who refused, too, to accept further tariff reductions for industrial goods until the Germans gave in on agriculture. Accordingly, the Council of Ministers in May was unable to agree to the second 10 per cent cut at the end of 1961 that had been envisaged in the original acceleration decision.

Thus something had to be done if the Community were to avoid the politically and psychologically damaging twin failures of being unable to complete the acceleration, and of having to admit that the goals of the first stage remained unachieved, so that all further progress toward the Common Market would have to be delayed for at least a year.

The French and Dutch representatives on the Special Committee pressed for early Council action on the Commission's draft regulations. It was becoming increasingly clear that if there were to be any agreement on a common agricultural policy, it could not come for a few products at a time, but would have to be on a "package deal" that would grant something to the special preoccupations of each of the Six. Accordingly, the Special Committee undertook to report on the draft regulations for grain and pork at the October session of the Council. It was also decided at the June meeting to ask the Commission to present additional detailed proposals for other products (fruit, vegetables, beef, dairy products, rice, fats, etc.) before the end of the year.[92]

There is little point in going into the incredibly complex and technical detail of the Commission's draft regulations.[93] It will suffice to say that the proposals were based on its own general program and on the Council's resolution on the levy system (see pp. 247–48 above). Despite opposition from governments and agricultural groups, the Commission continued to press for such controversial points as a *six-year* transition period leading to a *fusion* of national market organizations; the renunciation by the Member States of *all* other forms of protection, including duties, quotas, and minimum prices; and a Community price level between the current high price of the Germans and the low price of the French and Dutch.

The Council of Ministers began serious debates on the first draft regulations at its October session, debates that were to be the most difficult and drawn-out in the Community's history. Issues that remained unsolved in the Special Committee were brought to the Council. Concessions were offered, bargains struck, new points of conflict unearthed and referred back to the Special Committee. The Commission once again was an active participant and from time to time offered compromise solutions when deadlock threatened. A fuller account of the Council debates from October 1961 to January 1962, and of the part the Commission played in them, will be presented below. First, however, we must examine the roles played by the other Community institutions, as well as by Community-level and national interest groups, in the long process of preparation that the common agricultural policy involved.

THE ROLES OF OTHER COMMUNITY INSTITUTIONS AND
OF COMMUNITY-LEVEL INTEREST GROUPS

The EPA, the ESC, and Community-level interest groups tried to influence the Commission throughout the period it was developing its general proposals. Contacts were also maintained during 1961, as the Commission, the Special Committee, and the Council sought compromises on the specific draft regulations that would give effect to the general proposals. It is difficult to judge the success of these efforts to influence the proceedings, since they were not restricted to formal debates and resolutions or to issuing required opinions, but included an almost constant informal collaboration. Throughout the preparation period (1958–60), the Commission was in contact with the Agricultural Committee of the EPA, with the Specialized Agricultural Section of the ESC, and with representatives of interest groups. There were substantial differences in detail between the Commission's first draft and the final proposals, some of which can be attributed to pressure from such quarters. But this does not serve to alter our conclusion that these institutions are essentially tangential to EEC policy-making. The basic substance of the Commission's proposals was not changed, and most of the elements adopted from the resolutions of the EPA and ESC seem to have been chosen either to reinforce what the Commission already desired to do, or to effect a formal cooptation of certain groups. Not that the Commission ignored the views of interest group representatives and parliamentarians. Its proposals were certainly designed to achieve a maximum support from these quarters, but their views could have been as easily obtained through more standard lobbying activities.

It remains true, however, that the resolutions of the various institutions were far too general to have any significant influence on Commission policy-making. It is also clear that the Commission's final proposals were affected by formal and informal contacts with the Permanent Representatives, governmental experts, the representatives of third countries (the United States and Commonwealth countries), national interest groups, and so on. The changes made by the Commission in its specific draft regulations at the end of 1961 were made with a view to reconciling divergent standpoints within the Council, and not, except incidentally, in response to amendments suggested formally or informally by the EPA or the ESC. It follows that the studies, debates, and resolutions of such bodies as the EPA, the ESC, and COPA were of greater significance for the internal processes of these institutions than for the effects they may have had on the Commission's deliberations.

We have already discussed the activities of COPA with regard to the common agricultural policy and the internal developments that followed. Suffice it to repeat here that COPA representatives concentrated their lobbying efforts on the ESC, by which means they hoped to gain an assured hearing for the agricultural producers' point of view. The intensive negotiations within COPA to achieve a common position that could be defended in the ESC, as well as the negotiations within the Specialized Section on Agriculture to gain support from labor and industry, were of considerable significance for the development of a procedural consensus. Much the same conclusion may be drawn for the groups representing agricultural workers, commerce in agricultural products, and the foodstuffs industries, although the interests of these groups were perhaps closer together at the start.

With respect to the ESC, it issued two opinions on the Commission's general proposals. These were in turn based upon opinions from the Specialized Section on Agriculture, which had been discussing the Commission's proposals for eight months.[94] The ESC received the Commission's draft proposals in November 1959, and issued an opinion on its general provisions on May 6, 1960, and on its specific, product-by-product proposals on June 30, 1960.[95] The second of these opinions was largely beside the point, so far as influencing the Commission was concerned, since it was issued on the basis of the Commission's draft proposals, which had already been superseded by the definitive proposals. It was, however, available to the Commission during its 1961 work on the product-by-product draft regulations. The ESC was not *formally* consulted by the Commission regarding these specifics of application. Nevertheless, the Commission continued to keep the Special Section on Agriculture "informed" of progress being made.[96] Accordingly, all the draft regulations were circulated in the Special Section, which prepared "information reports" that were sent back to the Commission. No formal plenary sessions of the ESC were held.[97] This would seem to confirm our conclusion that the activities of the ESC *as an institution* have not had a substantial influence on policy. That the views of major interest groups will continue to be kept in mind, and that this may be conveniently accomplished by contact with them in the ESC or its special sections, is evident.

Both 1960 opinions were quite general, being an amalgam of concessions made by the various groups. Both substantially accepted the Commission's proposals, although there were numerous reservations and suggestions on matters of detail, and in spite of the fact that the debates had often been highly critical. The representatives of industry abstained on the first opinion,[98] and presumably they pursued their opposition through other channels. The same may be said of other interest groups that agreed to compromises on the final draft. There is no evidence to suggest that the participating groups had given up their specific demands, even though they had been willing to withdraw them in the interest of reaching a general agreement.

We shall not examine the details of these two opinions, except to indicate the major points that seem to have influenced the Commission's final proposals.[99] The ESC requested that a section on a common social policy in agriculture be included, that the Commission prepare an annual report on such questions as agricultural incomes and structures, and that the Consultative Committees for all the proposed European Offices be created. Each of these proposals had the effect of expanding the role of the central institutions. Similarly, the essence of the informal consultations carried on in 1961 was a recommendation that the role of the Agricultural Guidance and Guarantee Funds be expanded (they were to provide *Community* financing of export subsidies and internal market supports), and that they begin operation at once, rather than in three years as the Commission had proposed.[100]

As for the EPA, it has devoted more time and effort to the problems of the common agricultural policy than to any other aspect of the EEC. This has been the case even though, in a formal sense, it did not have an official role to play until early 1961. Recall that, according to Article 43 of the Treaty, the Commission, after consulting the ESC, makes proposals to the Council, which in turn issues implementing regulations, directives, decisions, or recommendations after consulting the Assembly. The Council did not consider any implementing measures until 1961, and hence did not formally consult the Assembly. But the Assembly was not prepared to take a minimal view of its functions, and sought instead to assert a continuing influence over Community policies regardless of specific Treaty provisions. In general, the Commission, the Council, and the governments acquiesced in this. The Assembly's discussions of agriculture took place in four distinct stages: before the Commission's draft proposals, between the draft and the definitive proposals, after completion of the definitive proposals, and after the Commission's submission of its specific draft regulations to the Council.

From March 1958 to December 1959, the Assembly, through the activities of its Agricultural Committee and by means of a number of formal debates, sought to exercise some sort of prior control over the Commission's proposals. Three reports, prepared by M. Troisi, H. A. Lücker, and H. Vredeling, were adopted by the Agriculture Committee and discussed by the Assembly.[101] André Boutemy, then President of the Agricultural Committee, stated the Assembly's position in unambiguous terms during a debate in June 1959. He observed that the reports and subsequent debates would enable the Assembly to set forth a basic political framework to which the Commission would be expected to adhere. As he pointed out, "The controlling agent must not be content with basing its opinions upon information supplied by the body it controls. Indeed, everyone should remember that the executive branches were intended to operate in the political framework established by the EPA."[102] The reports prepared by Troisi, Lücker, and Vredeling were fairly general, amounting to little more than statements of the problems and needs of agriculture, and of the general goals that a common agricultural policy ought to strive for.

In December 1959, the Council, having received the Commission's draft proposals, referred them to the EPA "by right of information." At the end of March, the Agriculture Committee presented eight detailed reports to the Assembly, paralleling the sections of the Commission's draft: the situation of agriculture and the general principles of a common agricultural policy; agricultural structures; grain; sugar; milk and milk products; meats, poultry, and eggs; fruit and vegetables; and wine.[103] These were discussed by the Assembly at the March–April session. As in the case of the ESC and COPA, the Commission's proposals were accepted as a valuable point of departure and as proof that a common agricultural policy was possible. Nevertheless, they were subjected to some sharp criticisms both in the reports and in the debates. It is important to note that the principle of a common agricultural policy was not only generally accepted, but repeatedly reaffirmed by speakers representing all political groups and economic interests. The reports and the debates dealt with questions of emphasis and detail corresponding to particular national or group preoccupations. The Commission was accused of having made it insufficiently clear whether the policy of the Community was to be liberal or "dirigiste," reasonably open or protectionist, with a high or a low price level. More specific proposals to cover the transitional period were called for. The Commission was accused of having concerned itself too much with overproduction and not enough with the standard of living for farmers. There must be a clearer Community preference for agricultural products. The Agriculture Committee's reports clearly favored a system of set minimum and maximum prices rather than the system of target prices proposed by the Commission, a position that received strong support in the Assembly.

The Commission's definitive proposals do not appear to have been significantly altered to meet the objections of the Assembly. More specific proposals for the transitional period were included, but the relative emphasis on the dangers of overproduction, and on the extent to which the Community was to be protectionist or liberal, remained essentially unchanged. Furthermore, the Commission retained its system of target and intervention prices, although it made a small change in the percentage range between the intervention price and the target price.[104] The Commission's definitive proposals were again transmitted "by right of information" to the Assembly's Agriculture Committee, which voted a resolution that it presented to the Assembly in October 1960. A lively, and often heated, debate ensued, one that revealed some basic policy differences between a majority of the Assembly and the Commission. The resolution was addressed to the Council and contained two particularly controversial articles (Articles 10 and 20), the first concerning the Community's import regulations, and the second the level of prices that should obtain in the Community.[105]

Article 10 of the resolution states that "in the Community organization of agricultural markets the system of imports under which import licenses are granted should be established on the basis of an annual balance sheet (production, needs, imports)."[106] This was directly at variance with the Commission's proposals for a system of compensatory levies and import certificates to be granted on demand. The Agriculture Committee challenged the effectiveness of these measures and recommended the use of quotas. According to one report, "In the Assembly the great majority of Christian Democrats supported this article and thought it deplorable that import licenses should be granted when requested. . . . In essence the majority of speakers thought that community preference was essential, and that unregulated imports would destroy the equilibrium of the European market."[107]

Article 20 states:

The approximation of prices with a view to the realization of a common price level for agricultural products should be carried out progressively and in relation to the flow of trade from the producing to the consuming areas, and *in the light* of the price levels existing in the country which is the Community's biggest customer [consumer] of agricultural products. This procedure would respect the principle of ensuring economic and social development in accord with the highest standard of living in the Community.[108]

This meant a commitment to the German price level, since it was the highest in the Six. It was an implicit rejection both of the Commission's program of price approximation and an ultimate price level between the highest and lowest, and of an important principle of its entire agricultural policy, namely that price policy ought not to be relied on for assuring farmers an ample return, for this would only lead to overproduction.

In spite of the active and categorical opposition of Mansholt, Vice-President of the Commission, as well as that of the Socialists and the Dutch, the Assembly adopted the resolution by a vote of 45 to 30 with four abstentions. Perhaps the worst aspect of the resolution from the Commission's point of view, however, was eliminated when the Assembly adopted an amendment proposed by René Charpentier (MRP, France), which excluded feed-grains from the terms of the Article.[109]

What were the implications of this resolution and debate? It is interesting to note first that Vice-President Mansholt made it clear during the debate that the Commission would not modify its proposals on prices regardless of what resolution the Assembly might adopt.[110] This bears out our thesis that the Assembly has relatively little direct influence on the Commission. Certainly the debate was important. Although the policy implications are obviously of major significance both internally and externally, the action taken by the Assembly in no way diminishes the integrative potential of the common agricultural policy. That there was considerable support for a protectionist agricultural policy and for one based on high prices for producers cannot have come as a surprise. The comment of Pierre Drouin in *Le Monde* is needlessly pessimistic: "After listening for seven or eight hours, one was indeed far from the Europe of the peoples or the fatherlands [l'Europe des peuples ou des patries], and arrived quite simply and shamelessly at the Europe of 'high agricultural prices.' "[111]

The process of political integration is not dependent upon particular policy formulations. There is no reason why an integrated Europe cannot have an agricultural policy based on protectionism and high prices, however inadvisable this might be as an economic policy. What is significant for political integration is the seeming unanimity with which the need for a common agricultural policy had been accepted. Except for the Dutch, the cleavages revealed in the Assembly's debates occurred on the basis of party affiliation and not nationality. The Socialists and Christian-Democrats were in direct opposition on a number of points, but both espoused positions involving increased centralization. All groups concentrated their efforts upon attempting to influence the content of agricultural policy, whether in a protectionist or liberal direction, whether in the interests of consumers or producers. They thereby contributed to the spill-over process and to political integration.

The first formal consultation of the Assembly by the Council came in January 1961. This concerned the draft regulation on the application of certain rules of competition to agriculture that the Commission had proposed as part of the package settlement on acceleration. The EPA also debated and passed two other resolutions on agriculture: a statement on the levy system, and a resolution on the establishment of objective criteria for the application of minimum prices in agriculture. The three reports presented by the Agriculture Committee once again revealed a significant difference of opinion from that of the Commission.[112] The chief issues revolved around the Committee's insistence that the rules on competition be applied concurrently with the introduction of the levy system for each product, that the system of minimum prices be an integral part of the common agricultural policy, and that the levy system be supplemented by quotas to assure a preference to Community producers. Vice-President Mansholt contested these positions, expressing the Commission's desire to keep the issues of rules of competition and minimum prices separate from that of the common agricultural policy *per se*, and to establish the principle that levies would replace all other forms of protection.[113] The resolutions finally voted by the Assembly contained some "compromises" between the Commission and the Agriculture Committee. It was agreed that competitive distortions "would be taken into account" when the levy systems were introduced, and that although minimum prices were not an integral part of the common agricultural policy, they should be applied "in the framework" of its transitional measures.[114] But otherwise the Assembly's resolutions were not much modified to accommodate the views of the Commission. This was particularly the case as regards minimum prices.* The resolution on the levy system also still insisted on the introduction of quotas as an additional protective device.

When the Assembly met in October 1961 to consider formal opinions on the draft regulations for grain, pork, poultry, and eggs, it was clear that

---

* We shall not deal further with the thorny and complex issue of objective criteria for minimum prices, nor, for that matter, with the problems of competition in agriculture. These continued to plague the Community throughout the year, but they are separable, at least for our purposes, from the common agricultural policy itself.

its January debates and resolutions had done little to change the Commission's position. Once again, in the report of the Agriculture Committee presented by Charpentier, in the debates that followed, and in the opinions agreed to, the EPA criticized certain details of the Commission's drafts as not offering sufficient guarantees to Community farmers. The Assembly favored, among other things, a floor on intervention prices, a system of quotas, and an "orientation price" below which the price of pork might not fall.[115] On the other hand, it stressed the need to strengthen the independent powers of the Commission in the administration of the levy system, especially in regard to the determination of price levels. In the Assembly's formal opinions on the market organization for fruit, vegetables, and wine, adopted in November, a similar emphasis was present. The Commission's proposals were just a first step and must be supplemented by more far-reaching measures, namely a European Bureau for fruit, vegetables, and wine, and a harmonization of legislation concerning wine production.[116]

Throughout the difficult months of November and December, the Assembly constantly reminded the Council of the importance of adopting the Commission's proposals before the end of the year. At the November "colloquy" between the Assembly, the Council, the EEC and Euratom Commissions, and the High Authority of the ECSC, the Assembly subjected the Ministers to lively attacks for their failure to demonstrate "a Community spirit."[117] It also protested vigorously against French efforts to diminish the role of the Commission in the administration of the levy system.[118]

It has been evident from the Assembly's debates, resolutions, and opinions that a majority of its members is unwilling to commit itself to anything but a high price level and a protectionist import policy. This reflects the considerable influence of farmers' organizations upon national parliamentarians, especially that of the Deutscher Bauernverband on the CDU/CSU. The position taken by the Christian-Democratic group has been attributable in part to a desire to help the CDU in the 1961 Bundestag elections, in which the farmers' vote played a vital role. Nevertheless, the energy with which agricultural groups from all countries have sought to influence the Assembly is impressive; in terms of the future, it suggests that the practical effectiveness of that body will vary in relationship to the extent that groups channel their expectations and demands through it. In this context it is interesting to contrast the ESC and the Assembly. In the former, the effort was to achieve as nearly unanimous an opinion as possible, with the result that the views of the interests represented effectively canceled each other out. The ESC's opinion had to be moderate and general. In the Assembly, on the other hand, a majority has passed resolutions and opinions that have included specific policy recommendations. These have a far greater likelihood of proving to be of eventual political significance.

It has also become clear that even in the area of agriculture the Assembly's commitment to political integration is basic. The Commission has been able to count on the Assembly's support at all times: when it comes to a confrontation with the Council of Ministers, when any of the long-range goals of the Community seem threatened, and even when the Commission has been unwilling to change its proposals along the lines urged by the Assembly. This is the paradox of the Assembly. The only way it can hope to play a significant role in Community affairs is by supporting the initiatives of the Commission and by urging the Member States to continue to delegate authority to it. But as yet its influence over matters of policy detail seems minimal.

THE SIX ADOPT
A COMMON POLICY FOR AGRICULTURE

How was the common agricultural policy received? And how were opposing interests finally accommodated? All through the preliminary work and throughout the long negotiations, one fact has stood out clearly: all those concerned, governments and interest groups alike, have recognized the need for a "Community solution."

The reactions of agricultural groups in the Six have left no doubt that while all are determined to protect their established positions and to achieve a maximum advantage, they are at the same time prepared to do so within the framework of a common agricultural policy. The rapid rate at which agricultural groups (producers, commercial groups, foodstuffs industries, and workers) have organized at the EEC level is powerful evidence of this. Most groups have realized that neither short- nor long-range goals can be achieved at the national level. They have therefore shown a willingness to accept common measures so long as positive bonuses are held out, and so long as they are able to exercise some influence over policy-making.

Thus COPA insisted on being associated in the continued efforts of the Community institutions to develop a common agricultural policy that would meet the practical objections of farmers to the Commission's proposals. Moreover, it stressed that a common agricultural policy was a necessity if farmers were to realize their legitimate aspirations, and that a common agricultural policy was inconceivable without common policies (especially toward third countries) and a Community organization or coordination of agricultural markets.[1]

For some groups, of course, organization at the Community level has probably resulted from a realization that it was impossible to block the common agricultural policy entirely—and a belief that the best obstructionist action could come from within. In any event, the result has been to enhance the role of the center, since a new framework for political action has been implicitly accepted, even by those groups seeking to limit such action. This does not mean that the proposals of the Commission have been received with unanimous approval. On the contrary, they have completely pleased no one and have been subjected to extensive criticism from all sides. The point is that they represent the basis for a joint agricultural policy that is being worked out within the EEC institutional system and in accordance with its characteristic procedural code.

Leaving aside the detailed, product-by-product criticisms of the Commission's proposals, which are far too complex to treat here, four issues have caused the most controversy: the question of prices, the relative emphasis to be given to structural policy as against market policy, trade relations with third countries, and the length of the transitional period. The positions taken by interest groups on these issues are summarized in the following table.

Of the various national groups, the German DBV, from the very beginning, took the most unequivocal position on the common agricultural policy. Enjoying the highest price level in the EEC, as well as the benevolence of the German government, it insisted upon retaining its advantages in the context of the Six. It criticized the Commission with some heat for favoring low agricultural prices in the interests of consumers who already enjoyed a higher standard of living than farmers. It rejected a Community structural policy as unnecessary, since it considered this an area of essentially national concern. It accepted the concept of the Common Market only if trade liberalization came gradually, categorically rejecting the Commission's proposed six-year transitional period. According to the DBV, the real problem was not the high level of German prices, but the fact that production costs in other EEC countries were kept artificially low by unfair competitive practices: e.g., the export subsidies and price controls of the Dutch. Action should therefore be taken to harmonize production costs before price approximation could be considered. The DBV called for a clearly preferential policy toward third countries, in which compensatory levies would be supplemented by quotas. As regards EEC trade, it rejected the Commission's proposed target and intervention prices in favor of a fixed minimum price.[2] The Commission's emphasis upon structural reforms as the best way to bring about an improvement in agricultural incomes was also rejected.

POSITIONS TAKEN BY INTEREST GROUPS ON THE FOUR MAIN ISSUES
OF THE COMMON AGRICULTURAL POLICY

Country	Group	View on what Community price level ought to be	Structural vs. price policy as means to improve income	Relations with 3d countries	Proposed 6-year transitional period
Germany	Farmers	High	Price	Preferential	Too short
	Bus & com	Low	Structural	Liberal	Too short
	Labor	Low	Structural	Liberal	—
Bel–Lux	Farmers	High	Price	Preferential	Too short
	Bus & com	Low	Structural	Liberal	—
	Labor	Low	Structural	Liberal	—
France	Farmers	Ave. to high	Both	Preferential	Accepted
	Bus & com	Low	Structural	Preferential	—
	Labor	Low	—	—	—
Italy	Farmers	Ave. to high	Both	Preferential	Too short (exc. fruit–veg)
	Bus & com	Low	Structural	—	Too short
	Labor	—	—	—	—
Neth	Farmers	Low	Structural	Liberal	Accepted
	Bus & com	Low	Structural	Liberal	Accepted
	Labor	Low	Structural	Liberal	Accepted

SOURCES: "L'Agriculture dans le Marché commun"; EPA, Direction de Documentation Parlementaire et de l'Information, *Prises de position*; "Le point de vue des organisations"; *Agriculture, The Commonwealth, and EEC*, pp. 18–25; *Agence Europe*, April 2, 6, 11, 1960; August 30, 1960; September 20, 1960; October 19, 1960; ECSC, *Informations Mensuelles*, August–September and October–November–December 1958; EPA, *Cahiers*, January 1960; April 1961; July 1961; August–September 1961; October 1961.

The Belgian Boerenbond was in substantial agreement with the DBV on the need for harmonizing national policies and suppressing unfair competitive practices, although its position on prices was less categorical. The need for an approximation between the highest and the lowest was accepted, but six years was not considered enough. Furthermore, the Commission ought to have stressed measures intended to bring production costs together.

French groups in general reacted favorably to the Commission's proposals, France having the most to gain from a Common Market in agriculture. In order to protect this advantage, they insisted on a clearly preferential European system, with both import levies and quotas against third countries. They were opposed to the Commission's proposal that minimum prices be replaced by a system of variable levies. The shortened transitional period was accepted so long as it was accompanied by a harmonization of legislation in the social field, in sanitation, and in standards of quality. "Necessary" price reductions were allowed, provided there were adequate safeguards to ensure the income of farmers while structural changes were being made. The French attitude was an opportunist one, and is probably best illustrated by the following statement:

Let us not forget the importance of the potential of French agricultural production, which must have markets. At our door there is a market of 170 million consumers which will become 180 million in ten years' time. . . . It would be a grave error not to profit from the occasion and to let ourselves be put off by the obstacles that the Common Market will meet. If this market did not come into existence, French agriculture would not find itself in a better situation with regard to third countries; it would face the competition of countries which have a permanent agricultural surplus to dispose of. Even if it does not give us complete satisfaction, the Common Market is still the lesser evil.[3]

The Italians also had a great deal to gain from a Common Market in agriculture, especially the fruit and vegetable growers of the Po Valley. The Confederazione Nazionale Coltivatori Diretti favored as rapid a liberalization as possible for these products, regarding even the Commission's timetable as too slow. Moreover, the institutions of the Community should be granted sufficient power to eliminate internal protective devices such as quotas, seasonal import calendars, and minimum price lists, which were still employed to bar Italian produce from the German, French, and Belgian markets.[4] For other products, however, Italian groups were less enthusiastic about rapid liberalization, maintaining that extensive structural reform must come first. They also expected to receive a large amount of structural aid from the EEC.

The most favorable reaction to the Commission's proposals came from the Dutch. The Landbouwschap agreed to the shortened transitional period and to the proposed system of levies, *provided* this were accompanied by the elimination of all other protective devices: import quotas, export aids, and minimum import prices. For the Dutch, internal trade liberalization was a necessary condition for the establishment of a Common Market in agricultural products. They had always favored a low price level, particularly for feed-grains, which are the basis of their transformation agriculture (meat, dairy products), and they considered the Commission's proposed system of import levies on feed-grains, as well as its provisions for export compensations, adequate to safeguard their interests. They also championed a liberal policy toward third countries, criticizing even the Commission's proposals as too preferential or protectionist.[5]

All agricultural groups, with the possible exception of the DBV, perceived immediate advantages from a common agricultural policy. The French and the Dutch were concerned primarily to guarantee their export markets, as were the Italians for fruit and vegetables, and possibly for wine. For the French this implied a strictly preferential policy with regard to third countries, whereas for the Dutch, with a large extra-Community trade in both agricultural and industrial goods, it meant a liberal commercial policy. The Belgians and Italians saw the common agricultural policy above all as a way to increase the efficiency of their agriculture through internal structural reforms. All farmers' groups were determined to improve their relative standard of living. Those with a high price level were loath to risk an eventual decrease that might or might not be made up by structural reform. Low-price countries expected a modest price rise, but saw the major advantage in an expanded production. Only the Dutch, with both low prices and an efficient production, wanted to keep prices low. Rapid internal trade liberalization was stressed by those countries expecting to gain from expanded exports (especially the Netherlands, and France and Italy for some products), and resisted by those whose gains were expected from structural reform (Germany, Belgium, and Italy). Similarly, although practically all groups accepted the need for some kind of European market organization, the Germans and Belgians regarded it as a necessary evil to be kept to a minimum, whose dirigistic and technocratic tendencies had at all costs to be avoided. Many of the goals of the Dutch, Italians, and French, on the other hand, depended upon the creation of European Offices and upon compulsory coordination of national market organizations. This is not to say that there was agreement on the specific powers the European Offices and the Commission should have with respect to setting prices and making purchases.

It ought to be kept in mind that agricultural groups are not the only ones actively concerned with the future common agricultural policy. The broad outlines of the policy must also correspond to some degree to the interests and demands of trade unions, consumers, commercial groups, foodstuffs producers, and industry. In general, the interests of these groups are served by a low Community price level for agricultural goods, by an emphasis on structural reform over market policy, and by a liberal commercial policy. Hence, they have acted as a counterweight to the farmers' organizations in the deliberations of those national and Community institutions engaged in formulating a common agricultural policy. We have seen an example of this in the ESC deliberations on the Commission's draft proposals.

Although opinion has been divided on the common agricultural policy, both among the several Member States and within each one, a degree of intergroup unity has developed among groups organized at the Community level, both as they themselves begin to perceive common interests and as the EEC moves to the stage of implementing the specifics of the policy. Such a pattern of converging interests has uniformly given rise to further demands for action, thereby enhancing the role of the central institutions and contributing to the process of integration.

NATIONAL REACTIONS: GOVERNMENTS

When the EEC Council of Ministers met in October 1961 to consider the Special Committee's report on the Commission's draft regulations, the views of the several governments were fairly clearly defined. Over a year had passed since the Commission had presented its general proposals for a common agricultural policy, and the essential details of its draft implementation regulations had been known for some months. The draft regulations presented more serious problems in that it was probably genuinely difficult for agricultural experts to anticipate what their exact impact would be on the administration of national programs in agriculture. Many of the problems that had vexed the meetings of the Special Committee and its multitude of study groups were of a purely technical nature, for the complexities of agricultural policy can hardly be overemphasized.

Nevertheless, some things were amply clear from the more general statements that had been made during 1960–61.[6] Of the Six, only Germany seemed to oppose the Commission's proposals categorically. Her unwillingness to move very far or very fast in agriculture has already been discussed in the context of the acceleration decision. With her determination to keep food prices high and to keep access to non-Community food suppliers open, it seems likely, despite protestations to the contrary, that she did not really want a common agricultural policy. It was not possible or prudent to oppose it frontally, for this would have been an explicit violation of the Community's procedural code. Therefore, her strategy was (and remains) to delay as long as possible by raising one set of technical objections after another, although she was doubtless aware that in the long run she would have to go along with the others. The government was under severe pressure from the DBV, and from all political parties except the SPD, to yield nothing in agriculture. Contrary to the situation in most of the Six, the demands of the farmers were supported by industry. Germany is the largest food importer in the Community (mainly from outside the EEC), and many of these imports are tied to industrial exports by various kinds of barter deals (e.g., German grain purchases from Argentina are linked to Argentine purchases of German manufactured products).[7]

In Community discussions the Germans pleaded for "understanding" and "patience." They declared that they did not wish to except themselves from their Treaty obligations, and had no counterproposals to those of the Commission, but felt that the Commission ought to have limited its proposals to pragmatic first steps to be followed by further proposals based on the results. Six years for the transition to the Common Market stage was far too short a time. The levy system could not be accepted as a substitute for other protective devices, such as minimum prices, compensatory charges, and long-term contracts. European Offices ought to be created only when and if needed. Furthermore, Germany could not accept the Commission's proposals for price reductions, for this would result in an unacceptable reduction in the income of farmers. An approximation of prices was not opposed in principle, but must be preceded by careful studies and made with considerable caution. At any rate, a harmonization of competitive conditions must precede all other Community action.

The Belgians were perhaps the closest to the German position in echoing this theme of "harmonization before liberalization," and in agreeing that a six-year transition period was too short. Agriculture had always been a sore spot in the Benelux economic union because of the relatively backward condition of Belgian agriculture. The Belgian position was not so rigid as the German, however, and the Commission's proposals for a price approximation and for the levy system were in general accepted, although the latter could not imply an abolition of minimum prices.

Luxembourg considered that the Commission had failed to give proper attention to the goal of trying to improve the lot of the individual farmer. There was too much concern for trade with third countries. It was too early to decide on a transitional period or to set up the European Offices, since production and marketing conditions were still so different. Price approximation must be preceded by cost reductions and the institution of compensatory provisions for those affected.

The Italians criticized the Commission's proposals as too dirigistic, too protectionist, and too autarkic. The length of the transition period could not be fixed rigidly. European market organizations were not necessary for all products and ought to be the exception and not the rule. For most purposes common rules of competition and the coordination of national market organizations would suffice. The provisions on structural policy were inadequate. Price and market policy could not be relied upon to assure agricultural incomes, for they would only lead to overproduction. The purchase of surpluses by the Community must only occur under exceptional circumstances, and not when the disequilibrium between supply and demand was the result of an autonomous initiative dictated by special interests. The variable levy system must be applied for all products (including fruit and vegetables).

The Dutch, as net exporters of agricultural products, had always insisted that a common market in agriculture be instituted parallel to the common market in other sectors. This meant that trade liberalization must not be delayed while waiting for common policy mechanisms. The variable levy system was accepted, but it must include the abolition of minimum prices or at least their severe restriction. The Commission's proposals on price levels were criticized for being based on a compromise between national price levels, rather than on an autonomous concept of what agricultural prices should be. This could only lead to permanent surpluses, disturbances in the Community's relations with third countries, and ever-increasing difficulties for the industries engaged in processing agricultural products. The Dutch were in favor of setting up European Offices, but felt this should be done gradually and only where other measures proved inadequate. The chief objective of the Dutch in the sector of agriculture was to force the other EEC countries, and especially Germany, to open their markets to Dutch food exports, primarily of dairy products. They were clearly willing to accept certain disadvantages, such as higher support prices and restrictions on the importation of cheap grain from outside the Community, to achieve this goal. But they were determined to have the common agricultural policy launched at once, and made this a condition of their agreement both on the so-called "second" acceleration and on the transition to the Common Market's second stage.

The French, too, wanted to secure outlets for their agricultural surpluses, as well as to use the common agricultural policy as a means to bring about structural reforms. Under heavy domestic pressure from farmers' organizations, including various forms of strikes, riots, and the like, the French government had proposed in its Four Year Plan for the French Economy (1962–65) to increase agricultural output by 28 per cent. Domestic consumption could hardly be expected to keep up with the increase, and hence a market would have to be assured in the Community. In many ways the position of the French was the closest to that of the Commission. They insisted on the rapid institution of the common agricultural policy, making this a condition for action in other areas, as did the Dutch. They agreed to the six-year transition period. Sufficient guarantees would have to be provided for farmers, and this required on the one hand that the common agricultural policy be clearly preferential, and on the other that the common market organizations be established as rapidly as possible. (They did favor more governmental control of these offices, however.) To this end they proposed that some of the measures envisaged by the Commission for the final stage should be instituted during the preparatory or transitional period. They also argued for a strict harmonization of trade policies, as well as sanitary legislation. On intra-Community trade they accepted the levy system, although they suggested that in exceptional cases levies should be accompanied by other safeguard measures such as minimum prices.

Thus France criticized the Commission for not going far enough or rapidly enough toward a strict European system of market organization, while all the other Member States thought that *coordination* of national market organizations would suffice for most products for the preparatory period. Italy seemed to reject the European Offices except under very special conditions. The Dutch and the Belgians and Germans were directly opposed in their views about the necessary balance between harmonization and liberalization. The French and the Dutch (and the Italians for some products) accepted the six-year transition period, which was opposed by Germany, Belgium, and Luxembourg. The Dutch complained that the EEC price level would be too high, whereas the Germans, Belgians, and Luxemburgers found it too low. The French, Belgians, and Luxemburgers stressed the need for a system of Community preference, while the Germans, Dutch, and Italians felt the Community should adopt a more liberal policy toward third countries. It remains now to indicate how these divergent views were eventually reconciled, and to outline and assess the main features of the decisions finally taken.

AGRICULTURE AND THE COUNCIL OF MINISTERS

"Nous sommes condamnés à réussir." In these words, spoken at the end of one of the dreary Council sessions on agriculture, Edgar Pisani, French Minister of Agriculture, gave expression to the basis of the dynamics of integration.[8] Agreement on a series of specific regulations involving the renunciation of purely national agricultural programs presented serious problems for each of the Six, and yet the price of failure was high. As is always the case in EEC politics, no issue could be treated in isolation. The timing of the Treaty and the specific material interests that the Member States seek to advance through integration mean that problems constantly impinge on each other, and that disadvantages must frequently be accepted in one area if advantages are to be realized in another. So it was with agriculture.

The stakes were high for the French, Dutch, and Italians, for whom the expected advantages of a common agricultural policy had been a major reason for embracing integration. Moreover, the French and the Dutch were prepared to deny their partners advantages in other areas if agreement were not reached in agriculture. This stand threatened the passage to the second stage of the transition period, the "second" acceleration, and the negotiations that were then being undertaken on British entry into the EEC.

Practically everyone had much to gain from the passage from the first to the second stage. It represented the point of no return—both legally and psychologically. Thereafter, only a unanimous vote of all the Member States could slow down the Treaty timetable and delay the steps called for in the second and third stages. Importers and exporters, industrialists and trade unionists, politicians and civil servants, could then have stable expectations for the future, for there would be no going back. In addition, as the "Europeans" emphasized, the second stage would bring a series of new policy areas under the majority voting procedures of the Treaty.[9] In every way it was an important milestone in the direction of economic and political unity.*

The second acceleration involved essentially the same play of interests as the original acceleration sequence: it was supported by businessmen who found the Treaty timetable too confining for national investment and sales planning, and by all those who for varied reasons wanted to speed up the execution of the Treaty.

The British negotiations, as before, represented both a threat and an attraction. The Germans, the Italians, and the Benelux countries had always favored some kind of arrangement with the British for commercial reasons. Moreover, in the eyes of Benelux and the Italian leaders, British membership would be a desirable counterweight to de Gaulle and his ambitions to create a Paris-Bonn axis. But all agreed, especially the "Europeans," that the British must not be permitted to write their own terms for entry, or to take advantage of divisions within the EEC. They would have to accept the Rome Treaty and all decisions taken by the Six over the first four years. It was necessary for the Six to present a united front in the negotiations, and nowhere was this more important than in agriculture. Furthermore, nothing could be worse than carrying on membership negotiations after the Community countries had themselves failed to implement their own Treaty. Hence progress in agriculture, passage to the second stage, and the British negotiations were closely connected, whether the goal was facilitating British entry (the Germans, Dutch, Belgians, and Italians) or making the price as high as possible (the French).

The scene was thus set for the usual hard game of reciprocal concessions so characteristic of EEC decision-making. The bargaining that ensued over agriculture was played out against this multifunctional background. But it ought also to be kept in mind that the common agricultural policy

---

* Two other issues bound up with the passage to the second stage are worth mentioning: the demand made by France that her partners fulfill their Treaty obligation to equalize pay for men and women, and the implementation of the first EEC regulation on restrictive business practices, a matter that was particularly close to the heart of the German Minister of Economic Affairs, Erhard.

itself was a very large and diverse package within which most groups and governments could find some advantages. It was with this consideration foremost that the Commission had drawn up its general proposals as well as its draft regulations (see pp. 261–69 above). And it was this consideration that governed the negotiations among the Council, the Special Committee, and the Commission, negotiations that sapped the energies of Community and national officials from October 1961 to January 1962.

These discussions centered on the draft regulations proposed by the Commission for the organization of markets for grain, pork, poultry, eggs, fruit, vegetables, and wine.* The Commission advocated moving toward the common agricultural policy in two stages: first, to unify the systems of internal supports and external protection while maintaining different national price levels and producer incomes; and, second, to move gradually toward the harmonization of price and income levels as the Community support mechanism made itself felt.[10] Since price harmonization was a particularly sensitive subject, especially in Germany, the Commission limited its 1961 proposals to the first set of objectives.† The key element here was the levy system, which was not only to take the place of all other forms of protection inside the Community during the transition period, but to be the basis of the permanent Community policy toward third countries (see pp. 247–48 above). The Commission insisted, as we have seen, that the levies should be the sole means of support. This insistence really amounted to an implicit rejection of the normal procedure of abolishing trade barriers under the Rome Treaty.[11]

Of all the draft regulations, the one on grain was perhaps the most important. It certainly provided the greatest difficulty for the negotiators. France was already a net exporter of grain and expected an ever-increasing surplus in the future. Securing a safe outlet in the Community was vital to her. But any common policy for grain was likely to result in lower prices than those prevailing in Germany and Italy, and this presented problems for the governments of those two countries, since wheat producers are influential in both the DBV and the Coltivatori Diretti. Furthermore, many products are based on the conversion of grain—namely, pork, poultry, eggs, beef, milk, and milk products—and the system and price level adopted will basically affect countries specializing in these products. This is particularly serious for countries like the Netherlands which import grain at low world prices and which will have to shift to higher-priced Community grain. As

---

* The problems of competition in agriculture, and objective criteria for minimum prices, were also being discussed at this time. But, as we have noted, these issues are separable from the common agricultural policy *per se.*

† Recall that the Commission had made tentative proposals for price harmonization in 1960.

COMPOSITION OF NATIONAL AGRICULTURAL PRODUCTION IN THE
SIX COUNTRIES (1955–56)

(In percentage of value of total national agricultural production)

EEC Product	Bel–Lux (4.9)[a]		Germany (23.0)[a]	France (39.4)[a]	Italy (26.3)[a]	Netherlands (6.4)[a]
	Belgium	Luxembourg				
Grain	9%	10%	11%	11%	25%	5%
Potatoes	4	5	7	2	2	6
Sugar beets	4	—	3	2	2	3
Wine	—	6	1	8	11	—
Fruit	5	1	3	4	10	4
Vegetables	11	—	3	9	7	8
Other	3	5	—	2	9	8
Total of vegetable products	36	27	28	38	66	34
Beef and mutton	17%	15%	14%	19%	8%	12%
Pork	12	24	26	11	4	15
Poultry	1	1	1	7	2	2
Eggs	11	4	6	5	5	11
Milk and products ..	25	28	25	19	12	26
Other	—	—	—	1	1	—
Total of animal products	66	73	70	62	32	66

SOURCE: Adapted from EEC Commission, *Recueil*, p. 130.

[a] Percentage of EEC production.

for the other products, the accompanying table on the composition of national agricultural production shows that pork was especially important for Germany and Luxembourg, poultry for France, eggs for Belgium and the Netherlands, and fruit, vegetables, and wine for France and Italy. The degree to which a country was affected varied also with the relative efficiency and productivity of its agriculture and with its prevailing price level (for details see pp. 220–25 above).

When the Council of Ministers met in October 1961 for their first formal examination of the Commission's drafts, small progress had been made toward agreement. The Special Committee on Agriculture had accomplished little more than drawing up lists of the areas of disagreement. Thus, despite additional lengthy Council sessions—November 29–December 2, December 12–13, December 18–21, and December 29–30—and the around-the-clock labors of the Commission, the Special Committee, and hundreds of national experts, agreement was not possible by the end-of-the-year deadline. Rather than permit the first stage to be automatically extended (as stipulated in the Treaty) and admit the failure of the negotiations, the Council agreed in effect to stop the clock, and to consider its Sixtieth Session merely recessed. Although it was not until January 14, 1962, after almost continuous session since January 4, that the final decisions on agriculture were made and the vote taken to pass to the second stage of the transition period, all documents were given a December 1961 date and all decisions were retroactive. As President Hallstein later told an American audience, "The courage of the ministers should not be underrated—nor, indeed, their endurance. Forty-five separate meetings, 7 of them at night; a total of 137 hours of discussion, with 214 hours in subcommittee; 582,000 pages of documents; 3 heart attacks—the record is staggering."[12]

The achievement was a major one. There is no precedent for the promulgation of such an extensive series of measures at one time even on a national scale, to say nothing of an agreement covering six countries. The texts agreed upon were as follows: a series of regulations on the organization of the markets for grain, pork, poultry, eggs, fruit, and vegetables; regulations on wine-growing and wine quotas for Germany, France, and Italy; a financial regulation setting up the Guidance and Guarantee Fund; a regulation on competition; a decision concerning certain goods manufactured from agricultural products; a decision on permissible import duties; a decision on objective criteria for the establishment of minimum prices; and resolutions on dairy produce, beef, and sugar.[13] The importance of these measures cannot be overemphasized. As the Commission points out, "By creating various market organizations for the most important products, by instituting, in the shape of a Guidance and Guarantee Fund, a Community system for the supply of finance, by applying rules of competition to all products, these decisions enable trade in agricultural products to take its full part in the Common Market, as has already been done in the case of industrial products."[14] Most of the regulations took legal effect on July 1, 1962.

The problems posed by agriculture were among the most difficult faced by the Community, and the governments were subjected to far more intense pressure from agricultural groups than they had ever faced from business or labor. As the *Financial Times* noted on January 15, "The fact that the six governments were able to reach a compromise shows that in the last resort they were willing to gamble with votes at home rather than stand accused of blocking the advance towards closer unity."

It seems clear that once again it was the mediatory and brokerage activities of the Commission that made the outcome possible. This, of course, is not to deny the fact that all concerned made substantial concessions (especially the Germans), or that certain national delegations played valuable mediatory roles (especially the Italians and Belgians). But it was the work of Vice-President Mansholt and the Commission staff that guided the discussions. Indeed, it is striking to note that the final regulations do not differ markedly from the Commission's original proposals.

Five sets of problems posed the greatest difficulty for the negotiators.* How was the adaptation to the common agricultural policy to be made? How was the common agricultural policy to be financed? At what level were Community prices to be harmonized? What would be the institutional arrangements, i.e., how would day-to-day affairs be organized? And by what date should the Common Market be completed?[15]

Adaptations. The Commission had proposed to solve the problem of adaptation for grain, and products based on grain conversion, by means of its system of variable levies.† These would differ substantially in detail from product to product, but their general effect would be the same, namely an increase in competition and a gradual loosening of purely national control over price and market policy. This loosening of national controls, and their replacement by Community controls, would be furthered by the Commission's insistence that the levy system replace all other protective devices that might be imposed by a Member State acting independently. In general, all except the Germans accepted the Commission's proposed methods of fixing the several kinds of prices upon which the levy system would be based (importing prices, threshold prices, target prices, intervention prices, reference prices, and sluice-gate prices).‡ The Germans insisted on "a more flexible" system that would ensure higher prices and greater protection; they dissented particularly vigorously on the Commission's target price proposals. There was a somewhat greater spread of opinion on the incompatibility of the levy system with other forms of protection, the French and Belgians, in particular, holding out for the retention of minimum prices; but the principle was accepted. The Germans, on the other hand, insisted on maintaining independent means for protecting their farmers, including the systematic use of quotas.

* In the discussion that follows we can hope to focus only on general problems common to all products. It is beyond the scope of this study to examine all the conflicts over matters of detail, or to compare the particulars of the original Commission drafts with the final regulations and decisions.

† For fruits, vegetables, and wine, adaptation would be provided by the introduction of common rules to govern competition, including the application of common quality standards.

‡ This was clearly true of grain. There were some reservations on matters of detail for other products, depending essentially on the competitive position of that particular product—e.g., Belgium for pork and France for poultry.

The Germans were clearly isolated, and there was little change in their position until after the new cabinet had been designated following the Bundestag elections of September 1961. At the Council's session of November 30, the Minister of Agriculture, Werner Schwarz, presented Germany's conditions for accepting the levy system. He pointed out that the Commission's proposals would result in a rapid drop in the income of the German farmer, and that the government could not be expected to acquiesce in this. But Germany would give her agreement if the system of target prices were not applied completely for a number of years, if subsidies could be paid to German farmers to compensate them for their losses, if special low transportation rates could be applied to grains, and if quotas were retained until the levy system had been proved effective. None of the other Member States was impressed by the German concessions, which were labeled as unworkable "bastard solutions." The French indicated, however, that they would be willing to engage in some bargaining. The Commission then offered to modify its proposals to take account of German problems. Mansholt urged the Germans to drop their insistence on quotas, and to accept instead a safeguard clause for intra-Community trade that would permit a Member State to suspend imports subject to a Community control. The French and Dutch objected to this derogation from the levy principle, but eventually accepted the compromise. There was considerable debate over the length of time that might pass until the Commission and Council could review a national action (important for perishable goods). The Germans also held out for minimum prices for fruit and vegetables, having renounced them for all other products. Such an arrangement, however, would have been a direct threat to the Italians, who refused to yield the point, and in this they were supported by the Dutch and the French.

After an emergency cabinet meeting in early January, the Germans offered another compromise. They would accept the ban on minimum prices and quotas in return for a safeguard permitting them to ban imports altogether in case of danger to the economy. The Commission would have a week to uphold or cancel. Cancellation could be appealed to the Council, and the ban would be restored pending decision. This timetable was opposed by the Italians, who wanted to limit any possible delay to five days, and the provision for reinstituting the ban was opposed by several delegations. The final formula accepted the principle that all existing protective devices would be abolished as of July 1, 1962, when the levy systems would be introduced. However, a Member State with acute difficulties arising from excessive imports could take measures to cut off or limit imports, or otherwise protect domestic producers. The measures were not spelled out, although it was stipulated that the level of protection could not exceed that applied on July 1, 1962, nor could frontiers be closed for a three-day period of grace. The Commission must be notified immediately of the measures taken, and it would decide within four days whether the national action was to be upheld, modified, or abolished. This decision would take effect immediately, although it could be appealed within three days to the Council, which would make a ruling by a qualified majority. The appeal would not suspend the Commission's decision except in the case of grain (for ten days). For top quality fruit and vegetables no autonomous protective measures of any kind could be taken unless authorized in advance by the Commission. Whatever protective measures were taken must be applied equally to third countries and in a manner to preserve a preference for Community products.

Financial Provisions. The Commission proposed the introduction of Community financial responsibility for two kinds of agricultural support: refunds to help Member States dispose of agricultural surpluses to non-member countries, and internal market support. For this purpose a Commission-directed Agricultural Guidance and Guarantee Fund was to be set up. Contributions to the Fund were to be in proportion to a country's share of agricultural imports from the outside world, since the receipts from the levies applied to extra-Community imports would go to the Community, in part at first, and completely after the transition period. This, of course, put the financial burden directly on the Germans and the Dutch, who imported substantial amounts from third countries, and would be an additional inducement to switch to Community sources.

The Germans were again alone in their complete opposition.* They would accept the idea of Community responsibility only for the final stages of the common agricultural policy, when prices and other costs were aligned. In their package compromise offer in November, they relented and accepted the immediate introduction of Community financing, insisting, however, that contributions be based on the regular budget allocations as established in the Treaty, rather than on imports. The Commission amended its proposals to lessen somewhat the burden on importing countries, without accepting the German condition. The French held out for a definitive regulation and for immediate application of levy receipts to the Fund. The Belgians offered a compromise formula, based on a proposal of the Commission, whereby in 1962 the whole of the Fund would be allocated according to the Treaty formula; in 1963, 90 per cent according to the Treaty formula and 10 per cent according to imports; in 1964, 80 per cent according to the Treaty formula and 20 per cent according to imports; and so on (the proportion calculated according to imports being increased by

* The Dutch stood to gain as well as lose, since they are net exporters of dairy produce.

10 per cent a year). The Germans insisted that any decision be made for three years only. The Italians insisted that a specified portion of the Fund be used for structural reform.

The regulation finally adopted represented significant concessions to the German position. In spite of strong objections by the French, the Fund will be financed by contributions from the Member States and will only gradually be adjusted in proportion to imports. The amount of money available will be set by the Council each year. The whole system will be reviewed in three years. Not until the Common Market stage has been reached will receipts from the levies go to the Community for Community expenditures. As for types of expenditure, no more than the main categories were spelled out: export subsidies, domestic market intervention, and long-term structural improvement. These costs will be met only gradually by the Fund: one-sixth in 1962–63, one-third in 1963–64, and one-half in 1964–65. Eventually, in the Common Market stage, all appropriate expenditure will be financed by the Fund.

Price Harmonization. As we have noted, the Commission, having decided this issue was too explosive, did not include any specific recommendations in its draft regulations. The Dutch and French, however, tried to get a commitment, if not on the actual price level, then on a timetable and on criteria for determining the level. But the Germans were adamant, and all that was accomplished was a commitment to freeze prices at their current level, to fix criteria for approximation before autumn 1962, and to begin actual approximation in 1963. It was agreed, though, that the future price policy would be "determined in relation to efficient and viable farming," and this provision helped to satisfy the Dutch. The Council will continue to decide in this area by unanimity until 1966, and it is questionable if anything will really be accomplished before then.

Institutions. The Commission had proposed that it should be made responsible for most of the tasks of administration, regulation, and day-to-day management. The Germans countered by insisting that all decisions should be taken by the Council, by unanimity for four years and by qualified majority thereafter. This would have given Germany a veto for four years and might have been enough to strangle the common agricultural policy at birth. The German position received no support from the other Member States, but they were not all agreed that the Commission should play the leading role. The French introduced a plan whereby a series of intergovernmental steering committees, composed of national and Commission representatives, would be set up and given the power to make most decisions. This proposal was vigorously criticized by Benelux and Italy not only as constituting a frontal attack on the status of the Commission, but as being inconsistent with the Treaty. The Commission in its 1960 general proposals had suggested the creation of Directors' Committees, but their functions were to be merely advisory. The Dutch were the strongest in defense of the Commission, maintaining that it should take all the decisions, but the others sought a compromise solution.

The final outcome was closer to the Commission's original conception. The Commission continues to have primary responsibility for the implementation and administration of the common agricultural policy, but in many cases it must consult with Management Committees (one for each product), made up of national representatives. In the event of a conflict between a decision of the Commission and a qualified majority of the relevant Management Committee, the Council is automatically seized with the issue and can amend the Commission's decision by a qualified majority vote within thirty days.[16] Much is left to authorities in the Member States, and to a large extent the Commission's chief function is to act as a coordinating body and a watchdog. Major decisions are of course taken by the Council on proposals from the Commission. For some decisions—e.g., approximation of prices and criteria for Community financing of refunds —unanimity is required until the third stage. For others—e.g., arrangements for products processed from grain and the coordination and unification of import systems in trade with nonmember countries—only a qualified majority is required.

The Timetable. The Commission had proposed to complete the Common Market in six years, that is, by 1967. The Germans maintained that they would need at least eight years. Most of the others came around to the Commission's view, but gave in to the Germans in exchange for concessions on the levy system and the safeguard clause. The transition period was finally set at seven and a half years.

The final "package" agreement also included a timetable for the introduction of the levy system and a Community market organization for additional products of particular interest to certain states, especially France and the Netherlands.[17] This was of special concern to the Dutch, whose final assent was assured only by an official commitment to institute a levy system and Community financial support for dairy produce. (For details of the measures envisaged for each product, see the accompanying table.)

CONCLUSIONS

The great integrative potential of the Rome Treaty lies in its generality, in the powers granted to the central institutions of the EEC to fill out the Treaty and in so doing to "legislate" for the Community as a whole. The case of agriculture suggests how such Community legislation is likely to be worked out. It has been our contention that it is not the policy content, but the method and the context, of decision-making that is of greatest interest.

Summary of Measures Envisaged for Each Product

	Commodity and date of entry into force									
Measure	Grain 7/1/62	Pig-meat 7/1/62	Eggs 7/1/62	Poul-try 7/1/62	Fruit & veg. 7/1/62	Wine 7/1/62	Dairy prod.[a] 11/1/62	Beef & veal[a] 11/1/62	Sugar[a] 11/1/62	Rice[a] (no date)
Levy	×	×	×	×	—	—	×	—	—	—
Target price	×	—	—	—	—	—	—	—	—	—
Intervention price	×	—	—	—	—	—	—	—	—	—
Threshold price	×	—	—	—	—	—	—	—	—	—
Sluice-gate price for nonmember countries	—	×	×	×	—	—	—	—	—	—
Intra-Community sluice-gate prices	—	×	—	—	—	—	—	—	—	—
Refunds	×	×	×	×	—	—	×	—	—	—
Approximation of prices	×	—	—	—	—	—	—	—	—	—
Standard of quality	—	—	—	—	×	×	—	—	—	—
Quotas	—	—	—	—	—	×	—	—	—	—
Import certificates	×	—	—	—	—	—	—	—	—	—
Customs duties	—	—	—	—	×	×	—	—	—	—
Annual forecast	—	—	—	—	—	×	—	—	—	—

SOURCE: EEC Commission, *A Farm Policy for Europe*, p. 27.

[a] Common agricultural policy was to be decided upon by the Council in 1962. However, according to the latest documents available (January 1963), agreement has not yet been reached on the schedule for these products.

We have found that all the governments and most of the interest groups have accepted the necessity of a common agricultural policy. They have furthermore recognized that only the Community's central institutions can work out such a policy, and that its administration and application will inevitably expand the role and responsibility of those institutions. Opposition as well as support for the Commission's proposals has been channeled through Community procedures.

The Commission espoused a distinct set of values in making its proposals: that liberalization in other spheres must go hand in hand with liberalization in agriculture; that structural reforms should take precedence over price supports; and that a lower price level ought to be achieved in the interests of consumers and to keep the Community competitive on the external market. Each of these positions had strong support in each of the Six, not so much from politically motivated "Europeans," but from almost all nonagricultural interest groups, and from most of the government ministries with which they had constituency relationships. Once again positions were taken on EEC issues not on the basis of nationality, but in line with changing perceptions of economic and political interest.

The Commission's proposals were based on the assumption that a satisfactory agricultural policy demanded centralized direction by Community institutions working *with*, but not under, national officials. These proposals were clearly expansive in nature. The Commission also recognized the need to take account of the centers of power and influence in the EEC environment, and its proposals were designed to elicit a maximum support from all interests concerned. This is particularly marked when we compare the draft proposals with the definitive ones. Both interest groups and government officials were formally coopted into the proposed machinery for agricultural policy-making.

As in the other cases we have examined, a multitude of goals was being pursued simultaneously. Support for a common agricultural policy rested on a convergence of policy goals. But once again the diverse goals were mutually interdependent, and convergence acted as a catalyst for the spill-over process. Germany's efforts to delay an acceleration in agriculture were responsible for the creation of a specific timetable for the common agricultural policy, and for the assertion by the Commission of an ever more active role. Both the levy system and the solutions to problems of competition in agriculture were introduced, at least in part, to overcome German objections to agricultural liberalization. The French wanted a well-defined Community preference and a rapid introduction of the Common Market in agricultural products, and hence were brought to give strong support to the creation of European Offices, which imply ultimately an expansion of central decision-making. They also continued to insist on harmonization of social and economic legislation. The Italians seemed in principle to oppose these European Offices as being "dirigistic," although they relied on massive Community "dirigism" to speed up liberalization for fruit and vegetables and to provide structural support funds for Italy.

The characteristic Community procedural code was observed throughout the negotiations. The inevitability of a compromise agreement was accepted, and sensitivity to each other's needs was demonstrated, as well as a willingness to make concessions when necessary. Divisive issues were postponed where possible, and the vital interests of all participants were accommodated. Even the Germans, who were called upon to make the most concessions, were able to view the results with considerable satisfaction.[18] This does not mean that the negotiations were always peaceful. As *Time* magazine reported with its usual flair, "The sessions were heated. Three officials collapsed with heart attacks, and stubble-bearded, trigger-tempered delegates fought long into the night, stoked with double whiskies brought to the conference table. Each point was conceded only after bitter argument. 'This isn't integration!' shouted a Netherlands minister, 'This is disintegration!' "[19] On the other hand, a certain bitterness during negotiation does not preclude a feeling of unity at the end.[20] Different, often divergent, interests existed, and were expressed and defended. But a final compromise acceptable to everyone was given ultimate priority.

Agriculture has provided yet another example of the fact that only through the active intervention of Community institutions can the basic demands of all concerned find a place in the final solution. It is premature to draw definitive conclusions about the accommodation pattern that it is prevail for agriculture. Substantively speaking, it would seem that to date the prevalent pattern has been one of "splitting the difference." But it looks as if the trend is toward an ever more important mediatory role for the Commission, and hence toward accommodation by "upgrading common interests." This will be increasingly true as the Six move closer to the Common Market stage of the common agricultural policy. As Vice-President Mansholt observed, "All of this is not to say that we need not expect any difficulties in the implementation of the regulations. They are certain to arise. In the short preparatory period at our disposal there are many difficult problems to solve. However, one thing is certain: there is no going back. We have consciously burnt our national boats behind us in order to steer a European course."[21]

Two institutional developments are of special interest. The first of these is the procedure, widely used in the regulations on agriculture, whereby the Council of Ministers acts as a kind of court of appeals from decisions of the Commission. This applies when the Commission acts contrary to the advice of a Management Committee, or when a Member State objects to Commission decisions with regard to use of the safeguard clauses. It is difficult to foresee the exact effect this will have on the work load of the Community institutions, or on the nature of the decisions. It does not seem to weaken the position of the Commission to any great extent, for in order to overturn a Commission decision a qualified majority of twelve out of seventeen is required. This means that if the Commission has the support of one major power plus the Netherlands or Belgium, its decisions will be sustained despite the opposition of the rest. Nothing short of the opposition of all three major powers, or of two plus both Belgium and the Netherlands, could reverse the Commission's ruling.

The other institutional development, and one that presents as many problems as opportunities, is the vastly increased work load that now devolves on the Commission. Once again in the words of Vice-President Mansholt:

There will be a marked change in the nature of our work. Instead of preparing a policy we shall have to implement it. We are moving from theory to action. In the coming months, the Commission will have to set up an effective machinery which can take daily decisions on—to quote only a few examples—the application or non-application of the safeguard clause, or the application of the levy system. It is clear that Brussels will become a centre of European market development.[22]

The heaviest load will be in the administration of the levy system, above all of that for grain. Every day the Commission will have to register over 2,000 facts on changes in the level of world prices; these will be used in establishing the free-to-frontier price, upon which the Member States base themselves in calculating the levies applied to imports from third countries. The Commission must also fix daily the price upon which the amount of the subsidy granted to Community exporters is calculated. The franco-frontier price is the basis of the intra-Community levy, and it will be fixed weekly by the Commission.[23]

The authority of the Commission may well be increased by this mush-rooming of detailed and technical functions. But the system could also become overloaded. Member States that wanted to delay or evade imple-mentation of the common agricultural policy could swamp the Commission with innumerable petty violations and appeals.* The continued coopera-tion and good will of the governments is certainly a requisite to the efficient functioning of the system.

The ability of the Commission to operate as a policy initiator, as a mediator, and as an honest broker might also be compromised because of this proliferation of routine tasks, and it could eventually become little more than a regulatory agency analogous to the Federal Trade Commission or to a cross between the FTC and the U.S. Department of Agriculture. This sort of evolution might come about anyway, as the unification of markets nears realization. In this regard it is instructive to view the experience of the High Authority of the Coal and Steel Community and of the Euratom Commission. Such a development would be disappointing to committed "Eurocrats," but would not necessarily impede integration, once the proc-ess were well under way. Little is known of the integrative function of complex organizations like the Department of Agriculture or the FTC in American society, but they are certainly not without political functions, nor are they neglected by politicians or interest groups.

* As can happen in other sectors, too, especially competition.

GENERAL CONCLUSIONS

WE ARE NOW in a position to advance some conclusions about the actual and potential impact of the EEC on decision-making patterns in the "Europe of the Six." We have examined the provisions of the Treaty to judge the extent and nature of the commitments formally entered into by the Six, paying special attention to the roles and competencies assigned to the central institutions. We have seen how this system evolved in response to organizational and environmental needs, and we have sketched out the reactions that the Common Market elicited both from individual firms and groups of firms and from trade associations and trade unions. We then proceeded to analyze the EEC in action, seeking to relate the domestic pursuit of political and economic interests to the conduct of groups, parties, and governments on the Community stage. And we examined four examples of decision-making to determine the way in which major conflicts of interest were resolved, and to assess the expansive potential of the EEC. It remains now to draw these materials together in the context of the considerations set forth in Part I. To what extent and with what kinds of variations are the two parallel processes of political integration set in motion?

Have the Six abandoned the desire and ability to conduct foreign and key domestic policies independently of each other, seeking instead to make joint decisions or to delegate the decision-making process to new central institutions? We have seen that in signing the Rome Treaty, these six countries committed themselves to establishing "the foundations of an ever closer union among the European peoples"[1] in the form of "a Common Market and progressively approximating the economic policies of the

Member States, to promote throughout the Community a harmonious development of economic activities, a continuous and balanced expansion, an increased stability, an accelerated raising of the standard of living and closer relations between its Member States."[2] The obligations accepted by the Member States are at times specified in the greatest detail for every particular, and at times stated only in the most vague and general terms. Thus whereas the features of the customs union (tariff and quota elimination, and the establishment of the common external tariff) are spelled out in detail with respect to *goals, policies, and rules,* the elaboration of policies regarding such matters as transport, competition, mobility of labor and services, state aids and state trading, capital movements and capital transfers, agriculture, and general commercial law is left to the central institutions, with only broad goals or policy alternatives stated in the Treaty. The central institutions are therefore endowed with a potentially far-reaching legislative power that can be exercised without the necessity of obtaining ratification from national parliaments.

Our analysis of this institutional system, and of decision-making in it, has revealed that there is a subtle mixture of delegated and shared policy-making. A vast and complex multinational bureaucracy has evolved, composed of national and Community civil servants and politicians. Policy-making, or the pattern of bargaining and exchanging of concessions that it has come to mean, involves not only six governments, but also an autonomous representative of the interests of the Community as a whole, the Commission. The Commission enjoys some unique advantages by virtue of its ability to embody the authority of a Community consensus. It can claim to speak for the common interests of all six countries, and has repeatedly demonstrated its capacity to precipitate unity by taking divergent demands and breaking them into their constituent parts, thus obliging each party to a conflict to re-examine its position in the perspective of the common interest.

The Commission has performed its supervisory functions (regarding the customs union provisions) diligently and at the same time with prudence, preferring to achieve government compliance by using persuasion than by exercising its power to bring suits before the Court of Justice, although this, too, has been done. In making policy proposals to the Council of Ministers, it has sought to engage national civil servants in policy preparation, yet it has not defined the interests of the Community as an average of those of the Member States. Instead, it has vigorously defended its own role as spokesman for Community interests, and has sought to expand this role in its specific proposals. It has grasped the initiative repeatedly in acting as a mediator or broker between the Member States in the Council of Ministers, as well as in the many special committees set up to achieve the maximum consensus possible below the ministerial level (e.g., the Committee of Permanent Representatives, the Special Committee on Agriculture, and the Rey Committee).

The Council of Ministers clearly considers itself a Community institution and not an intergovernmental body. Most issues that reach it involve basic conflicts of interest among Member States. Each member tries to influence the content of the final decision as much as it can, but all are agreed on the necessity of mutual concessions, since the normal practice is to exclude the possibility of not reaching an agreement at all. Agreements are reached on issues involving basic conflicts of interest when the cost of further delay becomes too great. Thus the pressures on the Community from GATT, the British, and the EFTA were largely responsible for forcing the Member States to come to quick agreements on the level of the common external tariff and List G, on acceleration, and on basic policy toward the outside world. In all these cases further procrastination or discussion would have called into question the integrity of the EEC itself. Such pressures also arise within the Community as different elites seek to achieve their own goals through action at the Community level, e.g., the initiation by business groups of the movement for accelerating the Treaty timetable, and the demands from French and Dutch agriculture for rapid implementation of the common agricultural policy.

Conflict resolution in the Council usually follows an upgrading-of-common-interests pattern, although other elements may be injected. This lack of clarity is due to the interpenetration of roles to which we have devoted so much attention. While the Council may reach agreement on the basis of a text submitted by the Commission, this text may itself incorporate a "splitting of the difference" from a lower level. The three types of conflict resolution we have employed are abstract types, and for the most part we can discuss only the *extent* to which a given decision approximates the abstract standard. The crucial ingredients are two: first, the participation of an institutionalized mediator with autonomous powers; and, second, a continued commitment of the Member States to the enterprise, and hence to the necessity of ultimately reaching a decision. We have already noted that the Commission participates as a *de facto* seventh member in all meetings of the Council and of its preparatory bodies. Here its role depends on the fact that the bulk of the work of the Council is based on a prior proposal from the Commission, the terms of which cannot be changed by the Council except by unanimity, or *by agreement between the Council and the Commission*. Even where the Treaty does not assign this role to the Commission the same pattern has prevailed.

Thus the Member States asked the Commission to prepare the common position on the free trade area, as well as the proposals on acceleration, precisely because they could not come to an agreement without its services. Once these tasks had been conferred, it was extremely difficult for the Council to resist the proposals made by the Commission. Moreover, it has proved far easier for Member States to give in to the Commission than it would have been for the Germans to give in to the French or vice versa; in other words, in justifying their actions, both to themselves and to their respective governments, Ministers have been able to defend major concessions on the ground that they were made in the interests of the Community.

The European Parliamentary Assembly and the Economic and Social Committee have been tangential to this evolving policy-making process. A procedural and substantive consensus is well developed in the EPA, and it possesses an important moral influence as a result of its strong pro-integration majority. At this stage, however, it seems to serve as little more than a sounding board for the Commission. In spite of its determined efforts to influence the policy-making process, there is little evidence that it has been successful. As we have seen, many in the EPA have been highly critical of the institutional developments we have described, partly, at least, because they felt their own role was being diminished. It is something of a paradox that one reason for the relative impotence of the EPA may be the strong dedication of the great majority of its members to a maximum of political and economic integration. In the present situation, and as long as these values are still relatively precarious, this forces it to give support to the Commission and to Community solutions even when its policy demands have not been met. The role played by the Assembly in the Community discussions on a common agricultural policy may hold interesting portents for the future. Should interest groups in the Six begin to channel their demands through the EPA (as occurred markedly in agriculture), it might endow that body with a broader base of support and hence of influence.

It was our expectation that as the Six began to share or delegate decision-making, political actors in these countries would begin to restructure their activities and aspirations accordingly. This has been most striking at the level of high policy-makers and civil servants, for the EEC policy-making process, by its very nature, engages an ever-expanding circle of national officials. There is strong evidence that this sort of interaction contributes to a "Community-mindedness," by broadening perspectives, developing personal friendships, and fostering a camaraderie of expertise, all of which come from being involved in a joint problem-solving operation. Such developments can be expected to occur in a rough correlation to the frequency of contact. Thus they are more marked in the Committee of Permanent Representatives, which meets twice a week or more and is in constant contact with European integration affairs, than in one of the committees of customs experts that meet once or twice a year. We may expect, however, that more and more officials will become deeply involved as the Community continues to negotiate common policies or coordinated and harmonized policies. This has certainly been the case in agriculture. As these negotiations proceed, we may expect to see accelerated the incipient processes whereby the distinction between domestic affairs and foreign affairs becomes eroded. Thus the technical ministers (transport, agriculture, economic and financial affairs, etc.) are already finding it necessary to meet on a regular basis and to extend their discussions beyond the obligations of the Rome Treaty.

There is also ample evidence of a restructuring of activities and expectations at the level of nonofficial political actors, although its incidence is less striking, owing primarily to the over-all phasing of the Treaty timetable. For the most part, the effect of the Treaty to date has been negative in the sense that it has involved the *elimination* of tariffs and quotas, and of obstacles to the free establishment of professions and services, and so on. Nevertheless, individual firms and groups of firms have certainly responded to their perceptions of the economic advantages to be gained from the creation of a large free market. They have also taken steps to protect themselves from what they take to be the possible disadvantages of the new market. This indicates that the Common Market has been accepted and that economic circles have come to define their interests in terms of it. This was particularly evident in the case of acceleration.

At the level of political organization and action, there is great surface activity, but in general it cannot be said that the coming of the Common Market has basically altered the behavior of national interest groups. The bulk of interest-group activity remains oriented toward national goals. But there is a great deal of new transnational contact: witness the creation of 222 EEC-level interest groups and the fairly regular participation of representatives of national interest groups in the ESC. Interest-group leaders are being involved in a pattern of interaction similar to that described for national officials. There is an unparalleled amount of traveling, meeting, and exchanging of views. Organizations that in the past balked at paying for the expenses of one delegate to some international meeting may now help to maintain a large, expensive staff in Brussels for the purpose of trying to influence the Community institutions. Yet these activities are not as yet oriented to any really significant joint problem-solving. Most of the EEC-level interest groups are merely liaison groups with essentially secretarial functions and no real role to play in coordinating national group views.

The most notable exception to these generalizations has been in the sector of agriculture, in which the immediate interests of agricultural producers, agricultural workers, and all the industries concerned with the transformation, trade, or marketing of agricultural products are involved. Here the incidence of political activity has been the highest, and here, too, EEC-level interest groups have begun to play a significant role. This leads us to anticipate that as the Community moves to major undertakings in other sectors of the economy, nationally organized interest groups will be compelled to channel more of their political activities through EEC-level groups, if only to establish some new constituency relationship and maintain routes of access to the policy-making process. This will doubtless also force them to engage in some kind of a negotiating process designed to achieve concerted action at this level.

It has been said that these developments are misleading, that they are merely a reflection of good times and could be overturned if there were an economic slump. It is maintained that integration is the product of an accidental and temporary marriage of convenience, that nobody has been hurt yet, and that support will disappear as soon as the shoe begins to pinch. Our findings lead us to reject such a judgment. Significant national powers have been thrust into a new institutional setting in which powerful pressures are exerted for "Community" solutions: that is, solutions which approximate the upgrading-of-common-interests type. Our case studies have revealed that important and divergent national interests have been consistently accommodated in order to achieve a decision.

Two important and related factors that might limit continued political integration have been singled out: namely, the autonomy of functional contexts, and the possibility of a major policy reversal on the part of one or several Member States. Experience over the first three years has confirmed our original hypotheses about the inherently expansive nature of the tasks assigned to the EEC. The case studies have illustrated in a striking fashion the operation of the spill-over principle. Community policies have resulted from a pattern of concession, a pattern that confirms the expansive potentialities inherent in the Treaty by virtue of its broad scope and generality. Practically all governments, parties, and groups perceive some likely advantage from the EEC. The reaction of business groups to the Common Market was more favorable than anyone had dared to hope. Much of the same can be said of farmers' and peasants' organizations.

Even General de Gaulle has come to consider at least some version of the Community of the Six as economically and politically indispensable to his vision of France's destiny.[3] His substantive policies with regard to internal EEC affairs have supported the Treaty of Rome. In fact, the French have been among the most insistent that the Common Market be realized more quickly. We have also noted that on a number of occasions the positions taken by the French were closest to those of the Commission. This has not implied that the long-range goals of the two are identical, related, or even necessarily compatible. As the following statement shows, de Gaulle continues to view the Commission as "mere technicians," useful for France but certainly not to be endowed with the chief role in integration: "These bodies have their technical value, but they have not, and cannot have, any political authority or consequently be effective."[4] And, again, "In Europe, legitimate power is the power which comes from national sovereignty, and against this power arbitrary outside tyrannies like the so-called 'supra-national' institutions can do nothing."[5] Nevertheless, in most EEC negotiations the French have accepted the developing procedural code of the Treaty. They have demonstrated a willingness to make concessions and have accepted the initiatory and brokerage activities of the Commission. But they have resisted direct efforts to increase the competence or prestige of the Commission, except when this seemed a necessary price for substantive agreement.

We have not argued that integration is supported for identical reasons, but for converging ones. The convergence of these pro-integration aims and expectations may be grouped as follows:

Integration as political unification. This group consists of a relatively small number of strategically placed "Europeans" in all walks of life and in all countries, mostly in Christian-Democratic parties, but some of them in Socialist parties, particularly in Belgium and the Netherlands; a majority of EPA members; the Commission; Adenauer, Schuman, Pella, Wigny, Romme, and Spaak; and Monnet and various "federalists."

Integration as economic unification. This group is composed of Socialist and Christian-Democratic parties and trade unions in all countries; other groups which consider themselves in a marginal position at the national level, or which have come to the conclusion that comprehensive welfare or planning programs cannot be achieved at the national level; Belgian industry; and Dutch agriculture.

Integration as economic and political cooperation. This head covers de Gaulle and the UNR; center parties in France; agricultural groups in France, Belgium, Italy, and Luxembourg; and high-cost industry in all countries.

Integration as free trade. Here we have free-trade-oriented parties; Liberals in Italy, Belgium, and the Netherlands; the FDP, the DP, and the Erhard wing of the CDU; low-cost and highly efficient industry in all countries, especially in Germany and the Netherlands; and commerce in all countries.*

The case studies have graphically demonstrated that none of these broad "visions" of a united Europe could be realized in practice without the others gaining some measure of realization as well. The unity and integrity of the Community have been preserved, the pace of integration has been accelerated, the role of the central institutions has been expanded, the notion of "Community preference" has been reasserted, and the Community is pledged to follow a liberal trade policy toward the outside world (at least in industrial products).

Once involved in an undertaking of this magnitude, the Six have found it difficult to avoid moving farther and faster than originally planned. This possibility was allowed for in the legislative powers granted to the central institutions. Furthermore, the Community has been forced to meet pressures from the outside. The inability of the governments to reach mutually acceptable agreements has repeatedly faced them with the alternative of admitting failure or delegating a larger role to the Commission. As Haas points out,

Once governments have committed themselves . . . to certain common measures of fundamental importance to the daily lives of their entire citizenry, they can resolve future problems of implementing the agreement only by means of further delegation of power to the center. . . . Since the range of issues which gave rise to the initial step is woven completely into the contemporary preoccupation with welfare, withdrawal would imply a sacrifice of economic advantage—a step not taken lightly by elected politicians.[6]

Businessmen, having accepted the Common Market as a *fait accompli*, found the timetable for its institution too leisurely and pressed for an acceleration of the customs union provisions. Such an acceleration was achieved, but only on the condition that the common agricultural policy be speeded up as well. This partial acceleration also gave rise to new demands for accelerated action in the realm of social policy, in the harmonization of social charges, in the coordination and approximation of commercial law, and so forth. All this has implied further increasing the tasks and the grant of power of the center.

Can we then say that the alternatives open to national policy-makers

---

* It ought to be pointed out that as yet the impact of the Common Market has not been felt by the groups that are perhaps the most likely to suffer, namely artisans and handicraft industries, and small and medium-sized retailers and manufacturers. There is some indication, however, that these groups will not oppose integration, but will rather demand their "slice." This has been demonstrably the case in agriculture.

have been so dramatically narrowed as to eliminate the possibility of a failure or breakdown of the EEC? There is always the possibility of a calamity. I refer to something short of the ultimate calamity of global nuclear war: e.g., Soviet trade overtures and a clear offer of reunification would severely strain Germany's devotion to European integration; France could be plunged into chaos when de Gaulle leaves the scene; a government of the extreme right or left could conceivably come to power in France, or of the extreme left in Italy. Barring this kind of occurrence, it would seem almost impossible for a nation to withdraw entirely from integration. The political and economic advantages are probably too compelling, and the processes too well-advanced. Moreover, the ability of any nation to exercise a formal veto over joint decision-making will be still further reduced as time goes on.

This cannot obscure, although it may modify, two realities of power. First, General de Gaulle is probably quite correct when he argues that only the positive action of legitimate political authorities (the nation-states) can be the ultimate basis of integration. It is clear that the Community's procedural code depends entirely on the willingness of the Member States to defer to each other's needs and interests, and to accept the mediating activities of the Commission. This will probably continue to be the case even when majority voting becomes the rule. The second reality is that the participants in the integration process, the Member States, are not equal in power, or, in other words, in their ability to give direction to the process. Most "Europeans" have always realized that the basis of European unity was the *rapprochement* between Germany and France. Whether this will mean ultimately that a Paris-Bonn axis will control the Community we cannot say. This has not been the case in the early years. Up to de Gaulle's abrupt and dogmatic action barring the door to British entry into the Community over the protests of the other five, none of the major powers had sought to impose its policy aims on the others to the detriment of their interests. The impact of this act on the Community is difficult to predict. It may settle the question, one way or the other, of whether one or two countries can effectively dominate the enterprise. It is unlikely to bring about its collapse, for all the Member States have too much invested.

Our studies of decision-making in the EEC have shown that no stable voting coalitions have appeared, and that the French and Germans have been on opposite sides in Council debates more often than not. It might be argued that this is beside the point, and that the essence of the Community's success is still German willingness to accede to French demands. But even if this were demonstrable, it would not prove that the Community is *dominated* by the French and Germans.

Up to 1962, all indications had been that the Six, including the French, were trying not to escape the logic of integration, but to embrace it. As noted, cooperation and coordination were being carried beyond what was specified in the Treaty to such areas as monetary and financial policy, business cycle policy, and taxation. De Gaulle's desire, expressed already in January 1960, to establish a machinery for broad political consultations among the Six was another example: "The solidarity created by the Common Market almost automatically leads the Governments to concert their actions in other fields, and above all in the field of international politics."[7]

Since the Six were obliged quite early to defend the Community against external attacks, the attempt to coordinate their positions in other international organizations followed naturally. The form this coordination takes varies according to whether they are elaborating a view to be given in the name of the Community, or merely working out common ideas to animate separate declarations, or attempting to avoid contradictory interventions. Prior coordination is achieved in Council meetings, and the results are also examined in the Council. When the Commission participates directly, it presents the Community position and even negotiates for the Community, as, for example, in the General Tariff Conference of GATT, and in the separate bilateral trade negotiations between the EEC and the United States and other third countries over the common external tariff. The Six carried on a coordinated defense in GATT in October 1957, April 1958, October 1958, and May 1959, and also in sessions of U.N. economic organs and affiliated agencies. In addition, the commitments to be undertaken by Member States in international commodity agreements are studied in the Council, and coordinated for possible inconsistencies with the Common Market (e.g., the common agricultural policy imposes limits on member participation in international wheat and sugar agreements).

To say it is unlikely that any Member State will withdraw from the EEC is not to say the process of political integration could not be slowed down and perhaps arrested. It is important to keep in mind the nature and limits of the conclusions we have drawn. Our main findings have concerned the nature and functioning of the EEC institutional system and the procedural code governing its decisions. This code is based upon willingness to compromise national positions and to confer certain tasks on central institutions that act in the name of the Community. Such willingness can be premised on one or both of two factors: a slowly emerging concept of "the rules of the game" of the Community, in which case one might be able to speak of a Community consensus; or a particular pattern of interest convergence.

A society generates support for a political system in two ways: through outputs that meet the demands of the members of society; and through the processes of politicization . . . through which attachments to a political system become built into the . . . member of a society. . . . When the basic political attachments become rooted or institutionalized, we say that the *system* has become accepted as legitimate. . . . What I am suggesting here is that support resting on a sense of legitimacy . . . provides a necessary reserve if the system is to weather those frequent storms when the more obvious outputs of the system seem to impose greater hardships than rewards.[8]

Both kinds of support underlie European integration, although it has been the convergence of interests and the interdependence of concrete goals that have been crucial. Integration is rooted in interest, in the perception of the actors that they can better satisfy their aspirations in this new framework. What is striking about the Treaty of Rome and the first years of the EEC is the *scope* of the tasks assigned to the central institutions, and the extent to which these tasks appear to be inherently expansive; that is, the extent to which integrative steps in one functional context spill over into another. An ever-widening circle of actors finds this system to be an effective, logical, and appropriate framework in which to pursue its goals, and this is one essential feature of a community.

It follows, as we have maintained, that the national decision-maker can still redefine his attitude toward European integration if the outcomes are no longer acceptable. We can claim that the alternatives open to him are limited, but not that the commitments are completely irreversible. We can claim that the price to be paid for withdrawal or for a manifest violation of the EEC procedural code is likely to be very high, but not that some decision-maker might not underestimate it or be willing to pay it. We can claim that so many individuals and groups have restructured their actions and expectations that a responsible politician would hesitate to reverse the process, but not that this would deter a de Gaulle from pursuing his particular vision. Such processes are binding only when individuals "channel their aspirations through permanent interest groups," when "these groups are habitually led by identifiable elites competing with one another for influence," and when the "relations among these elites are governed by the traditions and assumptions of parliamentary (or presidential) democracy and constitutionalism."[9]

There are a number of ways in which the processes of political integration might be interrupted. The most drastic, and therefore probably the least likely, would be the continued pursuit by de Gaulle of policies that the United States and some of the other Member States would define as seriously detrimental to their vital interests. This could confront France's partners with the choice between the United States and the Atlantic Alliance, and de Gaulle's Europe, be it that of Charlemagne or Alexander I. But the choice is unlikely to be so clear, and the reaction of

France's partners, as that of the United States, will more probably be to wait out de Gaulle and to apply such pressures as they can. These could take the form of denying the French certain desired outcomes from the EEC that are still dependent on unanimous consent: e.g., the new association agreement with France's former overseas territories, her promise to Algeria of some form of association with the Community, and continued progress in the common agricultural policy. Such steps would doubtless slow down the integrative process. It would not be completely arrested, however, because so much is now automatic, and it is highly unlikely that any of the Six would violate specific Treaty obligations to retaliate against the French.

A Member State wishing to limit the process of political integration (if not the creation of the customs union) can proceed in various ways. It can refuse to attend sessions of the Council of Ministers when subjects it wants to sidestep are discussed, or it can absent itself from the study groups and preparatory committees that play such an important part in developing policies and building acceptance of the system. One or several Member States could also act so as to reduce the independent political role of the Commission, which must be renewed every four years. This might be done by appointing "technicians" rather than "politicians," in which case the Commission's role might be reduced to that of a regulatory body like the Federal Trade Commission.* Or a Member State could subject the Commission to severe political pressure, threatening reprisals in case of resistance.† Without the vigorous and independent Communitarian initiatives of the Commission, and without its mediatory and brokerage activities, the progress of the Community, the spill-over dynamic, might well be arrested.

Another way in which the integrative processes might be slowed down, or even interrupted, is by increasing the membership of the Community. This possibility no longer appears to lie in the immediate future, but it certainly cannot be ruled out altogether. As we saw in the study of the free trade area negotiations, the French were not the only ones in the Six who had serious reservations about the effects of widening the Community. Many "Europeans" have had doubts about this, not only because they may have mistrusted British motives, but because they felt that an increase in the number of participants would both overload the already complex decision-making system and decrease the willingness of Member States to make concessions and to adhere to the Community's code. It is feared

* As has apparently happened to the High Authority of the ECSC.
† Such was the fate of the President of the Euratom Commission, Etienne Hirsch, who was not reappointed in 1962 because his policies had displeased the French government.

that many in the Six will perceive a much-reduced value in the EEC if it is broadened to include several countries to full membership, as well as perhaps having some attendant association for EFTA neutrals and Commonwealth countries. Furthermore, countries like Great Britain, Denmark, Norway, and Ireland have not shared in the previous integration experience. Political parties and interest-group elites have not experienced the patterns of interaction and value-sharing and consensus formation that have become established in such bodies as the European Parliament and the Economic and Social Committee. Their bureaucrats have not participated in the development of the Community's procedural code. Nor is it yet clear whether the majority of political actors in these countries expect anything from the EEC beyond possible commercial advantage.

Our analysis has shown that the decision-making powers given up by the Six are being exercised in a complex and amorphous bureaucratic structure in which it is extremely difficult to enforce responsibility and accountability. The national parliaments have doubtless been the chief losers. It is open to question whether countries with strong parliamentary traditions like the United Kingdom and Denmark will accept this trend to an "international technocracy." For this has been the dilemma of Community countries with traditions of parliamentary rule, and they have been living with the idea much longer. To date, however, they have felt that the ultimate goal of a united Europe was a justification for certain sacrifices, and that eventually the European Parliament would take its rightful place as a true parliament of Europe.

APPENDIXES

THE INSTITUTIONS OF THE EEC

DECISION-MAKING IN THE COUNCIL AND THE COMMISSION[1]

The Council acting alone

—requires unanimity to adopt *regulations* concerning:
  —any autonomous modification or suspension of duties of the common customs tariff during the transition period (Article 28).
  —the granting of exceptions to the principle of nondiscrimination in transport (Article 76).
  —the provisions on transport (common rules, conditions for admission, etc.), when these might seriously affect the standard of living and the level of employment in certain regions, and also the utilization of transport equipment (Article 75, paragraph 3).
—requires a qualified majority to adopt *directives* concerning:
  —the granting of specified mutual assistance to a Member State in balance of payment difficulties—a recommendation from the Commission (Article 108, paragraph 2).
—requires unanimity to make *decisions* concerning:
  —the granting of compensatory payments for excess prices paid for raw materials in comparison with the delivery prices of the same supplies obtained on the world market. For Member States that require raw materials for the production of goods destined for exports outside the Community in competition with producers in third countries (Article 45, paragraph 3).
  —whether and by what procedure appropriate provisions for common rules, etc., might be adopted for sea and air transport (Article 84, paragraph 2).
  —the compatibility with the Common Market of certain state aids under special circumstances, notwithstanding the general principles on the subject or a decision of the Commission to the contrary (Article 93, paragraph 2).
  —new tasks to be entrusted to the European Social Fund on opinion from the Commission (Article 126, paragraph 6).

—new provisions to be made for the association of the overseas countries and territories upon the expiration of the five-year Implementing Convention (Article 136).

—determination of the list of products (arms, war materials, etc.) considered necessary for the protection of national security, for which special measures may be taken (Article 223, paragraph 2).

—conclusion with a third country, a union of states, or an international organization of agreements creating an association embodying reciprocal rights and obligations, joint actions, and special procedures (Article 238).

—requires a qualified majority to make *decisions* concerning:

—the revoking or modifying of authorizations made by the Commission to a Member State to take specified protective measures in the case of disturbances in the capital market (Article 130).

—the granting of special assistance to a Member State in balance of payment difficulties (Article 108, paragraph 2).

—the revoking or amending of authorizations made by the Commission to a Member State to take specified measures of safeguard in the case of balance of payments difficulties (Article 108, paragraph 3).

—amendment, abolition, or supervision of measures of safeguard taken by a Member State to deal with a "sudden crisis" in the balance of payments (Article 109, paragraph 3).

—supervision of part or all of the assistance granted by the European Social Fund. At the expiry of the transitional period. On opinion from the Commission (Article 126, a).

—establishment of the draft budget of the Community (Article 203, paragraph 3).

—adoption of the budget after considering amendments proposed by the European Parliamentary Assembly and after discussion with the Commission (Article 203, paragraph 4).

—requires a simple majority to make *decisions* concerning:

—the calling of a conference of the representatives of the governments of Member States, for the purpose of determining in common agreement the Amendments to be made to the Treaty (Article 236).

—requires a special majority to make *decisions* concerning:

—adoption of that section of the budget relating to the European Social Fund (Article 203, paragraph 5).

—determination of the amounts to be devoted to the financing of various projects under the Development Fund. Consults the Commission (Implementing Convention Relating to the Association with the Community of the Overseas Countries and Territories, Article 4).

—requires unanimity to take *other actions* as follows:

—make a "confirmatory statement" to the effect that the essence of the objectives of the Treaty for the first stage have been achieved. Transition to the second stage is conditional upon this statement. Report from the Commission at end of fourth and fifth years. At the end of the sixth year the vote is taken by a qualified majority (Article 8, paragraph 3).

—assign to the Commission functions relating to the implementation of common measures in the field of social policy and particularly in regard to the social security of the migrant workers (Article 121).

—authorize the Commission to open tariff negotiations with third countries concerning the common external tariff, and to conduct these negotiations; appoint a special committee to assist the Commission; issue directives to serve as the framework for negotiation. To the end of the second stage (Article 111, paragraphs 2 and 3).

—conclude agreements on the behalf of the Community with third countries concerning the common customs tariff (Article 111, paragraph 2, and Article 114).

—conclude agreements on the behalf of the Community concerning the common commercial policy and after expiry of the transition period (Article 113, paragraph 3, and Article 114).

—determine the provisions it shall recommend to Member States for adoption concerning election of the European Parliamentary Assembly by direct universal suffrage (Article 138, paragraph 3).

—amend the number of members of the Commission (Article 157).

—decide not to fill vacancies on the Commission (Article 159).

—provisionally suspend a member of the Commission from his duties and make provision for his replacement pending a ruling of the Court of Justice regarding removal for a serious offense or nonperformance of duty (Article 160).

—increase the number of judges if requested by the Court (Article 165).

—increase the number of advocates-general if requested by the Court (Article 166).

—approve the rules of procedure adopted by the Court (Article 188).

—appoint the members of the Economic and Social Committee (Article 196).

—approve the rules of procedure of the Economic and Social Committee (Article 196).

—amend the scales of financial contributions for the budget and for the European Social Fund (Article 200, paragraph 3).

—fix the number of auditors and appoint them for five-year terms (Article 206).

—lay down the statute of service for officials and the conditions of employment for other employees of the Community (Article 212).

—determine the rules concerning the languages of the Community (Article 217).

—act on the application of any European state to become a member of the Community. On opinion of the Commission. The conditions of admission and the amendments to the Treaty necessitated thereby shall be the the subject of an agreement between the Member States and the applicant state (Article 237).

—appoint assistant rapporteurs on request of the Court and lay down a statute for them (Protocol on the Statute of the Court of Justice) (Article 12).

—change the statute of the Court (Protocol on the Statute of the Court of Justice) (Article 45).

—requires a qualified majority to take *other actions* as follows:

—make a "confirmatory statement" on passage to the second stage. At the end of the sixth year (Article 8, paragraph 3).

—in the case noted above (Article 111, paragraph 2).

—authorize the Commission to open negotiations where agreement with third countries is necessary with regard to the common commercial policy and after the expiry of the transition period; appoint a special committee to assist; issue directives for the negotiations (Article 113, paragraphs 3 and 4).

—fix the salaries, allowances, and pensions of the President and members of the Commission and of the President, judges, advocates-general, and registrar of the Court of Justice; also any allowances granted in lieu of remuneration (Article 154).

—give the Commission a discharge in respect of the implementation of the budget (Article 206).

—requires a simple majority to take *other actions* as follows:

—adopt its own rules of procedure (Article 151).

—request the Commission to undertake any studies which the Council considers desirable for the achievement of the common objectives, and to submit to it any appropriate proposals (Article 152).

—lay down the status of committees provided for in the Treaty (Article 153).

—lay down conditions and limits under which the Commission might collect information and verify situations (Article 213).

The Council acting on a proposition of the Commission

—requires unanimity to adopt *regulations* concerning:

—amendment of the timetable for the elimination of customs duties (Article 14, paragraph 7).

—the fixing of duties for the Common External Tariff for products on List G in the absence of agreement between the Member States. Up to end of second stage (Article 20).*

—amendment of the procedure for gradual increases in global quotas. During first stage. (Article 33, paragraph 8).*

—all measures for formulating and putting into effect a common agricultural policy. To end of second stage (Article 43, paragraph 2).*

—determination of the criteria for minimum systems for agricultural products and a procedure for their revision (Article 43, paragraph 2).

—measures necessary to effect free movement of workers, especially in the field of social security (Article 51).

—adoption of a general program for the abolition of restrictions on the freedom of establishment (Article 54, paragraph 1).

—extension of the provisions for the free supply of services to nationals of third states who are established in the Community (Article 59).

* After which unanimity is replaced by a qualified majority vote.

—adoption of a program for the abolition of restrictions on the free supply of services (Article 63, paragraph 1).

—adoption of common rules applicable to international transport, of conditions for the admission of nonresident carriers to national transport services, and of any other appropriate provisions. To the end of the second stage, when unanimity is replaced by a qualified majority vote (Article 75, paragraph 1).

—application of the principles and rules on competition laid down in Articles 85 and 86. For the first three years, when unanimity is replaced by a qualified majority vote (Article 87).

—harmonization of national fiscal legislation (turnover taxes, excise duties, other indirect taxation) (Article 99).

—appropriate measures to assure consultation with regard to policy on economic trends (Article 103, paragraph 2).

—enactment of "appropriate provisions" granting powers of action that may be required to achieve an aim of the Community and that are not otherwise provided for (Article 235).

—requires a qualified majority to adopt *regulations* concerning:

—the cases noted above in which unanimity prevails for a limited period only (Article 20; Article 33, paragraph 8; Article 43, paragraph 2; Article 75, paragraph 1; Article 87, paragraph 1).

—adoption of rules to implement the general prohibition on any discrimination based on grounds of nationality (Article 7).

—adjustments required to ensure the internal harmony of the common customs tariff, considering especially the degree of processing undergone by various goods (Article 21, paragraph 2).

—modifications or suspensions, not exceeding 20 per cent of the rate and for a six-month period, of any duty on the Common External Tariff. After expiry of the transitional period. (Article 28).

—determination of the extent of application of the rules of competition to the production and trade in agricultural products (Article 42).

—substitution of a common organization of agricultural markets for national market organizations (Article 43, paragraph 3).

—modification of minimum prices for agricultural goods where it has been impossible to establish objective criteria. From beginning of the third stage. (Article 44, paragraph 5).

—exceptions from the application of the provisions on the right of establishment (Article 55).

—implementation within two years of those provisions of the Treaty which call for the abolition of any discrimination existing in the application by a carrier of the transport rates and conditions that differ on the ground of the country of origin or destination of the goods carried (Article 79, paragraph 3).

—enforcement and application of Articles 92 and 93 concerning the aids granted by states (Article 94).

—implementation of a common commercial policy based on uniform principles in regard to tariff amendments, the conclusion of tariff or trade agreements, the alignment of measures of liberalization, export policy, and protective measures. After expiry of transitional period. (Article 113, paragraphs 1 and 2).

—adoption of provisions necessary for implementing the European Social Fund; in particular, fixing details concerning the conditions under which the assistance of the fund shall be granted and the categories of enterprises whose workers shall benefit (Article 127).

—determination of the particulars of the extension of the right of establishment to nationals and companies of Member States other than that state having special relations with the country or territory concerned (Implementing Convention Relating to the Association with the Community of the Overseas Countries and Territories, Article 8).

—requires a qualified majority of nine to adopt *regulations* concerning:

—determination of a system to replace minimum prices still in force at the expiry of the transitional period (Article 44, paragraph 6).

—requires a simple majority to adopt *regulations* concerning:

—adoption of measures necessary to effect progressively the free movement of workers (Article 49).

—establishment of general principles for implementing a common policy of occupational training (Article 128).

—requires unanimity to adopt *directives* concerning:

—implementation of the general program for abolishing restrictions on the right of establishment, or if no such program exists, to complete one stage toward the achievement of freedom of establishment for a specific activity. Until the end of the first stage (Article 54, paragraph 2).*

—mutual recognition of diplomas, certificates, and other qualifications for the exercise of non-wage-earning activities. Unanimity is required on matters that are subject to legislative provisions, and on measures concerning the protection of savings and the conditions governing the exercise of the medical, paramedical, and pharmaceutical professions. Otherwise to end of first stage (Article 57, paragraph 2).*

—implementation of the general program for freeing the supply of services, or if no such program exists, to complete one stage in the liberalization of a specific service. Until end of first stage (Article 63, paragraph 2).*

—implementation of provisions calling for the progressive abolition of restrictions on the movement of capital and any discriminatory treatment. To the end of the second stage (Article 69).*

—approximation of such legislative and administrative provisions of the Member States as have a direct incidence on the establishment or functioning of the Common Market (Article 100).

—elimination of distortions in the conditions of competition that are due to disparities existing between the legislative or administrative provisions of the Member States. To the end of the first stage (Article 101).*

—coordination of legislative and administrative provisions that lay down

* After which unanimity is replaced by a qualified majority vote.

special treatment for foreign nationals justified by reasons of public order, public safety, and public health. Unanimity for legislative provisions. For administrative provisions, to end of second stage (Article 56, paragraph 2).*

—progressive harmonization by Member States of measures to aid exports to third countries. To end of second stage (Article 112, paragraph 1).*

—progressive coordination of the exchange policies of Member States in respect of the movement of capital between those states and third countries (Article 70, paragraph 1).

—application of the principles and rules on competition laid down in Articles 85 and 86. For the first three years (Article 43, paragraph 2).*

—requires a qualified majority to adopt *directives* concerning:

—the cases noted above in which unanimity prevails for a limited period only (Article 54, paragraph 2; Article 56, paragraph 2; Article 57, paragraph 1; Article 57, paragraph 2; Article 63, paragraph 2; Article 69; Article 101; Article 112, paragraph 1; Article 43, paragraph 2; Article 87, paragraph 1).

—the fixing of the timing for the reductions of such customs duties between Member States as remain to be carried out in the course of the third stage (Article 14, paragraph 2c).

—the settling of any special problems raised by the application of the provisions governing the reduction of customs duties between Member States (Article 14, paragraph 5).

—any technical difficulties raised by the application of the provisions concerning the establishment of the Common External Tariff (Article 210).

—the particulars of application of measures decided upon with regard to policies on economic trends (Article 103, paragraph 3).

—implementation of a common commercial policy based on uniform principles. After expiry of the transition period (Article 113, paragraphs 1 and 2).

—requires a simple majority to adopt *directives* concerning:

—adoption of measures necessary to effect progressively the free movement of workers (Article 49).

—requires unanimity to make *decisions* concerning:

—all measures for formulating and putting into effect a common agricultural policy. To end of second stage (Article 43, paragraph 2).*

—extension or shortening of the second and third stages of the transition period (Article 8, paragraph 5).

—establishment of financial regulations, and of methods and procedures relative to implementation and execution of the budget (Article 209).

—amendments to a list of products (arms, war materials, etc.) considered necessary for the protection of national security, for which special measures may be taken (Article 223, paragraph 3).

---

* After which unanimity is replaced by a qualified majority vote.

—conditions for the application of certain provisions of the Treaty to Algeria and the French overseas departments (Article 227, paragraph 2).

—requires a qualified majority to make *decisions* concerning:

—the granting of tariff quotas at reduced rate of duty or duty-free for products on Lists B, C, and D in cases of insufficient supply (Article 25, paragraph 1).

—reductions of the minimum percentage of 10 per cent by which global quotas are to be increased annually, in the case of quotas representing more than 20 per cent of the national output of the product concerned (Article 33, paragraph 5).

—additions to the list of agricultural products in Annex II (Article 38, paragraph 3).

—corrections to be made in minimum prices that have been fixed by the states and that do not conform to the criteria established by the Council (Article 44, paragraph 4).

—modification or abolition of certain measures taken to deal with problems of capital movements as provided in Article 70, if they are found to restrict excessively the free movement of capital (Article 70, paragraph 2).

—authorization of a limited and temporary introduction of certain exemptions and drawbacks in respect of exports to other Member States (Article 98).

—implementation of a common commercial policy based on uniform principles. After expiry of the transition period. (Article 113, paragraph 2).

—adoption of proposals for implementing the general commitment on Member States to proceed by way of common action within the framework of any international organization of economic character. From the end of the transition period. (Article 116).

—authorization to Member States to take specified measures of safeguard in the event that France should fail to take measures requested by the Council to make uniform such charges and aids as apply in the franc area (Protocol Relating to Certain Provisions of Concern to France, Article 1, paragraph 2).

—abolition of this system of charges and aids in the event of the balance of current payments of the franc area having remained in equilibrium for more than one year, and of its monetary reserves having reached a satisfactory level (Protocol Relating to Certain Provisions of Concern to France, Article 1, paragraph 3).

—to what extent the derogations accorded to the Duchy of Luxembourg shall be maintained, amended, or abolished (Protocol Concerning the Grand Duchy of Luxembourg, Article 1, paragraph 2).

—abolition of special quota granted to Germany for importation of bananas (Protocol Concerning the Tariff Quota for Imports of Bananas, Article 4).

—requires a special majority to make *decisions* concerning:

—the distribution of the amounts available from the Development Fund between the various requests received for the financing of social institutions (Implementing Convention Relating to the Association with the

Community of the Overseas Countries and Territories, Article 5, paragraph 2).

—establishment of the particulars concerning calls for, and transfers of, financial contributions, budgeting, and the administration of the resources of the Development Fund (Implementing Convention Relating to the Association with the Community of the Overseas Countries and Territories, Article 6).

—requires unanimity to take other actions as follows:

—appoint an Arbitration Board to decide on passage to second stage after the sixth year (Article 8, paragraph 4).

—fix the procedure to be applied in the course of the transitional period for the establishment of common action and regarding the achievement of a uniform commercial policy (Article 111, paragraph 1 and 3).*

—amend proposals of the Commission (Article 149).

—lay down provisions under which the financial contributions of the Member States to the budget of the Community may be replaced by other resources of the Community itself; in particular, by revenue accruing from the common external tariff. It shall recommend adoption to Member States in accordance with their respective constitutional rules (Article 201).

—fix the system of social payments applicable to fonctionnaires and agents of the Community (Protocol on Privileges and Immunities, Article 14).

—requires a qualified majority to take *other actions* as follows:

—as noted above (Article 111, paragraphs 1 and 3).

—amend the statute of service for officials and the conditions of employment for other employees of the Community. After fourth year (Article 212).

—requires a simple majority to take *other actions* as follows:

—lay down a Community system of taxation on salaries, wages, and emoluments (Protocol on Privileges and Immunities, Article 12).

—determine to which categories of fonctionnaires and agents of the Community the provision of Articles 11, 12, and 13 shall apply (Protocol on Privileges and Immunities, Article 15).

—determine the form for permits and passes for Community officials (Protocol on Privileges and Immunities, Article 6).

The Commission acting alone

—may adopt *regulations* concerning:

—the methods of administrative cooperation to be adopted regarding the free movement of goods (Article 10, paragraph 2).

—the provisions applicable to trade between Member States, to goods originating in another Member State in whose manufacture products have been used on which the appropriate customs duties or charges with equivalent effect have not been levied (Article 10, paragraph 2).

* After which unanimity is replaced by a qualified majority vote.

—the determination of the extent to which customs duties of a fiscal nature shall be taken into account for calculating the arithmetical average that is to be the basis of the Common External Tariff (Article 22).

—the actions to be taken in cases of dumping (Article 91, paragraph 2).

—provisions as regards relations between Member States to ensure application of special Protocol Relating to Goods Originating in and Coming from Certain Countries and Enjoying Special Treatment on Importation into one of the Member States (Article 4).

—may adopt *directives* concerning:

—the timing of the abolition of charges having an effect equivalent to customs duties on importation (Article 13, paragraph 2).

—the procedure and timing according to which Member States shall abolish between themselves any measures that have an effect equivalent to quotas (Article 33, paragraph 7).

—the conclusion of long-term contracts for agricultural products (Article 45, paragraph 2).

—the application of the rules on competition as regards public enterprises and enterprises to which special or exclusive rights are granted (Article 90, paragraph 3).

—the elimination of discrimination in fiscal matters—internal charges, turnover taxes, or drawbacks granted on exported goods (Article 97).

—may make *decisions* concerning:

—authorizations to Member States in difficulty to retain certain customs duties of a fiscal nature (Article 17, paragraph 4).

—the granting of tariff quotas at reduced or null duties for products on Lists E and G and Annex II (Article 25, paragraph 2 and 3).

—authorizations to states encountering special difficulties to postpone the lowering or raising of certain headings of its tariffs (Article 26).

—abolition by a state of quotas for products where imports in two successive years have been below the level of the quota granted (Article 33, paragraph 4).

—authorizations to Member States to take protective measures in regard to capital movements in the event of disturbances in the functioning of the capital market. The Commission determines the conditions and particulars of such measures (Article 73, paragraph 1). In the event that a state should take similar measures independently, these can be modified or abolished by the Commission (Article 73, paragraph 2).

—the elimination of discriminations in transport from an examination of rates and conditions involving any element of support or protection in the interest of one or more particular transport enterprises (Article 80, paragraphs 1 and 2).

—the confirmation of the existence of infringements of the rules and principles on competition. Such decisions are published, and Member States can be authorized to take specified measures to remedy the situation (Article 89, paragraph 2).

—the application of the rules on competition as regards public enterprises (Article 90, paragraph 3).

—authorization to injured states to take specified protective measures against dumping (Article 91, paragraph 1).

—establishment of the compatibility of aids granted by states with the Common Market and to direct that they be abolished or modified (Article 93, paragraphs 2 and 3).

—the elimination of discrimination in fiscal matters (Article 97).

—authorization to Member States to take specified safeguard measures regarding exchange rates in the event of balance-of-payments difficulties (Article 107, paragraph 2, and Article 108, paragraph 3).

—authorization of specified protective measures in the case of difficulty in the application of the common commercial policy—diversions of commercial traffic, disparities between measures taken (Article 115).

—the granting of prior approval to plans for the reconversion of enterprises that are to receive funds from the European Social Fund (Article 125, paragraph 2c).

—determination upon request of specified measures of safeguard it considers necessary to deal with cases of serious economic difficulty likely to persist. This is the general safeguard principle, and may include certain temporary derogations from the provisions of the Treaty (Article 226).

—authorizations for France to take specified safeguard measures in the event that the basic level for overtime payment and the average overtime rates are not brought into line with those prevailing in France by the end of the first stage (Protocol Relating to Certain Provisions of Concern to France, II, paragraph 2).

—determination of the particulars by which quotas to be offered to other Member States by the territory of one shall be opened and increased; the determination of the volume of certain tariff quotas (Implementing Convention Relating to the Association with the Community of the Overseas Countries and Territories (Article 11, paragraph 3, and Article 15, paragraph 4).

—may take *other actions* as follows:

—take all appropriate steps in order that negotiations on List G be undertaken before the end of the second year and concluded before the end of the first stage (Article 20).

—convene a conference of Member States with a view to comparing their agricultural policies and drawing up a statement of their resources and needs (Article 43, paragraph 1).

—establish the conditions under which workers may live in the territory of a Member State after having been employed there (Article 48, paragraph 3d).

—administer the European Social Fund assisted by a Committee composed of representatives of governments, trade unions, and employers (Article 124).

—adopt its own rules of procedure with the view of ensuring its own functioning and that of its services in accordance with the Treaty (Article 162).

—administer the Development Fund for the Overseas Countries and Territories, establishing and executing programs for financing social institutions (hospitals, teaching and research establishments, etc.) and economic investments of a general interest (Implementing Convention Relating to the Association with the Community of the Overseas Countries and Territories) (Articles 1, 2, and 3, and Article 5, paragraph 1).

CASES IN WHICH THE COUNCIL MUST CONSULT THE ASSEMBLY[2]

—The adoption of rules to implement the general prohibition on any discrimination based on nationality (Article 7).

—the amendment of the timetable for eliminating customs duties (Article 14, paragraph 7).

—the formulation and implementation of the common agricultural policy (Article 43, paragraph 2).

—the substitution of a common organization of agricultural markets for national market organizations (Article 43, paragraphs 2 and 3).

—the adoption of a general program for the abolition of restrictions on the freedom of establishment (Article 54, paragraph 1).

—the implementation of the general program for the abolition of restrictions on the right of establishment, or, if no such program exists, the completion of one stage toward the achievement of freedom of establishment for a specific activity (Article 54, paragraph 2).

—the coordination of legislative and administrative provisions that lay down special treatment for foreign nationals justified by reasons of public order, public safety, or public health (Article 56, paragraph 2).

—the mutual recognition of diplomas, certificates, and other qualifications for the exercise of non-wage-earning activities (Article 57, paragraph 1).

—the coordination of legislative and administrative provisions of Member States concerning the engagement in and exercise of non-wage-earning activities (Article 57, paragraph 2).

—the adoption of a program for abolishing restrictions on the free supply of services (Article 63, paragraph 1).

—the implementation of the general program for freeing the supply of services, or, if no such program exists, to complete one stage in the liberalization of a specific service (Article 63, paragraph 2).

—the adoption of common rules applicable to international transport, and of conditions for the admission of nonresident carriers to national transport services, and any other appropriate provisions (Article 75, paragraph 1).

—the application of the principles and rules on competition laid down in the Treaty in Articles 85 and 86 (Article 87, paragraph 1).

—the approximation of such legislative and administrative provisions of the Member States as have a direct incidence on the establishment or functioning of the Common Market and that would involve amendment of legislative provisions (Article 100).

—suspension of part or all of the assistance granted by the European Social Fund (Article 126, paragraph a).*

* In these cases the Council acts alone.

—the formulation of new tasks to be entrusted to the European Social Fund (Article 126, paragraph b).*

—the adoption of provisions necessary for implementing the European Social Fund; in particular, fixing details concerning the conditions under which the assistance of the Fund shall be granted and the categories of enterprises whose workers shall benefit (Article 127).

—the formulation of provisions under which the financial contributions of the Member States to the budget of the Community may be replaced by other resources (Article 201).

—the adoption of the budget of the Community (Article 203, paragraphs 3 and 4).

—the laying down of the statute of service for officials and the conditions of employment for other Community employees (Article 212).[3]

—the enactment of "appropriate provisions" granting powers of action that may be required to achieve an aim of the Community and that are not otherwise provided for (Article 235).

—the calling of a Conference of the Member States for the purpose of amending the Treaty (Article 236).

—the conclusion with a third country, a union of states, or an international organization of agreements creating an association embodying reciprocal rights and obligations, joint actions, or special procedures (Article 238).

CASES IN WHICH THE COUNCIL OR COMMISSION MUST CONSULT THE ECONOMIC AND SOCIAL COMMITTEE

—The formulation and putting into effect of the common agricultural policy (Article 43, paragraph 2).

—the adoption of a general program for the abolition of restrictions on the freedom of establishment (Article 54, paragraph 1).

—the substitution of a common organization of agricultural markets for national market organizations (Article 43, paragraphs 2 and 3).

—the implementation of the general program for the abolition of restrictions on the right of establishment, or, if no such program exists, the completion of one stage toward the achievement of freedom of establishment for a specific activity (Article 54, paragraph 2).

—the adoption of a program for abolishing restrictions on the free supply of services (Article 63, paragraph 1).

—the implementation of the general program for freeing the supply of services, or, if no such program exists, to complete one stage in the liberalization of a specific service (Article 63, paragraph 2).

—the adoption of common rules for international transport, of conditions for the admission of nonresident carriers, etc. (Article 75, paragraph 1).

—the implementation of those provisions of the Treaty which call for the abolition of any discrimination existing in the application by a carrier in respect of the same goods conveyed in the same circumstances, and of transport

---

* In these cases the Council acts alone.

rates and conditions that differ on the ground of the country of origin or destination of the goods carried (Article 79, paragraph 3).

—the approximation of such legislative and administrative provisions of the Member States as have a direct incidence on the Common Market and that would involve amendment of the legislative provisions (Article 100).

—Commission efforts to promote close collaboration between the Member States in the social field (employment, labor legislation and working conditions, occupational and continuation training, social security, industrial hygiene, the law as to trade unions and collective bargaining) (Article 118).

—the implementation of common measures in regard to the social security of migrant workers (Article 121).

—the suspension of part or all of the assistance granted by the European Social Fund (Article 126, paragraph b).

—the adoption of new tasks for the European Social Fund (Article 126, paragraph b).

—the adoption of provisions necessary for the implementation of a common policy of occupational training (Article 128).

APPENDIX B

CHRONOLOGY OF EVENTS IN
THE FREE TRADE AREA NEGOTIATIONS

STAGE ONE

June 1955   Ministers of the Six at Messina.
Discussions start under Spaak.
British representative withdraws at end of 1955.

April 1956   Spaak Report.

May 1956   Spaak Report accepted by the Ministers of the Six as a basis for negotiation; Spaak entrusted with guidance of the negotiations.

July 1956   OEEC Council, on a *British* proposal, decides to establish a special *working party* to study forms and methods of association between the Six and the rest of the OEEC.

January 1957   OEEC Council reports free trade area "possible."

February 1957   British issue White Paper giving views on form of free trade area.
OEEC Council enters into negotiations to determine ways and means. Three work parties set up.

March 1957   Rome Treaty signed.

August 1957   Maudling appointed coordinator by U.K.
In *September* visits other OEEC countries.

October 1957   OEEC Council declares determination to secure establishment of a free trade area to include all members. Establishes intergovernmental committee at Ministerial level—the Maudling Committee—to negotiate on a Treaty.
(France without a government—Faure, representative.)

January–February 1958	Maudling Committee meets — French *preparing alternatives.*
	British memo on agriculture.
February 1958	French Conseil Economique unanimously rejects free trade area in OEEC form.
	French counterproposals for sector approach.
March 1958	Carli Plan presented at Maudling meeting.
	First Session of the EPA—Hallstein attacks concept of free trade area.
April–June 1958	End of Fourth Republic.
June 1958	Macmillan and de Gaulle meet.
July 1958	Maudling Committee meets.
September 1958	EEC Council asks European Commission to organize studies of sectors.
October 1958	Ockrent Report and Maudling meeting clarify differences existing among the Six.
	Decide on a second Maudling Committee to receive sector reports.
November 13–14, 1958	Soustelle announces French decision that a free trade area as conceived by Britain is not possible.

STAGE TWO

November 26, 1958	Bad Kreuznach meeting between Adenauer and de Gaulle.
	Hallstein touring capitals for exploratory talks on measures to be taken January 1, 1959.
December 3–4, 1958	Council meets. Authorizes Erhard to go to London to inform U.K. of the actions the Six have decided to take.
December 15, 1958	OEEC Council meeting—stormiest in history—tension between U.K. and France. Confrontation of Maudling Report and EEC Council proposals.
December 1958	Commission calls for a speed-up in completing the common external tariff.
December 1958	French financial reforms, liberalization, convertibility.
January 1, 1959	Rome Treaty goes into effect.
February 25, 1959	Commission submits First Memo at request of Council. Lively reaction from all sides.
	Six to inform Commission by April 15 of comments.
	Special Committee set up to make a further report.
April 1959	Benelux proposals.

April–May 1959   Meetings of Rey Committee—*hardened* French position.

July 1959   Stabilization Plan published.
                    French Patronat favors acceleration of the EEC Treaty
                    timetable.

September 1959   Second Memo (to Special Committee)—denies the need
                    for a European solution, the experience of summer
                    having brought Commission to this view. *U.S. sup-
                    port for Commission quite active*; balance-of-payments
                    problems.

October 1959   Wigny presents Acceleration Plan.

November 1959   Rey Committee studying Commission proposals. France
                    offers new *acceleration* proposals embarrassing to Be-
                    nelux.
                    Counterproposal—Luns Plan.
                    Diplomatic activity—Lloyd to Paris, Adenauer to London.

Late November   Council finally adopts most of Commission proposals.
1959   Dillon had endorsed Commission approach.

December 1959   Western Summit Meeting decides to call Special Economic
                    Conference (Dillon). Active U.S. involvement now.

STAGE THREE

January 1960   Special Economic Conference of Thirteen on January
                    12–13.
                    Conference of Twenty and EEC/EC.
                    OEEC Council meets.
                    Four Wise Men appointed to revise OEEC.

March 1960   Acceleration proposals made by Hallstein.
                    Council discusses, refers to Permanent Representatives
                    and Rey Committee.
                    Seven meet in Vienna, see acceleration as unfriendly move.
                    The Six complete the common external tariff two years
                    ahead of schedule with final agreement on List G.

End March 1960   Committee of Twenty-One meets in Paris for first discus-
                    sion of trade questions.
                    Macmillan leak in Washington, D.C. Violent reaction on
                    the Continent.

May 1960   Council session in Luxembourg—discussion on accelera-
                    tion. Declaration of intention re third countries. The
                    agricultural problem comes to a head. Acceleration
                    accepted contingent upon progress in forming a com-
                    mon agricultural policy.

June 1960	WEU meeting. Profumo hints U.K. would join ECSC and Euratom.
June 10, 1960	Committee on Trade Problems (Committee of Twenty-One) in Paris. Study group set up.
July 7–8, 1960	Study group meets—to report by September 10.
September 14, 1960	Preparatory committee for OECD meets. Completed main tasks of drafting Convention.
December 12, 1960	Special Committee on Trade Problems meets in Paris. Progress in EEC-EFTA discussions.
December 13–14, 1960	Meeting of Ministers of the 18 OEEC countries, U.S., Canada, Representatives of European countries. Approve draft Convention OECD.
December 20–21, 1960	Acceleration decision is fully implemented on basis of progress in agriculture. First steps toward a common agricultural policy.
January 11–14, 1961	Meeting of study group of Committee on Trade Problems —study list of products likely to be adversely affected.

NOTES

NOTES

Complete authors' names, titles, and publication data are given in the Bibliography. Full publication data for the documents of the European Communities are also given in the Bibliography, in the separate section on pp. 351–60.

CHAPTER ONE

1. For a full account, see Haas, *Uniting of Europe*, pp. 268–80, 283–317, 512–20.
2. Deniau, p. 6.
3. *Ibid.*, pp. 59–61.
4. EEC Treaty, Preamble.
5. Frank, p. 292.
6. Deutsch *et al.*, p. 5. See also Deutsch, *Political Community at the International Level*.
7. Haas, "Challenge of Regionalism," p. 443.
8. North, Koch, and Zinnes, p. 358.
9. Haas, "Persistent Themes," p. 627.
10. Haas, *Uniting of Europe*, p. 16.
11. Schokking and Anderson, p. 388.
12. Haas, *Consensus Formation*, p. 2. In this study of the Council of Europe, Haas also temporarily abandons his more precise definition.
13. Haas, *Uniting of Europe*, pp. 11 and 13.
14. Deutsch *et al.*, pp. 12–13.
15. Haas, "International Integration," p. 375.
16. North, Koch, and Zinnes, pp. 367–72.
17. Alger, pp. 128–45.
18. Haas and Whiting, p. 443.
19. Haas, "International Integration," p. 376.
20. North, Koch, and Zinnes, p. 355.
21. Haas, "International Integration," pp. 367–68.
22. *Ibid.*
23. *Ibid.*, p. 368.
24. Snyder, in Young, p. 20.

CHAPTER TWO

1. For a full discussion of the commercial aspects, see Frank, *passim*.
2. This discussion follows that of IRRI, pp. 410–515.
3. Hurtig, p. 344.
4. This is seen clearly in Article 226:
   "1. In the course of the transitional period, where there are serious diffi-

culties which are likely to persist in any sector of economic activity or difficulties which may seriously impair the economic situation in any region, a Member State may ask for authorization to take measures of safeguard in order to restore the situation and adapt the sector concerned to the Common Market economy.

"2. At the request of the State concerned, the Commission shall by an expedited procedure immediately determine the measures of safeguard which it considers necessary, specifying the conditions and particulars of application.

"3. The measures authorised under paragraph 2 may include derogations from the provisions of this Treaty, to the extent and for the periods strictly necessary for the achievement of the objects referred to in paragraph 1. Priority shall be given in the choice of such measures to those which will least disturb the functioning of the Common Market."

5. It should be noted that without the regulation of state trading these provisions are of little effect. This regulation is provided for in Article 37, but not very explicitly, as Hurtig (p. 347) rightly points out.

6. List A: duties that are to be substituted for purposes of calculating the arithmetical average (certain chemical products and textile machinery). Lists B, C, D, and E set maximum limits to duties even if the arithmetical averages are higher: List B at 3 per cent (mostly raw materials); List C at 10 per cent (mostly semi-manufactured products such as fats, marble, hides, paper, construction materials, and precious metals); List D at 15 per cent (mostly products relating to inorganic chemistry); and List E at 25 per cent (mostly products relating to organic chemistry). List F: headings in respect of which duties have been fixed by agreement (mainly agriculture). List G: headings yet to be negotiated between the member states (fish, cheese, bread, wine, salt, wood, aluminum, etc.).

These lists are dealt with in Article 19, paragraphs 2, 3, 4, and 5; and Article 20. See also Article 25, which permits special tariff quotas, notably in cases of traditional supply arrangements. Also Protocol Relating to German Internal Trade and Connected Problems, Protocol Relating to Goods Originally in and Coming from Certain Countries and Enjoying Special Treatment on Importation into one of the Member States, and Protocol Concerning Mineral Oils and Certain of Their Derivatives.

7. Defined as "products of the soil, stock-breeding, and of fisheries as well as products after first processing stage which are directly connected with such products." A list of these products is contained in Annex II.

8. Deniau, pp. 68–69.

9. Article 40 lists the following forms: common rules concerning competition, compulsory coordination of national market organizations, and European market organizations.

10. Article 44. Article 42 provides for safeguards in the form of aids in the case of enterprises handicapped by structural or national conditions. See also Protocol Concerning the Grand Duchy of Luxembourg.

11. Article 48, paragraphs 1 and 2. What this entails is spelled out in Article 48, paragraph 3.

12. Article 70, paragraph 2. "Appropriate measures" may be taken when the progressive coordination of exchange policies leads to discrepancies of such a magnitude as to permit "persons resident in one of the Member States to make use of the transfer facilities within the Community . . . in order to evade the rules of one of the Member States."

Article 73. In the event that capital movements lead to severe market disturbances, the Commission may authorize a Member State to take protective measures. Should such measures be of a "secret or urgent character," the Member State may itself take them without prior approval, although these can be later modified or abolished by the Community institutions.

13. Article 49 for free movement of workers; also Article 51, which calls for a uniform social security system. Articles 54 and 57 for right of establishment. Articles 60 and 63 for services. Article 69 for capital.

14. Article 74 and Article 75, paragraph 1. See major escape clause in Article 75, paragraph 3. Also Article 77 permitting state aids.

15. Article 84. "The Provision of this Title shall apply to transport by rail, road and inland waterway."

16. Certain exceptions may be allowed in the interests of "the requirements of a suitable regional economic policy, of the needs of underdeveloped regions seriously affected by political circumstances and . . . of the effects of such rates and conditions or competition between the different forms of transport" (Article 80, paragraph 2).

17. Deniau, pp. 81–85.

18. Such practices must not impose any restrictions that are not essential to the object, nor may they enable firms to eliminate competition.

19. These provisions are also binding on public enterprises and enterprises to which the states grant special or exclusive rights. Article 90.

20. Exceptions are allowed when aid is intended to stimulate underdeveloped regions; when it is intended to benefit Europe as a whole; or when it is of a social nature granted to individual consumers, such as emergency aid in the case of natural calamities, etc. Article 92, paragraphs 2 and 3.

21. Further specifications are found in Articles 96, 97, and 98.

22. Protocol Relating to Certain Provisions of Concern to France, Article 2, paragraph 1.

23. Deniau, pp. 89–90.

24. Each member shall pursue whatever economic policy is necessary to ensure the equilibrium of its over-all balance of payments and to maintain confidence in its currency, while ensuring a high level of employment and the stability of the level of prices. Article 104.

25. The Treaty also mentions the possibility of creating one or more agricultural orientation and guarantee funds. Article 40, paragraph 4.

26. Hurtig, p. 362.

27. Protocol on the Statute of the European Investment Bank, Article 4.

28. For a full discussion, see IRRI, pp. 495–502.

29. Although these must be given prior approval in the case of conversion plans. Article 125, paragraph 2.

30. Article 131. This covers the following: French West Africa; Senegal, the Sudan, Guinea, the Ivory Coast, Dahomey, Mauretania, the Niger and Upper Volta; French Equatorial Africa; the Middle Congo, Ubangi-Shari, Chad and Gabon; St. Pierre and Miquelon, the Comora Archipelago, Madagascar and the dependencies, the French Settlements in Oceania, the Southern and Antarctic Territories; the Autonomous Republic of Togoland; the French Trusteeship Territory in the Cameroons; the Belgian Congo and Ruanda-Urundi; the Italian Trusteeship Territory in Somaliland; and Netherlands New Guinea. Annex IV.

31. Implementing Convention Relating to the Association with the Community of the Overseas Countries and Territories, Article 1.

32. *Ibid.*, Article 8 and Article 11, paragraph 3.

33. *Ibid.*, Articles 1–7.

34. *Ibid.*, Articles 1 and 3, Annexes A and B. Hurtig, p. 371, gives the following figures (in dollars) for contributions made to the Development Fund by the six countries and received, in turn, by those possessing African territories:

Country	Contribution to be made	Contribution to be received	Total balance
France	200,000,000	511,250,000	+311,250,000
Germany	200,000,000	—	−200,000,000
Belgium	70,000,000	30,000,000	−40,000,000
Netherlands	70,000,000	35,000,000	−35,000,000
Italy	40,000,000	5,000,000	−35,000,000
Luxembourg	1,250,000	—	−1,250,000

35. Gaudet, p. 2.

36. *Ibid.*, p. 34. The Treaty would still seem to fulfill the requirements of Gehrels and Johnston (pp. 275–94) for real economic union: (1) agreement on gradual but complete elimination of tariffs, quotas, and exchange controls; (2) abandonment of the right to restore trade restrictions unilaterally; (3) provisions for joint action to deal with problems resulting from the removal of trade barriers and to promote more efficient use of resources; (4) some harmonization of national policies that affect price structures and resource allocation and of monetary and fiscal policies; and (5) provisions for the free movement of capital and labor.

CHAPTER THREE

1. Bebr, p. 67.

2. Reuter, "Affaires étrangères," p. 384.

3. Reuter, "Aspects II," p. 162. See also de Vreese, p. 194; and IRRI, pp. 468–78.

4. Article 189. Thus by implication, when the Treaty does not specify the form, the institutions concerned shall have the choice. Regulations, directives, and decisions are specifically called for in the Treaty in 35, 20, and 58 instances, respectively.

5. "Thus, in areas in which the power of issuing regulations is specified, there may be a real delegation of authority on the part of the Member States in the interests of the Community." *Savary Report*, p. 2365.

6. Article 192. "Decisions of the Council or of the Commission which contain a pecuniary obligation on persons other than States shall be enforceable.

"Forced execution shall be governed by the rules of civil procedure in force in the State in whose territory it takes place. The writ of execution shall be served, without other formality than the verification of the authenticity of the written act, by the domestic authority which the Government of each Member State shall designate for this purpose and of which it shall give notice to the Commission and to the Court of Justice."

7. The State has engaged itself in advance to accept the rulings of the Community institutions, but the realization of this engagement will involve national procedures. Thus a decision is legally the same as a directive when it refers to a state. *Savary Report*, p. 2366.

8. *Ibid.*, Annex D III, lists 14 cases involving complements to the Treaty:

Articles 44 (3), 51, 54 (1), 59, 63 (1), 84 (2), 121, 126 (b), 212, 217, 223 (2 & 3), and 235; Protocole sur les privilèges et immunités, Article 14; and Statut de la Cour, Articles 12 and 45. This does not represent an exhaustive list, since it is limited to provisions requiring unanimous votes in the Council of Ministers. It also excludes a number of items I would include, such as formation of a common agricultural policy, common commercial policy, provisions for a general harmonization of legislation, etc.

9. *Ibid.*, Annex D IV: Articles 8 (5), 14 (7), 136, 138 (3), 165, 166, 200 (3), 201, 237, and 238. See also Articles 33 (8), 157, and 227.

10. Article 236. These must then be ratified by all the Member States.

11. Article 138. Provision is made for possible direct elections.

12. Articles 165 and 167. The Court is also assisted by two advocates-general. Articles 166 and 167.

13. Ungerer, p. 275.

14. Articles 111 (2), 113 (2), 228, and 229. Article 6 of Protocol on Privileges and Immunities.

15. "The Council and the Commission shall consult each other and shall settle by mutual agreement the particulars of their collaboration." Article 162. See also Articles 147 and 152.

16. Behr, p. 69.

17. Van Ginderachter, p. 382. See also Ljubisavljevic.

18. "The right of veto accorded to any one of the six Member States by these provisions may not be as potentially paralyzing as would appear at first glance. . . . In the first (and most numerous) group of instances . . . the veto power is, after all, temporary only and vanishes upon the expiration of the transitional period. . . . In other instances, unanimity is required to *relieve* Member States of their Treaty obligations (93, 2–3). . . . In some instances the Treaty itself provides a means for circumventing a veto (54 [2]; 63 [2]) or at least makes available to Member States measures of safeguard and retorsion in case of paralysis (70 [2]; 107 [2])." Stein, "The New Institutions," in Stein and Nicholson, I, 36.

19. Most of the situations demanding unanimity do so only during part, or all, of the transition period.

20. *Savary Report*, p. 2364.

21. Article 148 (2). There is an exception in the case of determining the system to replace minimum prices in agricultural products at the end of the transitional period. In this instance the Council can decide by a majority of 9 out of 17. Article 44 (6).

22. Van Ginderachter, p. 387.

23. Behr, p. 70.

24. Article 203, paragraph 5.

25. Implementing Convention Relating to the Association with the Community of the Overseas Countries and Territories, Articles 3, 4, 5, and 6.

26. Gaudet, p. 8.

27. Gaudet, p. 9. Also van Ginderachter, p. 388.

28. Soldati, p. 25.

29. Gaudet, p. 15.

30. Reuter, "Aspects III," p. 313.

31. Behr, p. 70.

32. Gaudet, p. 15.

33. Ungerer, p. 274.

34. Ungerer also notes: "Another similar sign is the fact that a suit by one Member State introduced before the Court of Justice against an act of the Council is not considered 'inadmissible' because the representative of that Government approved the act in the Council." *Ibid.*, p. 275.

35. Reuter, "Aspects II," p. 164.

36. Reuter, "Aspects III," p. 315.

37. De Vreese, p. 196.

38. *Ibid.*

39. This treatment follows closely that of Soulé, "Comparaison II," pp. 208–12.

40. Gaudet, pp. 13–14.

41. *Ibid.*, p. 13.

42. Reuter argues that this amounts to the constitution of an internal juridical order. "Affaires étrangères," p. 372.

43. For the removal of judges, see Statute of the Court, Article 6.

44. Ungerer, p. 281.

45. *Ibid.*, p. 279.

46. Stein, p. 240. See also Wigny, pp. 63–64.

47. Reuter, "Aspects III," pp. 313–14.

48. Article 137. See also de Sainte Lorette, pp. 85–86; Ungerer, p. 280.

49. Article 203, paragraph 2. See also Soulé, "Comparaison I," pp. 101–2.

50. Article 201. Also Stein, p. 252.

51. See Pohle, pp. 11–14.

52. De Sainte Lorette, p. 94.

53. Van Ginderachter, p. 390.

54. Frank, p. 292.

55. Quoted by Stein, "An American Lawyer Looks at European Integration," in Stein and Nicholson, pp. 15–16.

56. *Ibid.*, p. 16.

57. Reuter, "Affaires étrangères," pp. 366–72.

CHAPTER FOUR

1. EEC Commission, *First Stage*, p. 12.

2. EEC Commission, *Bulletin*, No. 10 (1960), pp. 5–6.

3. EEC Commission, *General Report 1962*, pp. 95–96.

4. EEC Commission, *Bulletin*, No. 10 (1960), p. 14.

5. EEC Commission, *First Stage*, p. 17.

6. For details see *ibid.*, pp. 38–43.

7. *Ibid.*, pp. 43–51.

8. *Ibid.*, p. 13.

9. Haas, *Uniting of Europe*, pp. 451–85.

10. Stein, "The New Institutions," in Stein and Nicholson, p. 44.

11. Article 151.

12. EEC Council of Ministers, *Règlement intérieur*, Article 16.

13. "In the absence of a decision to the contrary, the Commission is invited to be present at the sessions of this Committee and of these working groups." *Ibid.*, Article 16.

14. The Commission may call the Council into session (EEC, *Treaty*, Article 147); it can enter questions on the Council's agenda (EEC Council of Ministers, *Règlement intérieur*, Article 2); and as a rule it participates in all deliberations of

the Council, unless expressly excluded (*ibid.,* Article 3). Under certain conditions the Council may make decisions out of session by means of a written procedure, but the Commission's approval must be obtained if the matter at hand concerns its competences (*ibid.,* Article 6).

15. Compiled from *Common Market,* II (March 1962), 56.

16. *Common Market,* II (April 1962), 79–80.

17. The total budgets of the three Communities (ECSC, EEC, and Euratom), including expenditures for the Overseas Development Fund, Euratom nuclear research funds, and ECSC funds for adaptation and research, was $314.7 million in 1961 and $398.7 million in 1962. The administrative budget of the three Communities was $46.9 million in 1961 and $53.5 million in 1962. *Ibid.* Compare this with the $63,149,700 that represented the total administrative budget of the United Nations for 1960. The budgets of the specialized agencies in 1961 were as follows (taken from United Nations, *Annual Report,* p. 101):

FAO	$ 9,225,500
ILO	9,003,909
UNESCO	12,957,763
WHO	16,889,760
Universal Postal Union	660,930
World Meteorological Organization	652,605
International Civil Aviation Organization	3,865,000
Intergovernmental Maritime Consultative Organization	225,000
International Telecommunications Union	2,211,860

See also *U.S. Participation in the U.N.,* pp. 217–19. Thus the total cost of the three European Communities was $314.7 million in 1961 and $398.7 million in 1962. This compares with the 1961 cost of the entire U.N. system—including the regular budget, the specialized agencies, the voluntary programs—of approximately $450 million. See Stoessinger.

18. EEC, *Projet de budget,* Titre I, Recettes. The U.S. contribution to U.N. expenses in 1960 was assessed at approximately $19 million, which represents 32.51 per cent of the total amount assessed against the Member States of the U.N. See *U.S. Participation in U.N.,* p. 217.

19. See EEC, *Projet de budget,* Titre III, and EEC Commission, *General Report 1960,* p. 72. The Commission's staff is composed as follows:

Category	In service April 1, 1960	Authorized in 1961 budget
A (administrators and policy-makers)	423	537
B (specialized technicians)	284	389
C (secretarial, etc.)	648	780
Translators	88	140
Totals	1,443	1,846

20. Stein, "The New Institutions," in Stein and Nicholson, p. 45.

21. *Ibid.,* p. 46.

22. "Réponse à la question écrite No. 81 posée au Conseil de la CEE par M. van der Goes van Naters," in EPA, *Annuaire-Manuel 1960–61,* pp. 688–90.

23. These figures are based on internal documents.

24. "Réponse à la question écrite No. 81," in EPA, *Annuaire-Manuel 1960–61,* p. 689.

25. See *Agence Europe*, July 26, 1960.

26. *Ibid.*, October 19, 1960.

27. EEC Commission, *Bulletin*, No. 8–9 (1960), p. 31.

28. See Chapter 8.

29. *Agence Europe*, April 17, 1960.

30. For the full text, see EEC Commission, *Bulletin,* Nos. 7–8 (1961), pp. 35–37.

31. "Les Réunions des Ministres des Finances," pp. 344–45.

32. *Agence Europe*, October 25, 1960.

33. "La Communauté à l'épreuve des faits I," p. 426.

34. Stein, "The New Institutions," in Stein and Nicholson, pp. 94–95.

35. See Camps, *First Year*, pp. 3–5; "La Communauté à l'épreuve des faits I," pp. 425–27; Margulies, pp. 292–94.

36. Camps, *First Year*, p. 4, n.5.

37. Quoted in *Agence Europe*, October 28, 1958.

38. These views were repeated by van der Goes van Naters, in November 1960, when he submitted a written question to the Council of Ministers asking for "a list of all the committees, subcommittees, work groups or expert groups, and *ad hoc* groups and committees, as well as mixed groups working entirely or in part under the Council, the Representatives of the governments of the Member States, the Council Secretariat, or the Committee of Permanent Representatives." "Question écrite No. 81," in EPA, *Annuaire-Manuel 1960–61*, p. 688.

39. This discussion is based on *Budgetary Control.*

40. Article 203.

41. The following chart, based on *Budgetary Control*, p. 12, Table 3, summarizes the results of the various negotiations on the 1959 budget (in millions of dollars):

	Original Estimates	Modifications at request of the experts	Experts' proposals	Final decision of Council
Council of Ministers	4.18	3.2	3.22	3.34
EEC Commission	21.60	18.2	15.74	16.94
European Parliament	3.60	—	—	3.68
Court of Justice	.88	—	—	.98

42. *Budgetary Control*, p. 27.

43. *Ibid.*, p. 31.

44. Gaudet, p. 7.

45. *Ibid.*

46. See Selznick, *TVA and the Grass Roots*, pp. 249–66.

47. Selznick, *Leadership in Administration, passim.*

48. For details see Haas, *Uniting of Europe*, pp. 268–80.

49. Speech before the EPA on October 12, 1960, reprinted in EEC Commission, *Bulletin*, No. 8-9 (1960), p. 15.

50. EPA, *Débats I*, November 1960, p. 179.

51. EEC Commission, *Bulletin*, No. 8-9 (1960), p. 16.

52. *Ibid.*, p. 17. For a recent full statement of Hallstein's view of the integration process and the Commission's role therein, see Hallstein, *passim.*

53. See the speech by Hallstein in EPA, *Débats I*, October 21, 1958.

54. EEC Commission, *General Report 1959*, p. 9 (italics mine).

55. *Ibid. 1958*, pp. 14–15 (italics mine).

56. "La Communauté à l'épreuve des faits I," p. 427.

57. Strictly speaking, the Treaty states merely that the Commission may not include more than two members of the same nationality. Article 157.

58. For example, the Council met 36 times in the period January 1, 1958, to September 30, 1960.

59. See the speech by the President of the Council, Pella, before the EPA, reprinted in *Agence Europe,* November 25, 1959 (Supplement). Pella pointed out that the respective national Parliaments could question the Foreign Minister about their government's position in the Council, and this has been a fairly common practice.

60. Speech by Pella before the EPA, November 24, 1959. EEC Council of Ministers, "Projet d'intervention du Président des Conseils," p. 5 (italics in the original). See also EPA, *Débats II,* November 24, 1959, pp. 1324–28.

61. EEC Council of Ministers, "Projet d'intervention du Président des Conseils," p. 6.

62. Speech by the President of the Council before the EPA, in EPA, *Débats II,* March 28, 1960, p. 19.

63. See Soldati, p. 25.

64. Gaudet, p. 17.

65. Quoted in EEC Commission, *Bulletin,* No. 1 (1961), p. 6.

66. Much of the information contained in this chapter is based on interviews.

67. EPA, *Débats I,* June 24, 1958, pp. 164–77.

68. A phrase used by Hallstein, *Agence Europe,* October 28, 1958.

69. Beloff, p. 539.

70. For details see Chapter 8 below.

71. *Agence Europe,* July 16, 1960.

72. For details see Chapter 11 below.

73. Haas, *Uniting of Europe,* p. 522.

74. Interviews with participants have convinced me that such a process is indeed under way.

75. "La Communauté à l'épreuve des faits I," p. 426.

76. By the terms of the personnel statute that came into force in 1962, so-called *agents temporaires* can occupy regular Commission posts for a maximum of two years plus one renewal of one year. Thereafter they must either resign or go through the process of becoming permanent EEC civil servants. See Règlement No. 31 (CEE) et No. 11 (CEEA), fixant le statut des fonctionnaires et le régime applicable aux autres agents de la CEE et de la CEEA, reprinted in European Communities, *Journal Officiel,* June 14, 1962.

77. Stein observes that this sort of evolution could weaken support for the Communities, and that it strengthens the case of those who would strengthen the EPA. "The New Institutions," in Stein and Nicholson, pp. 95–97.

78. "European Parliamentary Assembly," pp. 251–52.

79. Stein, "The New Institutions," in Stein and Nicholson, p. 60.

80. Stein, "European Parliamentary Assembly," p. 251.

81. Haas, *Uniting of Europe,* p. 413.

82. Stein, "European Parliamentary Assembly," p. 251.

83. EEC Commission, *General Report 1960,* p. 41 (italics mine).

84. *Agence Europe,* June 25, 1959.

85. This is provided for in Article 138 of the EEC Treaty. "The Assembly shall draw up proposals for election by direct universal suffrage in accordance with a uniform procedure in all member states. The Council, acting by means of a unanimous vote, shall determine the provisions which it shall recommend to member states for adoption in accordance with their respective constitutional laws."

86. *Direct Elections and the European Parliament*, p. 26.

87. This pattern was developed in the Common Assembly of the ECSC and has been carried over to the enlarged EPA. For details on its evolution and effects, see Kapteyn, in Lindsay, pp. 215–51. See also Haas, *Uniting of Europe*, pp. 390–450.

88. Compiled from EPA, *Annuaire-Manuel 1959–1960*.

89. Kapteyn, in Lindsay, p. 241.

90. "One aspect of the code [of conduct in the Assembly] is the habit of intra-party compromising which has been developed by both Socialists and Christian-Democrats into a fine art. . . . In both instances the acceptance of the code of intra-party compromise proceeded from an initial period of quasi-diplomatic relations to the evolution of a more truly party atmosphere, in which individual members argue with each other, seek to persuade one another, and eventually agree on a common formula without voting on it." Haas, *Uniting of Europe*, p. 438.

91. Haas, "Challenge of Regionalism," p. 453.

92. Kapteyn, in Lindsay, p. 248.

93. "First there is the creation of parliamentary groups, then the appearance of electoral committees, and finally the establishment of a permanent connection between these two elements. . . . There have usually been parliamentary groups before electoral committees. Indeed there were political assemblies before there were elections." Duverger, p. xxiv.

94. For brief accounts of the organization and functions of these groups, see "Méthodes et Mouvements pour unir l'Europe," pp. 51–54.

95. For an alternative evaluation see Zellentin, pp. 22–28.

96. The following table gives a general idea of the composition of the ESC. It seems to underrate the trade union representation, probably because of the difficulty of determining the specific position of some of the Italian appointees.

Categories	Germany	Belgium	France	Italy	Luxem-bourg	Nether-lands	Total
Agriculture	3	1	5	4	1	1	15
Trade unions	8	4	7	3	1	1	28
Industry	3	3	4	3	1	5	15
Artisans, commerce, and general interest	10	4	8	14	2	5	43
Totals	24	12	24	24	5	12	101

The trade union organizations list 34 new members of their movement in the ESC, and consider that at least half of the members represent employers and that most of the rest are not sympathetic to the trade unions. *Revue du Marché Commun*, 25 (May 1960), pp. 178–79.

The trade unions have continually complained of this imbalance and even threatened to boycott the Committee at the start. For details see Stein, "The New Institutions," in Stein and Nicholson, p. 48, and notes Nos. 74 and 75.

97. They included opinions on the following subjects: regulations concerning social security for migrant workers, directives on implementation of the right of establishment in overseas countries and territories, harmonization of commercial policy during the transition period, elimination of discrimination in transport rates, regulations for the European Social Fund, common agricultural policy, free movement of workers in the Community, a general program for the abolition of restrictions on the freedom of establishment and on the free supply of services, and regulations on rules of competition. For a complete listing see Rosenberg, in EEC Commission, *Bulletin*, No. 3 (1961), pp. 10–11.

98. EEC Economic and Social Committee, *Annuaire*, pp. 93–99.

99. Rosenberg, in EEC Commission, *Bulletin*, No. 3 (1961), p. 7.

100. For example, the opinion on the Commission's proposals for a common agricultural policy was adopted by a vote of 73 in favor and 19 abstaining. *Agence Europe*, June 24, 1960.

101. Stein, "The New Institutions," in Stein and Nicholson, p. 49.

102. See Haas, *Uniting of Europe*, pp. 340–54.

103. See Schumm; also Leclercq. The Dutch Economic and Social Council, on the other hand, has a very definite legal status as advisor to the government and as spokesman for interest groups, as well as certain rule-making and administrative functions. For details see Boshowers.

104. Haas, *Uniting of Europe*, p. 340.

105. EEC Council of Ministers, *Règlement intérieur*, Article 20; and EEC Economic and Social Committee, *Annuaire*, pp. 27–43. Also Rosenberg, in EEC Commission, *Bulletin*, No. 3 (1961), p. 6.

106. Rosenberg, in *ibid.*, pp. 6–8.

CHAPTER FIVE

1. See the numerous examples cited by Malvestiti in EEC Commission, *Bulletin*, No. 3 (1959), pp. 5–17. See also Hasbrouck, "Common Market at the Grass Roots."

2. See EEC Commission, *General Report 1960*, p. 131.

3. De Vleeschauer.

4. See Willemetz, pp. 38ff.; and ECIS, *Communautés Européenne*, August-September 1960.

5. Ouin, in Stein and Nicholson, p. 168.

6. ECIS, *Etudes et analyses*, No. 16.

7. EEC Commission, *General Report 1960*, p. 130.

8. Advertisement in *Le Soir*, January 3–4, 1960. An official of the store told me that the losses incurred in these price reductions were shared equally by the store and by the various suppliers, all of whom were anxious to get a foot in the Belgian economy.

9. Groups: Société Générale de Belgique, Amsterdamsche Bank, and the Deutsche Bank. See "Les Banques et Les Bourses dans le Marché Commun," in ECIS, *Communauté Européenne*, December 1960.

10. Groups: Banque Lambert, MM. Rothschild Frères, Berliner Handels Gesellschaft, la Compagnie Financière, Pierson-Helding-Pierson of Amsterdam, Medrobanca (Milan), la Compagnie d'Outre-Mer, and Bayerische Staatsbank. *Ibid.*

11. E.g., La Compagnie de l'Outre-Mer, Banca Commerciale Italiana, Crédit Lyonnais, etc. For an extensive list see ECIS, *Etudes et analyses*, No. 1.

12. E.g., Eurunion, with capital of one billion Belgian francs, created by members of Eurosyndicat (see note 11). For extensive lists of groups set up in each of the several countries, see citations in notes 10 and 11. Also "Les Banques belges, grande industrie dans le Marché Commun," *Le Monde*, April 14, 1960.

13. "Investissements américains dans la Communauté," in ECIS, *Communauté Européenne*, November 1960. Note the evolution in these figures on U.S. investment projects abroad (millions of dollars):

	1959	1960	1961
EEC	157.3	269.2	355.5
Other European countries	222.0	231.7	295.2
Total world	934.7	1,126.5	1,304.3

14. This trend is encouraged by the governments concerned, especially in France, where tax relief is given to firms wishing to regroup with a view to combating Common Market competition, and especially for the purpose of organizing exports on a joint basis. *Agence Europe*, January 2, 1959.

15. See EEC Commission, *Mouvements.* One of the services of the Commission tries rather unsuccessfully to keep up with these agreements by making lists of them as they occur. Long lists may be found in ECIS, *Communauté Européenne*, May, June, and July, 1960.

16. E.g., note the agreements between Renault and Alfa Romeo, Fiat and N.S.U., Peugeot and Mercedes-Benz, Montecatini and Pechiney, etc. For long lists see citations in note 15. For the incidence of such measures, see *Agence Europe*, October 9, 1961, which cites the following estimates from a study released by the Deutscher Industrie- und Handelstag: 880 affiliates created in other EEC countries; 610 agreements for technical cooperation; and 480 agreements for participation in EEC firms.

17. Most interest groups have specialized departments and staffs who are charged with the responsibility of following the work of the Community institutions, and of making contact with them and with the various national Ministries concerned.

18. See ECC Commission, *Bulletin*, No. 4 (1961), p. 11.

19. Organizations exist at the EEC level among medical, paramedical, and pharmaceutical professions (physicians, pharmacists, dentists, and veterinary surgeons); the legal profession (solicitors, tax consultants, etc.); and the technical professions (engineers, consultant engineers, chemical engineers, architects, chartered accountants, surveyors, and real estate agents). There is also a Standing Conference of the Chambers of Commerce of the EEC countries and a working party on European Integration of the Union of International Fairs. *Ibid.*, p. 13. See also *Agence Europe*, October 9, 1961.

20. For a full listing of all groups with summary information on members and purposes (exclusive of trade unions and agriculture), see EEC Commission, *Répertoire des organismes communs.*

21. EEC Commission, *Bulletin*, No. 4 (1961), p. 14. For a listing of these groups see EEC Commission, *Répertoire des organisations agricoles.*

22. "The European trade organizations are themselves a valuable instrument in the merging of the markets and in co-operation across the national frontiers." EEC Commission, *Bulletin*, No. 4 (1961), p. 15.

23. EEC Commission, *Bulletin*, No. 4 (1961), pp. 12–13.

24. See Stein, "The New Institutions," in Stein and Nicholson, p. 90.

25. There has been a similar development in the shoe industry, which has set up the "Comité de Liaisons et d'Etudes de la Chaussure," a committee with statutes permitting majority decisions in policy matters. Its aims are to present common opinions and to protect markets against third countries (especially Hong Kong, India, and Japan). Caze, pp. 409–16.

26. Haas, *Uniting of Europe*, pp. 353–54.

27. UNICE, *Statuts*, Article 5.

28. *Agence Europe*, November 10, 1960.

29. Haas, *Consensus Formation*, p. 5.

30. UNICE, *Statuts*, Article 12.

31. Nagels, p. 446. Also quoted in Stein, "The New Institutions," in Stein and Nicholson, p. 84.

32. For details see Haas, *Uniting of Europe*, pp. 355–89; Scheingold; Brouland; and Beever, pp. 93–204.

33. See Beever, pp. 70–77. Also Tessier, pp. 242–46.
34. Secrétariat Syndical Européen, "Rapport," p. 27.
35. Robinson, p. 136.
36. COPA, "Règlement intérieur."
37. COPA, "Position de l'Assemblée du COPA."
38. COPA, "Déclaration de l'Assemblée du COPA."

CHAPTER SIX

1. Haas, *Uniting of Europe*, p. 155.
2. *Ibid.*, pp. 287–89.
3. The first part of the discussion that follows is based on Ouin's analysis in Stein and Nicholson, pp. 102–3.

CHAPTER SEVEN

1. For a detailed account and analysis of the negotiations, see the following three studies by Camps, which have been relied on extensively: *Free Trade Area Negotiations*; *European Free Trade Association*; and *Division in Europe*. For texts of the documents relating to the negotiations from July 1956 to December 1958, see *Negotiations for a European Free Trade Area*. For a good discussion of the economic problems, see Ouin, in Stein and Nicholson, pp. 131–61. See also Snoy, pp. 569–623; and Rudolfsen, pp. 3–10.
2. Camps, *Free Trade Area Negotiations*, p. 38.
3. *Ibid.*, p. 31. "The British have tried to make it unmistakably clear, both at home and abroad, that the essential cause of the breakdown was the protectionist attitude of the French government."
4. For the views of Baron Snoy et d'Oppuers, former Secretary-General of the Belgian Ministry of Economic Affairs and Belgian delegate in the drafting of Rome Treaties and on the Maudling Committee, see *Revue générale belge*, February 1960; and Snoy, pp. 569–623, *passim*.
5. Camps, *European Common Market*, p. 21.
6. The President of the Council, Félix Gaillard, noted in a speech at Lille that if the problems of harmonizing competition were hard to solve in the framework of the Six, they would be harder still with Thirteen. *Revue du Marché Commun*, No. 1 (1958), p. 30.
7. Camps, *Free Trade Area Negotiations*, p. 6.
8. *Agence Europe*, March 17, 1958; Snoy, pp. 612–15; and Camps, *ibid.*, pp. 9–10.
9. Camps, *ibid.*, p. 38.
10. *Ibid.*, pp. 19–21.
11. *The Financial Times*, November 15, 1958, quoted in *ibid.*, p. 21.
12. Furniss, pp. 456–57.
13. Dogan, in Lindsay, pp. 160–61.
14. *Agence Europe*, May 19, 1959.
15. *Le Monde*, January 13, 1960. According to Camps (*Division in Europe*, p. 36), "The conference was held not as might have been expected at the Château de la Muette, the headquarters of OEEC, but in temporary quarters, and with tempo-

rary staff, made available by the French Government which was anxious to dramatize the fact that the conference was the beginning of a new relationship between the Six and the other European countries and North America, not simply a continuation of the post-war OEEC pattern."

16. Couve de Murville, in *Le Monde*, March 9, 1960.

17. CNPF, "Le projet de Marché commun européen," in ECSC, *Informations Mensuelles*, January 1957, p. 34.

18. See "La Zone de libre échange," pp. 30–36; and "L'Industrie chimique française," pp. 80–83.

19. De Sainte Lorette, p. 199.

20. Speech at the Institut International de la Presse, in EPA, *Cahiers*, November 1959, pp. 17–18.

21. "Les tricheurs," *L'Usine Nouvelle*, December 1960.

22. Views of François Peugeot, President of the Fédération des Industries Mécanique et Transformatrice de Métaux, in "Pourquoi les industriels français sont farouchement pour le Marché commun," *Entreprise*, March 5, 1960.

23. Dogan, in Lindsay, p. 62.

24. "Lettre adressé à M. Guy Mollet, Président du Conseil," *Europe-Agriculture*, Chambres d'Agriculture, Supplement to No. 118 (Paris: February 15, 1957), pp. 3–4. See also "Position de la CNMCCA," *L'Usine Nouvelle*, July 19, 1958.

25. See the position of the Comité Français des Relations Agricoles Internationales, which consists of representatives from the APPCA, CGA, and FNSEA, in EPA, Direction de la Documentation Parlementaire et de l'Information, *Prises de position*, p. 6.

26. Beever, p. 231.

27. *Ibid.*, p. 232.

28. ECSC, *Informations Mensuelles*, December 1957, p. 76. The Agriculture Committee was *a priori* hostile to the free trade area.

29. For examples see the statements by Senators Bonnefous (Left Democrat), Vanrullen (Socialist), and Poher (MRP), in EPA, *Cahiers*, January 1960, pp. 2–11. See also the report of the Finance Committee in *ibid.*, December 1959, pp. 10–13; and the statements by Pleven and Radius in the National Assembly, *ibid.*, July 1960, pp. 4–5.

30. See statement by Robert Schuman at European Industrial Conference organized by the U.K. Council for the European Movement in 1958. "Isn't there a certain incompatibility or contradiction between the two regimes? Personally, I fear that there is, in effect, a fundamental difference between these two systems that threatens to uniquely complicate the solution." *Report of the European Industrial Conference.*

31. Statement by Radius in the National Assembly, in EPA, *Cahiers*, July 1960, p. 5.

32. See statement by de la Malène, in *ibid.*, February 1960, pp. 3–4.

33. EPA, Direction de la Documentation Parlementaire et de l'Information, *L'Activité de l'Assemblée Parlementaire Européenne*, August-September 1960, I, 7–8.

34. Haas, *Uniting of Europe*, pp. 275–76.

35. Camps, *European Common Market*, p. 4.

36. Bundestag debate on July 5, 1957, ECSC, *Informations Mensuelles*, December 1957, p. 75.

37. Camps, *Free Trade Area Negotiations*, p. 24. Von Brentano, when questioned about the position of Germany on the dispute between France and the U.K.

over the FTA, stated that the solidarity between the six Community countries was unquestionable and unconditional, and that, moreover, there was no conflict between France and the U.K., but a divergence of views between the Six and the U.K. *Agence Europe*, December 19, 1958.

38. *Neue Zürcher Zeitung*, October 16, 1959.

39. Before CDU Congress in April 1960. *Die Welt* and *Frankfurter Allgemeine Zeitung*, April 28, 1960. Also von Brentano in the Bundestag, April 6, 1960, reported in EPA, *Cahiers*, May 1960, p. 2.

40. Adenauer and von Brentano also consistently supported all Commission initiatives in the FTA dispute, e.g., the idea of a "contact committee." See von Brentano's speech before the Bundestag on November 5, 1959, in EPA, *Cahiers*, December 1959, pp. 1–2.

41. Camps, *Free Trade Area Negotiations*, p. 34.

42. Erhard, *Prosperity Through Competition*, p. 223.

43. *Ibid.*, p. 252.

44. See Erhard's speech in the Bundestag, reported in EPA, *Cahiers*, June 1960, pp. 2–3; also *Die Welt* and *Frankfurter Allgemeine Zeitung* of May 5, 1960. Shortly after publication of the Commission's Second Memorandum, on October 5, 1959, *Die Welt* and *Frankfurter Allgemeine Zeitung* published half-page advertisements consisting of a picture of Erhard and a text that warned against a divided Europe. According to *The Financial Times* of October 6, anonymous supporters of Erhard bore the cost of the advertisements.

45. *Industriekurier*, November 17, 1959.

46. *Le Monde*, April 26, 1960.

47. Erhard, "Was wird aus Europa?"

48. *Ibid.*

49. *Ibid.* Such a plan was proposed by the State Secretary, Müller-Armack. See "Der Plan für eine gesamteuropäische Zollunion," *Frankfurter Allgemeine Zeitung*, January 2, 1961.

50. Statements that Germany had come off the worst in the negotiations on the free trade area occurred as early as the winter and spring of 1957. E.g., *Deutsche Zeitung Wirtschaftszeitung*, quoted in *Agence Europe*, February 8, 1957; *Frankfurter Allgemeine Zeitung*, February 13, 1957; *Handelsblatt*, April 3, 1957.

51. "Les Industriels allemands contre le Marché Commun," *Entreprise*, April 16, 1960, pp. 26–35. This study is based on interviews with German industrialists in the mechanical construction, automobile, metallurgy, textile, optical, electrical construction, and electronic industries.

52. Bundesverband der Deutschen Industrie, *Jahresbericht* (1959), p. 50.

53. *Frankfurter Allgemeine Zeitung*, December 5, 1959. See also Berg's speech at International Press Institute, October 5, 1959. Münchmeyer has also advocated that the EEC become the eighth member of the EFTA; see *Europa Nachrichten*, November 19, 1960.

54. *Frankfurter Allgemeine Zeitung*, March 10, 1960; *Die Welt*, April 6, 1960.

55. *Europa Nachrichten*, March 9, 1960. See also Hasbrouck, "Toward One Europe," April 26, 1960.

56. See *Die Welt*, May 5, 1960. "We hope that Erhard will succeed in convincing a big majority in the Bundestag, and also a majority within his own party, of the necessity of implementing his own liberal ideas on European economic integration. Erhard will have to refer particularly to the Hallstein plan [acceleration] sponsored by the French-influenced EEC headquarters in Brussels." *Frankfurter Allgemeine Zeitung*, May 4, 1960.

57. See, e.g., *Handelsblatt,* September 27, 1960.

58. Münchmeyer, in *Frankfurter Allgemeine Zeitung,* January 5, 1959.

59. Camps, *Division in Europe,* p. 63. According to *Industriekurier,* October 29, 1959, "Excessive accentuation of the EEC Treaty's political aims risks endangering the large free trade area. Hallstein assumes that the EEC is in a position to follow a policy of its own; that is by no means the case." H. J. Abs, however, of the Deutsche Bank, has said that although an agreement between the Six and the Seven is crucial, it must not mean any modification of the Treaty of Rome or of its goals. *Agence Europe,* September 22, 1960.

60. *Opinion économique et financière,* October 22, 1959.

61. Beever, pp. 219–20.

62. *Ibid.,* p. 218. See also Brouland, p. 83.

63. Beever, p. 220.

64. EPA, Direction de la Documentation Parlementaire et de l'Information, *Prises de position,* p. 3.

65. ECSC, *Informations Mensuelles,* December 1957, p. 73.

66. *Ibid.,* pp. 89–92.

67. In EPA, *Cahiers,* November 1959, p. 14.

68. See the speech by Furler in the Bundestag, reported in *ibid.,* December 1959, p. 2. Also by Birrenbach, in *ibid.,* June 1960, p. 3.

69. See the speeches of Starke and Margulies in the Bundestag, in *ibid.,* June 1960, pp. 1–5.

70. Bundestag debate, November 5, 1959, reported in *ibid.,* December 1959, p. 2.

71. *Ibid.,* June 1960, pp. 1–4.

72. *Agence Europe,* November 20, 1958.

73. *Ibid.,* April 23, 1959; see Camps, *Division in Europe,* p. 16.

74. Statement by van Offelen, quoted in *Le Soir,* November 4, 1959.

75. *Agence Europe,* May 22, 1958.

76. *Informec,* No. 9, October 1, 1959.

77. *Occident,* November 1959. This position has been repeated in substantially the same form in the 1960 Annual Report of the FIB summarized in *Agence Europe,* "Documents," June 24, 1960. See also *Bulletin de la Fédération des Industries Belges,* September 10, 1960.

78. Beever, pp. 256–57.

79. ECSC, *Informations Mensuelles,* April 1957, p. 8.

80. *Agence Europe,* February 7, 1958.

81. See EPA, *Cahiers,* January 1960, pp. 25–27.

82. ECSC, *Informations Mensuelles,* January 1958, pp. 65–66. Senator Struye also spoke of the risk that free trade area countries, especially the United Kingdom, would become the recipients of most of the new foreign investment because they would enjoy the double advantage of Commonwealth preference and association in an FTA.

83. Debates in the Chamber of Representatives on January 20, 26, 27, and 28 and on February 2, 3, 4, 9, 10, and 11, 1960, reported in EPA, *Cahiers,* March 1960, pp. 1–4.

84. Statement by the President of the Council, Bech, in ECSC, *Informations Mensuelles,* pp. 66–67 (January 1958).

85. Haas, *Uniting of Europe,* pp. 148–50.

86. Daalder, in Lindsay, p. 116.

87. *Ibid.,* p. 130. The idea of a special Minister for European Affairs was advanced. During the negotiations for the formation of a cabinet in 1959, there was

a strong conflict between the Minister for Foreign Affairs and the Minister for Economic Affairs over European policies. *Ibid.*, p. 116.

88. *Agence Europe*, October 20 and 21, 1959. The Dutch felt that the Commission had shown itself unable to develop a Community policy of its own, that it could not go beyond what the French wanted. *Nieuwe Rotterdamse Courant*, September 29, 1959.

89. "The result of accepting the French suggestion would have been not only to increase the difference in treatment between Community countries and other European countries, more than would the Commission's original proposal, but it would also have meant an absolute increase in the tariff, the low tariff countries levied on goods coming from outside the Community." Camps, *Division in Europe*, p. 23.

90. *Ibid.*, pp. 23–24. See also *Agence Europe*, November 24, 1959.

91. Camps, *Division in Europe*, p. 7. Note, however, that C. P. M. Romme, head of the ruling Catholic People's Party, stated in a parliamentary debate late in 1960 that he was in favor of the de Gaulle suggestions. *Le Monde*, October 7, 1960.

92. *Christian Science Monitor*, March 1, 1960.

93. Quoted in Fontaine, pp. 61–64.

94. *Agence Europe*, February 23, 1961. The Dutch also proposed that the Secretariat be situated in Brussels rather than in Paris.

95. Haas, *Uniting of Europe*, pp. 205–6.

96. *Handels -en Transport Courant*, March 23, 1957. Another report pointed out that since there were no adequate assurances for either transport or agriculture, and since it was certain that trade with third countries would be endangered, the Netherlands should have made signing of the Treaty dependent upon the constitution of a free trade area. *Economisch-Statistische Berichten*, March 20, 1957.

97. See *Financiel Dagblad*, January 21, 1960; and *Algemeen Handelsblad*, October 26, 1959.

98. *Handels -en Transport Courant*, November 24, 1959.

99. *Agence Europe*, February 9, 1960.

100. "De Katolieke Werkgever," in EPA, *Cahiers*, December 1959.

101. In *Agence Europe*, "Documents," June 21, 1960.

102. *Ibid.*

103. Beever, pp. 262–65.

104. Robinson, pp. 156–57.

105. Sociaal-Economische Raad, in EPA, Direction de la Documentation Parlementaire et de l'Information, *Prises de position*, p. 5.

106. *Agence Europe*, July 5, 1960.

107. *Ibid.*, September 25, 1959. See also the statement by Blaisse.

108. Camps, *Division in Europe*, p. 17.

109. Haas, *Uniting of Europe*, p. 275.

110. *Agence Europe*, December 14, 1957.

111. "Italy, the Common Market, and the Free Trade Area," pp. 160–62.

112. De Sainte Lorette, p. 200.

113. For details see Camps, *Free Trade Area Negotiations*, p. 10.

114. The French found no difficulty in accepting the Carli Plan in its entirety. *Agence Europe*, March 17, 1958.

115. In EPA, *Cahiers*, August-September 1960, pp. 15–16.

116. *The World Today* (April 1958), p. 154.

117. Statement by Giuseppe Pella, then Foreign Minister, *Corriere della Sera*,

January 19, 1960; also by Amintore Fanfani, President of the Council, and Foreign Minister Antonio Segni, *Le Monde*, September 4–5, 1960.

118. E.g., *Corriere della Sera*, December 3, 1959; and *Messagero*, December 3, 1959.

119. *Agence Europe*, November 24, 1958, and November 18, 1958.

120. *Ibid.*, "Documents," February 19, 1960.

121. Beever, pp. 235–46.

122. *Ibid.*, pp. 246–47.

123. *Ibid.*, pp. 243–44.

124. See *The World Today* (April 1958), pp. 154–55. The agricultural groups do not seem to have taken a very active role in free trade area discussions, and do not seem to have made any significant policy statements. See the discussion of EEC agricultural policy on pp. 261–66.

125. See EPA, *Cahiers*, July 1960. The same general conclusions can be drawn from the statements of Italian representatives to the EPA.

126. Camps, *Free Trade Area Negotiations*, p. 39.

CHAPTER EIGHT

1. *IRRI*, pp. 444–45. The members of the Interim Committee were Baron Jean-Charles Snoy et d'Oppuers, Belgium (President); Félix Gaillard, France; Carl Ophüls, Germany; Ludovico Benvenuti, Italy; Lambert Schaus, Luxembourg; and Gerard Verryn-Stuart, Netherlands.

2. *Agence Europe*, April 19 and May 24, 1957.

3. *Ibid.*, July 19, 1957.

4. *Ibid.*, October 11, 1957, and March 6, 1958.

5. Considerable efforts were made to reach a common position in the Maudling discussions, and one member habitually presented the group position (if there was one). The French and Italians adopted different positions on the harmonization of economic and social policy, and the free circulation of labor, respectively. *Ibid.*, November 29, 1957.

6. Made up of Baron Snoy (Belgium), Müller-Armack (Germany), Mille (France), Cattani (Italy), Schaus (Luxembourg), Linthorst-Homan (Netherlands). *Ibid.*, January 18, 1958.

7. Up to this time in the Maudling Committee negotiations, the Six were unable to present a common front on the question of origin, about which wide differences existed between protectionist and liberal points of view, as well as on U.K.-Commonwealth relations, institutions, and safeguards. *Ibid.*, March 10, 1958.

8. For the major points in the French Memo, see above p. 119.

9. *Agence Europe*, March 20, 1958; EEC Commission, *General Report 1958*, pp. 115–16.

10. *Agence Europe*, September 6, 1958.

11. *Ibid.*, October 8, 1958; EEC Commission, *General Report 1959*, pp. 27–28.

12. Camps, *Free Trade Area Negotiations*, pp. 17–19. The text of the Ockrent Report can be found in *Revue du Marché Commun*, No. 8 (1958), pp. 369–74.

13. See especially the views of Baron Snoy in "Les Etapes," pp. 611–17, and in *Revue générale belge*, February 1960.

14. *Agence Europe*, November 20, 1959.

15. EEC Commission, *General Report 1959*, pp. 3–31.

16. Camps, *Free Trade Area Negotiations*, p. 13.

17. *Agence Europe*, March 18, 1958.

18. EEC Commission, *General Report 1958*, pp. 121–22. The idea had first been noted in March.

19. *Ibid.*, p. 116 (italics mine).

20. *Agence Europe*, September 3, 1958.

21. *Ibid.*, August 1, 1958.

22. EEC Commission, *General Report 1959*, pp. 27–28.

23. *Ibid.*, p. 29.

24. Camps, *Free Trade Area Negotiations*, pp. 23–24.

25. EEC Commission, *General Report 1958*, pp. 17–18.

26. Camps, *Free Trade Area Negotiations*, p. 36n.

27. *Ibid.*, p. 28.

28. *Agence Europe*, January 5 and 15, 1959. It was finally agreed that Member States could open bilateral talks on the 3 per cent quotas only by agreement among the Six.

29. EEC Commission, *First Memorandum*, p. 5.

30. *Ibid.*

31. *Ibid.*, p. 6.

32. *Ibid.*, p. 7.

33. *Ibid.*, pp. 16–17.

34. *Ibid.*, p. 33.

35. *Ibid.*, pp. 34–37.

36. EEC Commission, *General Report 1958*, pp. 117–22.

37. EEC Commission, *First Memorandum*, pp. 17–18. This departs from the position taken by the Community in the Ockrent Report.

38. *Ibid.*, p. 19.

39. EPA, *Débats I*, January 13, 1959, pp. 223–80.

40. *Ibid.*, in *Agence Europe*, January 13, 1959.

41. EEC Commission, *First Memorandum*, p. 12.

42. *Ibid.*, p. 41. According to Camps (*Division in Europe*, p. 15), "This suggestion, like some of the other references to the desirability of a 'wider arrangement,' shows signs of having been added at the last moment to make the memorandum more palatable to those within the Community who were pressing for a broader arrangement, as well as to the other European countries."

43. EEC Commission, *General Report 1959*, p. 32.

44. *Agence Europe*, March 19, 1959.

45. *Ibid.*, March 20, 1959.

46. *Ibid.*, March 21, 1959.

47. "Resolution adopted by the Council of the EEC, March 19, 1959," in EEC Commission, *First Memorandum*, p. 42.

48. Camps, *Division in Europe*, p. 17.

49. *Agence Europe*, April 29, 1959.

50. Erhard is reported to have said that the Treaty of Rome should not be regarded as standing for all time, and that the Six might well consider changing it, should this be necessary to achieve a wider association. *Ibid.*, April 29, 1959.

51. *Ibid.*, May 19, 1959.

52. EEC Commission, *Second Memorandum*, reprinted in EEC Commission, *Bulletin*, No. 4 (1959), pp. 13–14.

53. *Ibid.*, pp. 16–20. See also Camps, *Division in Europe*, pp. 20–21.

54. Reported in *Agence Europe*, September 24, 1959.

55. Reported in *ibid.*, September 25, 1959.

56. Camps, *Division in Europe*, p. 18. Mrs. Camps comments: "One of the most obvious signs of the 'reality' of the Community was the fact that industries . . . were now planning on the assumption that the Common Market, and only the Common Market, would become a reality. . . . A wider arrangement, by removing the 'difference' in treatment, would inevitably have dissipated some of the industrial support for the Community."

57. *Ibid.*, p. 20.

58. *Agence Europe*, October 21, 1959.

59. Camps, *Division in Europe*, p. 23. See also the speeches by Blaisse and van der Goes van Naters in the EPA session of September 24–25, 1959, *Agence Europe*, September 24 and 25, 1959.

60. See speeches of René Pleven and Christian de la Malène, EPA, September 25, *Agence Europe*, September 25, 1959.

61. *Agence Europe*, October 21, 1959.

62. *Ibid.*, October 20, 1959. Substantial support on these lines came from the Christian-Democratic group of the EPA; see statements by Jean Duvieusart and Hans Furler, September 1959.

63. See Chapter 9 below.

64. EEC Commission, *Second Memorandum*, p. 20.

65. EEC Commission, *General Report 1960*, pp. 28–29.

66. *Agence Europe*, November 17, 1959.

67. *Ibid.*

68. Camps, *Division in Europe*, pp. 24–25.

69. EEC Council of Ministers, "Projet d'intervention du Président du Conseil," p. 10.

70. Camps, *Division in Europe*, pp. 30–31.

71. See also *ibid.*, p. 34.

72. In Camps, *Division in Europe*, p. 39n. EEC Commission, *General Report 1960*, pp. 243–44. There was considerable conflict between the Six and the United States, on the one hand, and between the Seven and other OEEC countries, on the other, over the substance of these various decisions. The splits within the Six were also revealed. For a full discussion of this subject, see Camps, *Division in Europe*, pp. 35–41.

73. *Ibid.*, pp. 39–40.

74. Quoted by Hasbrouck, "Toward One Europe," March 29, 1960.

75. EEC Commission, *Bulletin*, No. 2 (1960), p. 24; and *Agence Europe*, February 8, 1960.

76. See Chapter 9 for details.

77. EEC Council of Ministers, *Decision*.

78. There are several exceptions: (1) Member States may request that products on List G be exempted and that the agreed common external tariff be used instead; (2) if by using the common external tariff (reduced by 20 per cent) the resultant tariff is below that of the *agreed* common external tariff, the rate will be reduced only as far as the latter rate; and (3) a special concession was made to Germany in view of German tariff reductions carried out in 1957.

79. *Agence Europe*, May 11, 1960.

80. In EEC Commission, *Bulletin*, No. 4 (1960), pp. 23–24.

81. Camps, *Division in Europe*, p. 55.

82. *Agence Europe*, May 31 and June 8, 1960.

83. In EEC Commission, *Bulletin*, No. 5 (1960), pp. 15–17.

84. For a discussion of the work of this study group since its creation, see *ibid.*, No. 3 (1961), pp. 24–26.

85. EEC Commission, *General Report 1960*, p. 10.

86. *Ibid.*, p. 11 (italics mine).

87. See *First Year*, pp. 15–16, in which she comments: "It is an issue that focuses attention on fears and on contingencies and on things that may never happen. . . . The negotiations have also taken the time and energy of those who must give precise content to the Treaty and establish the basic policies of the Community." See also Camps, *Division in Europe*, p. 28.

88. This is also the conclusion of Stein, "The New Institutions," in Stein and Nicholson, p. 94.

CHAPTER NINE

1. EEC Commission, *General Report 1960*, p. 27 (italics mine).

2. For details see Courtin, pp. 291–309. Also Furniss, p. 255.

3. Reported in *Agence Europe*, January 9, 1957.

4. For details see Chapter 4 above.

5. EEC Commission, *Recommendations*, p. 2.

6. *Ibid.*, pp. 2–5.

7. Camps, *Division in Europe*, p. 9. Also Stein, "An American Lawyer Looks at the Common Market," in Stein and Nicholson, p. 13.

8. For details see Chapter 10 below.

9. Fry, p. 1.

10. Stein, "An American Lawyer Looks at the Common Market," in Stein and Nicholson, p. 12.

11. *Ibid.*, pp. 12–13.

12. Fry, p. 12. Mr. Fry is Financial Editor of *The Guardian*, and these articles are based on a series of interviews with industrialists and businessmen in each of the Member States of the EEC.

13. For details on the "Truth and Austerity" program, see Furniss, Chapter 17.

14. Camps, *Division in Europe*, p. 9.

15. Fry, pp. 3–4.

16. *Agence Europe*, June 2, 1959.

17. "Faut-il accélérer la mise en application du Marché commun?" *Bulletin de la CNPF*, July 1959, p. 23.

18. Camps, *Division in Europe*, pp. 8–10.

19. EEC Commission, *General Report 1960*, p. 28 (italics mine).

20. *Agence Europe*, September 7, 1959.

21. *Ibid.*, September 30, October 10, and October 12, 1959.

22. This summary is based on that in *Agence Europe*, "Supplement," October 10, 1959, and Hasbrouck, "Toward One Europe," October 15, 1959.

23. Articles 15, 24, and 35 expressly provide for this possibility.

24. EPA, *Débats I*, September 23, 1959.

25. Quoted in *Le Soir*, October 22, 1959.

26. See the discussion of the common external tariff, pp. 206–10 below.

27. *Agence Europe*, November 26, 1959.

28. EEC Commission, *General Report 1960*, p. 29.

29. *Agence Europe*, February 23, 1960.

30. Baron Snoy et d'Oppuers had reportedly argued that new talks on the free trade area should be a condition for acceleration. *Agence Europe*, October 12, 1959.

31. The Dutch formally proposed that the level of the common external tariff be reduced by 20 per cent.

32. *Agence Europe*, November 11, 1959, December 3, 1959, and February 9, 1960; *Neue Zürcher Zeitung*, December 29, 1959; *Frankfurter Allgemeine Zeitung*, November 12, 1959; EPA, *Cahiers*, January 1960, pp. 24–25; *Bulletin du CNPF*, November 1959, pp. 16–17; and Hasbrouck, "Toward One Europe," October 15, 1959.

33. Haas, "Challenge of Regionalism," p. 448.

34. Hasbrouck, "Toward One Europe," October 15, 1959.

35. *Agence Europe*, February 23, 1960.

36. Article 8, paragraph 5.

37. EPA, *Débats II*, March 28, 1960, p. 25.

38. EEC Commission, *Bulletin*, No. 3 (1960), p. 19.

39. *Ibid.*, pp. 19–24.

40. *Ibid.*, p. 20 (italics mine).

41. Camps, *Division in Europe*, p. 43.

42. EEC Commission, *Bulletin*, No. 3 (1960), p. 18.

43. Article 14, paragraph 7; Article 33, paragraph 8. The Council acts by means of unanimity on a proposal of the Commission, and after the Assembly has been consulted for Article 14.

44. Article 24, "With a view to aligning their duties with the common customs tariff, Member States shall be free to modify these duties more rapidly than is provided for in Article 23."

45. In Article 18 the Member States "declare their willingness to contribute to . . . the reduction of barriers to trade by entering into reciprocal and mutually advantageous arrangements directed to the reduction of customs duties below the general level which they could claim." A similar commitment is made in Article 110. A procedure is provided in Article 28, according to which "any autonomous modification or suspension of duties of the common customs tariff shall be decided upon by the Council acting by means of a unanimous vote."

46. Article 15. "Member States hereby declare their willingness to reduce their customs duties in regard to other Member States more rapidly than provided for . . . if their general economic situation . . . permit[s]." Article 35 provides the same thing for quotas.

47. EEC Commission, *Bulletin*, No. 3 (1960), p. 18.

48. EPA, *Débats II*, March 28, 1960, p. 29.

49. *Ibid.*, p. 30.

50. *Ibid.*, p. 21.

51. *Ibid.*, p. 22.

52. EPA, *Débats II*, March 28, 1960, pp. 38–39.

53. See *ibid.*, March 28, 29, 30, 31, 1960.

54. See the speeches of de la Malène and Peyrefitte, in *ibid.*, March 28, 1960, pp. 41–44; March 29, 1960, pp. 88–91.

55. EPA, *Proposition*.

56. *Agence Europe*, March 11, 1960.

57. *Ibid.*, March 9, 1960.

58. See *Algemeen Handelsblad*, March 4, 1960, and *Handels en Transport Courant*, March 5, 1960. The acceleration proposals were described as "iniquitous" and as "evoking a serious situation for the Netherlands."

59. See, e.g., *Die Welt*, March 10, 1960.

60. *Agence Europe*, March 24, 1960.

61. *Europa Nachrichten,* March 11, 1960.

62. *New York Herald Tribune* (Paris), March 21, 1960; *Le Soir,* March 21, 1960; and *Die Welt,* March 21, 1960.

63. *Frankfurter Allgemeine Zeitung,* March 10, 1960.

64. Quoted in *Agence Europe,* March 21, 1960.

65. EEC Commission, Press Communiqué, March 24, 1960.

66. *Le Monde,* March 23, 1960.

67. *Handelsblatt,* March 10, 1960.

68. In the interim, in the Rey Committee discussions, the German delegate, State Secretary for Economic Affairs, Müller-Armack, described the idea of a more rapid alignment to the common external tariff as a "painful operation." He proposed that this first alignment be limited to five-eighths, since it was to be made only two and a half years after the Treaty came into force, which was five-eighths of the four-year time limit laid down in the Treaty. *Agence Europe,* March 23, 1960.

69. *Frankfurter Allgemeine Zeitung,* April 6, 1960; *Die Welt,* April 6, 1960.

70. *The Times* (London), April 6, 1960.

71. *Die Welt,* May 5, 1960.

72. Bundestag debates, May 4–5, 1960, in EPA, *Cahiers,* June 1960, pp. 1–7.

73. Camps, *Division in Europe,* p. 48.

74. See *Frankfurter Allgemeine Zeitung,* March 31, 1960. *Deutsche Zeitung,* March 31, 1960, carried headlines "England wants to torpedo the EEC," and "Macmillan against Napoleon and Hallstein." *Süddeutsche Zeitung,* March 31, 1960, commented: "Not a shot across the bows of EEC Europe, but a shot straight into them."

75. The Continental reaction . . . was immediate and violent. . . . In the short term the Prime Minister's intervention, rather than encouraging second thoughts, strengthened support on the Continent and in Washington for accelerating the Common Market." Camps, *Division in Europe,* p. 49.

76. See speeches of Blaisse, Starke, Müller-Hermann, Friedensburg. EPA, *Débats II,* March 28, 1960, pp. 33–38, 45–50, and 51–53.

77. *Revue du Marché Commun,* No. 23 (1960), p. 90. See the positions of the CNPF and the Fédération des Industries Mécaniques et Transformatrices de Métaux, *Entreprise,* March 5, 1960, p. 47.

78. *Agence Europe,* March 23, 1960.

79. *Revue du Marché Commun,* No. 23 (1960), p. 90.

80. *Agence Europe,* March 10, 1960.

81. *Ibid.*

82. *Ibid.,* March 26, 1960.

83. *Ibid.,* April 25, 1960.

84. *Ibid.,* March 24, 1960.

85. See Robinson, pp. 113–14.

86. See the position of the DBV in *Rheinische Bauernzeitung,* April 9, 1960, in EPA, *Cahiers,* May 1960, pp. 14–15.

87. Camps, *Division in Europe,* p. 51.

88. *Agence Europe,* May 9, 1960.

89. The following discussion is based on information drawn from interviews, internal documents of the several EEC institutions, and the following press reports: *Agence Europe,* May 10, 11, 12, 13, 1960; *La Libre Belgique,* May 10, 11, 12, 13, 1960; *Le Soir,* May 10, 11, 12, 13, 1960; and *Le Monde,* May 10, 11, 12, 13, 1960. For the text of the final decision, see EEC Council of Ministers, *Decision.* For a partial text, see EEC Commission, *Bulletin,* No. 4 (1960), pp. 19–22.

90. *Agence Europe,* April 7, 1960. Trade union representatives were on the whole in favor of acceleration, but regretted the "disequilibrium" in the Commission's proposals.

91. See *Agence Europe,* May 11, 1960.

92. By the end of 1960, France and Italy had invoked this provision and submitted a number of requests to the Commission. Approximately two-thirds of these requests were approved (13 of 20 listed), the Commission having examined "the legal, political and economic effects which would result from a favourable or unfavourable decision on its part." See EEC Commission, *Bulletin,* No. 1 (1961), pp. 49–50.

93. *Agence Europe,* May 13, 1960.

94. See *Het Parool,* May 14, 1960, and *De Volkskrant,* May 14, 1960. Also Robinson, p. 71.

95. EEC Commission, *General Report 1960,* p. 27.

96. Statement by Commission President Hallstein, *Agence Europe,* May 13, 1960.

97. ECIS, *Communautés Européennes,* June 1960.

98. See *Le Monde* editorial, May 14, 1960.

99. *Le Monde,* May 14, 1960.

100. *Frankfurter Allgemeine Zeitung,* May 16, 1960.

101. "No one need feel beaten. According to the experts, the compromises made are by no means so costly as they might have been." *Handelsblatt,* May 16, 1960. Also, "The ultimate compromise on agriculture should be measured not only by what Germany has conceded and what concession can be wrenched from the Netherlands. What has been conceded—and it is not a trifle—is the price for setting acceleration in motion." *Frankfurter Allgemeine Zeitung,* May 14, 1960.

102. See *Telegraaf,* May 14, 1960.

CHAPTER TEN

1. Deniau, p. 66.

2. EEC, *Treaty,* Article 19, paragraph 1. The duties in force on January 1, 1957, are used as the base. *Ibid.,* paragraph 2.

3. See the amusing account in Snoy, pp. 596–97.

4. Article 20.

5. *Ibid.*

6. Article 21.

7. Statement by Caron. Press release, Brussels, February 13, 1960.

8. *Les Echos,* February 15, 1960.

9. *Frankfurter Allgemeine Zeitung,* March 7, 1960.

10. Article 28. After the expiration of the transition period, modifications or suspensions of not more than 20 per cent and limited to six months in duration may be made by the Council voting by qualified majority on a Commission proposal.

11. This discussion follows that of Ouin, in Stein and Nicholson, pp. 131–37. See also EEC Commission, *General Report 1958,* pp. 56–57; *ibid. 1959,* pp. 73–74; and *ibid. 1960,* pp. 237–38.

12. EEC Commission, *General Report 1958,* p. 56.

13. *Ibid. 1959,* p. 74. EEC Commission, *Bulletin,* No. 2 (1959), pp. 38–39.

14. Gimon, pp. 20–23. The common external tariff represents for France *decreases* in 71.4 per cent of tariff positions, *increases* in 14.1 per cent, and *no change*

in 14.5 per cent. For Germany the figures are, respectively, 9.2 per cent, 79.5 per cent, and 11.3 per cent. *Revue du Marché Commun,* No. 22 (1960), p. 50.

15. Article 20. Being negotiations between Member States, the delegations could, if need be, evade the legal provisions of the Treaty in order to establish everything *ad hoc.* Corson, p. 140.

16. Article 20. The Commission is to make proposals after the first stage (italics mine).

17. Ouin, in Stein and Nicholson, p. 138.

18. EEC Commission, *Bulletin,* No. 3 (1960), p. 33. These products include wood (20 per cent by value), fats (11 per cent), paper pulp (11 per cent), aircraft and aircraft parts (8 per cent), lead and zinc and their ores (5.5 per cent), and engines for motor vehicles and aircraft, and parts thereof (5 per cent).

19. Ouin, in Stein and Nicholson, pp. 137–38.

20. Hasbrouck, "Toward One Europe," September 22, 1959.

21. Much of this chapter is based on interviews conducted in Brussels in 1959–61.

22. EEC Commission, *General Report 1958,* pp. 57–58.

23. EEC Commission, *Bulletin,* No. 3 (1960), p. 33.

24. *Agence Europe,* January 3 and 26, 1959.

25. *Ibid.,* January 31, 1959.

26. *Ibid.,* March 14, 1959.

27. *Ibid.,* March 14 and April 8, 1959. *Working Party I* (chairmen from Italy and Holland) was to study all agricultural products, including alcohol and spirits; also wood, cork, paper pulp, silk, and jute sacks. *Working Party II* (chairmen from France and Luxembourg) would deal with synthetic rubber. *Working Party III* (chairmen from Germany and Belgium) was to study lead and zinc ores, glass pearls, all metals, engines for motor vehicles, ships, and boats, the parts of such engines, accessories and parts of motor engines, and all the other products of the engineering industry.

28. *Ibid.,* March 18, 1959. EEC Commission, *Bulletin,* No. 2 (1959), p. 35.

29. *Agence Europe,* March 20, 1959.

30. *Ibid.,* April 8, 1959.

31. *Ibid.,* May 26, 1959.

32. *Ibid.,* June 23, 1959.

33. *Ibid.,* July 10, 1959. Agreement had been reached on tea, coffee, maté, wood (except tropical), bismuth, and cobalt.

34. *Ibid.,* September 17, 1959.

35. A few specific examples will serve to illustrate the differences after five months of negotiation:

Aluminum: Benelux wanted exemption, Germany a very low duty, and France and Italy at least 12 per cent.

Machine tools: France and Italy, 17 per cent; Germany, exemption.

Auto parts: Belgium, 13 per cent; others, 24 per cent.

Borates: Italy, 22 per cent; others, 12 per cent or exemption.

Bromides: France, 20 per cent; Italy, 25 per cent; Germany, 15 per cent; Benelux, exemption.

The problem of Italy's marginal industries still eluded solution (silk, lead, zinc, iodine, etc.).

36. *Agence Europe,* October 13, 1959.

37. *Ibid.* The Netherlands submitted a list of 28 products, for all of which

decreases were asked. Similarly, the German list asked for decreases mostly on food products. The Italian list mainly involved increases (*Agence Europe*, October 22, 1959).

38. *Ibid.*, November 12, 1959.

39. *Ibid.*, November 18, 1959.

40. *Ibid.*, November 30, 1959.

41. *Ibid.*, December 2, 1959.

42. *Ibid.*, December 15, 1959.

43. Paper pulp, aluminum, magnesium, auto parts, lead, and zinc. Recall that the negotiations on the four positions for petroleum products were suspended, and have not yet been settled. Each Member State will thus continue to apply its separate national tariffs to third countries. The solution rests on the development of a common energy policy for the Community, but mostly it is France's request for Community preference for Saharan oil (and the future of Algeria) that have frustrated agreement.

44. As permitted in Article 25, paragraphs 1 and 2, of the Treaty. Note, however, that recourse to tariff quotas is usually subject to approval and/or periodic review by the Commission.

45. EEC, Conférence des Représentants des Etats Membres de la CEE, *Accord.* See also Corson, pp. 140–41.

46. Ouin, in Stein and Nicholson, p. 139.

47. E.g., the Association of Fish Canning Industries of the Six Countries of the Community. *Agence Europe*, June 1, 1959.

48. Corson, p. 142.

CHAPTER ELEVEN

1. EEC, *Treaty*, Article 38.

2. *Ibid.*, Article 39, paragraph 1.

3. *Ibid.*, paragraph 2.

4. EEC Commission, *Recueil*, p. 134.

5. Deniau, p. 69.

6. EEC, *Treaty*, Article 40, paragraph 2.

7. EEC Commission, *General Report 1958*, p. 65.

8. Compiled from EEC Commission, *Report on the Economic Situation*, pp. 62 and 64.

9. EEC Commission, *Proposals*, Part I, p. 15.

10. *Ibid.*

11. *Agricultural Policy in the EEC*, pp. 4–5.

12. *Ibid.*, p. 5.

13. *Ibid.*

14. This part of the discussion relies heavily on *Agricultural Policy in the EEC*, pp. 6–13. Also EEC Commission, *Recueil*, pp. 125–77.

15. EEC Commission, *Recueil*, p. 130.

16. *Agricultural Policies in Western Europe*, p. 27.

17. Lipset, pp. 112–13 (and footnote).

18. Compiled from EEC Commission, *Report on the Economic Situation*, p. 62.

19. See Robinson, pp. 53–69.

20. For details see Boshouwers.

21. Robinson, p. 57.

22. *Ibid.*, pp. 57–58.

23. *Ibid.*, p. 173. "Each has then sought to promote the shared agricultural point of view in the policies of the Government as a whole, the one by working within the Government structure, the other by obtaining the support of the Central Organ for Foreign Economic Relations, the Social and Economic Council and the Second Chamber" (p. 172).

24. Hirsch-Weber, in Ehrmann, *Interest Groups*, p. 101. See also "Les Forces qui font l'Europe," pp. 47–54.

25. Deutsch and Edinger, p. 103.

26. See *Die Welt*, February 12, 1960. See also Teichmann.

27. Deutsch and Edinger, p. 94. For details on the Deutscher Bauernverband and German politics, see also Kitzinger.

28. Beer and Ulam, p. 576.

29. See *Belgian Boerenbond*.

30. For this treatment I have relied heavily on Kogan, pp. 67–69. For the Coltivatori Diretti, see also *The World Today* (April 1958), pp. 154–55.

31. *Federazione italiana dei consorzi agrari.*

32. LaPalombara, "Utility and Limitations," p. 40.

33. Kogan, p. 68.

34. For full discussions, see Mendras, pp. 735–60; and Fauvet and Mendras.

35. Brown, "Pressure Politics," pp. 702–19.

36. Meynaud, pp. 56–62.

37. For a fascinating account of their influence, see Brown, "Alcohol and Politics," pp. 976–94.

38. Brown, "Pressure Politics," pp. 702–19.

39. Ehrmann, "Pressure Groups," pp. 146–47.

40. Beer and Ulam, p. 420.

41. *Ibid.*, p. 384.

42. Mendras, p. 742.

43. *Ibid.*, esp. pp. 749–60.

44. Fauvet and Mendras, pp. 20–22.

45. Article 40, paragraph 1.

46. EEC, *Treaty*, Article 44.

47. For a discussion of some of the technical difficulties involved, see *Agricultural Policy in the EEC*, pp. 14–15; and Niehaus, pp. 289–312.

48. EEC, *Treaty*, Article 45.

49. For details, see *Agricultural Policy in the EEC*, p. 16.

50. EEC, *Treaty*, Article 43.

51. Member States in this position could ask for "equivalent guarantees regarding the employment and standard of living of the producers concerned, due account being taken of the time-factor in respect of possible adjustments and of necessary specialisations, . . . [and the assurance of] conditions similar to those existing in a domestic market." *Ibid.*, paragraph 3.

52. Statement by the French Minister of Agriculture, Roger Houdet, quoted in *Agricultural Policy in the EEC*, p. 25.

53. EEC Commission, *General Report 1958*, pp. 74–78.

54. See EEC Commission, *Recueil*, pp. 119–214. Also *Agricultural Policy in the EEC*, pp. 17–18.

55. For the list, see the final resolution in EEC Commission, *General Report 1958*, pp. 76–77.

56. *Ibid.*, p. 77.

57. *Ibid.*, p. 66.

58. *Ibid.*, pp. 66–68.

59. *Ibid.*, p. 70.

60. *Ibid.*, p. 71 (italics mine).

61. *Ibid.*

62. For the list, see EEC Commission, *Recueil*, p. 250.

63. For details, see EEC Commission, *Bulletin*, No. 2 (1959), pp. 44–45, and No. 3 (1959), p. 59; also *Agence Europe*, May 22 and 27, June 5 and 15, July 4, and August 7 and 8, 1959.

64. Mansholt warned the EPA in June 1959 against usurping the role of the executive. *Agence Europe*, June 24, 1959.

65. For details, see *Opera Mundi Europe*, No. 23, October 28, 1959.

66. EEC Commission, *Bulletin*, No. 1 (1960), pp. 46–47.

67. For the full text of the Commission's proposals, see EEC Commission, *Proposals.* The Commission also published summaries of both the draft and the final proposals: ECIS, *Towards a Common Agricultural Policy*; and ECIS, *Proposals for a Common Agricultural Policy.* I have also relied heavily on the excellent summaries of the two sets of proposals (and of the differences between them) in *Proposals for a Common Agricultural Policy* (published by PEP), pp. 4–15; and on *Agriculture, the Commonwealth, and EEC* (another PEP publication), p. 4.

68. ECIS, *Towards a Common Agricultural Policy*, p. 4.

69. EEC Commission, *Proposals*, Part II, pp. 6–7.

70. *Ibid.*, Part III, p. 6.

71. *Ibid.*, p. 7.

72. *Ibid.*, p. 18.

73. *Ibid.*, p. 17.

74. ECIS, *Proposals for a Common Agricultural Policy*, p. 3.

75. *Ibid.*, p. 4.

76. *Agence Europe*, July 16 and 29, 1960. EEC Commission, *Bulletin*, Nos. 6-7 (1960), p. 49.

77. *Agence Europe*, September 12 and 13, 1960. The members of the Special Committee on Agriculture were as follows:

Germany: Lahr, head (Foreign Affairs); Schlebitz (Agriculture); and other experts.

Belgium: Forthomme, head (Foreign Affairs); Doumont and Gerrebos (Economic Affairs); Forget and Blero (Agriculture); and Wendelen and Gaudy (Permanent Representatives).

France: Gorse, head (Permanent Representative, Foreign Affairs); Wallon (Agriculture); Mayoux (Interministerial Committee on European Economic Cooperation Questions); and representatives of the Ministry of Finance and Economic Affairs.

Italy: Cattani, head (Permanent Representative, Foreign Affairs); Albertario and Montanari (Agriculture); Ferlesch (Foreign Trade); and other experts.

Luxembourg: Buchler, head (Agriculture); Duhr (Foreign Affairs); Guill (Finance); and Wunsch (Economic Affairs).

Netherlands: Staf, head (former Minister of Defense); Franke and Le Mair (Agriculture); von Asbeck (Foreign Affairs); Hoogwater (Economic Affairs); and van Ooster (Permanent Representative).

78. *Agence Europe*, July 29, 1960.

79. For details, see EEC Commission, *Bulletin*, Nos. 6-7, 8-9, and 10 (1960), and No. 1 (1961).

80. See *Agence Europe*, November 17, 1960; and EEC Commission, *Bulletin*, No. 1 (1961), pp. 22–23.

81. Details of the German list are given in *Agence Europe*, November 21, 1960.

82. *Ibid.*, November 7 and 18, 1960.

83. EEC Commission, *Bulletin*, No. 10 (1960), pp. 46–47. *Agence Europe*, December 21, 1960.

84. "Resolution of the Council Concerning the Principles to Be Taken as a Basis for a System of Levies for a Certain Number of Products to Be Defined," *Agence Europe*, "Documents," No. 69, December 31, 1960 (italics in the original).

85. For more details see *ibid.*, November 21, 1960.

86. *Ibid.*, November 18 and 21, 1960.

87. EEC Commission, *Bulletin*, No. 10 (1960), pp. 46–47; No. 1 (1961), pp. 24–25.

88. *Ibid.*, December 20 and 21, 1960.

89. EEC Commission, *Bulletin*, No. 6 (1961), p. 47.

90. "Transition from the first to the second stage shall be conditional upon a confirmatory statement to the effect that the essence of the objectives specifically laid down in this Treaty for the first stage has been in fact achieved and that . . . the obligations have been observed. This statement shall be made at the end of the fourth year by the Council acting by means of a unanimous vote on a report of the Commission." EEC, *Treaty*, Article 8, paragraph 3.

91. See the statements by the Finance Minister, Baumgartner, and the Agriculture Minister, Rochereau, before the French National Assembly on May 14, 1961, in EPA, *Cahiers*, July 1961, pp. 10–12.

92. *Agence Europe*, June 13, 1961.

93. For explanatory memoranda and the texts of the draft regulations for pork and grain, see EEC Commission, *Bulletin*, No. 7-8 (1961), pp. 105–32.

94. The representation of interest groups on the Specialized Section is as follows (taken from "L'Avis du Comité Economique et Sociale," p. 173):

Group	Germany	Belgium	France	Italy	Luxembourg	Netherlands	Totals
Agriculture	3	1	5	4	1	1	15
Trade unions	2	2	2	2	—	1	9
Industry	1	1	1	1	—	1	5
Artisans, commerce, and consumers	2	—	—	1	1	1	5
Totals	8	4	8	8	2	4	34

95. For the texts of these opinions, as well as the report and opinions of the Specialized Section on Agriculture, see EEC, Economic and Social Committee, Section Specialisée pour Agriculture, *Rapport General*.

96. *Agence Europe*, September 23, 1961.

97. With the single exception of a formal opinion given by the ESC on the Commission's proposals for a common agricultural policy for rice, a product that had not been covered in the 1960 proposals. See *Agence Europe*, October 26, 1961.

98. The vote was 73 in favor, none against, and 19 abstentions. On the second opinion the vote was unanimous.

99. For a more detailed comparison, see EEC, Economic and Social Committee, "Aperçu comparatif."

100. COPA and the EPA had also proposed three years. *Agence Europe*, October 2, 1961.

101. EPA, *Troisi Report I*; EPA, *Lücker Report I*; and EPA, *Vredeling Report*.

102. EPA, *Débats I*, June 1959, p. 63.

103. EPA, *Lücker Report II*; EPA, *Carcassonne Report*; EPA, *Van Dijk Report*; EPA, *Legendre Reports I and II*; EPA, *Troisi Report II*; EPA, *Richarts Report*; and EPA, *De Vita Report*.

104. "The intervention price was to be 5–7 per cent below the target price instead of 5–10 per cent.

105. The Committee also recommended that the European Offices be set up after a transitional phase, whereas the Commission proposed their immediate creation.

106. EPA, *Annuaire-Manuel 1960–61*, p. 449.

107. *Agriculture, the Commonwealth, and EEC*, pp. 25–26.

108. EPA, *Annuaire-Manuel 1960–61*, p. 450 (italics mine).

109. The amendment was adopted by a vote of 12 to 7, with 50 abstentions! See *Nieuwe Rotterdamse Courant*, October 15, 1960.

110. *Agence Europe*, October 14, 1960.

111. Quoted in *Agriculture, the Commonwealth, and EEC*, p. 25.

112. EPA, *Schmidt Report*; EPA, *Charpentier Report I*; and EPA, *Thorn Report*.

113. EPA, *Débats I*, January 18, 1961, pp. 96–101.

114. For the texts, see EPA, *Annuaire-Manuel 1961–62*, pp. 471–72, for the opinion on rules of competition, and pp. 394–400, for the resolutions on minimum prices and levies.

115. See EPA, *Charpentier Report II*; also EPA, *Débats I*, October 17, 1961, pp. 48–61, and October 18, 1961, pp. 66–124, 128–52. For the texts of the final opinions, see EPA, *Annuaire-Manuel 1961–62*, pp. 489–531.

116. For the texts, see EPA, *Annuaire-Manuel 1961–62*, pp. 531–45.

117. EPA, *Débats I*, November 20, 1961, pp. 6–44, especially speeches by Boscary-Monsservin, Bohy, Pleven, and Legendre.

118. See Assembly Resolution 157, in EPA, *Annuaire-Manuel 1961–62*, pp. 468–69.

CHAPTER TWELVE

1. *Le Journal de la France Agricole*, October 20, 1960.

2. *Agriculture, the Commonwealth, and EEC*, p. 20.

3. Statement by the Vice-President of the FNSEA, quoted in *ibid.*, p. 24.

4. *Ibid.*, p. 24–25.

5. Robinson, pp. 118–19.

6. The following account is based on *Agence Europe*, July 27, 1960, October 10, 1960, October 9, 1961; *Agriculture, the Commonwealth, and EEC*, pp. 19–25; and *Common Market*, I (August–September 1961), 151–52.

7. *New York Herald Tribune* (Paris), January 10, 1962.

8. Quoted in *Agence Europe*, December 1, 1961.

9. These new policy areas included the elimination of competitive distortions caused by legislative or administrative regulations, the implementation of the programs for the right of establishment and the freedom of services, the abolition of quotas, the coordination of municipal law on access to and pursuit of non-wage-

earning activities, etc. For a complete list of the legal consequences of entry into the second stage, see EEC Commission, *Bulletin*, No. 4 (1962), pp. 8–12.

10. *Common Market*, I (July 1961), 135–37.

11. According to some, it represented a recognition that the normal procedures had not worked in agriculture. Trade in agricultural products lagged behind that in industrial goods in the acceleration decision. The quota increases called for in the Treaty had not materialized. Minimum prices had been used on a large scale to dissipate the effects of even the minimal drop in tariffs. Practically no progress had been made on harmonizing commercial relations with third countries. The German Bundestag had refused to honor its commitment under the acceleration decision regarding nonliberalized agricultural goods, and Germany had refused to open and enlarge global quotas for imports of live calves, canned meats, sausages, and veal. See *Common Market*, I (July 1961), 136; *ibid.*, I (November 1961), 195–96; *ibid.*, II (February 1962), 27; and *ibid.*, II (March 1962), 49–54.

12. Hallstein, p. 55.

13. For further details, see EEC Commission, *First Stage*, pp. 27–38. For the texts, see European Communities, *Journal Officiel*, April 20, 1962.

14. EEC Commission, *First Stage*, p. 24.

15. In the following treatment I have relied principally on Mayoux; *Common Market*, II (March 1962), 49–53; *Agence Europe*, October 9, 10, 25, 31, November 22, 28, 30, December 1, 2, 12, 13, 14, 19, 1961; and *Le Soir*, December 28, 29, 30, 31, 1961, and January 2, 3, 5, 6, 10, 16, 1962.

16. These provisions were criticized by the Assembly in a strongly worded resolution. See EEC Commission, *Bulletin*, No. 2 (February 1962), p. 104.

17. The timetable for 1962 was as follows (according to EEC Commission, *A Farm Policy for Europe*, p. 25):

	Proposals by Commission before:	Decisions by Council before:	Entry into force:
Rice	Apr. 30	July 1	——
Dairy produce	May 1	July 31	Nov. 1
Beef and veal	May 1	July 31	Nov. 1
Veterinary system	July 1	——	——
Sugar	July 15	Nov. 1	Jan. 1 (1963)

18. Rolf Lahr, German Secretary of State, described the agreement as "a new Treaty of Rome," in *Bulletin from the European Communities* (Washington, D.C., March-April 1962), p. 1.

19. January 26, 1962.

20. This is not always understood by "outsiders." As one observer wrote of the negotiations between the EEC and Great Britain, "The British delegation has not yet acquired that Continental lack of consideration for their opponent's feelings when it comes to hard bargaining which some of the Six have acquired and which others never lacked. They are still reluctant to share the experience of the Six that tough and sometimes even unfriendly negotiations do after all create the closest ties." *Common Market*, II (May 1962), 81.

21. EEC Commission, *Bulletin*, No. 3 (March 1962), p. 6.

22. *Ibid.*

23. For these and other examples see *Agence Europe*, July 30, 1962.

CHAPTER THIRTEEN

1. EEC, *Treaty*, Preamble.
2. *Ibid.*, Article 2.
3. "Concerning Franco-German and European solidarity, our basic belief is one of deep and profound faith in the fundamental necessity for the joint reconstruction of Europe. . . . There are the Treaties, and the most important is the EEC Treaty which is of the greatest value to the French economy. If the Community continues as it has begun it could prove even more valuable . . . at present and in the days to come our policy genuinely hinges on this European Community and very many of our decisions turn on it." Statement by Michel Debré on 24 October 1960 in the National Assembly, in *France and the European Community*, p. 18.
4. Statement made by General de Gaulle at his Paris Conference of 5 September 1960, *ibid.*, p. 10.
5. Statement made by Michel Debré at Metz on 2 October 1960, *ibid.*, p. 12.
6. Haas, "Challenge of Regionalism," p. 454.
7. Statement of Couve de Murville, in *Agence Europe*, January 21, 1960.
8. Easton, in Macridis and Brown, pp. 93–94.
9. Haas, *Uniting of Europe*, pp. xv–xvi.

APPENDIX A

1. This analysis is based largely on *Savary Report*, Annexes A–M.
2. Based on Soulé, "Comparaison (I)," p. 102. Wigny, pp. 109–10. *Savary Report*, Annex J.
3. The Assembly is not specifically mentioned: "The Council . . . after consulting the other institutions concerned . . ." (Article 212).

BIBLIOGRAPHY

Agricultural Policies in Western Europe. Occasional Paper No. 3. London: Political and Economic Planning, May 11, 1959.

Agricultural Policy in the European Economic Community. Occasional Paper No. 1. London: Political and Economic Planning, November 21, 1958.

"L'Agriculture dans le Marché commun," *Le Marché Commun Européen*, Agence Internationale de Documentation "Pharos." October 15, 1959. Entire.

Agriculture, the Commonwealth, and EEC. Occasional Paper No. 14. London: Political and Economic Planning, July 10, 1961.

Alger, Chadwick F. "Non-Resolution Consequences of the United Nations and Their Effect on International Conflict," *Journal of Conflict Resolution*, V (1961), 128–45.

"L'Avis du Comité Economique et Sociale de la CEE sur la politique agricole commune," *Revue du Marché Commun*, No. 25 (1960), p. 173.

Bebr, Gerhard. "The Balance of Power in the European Communities," *Annuaire Européen*, V, 53–79. The Hague: Nijhoff, 1959.

Beer, Samuel H., and Ulam, Adam B. (eds.) Patterns of Government. 2d ed. New York: Random House, 1962.

Beever, R. Colin. European Unity and the Trade Union Movement. Aspects Européens. Série D. Etudes Sociales. Leyden: Sythoff, 1960.

The Belgian Boerenbond: Each for One, All for Each. Published on the occasion of the International Exposition at Brussels. Brussels: Boerenbond, 1958.

Beloff, Max. "National Government and International Government," *International Organization*, XIII (1959), 538–49.

Boshouwers, Henk. "Industrial Organization in the Netherlands," *Cahiers de Bruges*, Vols. III–IV (1958).

Brouland, Paul. "Les Syndicats ouvriers et l'Europe des Six." Thèse, Faculté de Droit et des Sciences, Université de Strasbourg, 1958.

Brown, Bernard E. "Alcohol and Politics in France," *American Political Science Review*, LI (1957), 976–94.

———. "Pressure Politics in France," *Journal of Politics*, XVIII (1956), 702–19.

Budgetary Control in the European Economic Community: A Case Study in "Supra-National" Administration. Occasional Paper No. 6. London: Political and Economic Planning, March 28, 1960.

Bundesverband der Deutschen Industrie. *Jahresbericht, 1959.* Cologne: 1959.

Camps, Miriam. Division in Europe. Occasional Paper No. 8. London: Political and Economic Planning, June, 1960.

———. The European Common Market and Free Trade Area. Policy Memorandum No. 15. Princeton, N.J.: Center of International Studies, 1957.

———. The European Free Trade Association: A Preliminary Appraisal. Occasional Paper No. 4. London: Political and Economic Planning, September 7, 1959.

———. The First Year of the European Economic Community. Policy Memorandum No. 17. Princeton, N.J.: Center of International Studies, November 10, 1958.

———. The Free Trade Area Negotiations. Occasional Paper No. 2. London: Political and Economic Planning, April 6, 1959.

Caze, L. "Vie d'un comité syndical de liaisons et d'études dans le cadre du Marché Commun," *Revue du Marché Commun,* No. 19 (1959), pp. 409–16.

[COPA]. Comité des Organisations Profesionnelles agricoles de la Communauté Economique Européenne. "Déclaration de l'Assemblée du COPA réuni à Paris le 13 octobre 1960." Paris, October 1960. Mimeographed.

———. "Position de l'Assemblée du COPA réuni à Bruxelles le 8 décembre 1960." Brussels, December 13, 1960. Mimeographed.

———. "Règlement intérieur." Brussels, December 13, 1960. Mimeographed.

"La Communauté à l'épreuve des faits I. La Commission et les Gouvernements," *Revue du Marché Commun,* No. 20 (1959), pp. 425–27.

"La Communauté à l'épreuve des faits II. Le Marché Commun et les Pays Tiers," *Revue du Marché Commun,* No. 21 (1960), pp. 5–8.

Corson, Henri. "L'Etablissement de la Liste G," *Revue du Marché Commun,* No. 24 (1960), pp. 136–42.

Courtin, René. "L'Echelonnement des mesures de libération et les clauses de sauvegarde," *Revue d'Economie Politique* (January-February 1958), pp. 291–309.

Daalder, H. "The Netherlands," in Lindsay, European Assemblies. London: Stevens, 1960.

Deniau, J. F. The Common Market: Its Structure and Purpose. London: Barrie and Rockliff with Pall Mall Press, 1960.

Deutsch, Karl W., and Edinger, Lewis J. Germany Rejoins the Powers. Stanford, Calif.: Stanford University Press, 1959.

Deutsch, Karl W., *et al.* Political Community and the North Atlantic Area: International Organization in the Light of Historical Experience. Princeton, N.J.: Princeton University Press, 1957.

Direct Elections and the European Parliament. Occasional Paper No. 10. London: Political and Economic Planning, October 24, 1960.

Dogan, Mattei. "France," in Lindsay, European Assemblies. London: Stevens, 1960.

Duverger, Maurice. Political Parties. London: Methuen, 1955.

Ehrmann, Henry W. "Pressure Groups in France," *Annals of the American Academy of Political and Social Science,* CCCXIX (1958), 141–48.

Ehrmann, Henry W. (ed.). Interest Groups on Four Continents. Pittsburgh, Penna.: University of Pittsburgh Press, 1958.

Erhard, Ludwig. Prosperity through Competition. London: Thames and Hudson, 1958.

———. "Was wird aus Europa?" *Handelsblatt,* December 23–24, 1960.

Fauvet, Jacques, and Mendras, Henri (eds.). Les Paysans et la politique dans la France contemporaine. Paris: Colin, 1958.

Federazione Italiana dei Consorzi Agrari, 1892–1952. Rome: L'Etablissement Typographique de la Société Affiliée "Brandie Editoriale des Agriculteurs," n.d.

Fontaine, André. "L'Europe politique," *Revue du Marché Commun,* No. 33 (1961), pp. 61–64.

"Les Forces qui font l'Europe," *Réalités,* No. 161 (1959), pp. 47–54.

France and the European Community. Occasional Paper No. 11. London: Political and Economic Planning, January 30, 1961.

Frank, Isaiah. The European Common Market: An Analysis of Commercial Policy. New York: Praeger, 1961.

Fry, Richard. The Common Market in Action. Reprinted from *The Guardian,* April, 1960.

Furniss, Edgar S., Jr. France, Troubled Ally: De Gaulle's Heritage and Prospects. New York: Harper, 1960.

Gaudet, Michel. "The Legal Framework of the Community." Address before the Conference at the Law Society. London, September 29, 1960. Mimeographed.

Gehrels, Franz, and Johnston, Bruce F. "The Economic Gains of European Integration," *Journal of Political Economy* (August 1955), pp. 275–94.

Gimon, Jean. "Le nouveau Tarif douanier français," *Revue du Marché Commun,* No. 32 (1961), pp. 20–23.

Ginderachter, J. van. "Les Modes de vote dans les institutions européennes," *Revue du Marché Commun,* No. 30 (1960), pp. 382–91.

Haas, Ernst B. "The Challenge of Regionalism," *International Organization,* XII (1958), 440–58.

———. Consensus Formation in the Council of Europe. Berkeley and Los Angeles: University of California Press, 1960.

———. "International Integration: The European and The Universal Process," *International Organization,* XV (1961), 366–92.

———. "Persistent Themes in Atlantic and European Unity," *World Politics,* X (1958), 614–29.

———. The Uniting of Europe: Political, Social, and Economic Forces, 1950–1957. Stanford, Calif.: Stanford University Press, 1958.

Haas, Ernst B., and Whiting, Allen S. Dynamics of International Relations. New York: McGraw-Hill, 1956.

Hallstein, Walter. United Europe: Challenge and Opportunity. Cambridge, Mass.: Harvard University Press, 1962.

Hasbrouck, Jan. "Common Market at the Grass Roots," *New York Herald Tribune* (Paris), June 7 and 9, 1960.

————. "Toward One Europe," *New York Herald Tribune* (Paris), September 22, 1959, October 15, 1959, March 29, 1960, and April 26, 1960.

Heidenheimer, Arnold J. The Governments of Germany. New York: Crowell, 1961.

Hurtig, Serge. "The European Common Market," *International Conciliation*, No. 517 (March 1958), pp. 321–81.

————. "L'Industrie chimique française devant l'Association Economique Européenne," *Revue du Marché Commun*, No. 11 (1959), pp. 80–83.

[IRRI]. L'Institut Royal des Relations Internationales. "Le Marché Commun et l'Euratom," *Chronique de Politique Etrangère*, X (July–November 1957), 406–933.

"Italy, the Common Market, and the Free Trade Area," *The World Today*, XIV (April 1958), 152–62.

Kapteyn, P. J. G. "The Common Assembly of the ECSC as a Representative Institution," in Lindsay, European Assemblies. London: Stevens, 1960.

Kitzinger, U. W. German Electoral Politics. Oxford: Clarendon Press, 1960.

Kogan, Norman. The Government of Italy. New York: Crowell, 1962.

LaPalombara, Joseph. "Political Party Systems and Crisis Government: French and Italian Contrasts," *Midwest Journal of Political Science*, II (May 1958), pp. 117–42.

————. "The Utility and Limitations of Interest Group Theory in Non-American Field Situations," *Journal of Politics*, XXII (1960), 29–49.

Leclercq, Jean. Les Conseils économiques nationaux en Belgique, en France et aux Pays-Bas. Brussels: Conseil Central de l'Economie, 1954.

Lindsay, Kenneth. European Assemblies: The Experimental Period 1949–1959. London: Stevens, 1960.

Lipset, Seymour Martin. Political Man: The Social Bases of Politics. Garden City: Doubleday, 1960.

Ljubisavljevic, Bora. Les Problèmes de la pondération dans les institutions européennes. Aspects Européens. Série C. Politique. Leyden: Sythoff, 1959.

Macridis, Roy C., and Brown, Bernard E. (eds.). Comparative Politics. Homewood, Ill.: Dorsey Press, 1961.

Malvestiti, Piero. "Les Entreprises dans le Marché commun," *Bulletin of the EEC*, No. 3 (1959), pp. 5–17.

Margulies, R. "Die Kosten der Kleineuropäischer Gemeinschaften," *Europäische Wirtschaft*, No. 12 (1959), pp. 292–94.

Mayoux, Jacques, "L'Etablissement de la politique agricole commune," *Revue du Marché Commun*, No. 43 (1962), pp. 7–19.

Mendras, Henri. "Les Organisations agricoles et la politique," *Revue Française de Science Politique*, V (1955), 736–60.

"Méthodes et mouvements pour unir l'Europe," *Bulletin du Centre Européen de la Culture*, Vol. VI, No. 2 (May 1958), entire issue.

Meynaud, Jean. Les Groupes de pression en France. Paris: Colin, 1958.

Nagels, N. N. "Die Zusammenarbeit der industriellen Spitzenverbände in Europa," *Europäische Wirtschaftsgemeinschaft*, No. 22 (1958).

Negotiations for a European Free Trade Association. Cmnd. 641. London: HMSO, January, 1959.

North, Robert C., Koch, Howard E., Jr., and Zinnes, Dina A. "The Integrative Functions of Conflict," *Journal of Conflict Resolution*, IV (1960), 355–74.

Ouin, Marc. "The Establishment of the Customs Union," in Stein and Nicholson, American Enterprise in the European Common Market. Ann Arbor: The University of Michigan Law School, 1960.

Pohle, Wolfgang. "Beratend für Rat und Kommission tätig: Die Aufgabe des Europäischen Wirtschafts- und Sozialauschusses," *Europäische-Wirtschaft*, January 15, 1960, pp. 11–14.

"Le Point de vue des organisations sur les propositions de politique agricole commune, *Revue du Marché Commun*, No. 28 (1960), pp. 280–81.

Proposals for a Common Agricultural Policy in the EEC. Occasional Paper No. 5. London: Political and Economic Planning, February 1, 1960.

Report of the European Industrial Conference. London: United Kingdom Council for the European Movement, February 1958.

"Les Réunions des Ministres des Finances des Six pays du Marché Commun," *Revue du Marché Commun*, No. 18 (1959), pp. 344–45.

Reuter, Paul. "Affaires étrangères et Communautés Européennes," in Centre de Sciences Politiques de l'Institut d'Etudes Juridiques de Nice, Les Affaires étrangères. Paris: Presses Universitaires de France, 1959.

——. "Aspects de la Communauté Economique Européenne," *Revue du Marché Commun*, No. 1 (1958), pp. 6–14.

——. "Aspects de la Communauté Economique Européenne II," *Revue du Marché Commun*, No. 3 (1958), pp. 161–68.

——. "Aspects de la Communauté Economique Européenne III," *Revue du Marché Commun*, No. 6 (1958), pp. 310–16.

Robinson, Alan D. Dutch Organised Agriculture in International Politics, 1945–1960. The Hague: Nijhoff, 1961.

Rosenberg, Ludwig. "The Activities and Importance of the Economic and Social Committee," *Bulletin of the EEC*, No. 3 (1961).

Rudolfsen, E. "Zusammenleben in Europa—Aber wie?" *Europäische Wirtschaft*, January 15, 1960, pp. 3–10.

Sainte Lorette, Lucien de. Le Marché Commun. Paris: Colin, 1958.

[Savary Report]. France. Journal Officiel. Documents, Assemblée Nationale. Annexe N° 5266. Session ordinaire de 1956–57. Séance du 26 juin 1957. Rapport fait au nom de la commission des affaires étrangères sur le projet de loi autorisant le Président de la République à ratifier: 1° le traité instituant la Communauté Economique Européenne; 2° le traité instituant la Communauté Européenne d'Energie Atomique; 3° la convention relative à certaines institutions communes aux communautés européennes, signés à Rome le 25 mars 1957. "Dispositions relatives à la CEE," par M. Savary député.

Scheingold, Stuart A. "International Labor: The Regional Challenge." Unpublished Master's dissertation, Department of Political Science, University of California, Berkeley, Calif., 1959.

Schokking, Jan J., and Anderson, Nels. "Observations on the European Integration Process," *Journal of Conflict Resolution*, IV (1960), 385–410.

Schumm, Siegfried. "Interest Representation in France and Germany," *Cahiers de Bruges*, Vols. III–IV (1958).

Secrétariat Syndical Européen. "Rapport du Secrétariat à la deuxième Assemblée Générale des Syndicats Libres des Etats Membres des Communautés Européennes." Brussels, 1959. Mimeographed.

Selznick, Philip. Leadership in Administration: A Sociological Interpretation. Evanston, Ill.: Row, Peterson, 1957.

———. TVA and the Grass Roots: A Study in the Sociology of Formal Organization. Berkeley: University of California Press, 1953.

Snoy et d'Oppuers, Baron Jean-Charles. "Les Etapes de la cooperation européenne et les négotiations relatives à une zone de libre échange," *Chronique de Politique Etrangère*, (September–November 1959), pp. 569–623.

Soldati, A. "Le Fonctionnement de la CEE. L'Exécutif à deux branches," in Brückenschlag EWG–EFTA. Schweizerisches Institut für Aussenwirtschafts- und Marktforschung an der Handels Hochschule St. Gallen. Zurich and St. Gallen: Polygraphischer Verlag, 1960.

Soulé, Yves-Pierre. "Comparaison entre les dispositions institutionnelles du traité CECA et du traité CEE (I)," *Revue du Marché Commun*, No. 2 (1958), pp. 95–102.

———. "Comparaison entre les dispositions institutionnelles du traité CECA et du traité CEE (II)," *Revue du Marché Commun*, No. 4 (1958), pp. 208–16.

Stein, Eric. "The European Parliamentary Assembly: Techniques of Emerging 'Political Control,'" *International Organization*, XIII (1959), 233–54.

Stein, Eric, and Nicholson, Thomas L. (eds.). American Enterprise in the European Common Market: A Legal Profile. 2 vols. Ann Arbor: The University of Michigan Law School, 1960.

Stoessinger, John G. "Financing the United Nations," *International Conciliation*, No. 535 (November 1961), pp. 3–72.

Teichmann, Ulrich. Die Politik der Agrarpreisstützung. Cologne-Deutz: Bund-Verlag, 1955.

Tessier, Jacques. "L'Organisation du syndicalisme ouvrier dans le cadre européen," *Revue du Marché Commun*, No. 15 (1959), pp. 242–46.

Ungerer, Werner. "Le Régime institutionnel des communautés européennes," in Collège d'Europe, Sciences humaines et intégration européenne. Leyden: Sythoff, 1960.

[UNICE]. Union des Industries de la Communauté Européenne. Statuts. Brussels, 1959.

United Nations. Annual Report of the Secretary-General on the Work of the

Organization, June 16, 1959–June 15, 1960. General Assembly, Official Records, Fifteenth Session, Supplement No. 1. New York, 1960.

U.S. Participation in the United Nations. Report by the President to the Congress for the year 1959. 80th Congress, 2d Session, House Document No. 378.

Vleeschauer, R. de. "L'Adaptation des entreprises au Marché Commun," *Le Soir* (Brussels), October 25–26, 1959.

Vreese, Alphonse de. "Perspective pour un droit européen," in Collège d'Europe, Sciences humaines et intégration européenne. Leyden: Sythoff, 1960.

Wigny, Pierre. L'Assemblée parlementaire dans l'Europe des Six. [Luxembourg?]: Communauté Europèenne du Charbon et de l'Acier, n.d.

Willemetz, L. "Une Société de type européen," *Revue du Marché Commun*, No. 21 (1960), pp. 38–40.

Young, Roland (ed.). Approaches to the Study of Politics. Evanston, Ill.: Northwestern University Press, 1958.

Zellentin, Gerda. "The Economic and Social Committee," *Journal of Common Market Studies*, I (1962), 22–28.

DOCUMENTS OF THE EUROPEAN COMMUNITIES

[ECIS]. European Community Information Service. *Communauté Européenne*. Paris. Monthly.

———. Etudes et analyses. Brussels and Luxembourg.

———. Proposals for a Common Agricultural Policy. Brussels, July 1960.

———. Towards a Common Agricultural Policy. Brussels, January 1960.

[ECSC]. European Coal and Steel Community. Common Assembly. *Informations Mensuelles*. Luxembourg. Monthly.

[EEC]. European Economic Community. Conférence des Représentants des Etats Membres de la CEE. Accord concernant l'établissement d'une partie du tarif douanier commun relative aux produits de la liste G prévue au Traité instituant la CEE. Annexe contenant les taux des droits fixés pour les produits de la liste G. Protocoles. Acte Finale. Brussels, May 12, 1960.

———. Projet de budget de la Communauté pour l'exercise 1961 établi par le conseil. Brussels, n.d.

———. Treaty Establishing the European Economic Community and Related Documents. English edition. Brussels: Secretariat of the Interim Committee for the Common Market and Euratom, 1957.

———. Commission. *Bulletin of the European Economic Community*. Brussels. Monthly or bimonthly. Editions in several languages.

———. ———. A Farm Policy for Europe. Brussels, January 1962.

———. ———. First Memorandum from the Commission of the EEC to the Council of Ministers of the Community. Brussels, February 26, 1959.

———. ———. The First Stage of the Common Market: Report on the

Execution of the Treaty (January 1958–January 1962). Brussels, July 1962.

———. ———. General Reports on the Activities of the Community. Brussels, September 1958, March 1959, May 1960, May 1961, and June 1962.

———. ———. Mouvements dans l'industrie et le commerce en vue du Marché commun européen. 2d ed. Brussels, June 19, 1959.

———. ———. Proposals for the Working out and Putting into Effect of the Common Agricultural Policy in Application of Article 43 of the Treaty Establishing the European Economic Community. Brussels, June 30, 1960.

———. ———. Receuil des documents de la conférence agricole des états membres de la Communauté Economique Européenne à Stresa du 3 au 12 juillet 1958. Brussels, n.d.

———. ———. Recommandations de la Commission en vue de l'accélération du rythme du Traité. Brussels, February 26, 1960.

———. ———. Répertoire des organisations agricoles non gouvernementales groupées dans le cadre de la Communauté Economique Européenne. Direction Générale de l'Agriculture. 2d ed. Brussels, December 1960.

———. ———. Répertoire des organismes communs créés dans le cadre de la CEE par les associations industrielles, artisanales et commerciales des six pays. Brussels, May 1960.

———. ———. Report on the Economic Situation in the Countries of the Community. Brussels, September 1958.

———. ———. [Second Memorandum]. Memorandum from the Commission to the Special Committee for the Study of a European Economic Association. Brussels, October 1959.

———. Council of Ministers. Decision on the Acceleration of the Implementation of the Treaty Taken by the Representatives of the Governments of the Member States of the EEC Meeting in Council. Brussels, May 12, 1960. Press communiqué.

———. ———. "Projet d'intervention du Président des Conseils." Brussels, November 18, 1959. Mimeographed.

———. ———. Règlement intérieur provisoire du conseil. Brussels, 1960.

———. Economic and Social Committee. Annuaire. Brussels, 1960.

———. ———. "Aperçu comparatif des modifications introduites dans les propositions définitives de la Commission concernant la politique agricole commune par rapport à l'avis au Comité Economique et Social relatif à ces propositions." Brussels, September 26, 1960. Mimeographed.

———. ———. Section Specialisée pour Agriculture, Rapport général au sujet du projet de propositions concernant l'élaboration et la mise en oeuvre de la politique agricole commune en vertu de l'article 43 du Traité instituant la CEE. Brussels, July 1960.

[EPA]. European Parliamentary Assembly. Annuaire-Manuel de l'Assemblée parlementaire européenne. Luxembourg, 1958–59, 1959–60, and 1960–61.

———. [Cahiers]. *See below under* EPA, Direction de la Documentation Parlementaire et de l'Information.

————. [Carcassonne Report]. Rapport fait au nom de la commission de l'agriculture sur les propositions de la Commission de la CEE relatives à une politique commune dans le secteur du vin. Rapporteur R. Carcassonne. Doc. No. 4, 1960.

————. [Charpentier Report I]. Rapport présenté au nom de la commission de l'agriculture sur l'application d'un système de prélèvements aux échanges commerciaux de produits agricoles. Rapporteur René Charpentier. Doc. No. 108, 1960–61.

————. [Charpentier Report II]. Rapport présenté au nom de la commission de l'agriculture sur les consultations relatives aux propositions de règlement portant institution d'un régime de prélèvements et établissement graduel d'une organisation commune des marchés dans le secteur des céréales, de la viande porcine, de la viande de volaille, et des oeufs. Rapporteur René Charpentier. Doc. No. 72, 1961–62.

————. [Débats I]. Débats. Edition de langue française, compte rendu in extenso des séances. Luxembourg. Serial.

————. [Débats II]. Débats. Edition provisoire, compte rendu in extenso des séances. Luxembourg. Serial.

————. [Deringer Report]. Rapport fait au nom de la commission des questions juridiques, de règlement et des immunités sur la coordination des travaux des commissions parlementaires et sur la procédure à suivre en ce qui concerne les questions posées aux organes exécutifs et aux Conseils auxquelles une réponse orale est demandée (article 44.2 du règlement). Rapporteur A. Deringer. Doc. No. 2, 1960–61.

————. [De Vita Report]. Rapport fait au nom de la commission de l'agriculture sur les propositions de la Commission de la CEE pour une politique commune en matière de structure agricole. Rapporteur F. de Vita. Doc. No. 10, 1960.

————. [Legendre Report I]. Rapport fait au nom de la commission de l'agriculture sur les propositions de la Commission de la CEE pour une politique commune dans le secteur du sucre. Rapporteur J. Legendre. Doc. No. 6, 1960.

————. [Legendre Report II]. Rapport fait au nom de la commission de l'agriculture sur les propositions de la CEE pour une politique commune dans le secteur des céréals. Rapporteur J. Legendre. Doc. No. 7, 1960.

————. [Lücker Report I]. Rapport fait au nom de la commission de l'agriculture sur la politique agricole dans la CEE. Rapporteur H. A. Lücker. Doc. No. 39, 1959.

————. [Lücker Report II]. Rapport fait au nom de la commission de l'agriculture sur la situation de l'agriculture et les principes de base d'une politique agricole commune. Rapporteur H. A. Lücker. Doc. No. 3, 1960.

————. Proposition de résolution relative à l'accélération du rythme du Traité de la CEE. Doc. No. 20, 1960–61.

————. [Richarts Report]. Rapport fait au nom de la commission de l'agriculture sur les propositions de la Commission de la CEE pour une politique commune du marché de la viande de boeuf, de la viande de porc, de la viande de volaille et des oeufs. Rapporteur H. Richarts. Doc. No. 9, 1960.

———. [Schmidt Report]. Rapport intérimaire présenté au nom de la commission de l'agriculture sur la consultation relative à un premier règlement concernant l'application de certaines règles de concurrence à la production et au commerce des produits agricoles en vertu de l'article 42 du traité. Rapporteur Martin Schmidt. Doc. No. 107, 1960–61.

———. [Thorn Report]. Rapport présenté au nom de la commission de l'agriculture sur la détermination de critères objectifs pour l'établissement de systèmes de prix minima et pour fixation de ces prix. Rapporteur Gaston Thorn. Doc. No. 109, 1960–61.

———. [Troisi Report I]. Rapport sur le chapitre IV du premier rapport général sur l'activité de la CEE. Rapporteur M. Troisi. Doc. No. 63, 1958.

———. [Troisi Report II]. Rapport fait au nom de la commission de l'agriculture sur les propositions de la Commission de la CEE en vue d'une politique commune dans le secteur des fruits et légumes. Rapporteur M. Troisi. Doc. No. 8, 1960.

———. [Van Dijk Report]. Rapport fait au nom de la commission de l'agriculture sur les propositions de la Commission de la CEE européenne pour une politique commune dans le secteur laitier. Rapporteur F. G. van Dijk. Doc. No. 5, 1960.

———. [Vredeling Report]. Rapport fait au nom de la commission de l'agriculture sur les problèmes de structure, y compris les problèmes sociaux propres à l'agriculture dans la CEE. Rapporteur H. Vredeling. Doc. No. 41, 1959.

———. Direction de la Documentation Parlementaire et de l'Information. *L'Activité de l'Assemblée Parlementaire Européenne.* Luxembourg. Monthly or bimonthly.

———. ———. *Cahiers mensuels de documentation européenne.* Luxembourg. Monthly.

———. ———. Prises de position des organisations professionnelles sur le projet des propositions de la CEE concernant la politique agricole commune. Luxembourg, March 14, 1960.

European Communities. *Journal Officiel des Communautés Européennes.* Edition de la langue française. Brussels and Luxembourg. Serial.

INDEX